D0880800

SUPERSTARS

SUPERSTARS

BY FRANK LITSKY

Introduction by Howard Cosell

derbibooks inc. SECAUCUS, NEW JERSEY

TO

Arlene and Charlie,
the Superstars at home

Picture credits: Jacket photos by UPI except those of Wilt Chamberlain and Olga Korbut by Bruce Curtis; UPI (pp. 1, 2, 3, 5, 6, 7 right top and bottom, 8, 9, 10, 12, 13, 14, 15, 16, 17, 18, 19, 20, 21, 22, 23, 24, 25, 26, 28, 29, 30, 31, 32, 33, 34, 35, 36, 37, 38T, 39, 40, 41, 42, 43, 44, 45, 46, 47, 48T, 49, 50, 51, 52, 53, 54, 55, 56, 57, 58, 59, 60, 61, 63, 64, 65, 66, 67, 68, 70, 71, 72, 73, 74, 75, 77, 78, 79, 80, 81, 82, 84, 85, 86, 87, 88, 89, 90, 92, 93, 94, 95, 97, 98R, 99, 100, 101L, 102, 103, 104, 107, 108, 109, 110, 111, 112, 113, 114, 115B, 117, 118, 120, 123, 124, 125, 126L, 127, 129, 130, 131, 132, 133, 134, 135, 136, 137, 138, 140, 141B, 142B, 144, 145B, 146, 147, 148, 150, 151, 152, 153, 154, 155T, 156, 157B, 158, 159, 160, 161, 164, 165, 168, 169, 170, 171, 172, 173, 174, 175, 176, 177, 178, 179, 180, 181, 182, 183, 184, 185, 186T, 187T, 188, 189, 190, 192, 193, 194, 195, 196, 197, 198B, 199, 200, 201, 202, 203, 204, 205, 206, 207, 208, 209, 210B, 211, 212, 213, 214, 216, 217, 218, 219T, 220, 222, 223, 224, 225, 226, 227, 228, 229, 230, 231B, 232, 233, 234, 235, 236, 237, 238T, 239, 240B, 241, 242, 243B, 245, 246T, 247B, 248, 249, 250, 251, 252, 253B, 254, 255B, 256, 257, 258, 259, 260, 261, 262, 263, 264, 265, 266, 267B, 268T, 269, 270, 271, 272, 273B, 275, 276, 277, 278T, 280, 282, 283, 284, 285, 287, 288, 289R, 290, 291, 292, 293, 294, 295B, 298, 299, 300, 301, 302, 303, 304, 305, 306, 307, 308, 309, 310, 311, 312, 313, 314, 315T, 316, 317, 318, 319, 320, 321, 322, 323R, 324T, 325, 326, 327, 328, 329, 330R, 331B, 332, 333, 334B, 335, 336, 337, 338T, 339B, 340, 341, 342, 345, 346, 347, 348, 350, 351, 352); Wide World Photos (pp. 2 [Pelé], 71, 9 [Nicklaus], 38B, 48B, 76, 91, 115T, 116, 121, 126R, 141T, 142T, 143, 149, 155B, 157T, 162B, 166, 167, 187B, 210T, 215, 238B, 240T, 243T, 244, 246B, 253T, 255T, 267T, 268B, 273T, 286, 289L, 295T, 296, 297, 315B, 323L, 324B, 331T, 334T, 338B, 339T, 343, 344, 349); U.S. Trotting Association (pp. 83, 101R, 139T, 231T); Harness Racing Institute (pp. 139B, 247T); Bruce Curtis (pp. 7 [Killy], 27, 62, 98L, 186B, 191, 198T); Bettmann Archive (p. 69B); Sporting News (p. 69T); Culver Pictures (pp. 96, 105); National Baseball Hall of Fame (p. 119); 20th Century-Fox (p. 145T); United Artists (p. 281); New York Daily News (p. 279); SPORTS ILLUSTRATED photos by Fred Kaplan (Black Star) (pp. 162T, 163), Neil Leifer (p. 11, 106) James Drake (p. 274) and Mark Kauffman (p. 221), © Time Inc.; AMF Inc. (p. 330L); Peter Simon (p. 278B).

Published by

DERBIBOOKS INC.

Secaucus, New Jersey

An original work created and produced by

VINEYARD BOOKS, INC.

159 East 64th Street

New York, N.Y. 10021

Manufactured in the United States of America

Library of Congress Cataloging in Publication Data

Litsky, Frank.
  Superstars.

  "A Vineyard book."
  1. Athletes—Biography. I. Title.
GV697.A1L57   796'.092'2[B]   75-7753
ISBN 0-89009-044-0

CONTENTS

6

Introduction

My wife, Emmy, and I bumped into Sid Luckman in a Miami Beach restaurant the other day and the memories came flooding back. We had grown up together in Brooklyn. He went to Erasmus Hall High School and I went to Alexander Hamilton. Then he went to Columbia and I to New York University. I followed his pro-football career avidly, and then during World War II our paths crossed again. But in the sweep of life, and during the long passage of years, Sid Luckman became a distant figure lodged subconsciously in the inner recesses of my mind.

We talked briefly, remembered the time he led Erasmus to the New York City title with a victory over Flushing, and then he was gone.

"What was he like?" Emmy asked me. "He seems small for an NFL quarterback." I started to tell her but found myself wandering into a long dissertation that simply didn't get to the heart of the man as a person and as a player. Too much time had elapsed.

I won't have that problem anymore. This book has solved it.

Frank Litsky, with painstaking effort and indefatigable research, has produced an invaluable volume for the sports-media professional, for the devoted sports fan and, above all, for everyone who has just a touch of curiosity about some of the most renowned people of our society, past and present. Frank capsulizes 280 famous sports figures in this book and, almost uncannily, captures each and every one of them. He is able to do this because he is a dedicated reporter who quests for truth and who has scant patience with the all too frequent tendency to lionize athletic heroes. I know, because I have known Frank for more than 20 years, and he has never wavered in this regard. And I have known all, or nearly all, of the people in this book.

I know, too, because every day new sports biographies cross my desk to the point where my bookshelves are cluttered with more sports tomes than one could find at the New York Public Library. In the main, they are superficial paeans of praise, hastily composed, designed to capitalize on an athlete's prominence while he is a hot commodity in the market. The net result is that the reader learns little, if anything, about the subject as a human being—what kind of person he or she really is, what his character strengths and weaknesses are, what kind of life he leads outside of the arena.

But that is not the case here. If you want to learn about Kareem Abdul-Jabbar, a complex, moody and thoughtful man, you will discover this revealing quote: ''The Bible and its teachings had produced all these hate-filled people in Los Angeles. It seemed to me that there was nothing in the world as unlike Christ as Christians.'' Yet, before one gets too glowing a view of Jabbar, there is on the same page an incisive quote by a sportswriter: ''He is one of the smallest men I have ever met.'' In his meticulous, journalistic way, Frank Litsky takes all views into account. He wants to ''tell it like it is.''

I don't suppose that anyone has had the continuity and depth of association that I have had with Muhammad Ali during the past 15 years. The torturous twists of the man's life, his mercurial nature, the diversification of his talents, the bewildering successes that have followed what seemed to be disasters are all inextricably interwoven with my own life because of the hundreds of shows I have done with him. He is almost impossible to describe. Still, in a marvel of succinct perception, Litsky in two pages has documented the essence of Ali as I know him.

How do you decide on 280 people and why these 280? It's not easy, and some might quarrel over an omission here and there. All I can say is that no book can or should go on forever, and the very selection of the names in this opus is just another evidence of journalistic competence.

I can't wait to put it in one of my bookcases and clean out a couple of dozen worthless biographies. I think it's that good.

Besides, I'll be able to tell Emmy about Sid Luckman and many others. With her interest in women in sports she should know about Florence Chadwick, Dawn Fraser and Shane Gould. A lot of other women should too.

March 1975   HOWARD COSELL

Foreword

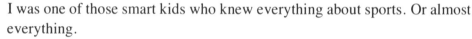

I was one of those smart kids who knew everything about sports. Or almost everything.

One summer day, when I was nine years old, I was playing baseball across the street from my grandmother's house when some older men (they must have been 14 or 15) put me to the test.

''You know a lot about baseball?'' asked one man.

''Sure,'' I said modestly.

''O. K. What's a ball?''

''Huh?''

''What's a ball?''

''What kind of question is that? A ball is the thing you hit with the bat.''

''No, not that kind of ball.''

''That's the only kind of ball I ever heard of.''

''You mean you don't know that if a pitch isn't a strike it's a ball?''

''No, it isn't,'' I answered triumphantly, my honor saved. ''If it isn't a strike, it's a do-over.''

In time I learned that a pitch that is not a strike is not a do-over. I learned many other things about many sports, and by 1946, when I started writing and editing professionally, I had a sound background of facts and figures.

I soon learned that there was more to writing. It was important to tell who, what, when, where and how, but equally important to tell why. It usually made for more interesting reading, too.

The importance of the ''why'' became the prime concern of a young group of sportswriters known as chipmunks (so named by Jimmy Cannon, an old-school writer, who one day had trouble hearing himself think in the press box, turned to a companion and said, ''Look at those young guys over there, jabbering like a bunch of chipmunks'').

The chipmunks were more concerned with the people who played the game than with the game itself. They wanted to know everything about these people, especially their motivation. They were not the first writers to talk to athletes, to spend time with them, to try to understand them as people rather than as numbers. But they made it a crusade, and they helped make the sports pages less dreary and more fun.

Not everyone accepted their philosophies. One year, during the Masters golf tournament in Augusta, Georgia, Jack Nicklaus had just finished his round and was entering the press interview room. As I headed there, I passed an old-time golf writer at his typewriter. I was sure he had not heard the announcement that Nicklaus was arriving, and I repeated it. He thanked me.

After the interview with Nicklaus, I returned to the press room and saw the old-timer still at his desk. Why did he pass up an opportunity to hear Jack Nicklaus recount his round, stroke by stroke? "He has been writing golf for 40 years," a colleague said later. "He feels that his readers are more interested in what he has to say about Jack Nicklaus than in what Jack Nicklaus has to say about Jack Nicklaus."

Perhaps he was right, but I think not. No one can probe a mind nearly as well as the man or woman who owns that mind. An interviewer with a feel for people and for the humanity of people can entrance his reader or listener or viewer in a way that no old-time writer could do.

With the advent of television and its seemingly endless sports presentations, a writer no longer can present merely the facts that his readers already know. He must look beyond the facts to the people who created them. He must tell his readers how these people function, what makes them distinctive, how they got the way they are, what motivates them, why they did what they did. He must also present these people as they really are and not the way he or his readers or the sports establishment would like them to be.

Year after year, bookstores overflow with collections of sports biographies that tell in endless detail what each athlete did year after year. There are paragraph after paragraph of the athletes' words. These books are fine. I collect them and read them and cherish them. But I have always wished that at least one of them would boil down the facts and the thoughts and combine the athlete's assessment of himself with the way others see him and do it all in a page or two of easy reading.

This is what I have tried to do in this book. In the words of my friend Howard Cosell, I have tried to "tell it like it is."

The telling was much easier than the picking. This book tells the stories of 280 superstars, and the greatest problem was trimming in half a preliminary list of more than 500 candidates. Why were some people included and some not? We tried to choose those who by performance or personality or both had risen above the high level of their peers, the true superstars such as Muhammad Ali, Arnold Palmer, Joe Namath, Billie Jean King and Bobby Fischer (we're still not sure if chess is a sport, but Bobby Fischer is too unusual a character to pass up).

In other words, here are the stories of the superstars of the Superstars.

FRANK LITSKY

March 1975

SUPERSTARS

Aaron, Henry Louis

(1934–   )

Early in the 1974 baseball season, when Hank Aaron of the Atlanta Braves hit the 715th home run of his 21-year major-league career, he became the leading home-run hitter of all time. He broke the legendary record of the legendary Babe Ruth, exciting much of a nation but infuriating and saddening many older people who felt that something of their past was being wrenched from them—and by a black man.

In the final days of the 1973 season Aaron said, "Earlier this year, some people in the older generation had the idea that they didn't want me to break it. But in other letters, people in the younger generation want me to do something they can relate to, instead of what their daddies talked about 30 or 40 years ago."

Aaron was flooded by mail, delivered twice a day. At one point cartons in the Braves' office held more than 3,000 letters, including one from a little boy who wrote, "I hope you catch up with Baby Root." There were also hate letters, many of which started "Dear Nigger," and death threats. "I can't go into hibernation," said the placid Aaron. "I've said that all I have to do to break Babe Ruth's record is to stay alive, but I got to live my life."

The tension that had become so acute in late 1973, when Aaron neared the record, vanished quickly in early 1974. On April 4, in Cincinnati, he hit his 714th home run, tying Ruth. On April 8, before a reverential home-town crowd in Atlanta and a national television audience of 35 million, he hit his 715th. Before sending the ball to the Baseball Hall of Fame, he loaned it to the Magnavox company for display. Magnavox had given him a five-year, $1 million contract to make television commercials and personal appearances, a rare ancillary benefit for a black athlete.

By that time Aaron was earning $200,000 a year from the Braves, the only major-league team he had ever played for. His first salary was $3 a game from a semi-pro team in his native Mobile, Alabama. In 1952 he joined the Indianapolis Clowns of the Negro American League as a shortstop. In his first appearance, batting cross-handed, he hit into a double play but then made 10 hits in 11 times at bat in the double-header. He was paid $100 on the first of each month and $100 on the 15th, and each month he sent home $175 of that $200.

In 1952 the Braves, then in Boston, bought him as a second baseman. In 1954 they moved to Milwaukee and brought him up, giving him a locker with his name spelled ARON. He played third base and second base before moving to the outfield, where he played most of his career (in later years he also played first base). From the start he was a .300 hitter, good on defense, swift on the bases. He was a natural player, but few people acclaimed him until his final seasons. Other players received the headlines. "Henry Aaron," wrote Jim O'Brien, "simply lacks magnetism."

He lacked little else. "With those wrists," said Rogers Hornsby, "he can be fooled a little and still hit the hell out of the ball." Roger Kahn wrote, "Henry Aaron's special technique is to swing at the ball and whack the daylights out of it." Curt Simmons said, "Throwing a fast ball by him is like trying to sneak the sun past a rooster." Joe Torre remarked, "Henry has the most ferocious swing with the least amount of effort that I have ever seen." Tommy Davis cited another virtue, saying, "He waits on a pitched ball better than anybody I ever saw." Ron Perranoski cited another, commenting, "He not only knows what the pitch will be but where it will be."

These skills resulted from hard work. "I try to keep my mind clear when I hit," Aaron said early in his career. "I don't want to think of anything but the baseball. Except for one thing. I try to remember not to swing too hard. I hit a home run, I want to hit another and I start to swing too hard. . . . This game looks easy. But it's not a guessing game but a thinking game. . . . I play my own natural way. I know I'm not flashy. I don't try to be. I want to be remembered as just plain Henry Aaron."

He will be remembered for much more—for his quiet efficiency, his dignity, his lack of pretense. (When an interviewer once asked, "What do you look for when you hit?" Aaron replied, "The baseball.")

Apparently the Braves did not remember him the way he wanted. He planned to retire after the 1975 season and become a Braves executive. But the Braves offered far less responsibility and money than he had expected, and he decided to keep playing, but only for the Milwaukee Brewers of the American League. The Braves traded him there, and he became a designated hitter. He was back home. Milwaukee remembered.

Aaron holds more important career records than anyone except Ty Cobb. At the close of the 1974 season he was the all-time leader in home runs (733), games played (3,076), at bats (11,628), plate appearances (13,058), extra-base hits (1,429) and total bases (6,591), and he ranked second or third in hits, runs scored and runs batted in. Perhaps, as William Leggett wrote in *Sports Illustrated*, "It is a matter of Ruth chasing Aaron."

Henry Aaron watches his record-breaking 715th home run sail over the fence.

14

Abdul-Jabbar, Kareem (1947–   )

In basketball annals, he will surely be one of the sport's all-time great "big men." Bill Russell called him "the greatest player to play this game," a distinction some had reserved for Russell himself. Bob

Cousy, another celebrated player and coach, said, "They can talk theory all they want, but if he comes to play we can just go home."

Hailed as a fledgling superstar since his childhood, he is, as *Sport* magazine said, "a man almost everyone appreciates and almost no one knows." He is bright and, when he chooses to be, well-spoken, but he is a private person, aloof, moody and at times discourteous. "He is one of the smallest men I have ever met," wrote Joe Falls.

When he was born, he was 22½ inches long and weighed 12 pounds 11 ounces. When he started school he was already a head taller than his classmates. He stood 6-3 in seventh grade, 6-11 in ninth grade, and he grew to an official 7-2 but is probably 7-4.

He led his high-school teams to a 95–6 record and three New York City championships. At UCLA he led the Bruins to an 88–2 record and three NCAA titles and was three times an All-American and three times the most valuable player in the NCAA championships. In 1969 he signed with the Milwaukee Bucks of the National Basketball Association for a $1.4 million, five-year contract. He was an instant star, winning player-of-the-year honors many times, and his salary reached $500,000 a year.

He was born and raised a Roman Catholic with the name Lew Alcindor, but he became a Sunnite Muslim. "The Bible and its teachings," he said, "had produced all these hate-filled people I saw in Los Angeles. It seemed to me that there was nothing in the world as unlike Christ as Christians."

Writing in *Sports Illustrated* in 1969, he said, "A long time ago I learned to accept the idea that people have no interest in me except as a jock. But I'm also a person, a human being, just like those other black men who walk about invisible to many of their fellows. . . . I'm black and I'm proud of being black and here it is, man, you can take it or leave it. This is me. . . . But I could no longer believe that the white man was evil and cruel, and black men inherently superior, as some of the other blacks are teaching nowadays. That is just the flip side of the old racism. I realized that black was neither best nor worst; it just was."

Alexander, Grover Cleveland (1887–1950)

bases. The batter was Tony Lazzeri. The Cardinals signaled to the bullpen for Alexander. According to legend, he was asleep, drunk or hung over, though he later said he was none of these. He trudged to the mound, 39 years old, weather-beaten and weary, and proceeded to strike out Lazzeri on four pitches and save the game, as the Cardinals won their first World Series.

Life after the major leagues was anything but bright for Alexander. He pitched for the House of David touring team until he was 50, appeared at a 42nd Street flea circus in New York (between the snake charmer and the penny slot machine) and drank. In 1949, in the early-morning hours of the day before Christmas, he was found in a Hollywood alley, unconscious and missing an ear. A year later he was dead. "He kept falling down and getting up again," Jack Sher wrote, "a proud, stubborn, unbelievably courageous man."

Though he was one of the most successful pitchers ever, Grover Cleveland Alexander, Old Pete, was better remembered for his drinking. "He had no interest in any form of training," wrote Grantland Rice. "Alex always thought he could pitch better after a hangover," said his wife. He also suffered from epilepsy.

In 20 seasons, from 1911 to 1930, Alexander pitched for the Philadelphia Phillies, Chicago Cubs and St. Louis Cardinals. He won 373 games (only Cy Young and Walter Johnson have won more), and he still holds the National League career records for complete games since 1900 (437) and shutouts (90). He pitched right-handed and threw mostly curves, seldom a fast ball. "These kids throw away their arms before they are mature," he said. "I got myself into the Hall of Fame without even trying."

He is best remembered for his heroics in the seventh game of the 1926 World Series. The Cardinals were leading the New York Yankees, 3–2, in the seventh inning when the Yankees loaded the

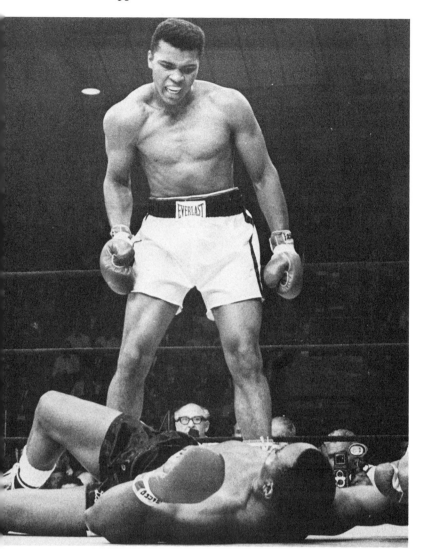

Cassius Clay taunts Sonny Liston after knocking him out in the first round of their Lewiston, Maine, rematch in 1965.

Ali, Muhammad (1942–)

He became the best-known athlete in the world, loved by millions as a black man who stood up to the white man, hated by countless others as an arrogant, bombastic braggart.

He is the fastest heavyweight boxing champion ever and, in the opinion of some, one of the best. He is by far the greatest box-office attraction in boxing history, and he has received the largest purses ever—$2.5 million for a 1971 loss to Joe Frazier, $2.6 million for beating Frazier in 1974, $5 million for beating George Foreman and regaining the title in 1974.

But his athletic talent is only half of his renown. He is colorful and charismatic, charming and abrasive, fascinating and mischievous, loud, antagonistic, magnetic. For years he was forever saying, "I am the greatest," and perhaps he spoke the truth. He is a Pied Piper who attracts crowds as a campus speaker or simply by walking down a street in any country.

Yet no one pretends to know what he is all about. *Sports Illustrated* called him "an enigma even to those closest to him." As his biographer, Jack Olsen, wrote, "His life is a symphony of paradoxes, and the biggest of all is that hundreds of thousands of words have been written about him, and yet his essential character, his attitudes, the fears and forces that drive him, remain unknown."

In 1960, when he was known as Cassius Marcellus Clay, he won the Olympic light-heavyweight championship. Four years later, as an unbeaten professional, he fought Sonny Liston for the heavyweight title. Clay was a 7–1 underdog, but he beat Liston and became champion.

Then he disclosed that he had become a member of the Nation of Islam, the so-called Black Muslims, a religious group that advocates racial separation. He often preached for the Black Muslims, and in 1967 he refused induction into the Army, contending that he was entitled to exemption as a Black Muslim minister. In addition, he said, "I don't have no quarrel with them Vietcongs."

He was convicted of draft evasion and sentenced to five years in prison. Though he appealed the conviction and never went to prison, boxing officials stripped him of his title. Conservative columnist William F. Buckley, reflecting the anti-Ali sentiment, wrote, "He is likely to hurt the sport badly by his ideologization of it. I can only hope that, to put it ineptly, someone will succeed in knocking some sense into his head before he is done damaging the sport and the country, which, however much he now disdains it, gave him the opportunity to hate it from a throne."

The Supreme Court overturned his sentence in 1970, and he fought champion Joe Frazier in 1971 in a bout that grossed $20 million. His three and a half years away from the ring showed, and Frazier won. But in 1974 he beat Frazier and the heavily favored Foreman and he was again champion. George Plimpton called his knockout of Foreman "the triumph of the underdog, the comeback from hard times and exile, the victory of an outspoken nature over a sullen disposition, the prevailing of intelligence over raw power, the success of physical grace, the ascendance of age over youth."

"He has emerged as more than a folk hero in the broad realm of fun and games," Will Grimsley wrote. "He is a social force. He has entrees to the palaces and government seats of the world. Presidents and potentates fawn over him. Kings and princes embrace him. Scholars court him. Children tug at him. Little people, from Bangkok to Baghdad, cry out his name."

While he relishes his regained position, he seems curiously removed from the limelight. "In the very private world in which he lives, he is subdued, earnest, quiet, even tender," wrote Bob Stewart. "He seems not to understand the harm he may be doing. . . . He does not hate, though he preaches on the edge of hatred. He does not mean literally all that he says."

He talked of retirement, but his vision of privacy was difficult to accept. "When I am through," he said, "I can say I have had my fun. I have seen the world. I have earned the most that I could earn, and I can't stay forever. . . . And I am so tired of publicity and things and people mobbing you and you have no freedom. You don't belong to yourself, you know? You don't own yourself. Everybody's watching you. I'm glad when the day comes when I can walk around and not be noticed."

That day will never come. Muhammad Ali will always be noticed.

Ali regains his crown as George Foreman crawls to his feet after losing their 1974 fight in Zaire.

Allen, George Herbert (1922–   )

George Allen is a football coach unlike any other. "His mind," Alfred Wright wrote, "is almost solely devoted to winning football games and how it can be done more efficiently." Allen's quarterback on the Los Angeles Rams, Roman Gabriel, agreed, saying, "I've never known a man who concentrated his energy so totally on one goal."

He is a spokesman for and example of the work ethic, devoted to inspiring messages. In an article written for *Sports Illustrated* he said, "If I've succeeded, it's because I outwork most people. Work is simply a synonym for effort, and as I tell my players, 'A hundred percent is not enough.' . . . The world belongs to those who aim for 110 percent." As John Underwood wrote, "Almost everything he says has been, or should be, on a wall somewhere."

From 1948 to 1956 he was head coach at Morningside College and Whittier College. He became celebrated as a defensive coach for eight years (1958–65) with the Chicago Bears. When the Los Angeles Rams sought him as head coach, Bears owner-coach George Halas charged "tampering" and tried to keep him. But he lost the fight, and Allen coached the Rams to two division titles in five seasons (1966–70).

He moved to the Washington Redskins in 1971 as head coach at $125,000 a year for seven years. He quickly traded for older, experienced players (sometimes he even traded draft choices he did not own) and paid them high salaries. Edward Bennett Williams, the lawyer and Redskins president, said, "I have given him an unlimited budget, and he's already exceeded it." The Redskins were called the Over the Hill Gang, but they became winners.

Though Allen became a Washington notable who dined at the White House and received play suggestions from Presidents, he strived to maintain his Boy Scout image. As William Barry Furlong wrote, "He has a boyish, diffident 'push' about him . . . though he labors hard to appear humble." His favorite food was still ice cream, and his wife, Etty, explained why: "I think it's because he doesn't have to chew. Chewing would take away his concentration from football."

Lest one think that he is all work and no play, he once said, "Nobody should work all the time. Everybody should have some leisure, and the early-morning hours are best for this. You can combine two good things at once—sleep and leisure. Leisure time is that five or six hours when you sleep at night."

The Washington Redskins carry their jubilant coach off the field after clinching the National Football Conference title in 1972.

Allen, Richard Anthony (1942–   )

Throughout his baseball career, Dick Allen has been a brooding enigma. Emotional, intense and unpredictable, he is determined to live by his own rules. When he feels he does not need batting practice, he does not take batting practice. When he feels he does not have to get to the park until 30 minutes before game time, that is when he gets there.

"He takes orders from no one, not even his manager," Will Grimsley wrote. "He is subject to none of the normal niceties that go with being a public figure." "He is one of a small number of great athlete-celebrities who have curled up inside cocoons rather than risk exposure," Larry Merchant said.

Since his major-league debut in 1963, he has played for the Philadelphia Phillies, St. Louis Cardinals, Los Angeles Dodgers and Chicago White Sox, driving managers to distraction at every stop. He has played the outfield and every infield position, always hitting with power and for high average. Extremely talented and hard-driving, he could afford to be individualistic. His salary of $225,000 a year is the highest in baseball history.

When he won the American League's most-valuable-player award in 1972, he put the trophy not in his home but in the White Sox clubhouse, an unusually generous gesture. Bill White, his roommate for two years with the Phillies, said, "All he wanted was somebody to give him a ball and a bat and let him go." His problem, wrote Sandy Padwe, was that "he has never been able to understand, or accept, baseball's impersonal nature."

He also couldn't accept losing. After the 1974 season he retired, saying, "I wasn't satisfied to have all those home runs and still lose." The White Sox traded him to the Atlanta Braves, but he refused to play for them, saying Atlanta was no place for a black man. One month into the 1975 season, the Braves traded him to the Phillies, and he started playing again.

He suspected that winning was eclipsed by other goals in the big-league stadiums. "With 162 games and all that travel, a baseball player becomes a piece of meat. . . . I don't want to be a slave to money.

The Lord gave me two good hands. I could go out and earn an honest living if I had to. . . . "

And there was a new generation of independent Allens on the march. "My nine-year-old boy threw a bat. He was suspended from Little League. The teachers say he won't answer questions he knows the answers to. I can see a lot of me in him. I'm going to have a six-foot-two monster on my hands some day."

Alston, Walter Emmons
(1911–   )

Only Connie Mack (50 years) and John McGraw (31 years) managed the same team longer than Walter Alston, and Mack had the advantage of owning his team.

Alston's major-league playing career consisted of one time at bat in 1936. For 13 years he was a successful minor-league manager. In 1954, when Charlie Dressen insisted on a multi-year contract as manager, the Dodgers let him go and hired the obscure Alston for one year. He has managed them ever since, in Brooklyn and Los Angeles, always signing blank one-year contracts at the season's end and not knowing until the following April how much money he would be earning (it is now $75,000 a year). Dressen said, "The Dodgers never plan to fire Alston. All they want to do is torture him." The torture has been infrequent because his teams have won seven National League pennants and four World Series.

Walter Alston, known to friends back home in Ohio as Smokey, is a big, sturdy man, calm, sincere, honest, tolerant, quick to admit errors and disdainful of players who do not. He is generally a conservative manager. When he got the job a New York writer said, "The Dodgers do not need a manager. That is why they got Alston." The Dodgers thought differently. "You'd go into a slump and Dressen would ignore you," one player said. "But this fellow comes around, tells you to hang in there and tries to pick up your spirit."

Despite the apprehensions, Alston proved a craftsman. "He treats his players like men," said Fred (Dixie) Walker, a Dodger coach and former outfielder. "He is patient and knows how to use his men," said Grady Hatton, a managerial rival. "He has kept his job," said Walter O'Malley, the long-time Dodger president, "first because he is non-irritating and second because he's competent."

"I like this job of managing," Alston has said. "If I do the best I can possibly do, there's not a helluva lot more I can do. If you're going to be fired, you're going to be fired. I'm not going to worry till the boss tells me."

The late Fresco Thompson, a Dodger vice-president, explained Alston's success this way: "Some fellows, when they're appointed big-league managers, become one of the 12 Apostles. They become John McGraw. The club hired Joe Zilch, not John McGraw. Walter Alston has the good sense to remain Walter Alston."

Anderson, Paul

(1932–   )

He became the strongest man in the world, and he has an Olympic gold medal to prove it. Ed Linn wrote, "In the natural development of the race, he had no justification for coming along for about 500 more years." Jim George, a weightlifting contemporary, said, "Any man that big shouldn't be able to move at all."

He is certainly big, except for his height (he stands 5 feet 10 inches). He weighed 310 pounds at age 21, competed usually between 330 and 350 pounds and went as high as 370. He has a 59-inch chest (Jack Dempsey's was 43), a 47-inch waist (Jess Willard's was 35), 36-inch thighs (Joe Louis' were 23) and a 23½-inch neck (Primo Carnera's was 20). He waddles when he walks and looks the way people think a strongman should look.

He smiles easily and is soft-spoken. His appetite is legendary. He drinks up to six quarts of milk a day, and his snacks include a quart of ice cream or a milkshake with three eggs.

In 1955, a year before the Olympics and long before he made the Olympic team, a made-to-order uniform was arranged for him. He was Olympic champion and world record-holder in 1956, a professional strongman in 1957, a professional wrestler in 1958 and a professional boxer in 1960 (he retired after three rounds of his first fight). He went on to perform strongman feats all over the nation and crusade for Christian youth groups.

His mother was 5-2 and ample, his father 5-10½ and 178 pounds. In high school, before he weighed 200 pounds, he lifted the rear end of cars just for fun. By his senior year he was a 230-pound single-wing blocking back—except in crucial situations. James (Red) Boyd, his high-school coach, recalled, "We used to line up in the T formation to give him the ball on the quarterback sneak. It was like turning a herd of elephants loose on the field."

He started working with weights to get in condition for college football. He was a surprisingly mobile 250-pound guard, but after one season of freshman football at Furman University he quit school and kept lifting. Eventually he could raise 5,000 pounds with a back lift and 3,500 pounds with a hip belt. He lifted a concrete-filled safe, full-grown

horses and a table with 6,270 pounds in weight.

"He is almost a frightening sight in action," wrote Furman Bisher. "He puffs and blows like a steam engine, and sometimes the muscles in his neck swell so enormously that it seems the arteries will come tearing through his hide."

Anderson believed weightlifting had practical values. "Strength can help a man in almost anything he wants to do. The average person is ridiculously weak compared with the strength he could build up in himself within just two months. Any young man might follow my pattern and become a champion. He might, but I don't think he could without natural strength. . . . It's got to be your life, as it's been with me. I've made weightlifting my life. That's how I was able to do it."

22

Andretti, Mario

(1940–   )

He is a supremely accomplished race driver. In recent years he has won in Formula One Grands Prix, Indianapolis, Formula 5000, sprint, midget, sports and stock cars. He set a world closed-course speed record of 214.158 miles an hour, and his auto-racing victories include the Indianapolis 500 and Daytona 500, three United States Auto Club season titles and three Twelve Hours of Sebring races.

In spite of his daredevil career, he remains a simple, private person, calm, unruffled, boyish and

handsome, with a crooked nose and dark curly hair. He is a small man, 5 feet 6 inches and 138 pounds, but size means little in auto racing. "He's just a nice guy," said Jacques Passino, director of Ford's racing program. "He doesn't call collect, he doesn't send bills and he doesn't bug you."

Born in Trieste when it belonged to Italy, he came to America with his family at the age of 15. He entered racing with determination, and, as one observer wrote, he has retained an almost childlike enthusiasm for the sport. The former sponsor of his Indy cars, Al Dean, said, "He's hungry. He's after something and he won't let go until he gets it." Clint Brawner, his mechanic, cited his "guts and ability and tremendous confidence."

The young Mario Andretti was impetuous. "I'm too eager," he once said. "I'm always fighting myself. I like to drive the car at the limit all the time." After years on the racing circuit he had mellowed. "I used to question whether I was really getting everything out of the car. Now, I just go as fast as I feel I can, and beyond that, well, I'm just not going to find out. I have just as much drive to win as I ever had, but I don't have stars in my eyes anymore."

He has earned hundreds of thousands of dollars for using and testing Firestone tires. He is an avid competitor of whom Bill Libby wrote, "He seems driven by natural desire. He has snarling confidence and the killer instinct. He is a professional race driver to whom other things in life do not seem to matter much."

Andretti confirmed that, saying, "Why do I race? I don't know. I really don't. I don't think anybody except me can understand it. Whenever I get bored with racing, I start thinking about how much I wanted to be where I am now. I would give up everything—my home, my family, everything I've gained—to stay in racing."

Andy Granatelli congratulates Mario Andretti after he won the 1969 Indy in a Granatelli-owned car.

Anson, Adrian Constantine

(1851–1922)

His nicknames—Cap because he was team captain and Pop because he was a major-league baseball player until the age of 47—reflected the respect and love of a nation.

Cap Anson was a major-league player, mostly a first baseman, for 22 years. For five years before that he played in the National Association for the Rockford (Illinois) Forest Cities and the Philadelphia Athletics. When the National League was founded in 1876 he jumped to the Chicago White Stockings (later the Cubs). He played for them and doubled as their playing manager from 1879 until he was fired in 1897.

Anson batted over .300 in 20 seasons, a National League record. His lifetime batting average was .339, and he was the first major-league player to make 3,000 hits. He was elected to the Baseball Hall of Fame in 1939. With all that, Cap Anson the man, rather than Cap Anson the baseball player, inspired purple prose. Ed Burns wrote, ''He was a man of strength, spiritual as well as physical. He didn't drink, he didn't smoke, and he lived according to a personal code of rigid honesty and unyielding pride.'' Lee Allen and Tom Meany said, ''He stood at first base like a mighty oak . . . the symbol of all that was strong and good in baseball.'' John B. Sheridan, in *The Sporting News,* called him ''the giant of giants . . . a man who had the finest conception of the honor and dignity of his profession.'' Hyder Ali wrote in verse, ''How old is Anson? When the ark first found once more a resting place, Old Noah, groping in the dark, found Anson on first base.''

Anson was a sober, tough, physically imposing man who treated his players well, put them up in the best hotels and had them driven to the ball park in carriages. A candy bar and a cigar were named for him. But when he left baseball he lost his life savings of $80,000 running a billiards parlor and had the mortgage on his home foreclosed. The National League offered him a pension, a rarity in those days, but he declined, saying, ''I don't want any charity.''

Eddie Arcaro in the winner's circle atop Native Dancer.

Arcaro, George Edward

(1916–   )

One of the golden names of horseracing, Eddie Arcaro was, according to *Life* magazine, "a power, pressure rider, hand-riding a horse through the stretch, scrubbing and kicking and elbowing it." His racing poise and confidence were unique and his success dazzling. For Emmett Watson he was "the greatest figure to mount a horse since Phil Sheridan upset the morning line at Winchester, Virginia."

Eddie Arcaro quit high school after one year to exercise horses at Latonia for $15 a week. He rode his first winner in 1932 as a 15-year-old apprentice at Caliente, Mexico. In 1934 Calumet Farm bought his contract and raised his pay to $350 a month. Soon after he was earning $100,000 and more a year.

During his 31 years as a jockey he rode in 24,092 races. He won 4,779, trailing only Willie Shoemaker and Johnny Longden in the all-time standing. His horses earned $30,039,543, a figure exceeded only by Shoemaker and Braulio Baeza.

He set an all-time record of 549 stakes victories and set another by riding ten "horses of the year." His 17 triple-crown victories (five Kentucky Derbies, six Preaknesses and six Belmont Stakes) are still a record. He is also the only jockey to ride two triple-crown winners (Whirlaway in 1941 and Citation in 1948). His other celebrated mounts include Nashua, Kelso and Bold Ruler.

He stood 5 feet 2½ inches and weighed 111 pounds. He had large hands, strong arms and shoulders and thin legs. His big nose led to the nickname used by the $2 bettor—Banana Nose. He was cool, honest and unpretentious. Respected in and out of racing, he was also bright, urbane, well-spoken and interested in the world around him.

He had friends everywhere, but he did not fraternize often with other jockeys. "It isn't easy," he explained, "to go out socially with a man one night and then have to take a mount away from him the next morning."

As a youth he was rough and hot-tempered. In late 1942 he was suspended for a year for trying to drive another jockey into the rail. But in later years his anger was replaced by poise, and when trainers wanted a jockey for a big race they invariably turned to him.

"When the big money is up, he's the rider you want," said trainer Max Hirsch. "Having the big money up is like giving him a shot of hop at the top of the stretch." Arcaro agreed. "I honestly believe there isn't anybody who can get the job done any better than I can. And I really believe I have the best judgment when the money is hanging up there."

The money was always hanging up there, and he resisted retirement. "If I quit," he said, "I'd just be another little man." But in 1962, aching from bursitis in his right arm, he retired at the age of 46. His wife, Ruth, was overjoyed.

"I can't recall being this happy in oh so long," she said. "These last few years I've been terribly afraid for him, and so have the children. Some Saturdays I'd get up just enough nerve to put on the television set to watch him ride, but then I couldn't. I'd look the other way and hope that nothing went wrong."

Why was he so successful? Ben Jones, the Calumet Farm trainer, thought it was a question of touch, "like with a piano player." Willie Shoemaker said he looked perfect on a horse: "The way he rides, he looks like part of the horse." "The best instrument to explain the genius of Eddie Arcaro is not a human collaborator at all," wrote Roger Kahn. "The best instrument is a horse. Unfortunately, Whirlaway and Citation keep their counsel, and the rest of us are left to guess."

Arcaro insisted that neither horse nor jockey could win by himself. "The fastest horse should win," he said. "But his speed alone won't get him the money. . . . I believe that 80 percent of the time the outcome of a race depends on the individual thinking on the part of the jockey on the best horse. . . . You don't win on bums."

He often had to coax his horses. "Of all the horses I ride," he said, "maybe 70 percent of them don't want to win. They don't like to run out by themselves, or they don't like moving up and getting dirt kicked at them, or they don't like something else. . . . When you get a horse like that, you've got to fool him. You try to time it so he's just up at the finish."

If his horses frequently didn't want to win, Arcaro did. He and his horses were often up at the finish.

Arcaro and Citation after winning the Preakness, the second leg of their 1948 Triple Crown victory.

Armstrong, Henry Jackson, Jr.
(1912–   )

Henry Armstrong, the man, was a humble, lonely introvert. As a fighter, his head bobbing constantly, his body in a semi-crouch, he was a buzzsaw and the only man to hold three world championships simultaneously.

In October 1937 he won the featherweight title; in May 1938, the welterweight title; in August 1938, the lightweight title. He gave up the featherweight crown in December 1938 because he had trouble making weight. He lost the lightweight title in 1939, almost won the middleweight title in 1940 and lost the welterweight title the same year.

In 1945 he retired after a 14-year professional career that encompassed 175 fights, 100 face stitches, scar tissue over both eyes, sore hands from fighting too often and a nervous breakdown. He was soon penniless and drunk. Then he started reading the Bible. In 1951 he was ordained a Baptist minister and became an evangelist and, in his words, "a humble worker for the Lord." He finally found peace.

Henry Armstrong punches his way to the featherweight title against Petey Sarron in 1937.

Al Stump wrote, "Peace was something he . . . never was able to find through nearly two decades of struggle, tragedy, success and disillusionment. He was the dupe of some of the most vicious rascals who ever threw a preliminary boy into three fights on the same card. . . . He was used, abused and confused by a succession of tinhorn handlers." And Barney Nagler said, "In his glory, he expressed himself in the violent poetry of strength and stamina and speed. . . . He drove fast cars and ran with fast women, and the money that came to him went away even faster." Stump also wrote, "He was a merciless meat-chopper because ambition, along with the fear that he might slip back to the poverty he had known most of his life, rode him hard."

Jack Dempsey described his fights as "a million punches thrown as fast and hard as he could let them go" and called him "a human piston." But in his later years, Armstrong had "found love of mankind." In 1943 he wrote this poem: "Thrown into a turbulent sea/ Of sharks and whales,/ But yet unharmed./ Put into a fiery furnace/ And yet unburned./ The faith in God/ Won't let His child go wrong/ Somehow: Because I meant to do good."

Ashe, Arthur Robert, Jr.
(1943–   )

He is the only black in the big-time world of white tennis. "A lump of coal in the snowbank," he says of himself. Tony Kornheiser wrote, "He has become the white man's black man—the crowd favorite, the highly visible, highly rich token." Frank Deford wrote that "He is invariably pestered by fawning Negroes whom he does not know and by patronizing whites keen to display their latent brotherhood now that they have a colored boy right here at the club." Such elements of irony and distinction were present early in his career. "I am often invited to clubs where other Negroes are admitted only as busboys," Ashe observed.

Lean (6 feet 1 inch, 158 pounds), handsome and clean-cut, he is an intellectual and an extrovert, witty and popular. In 1968 he became the first black man to win the United States championship (it was the first U.S. Open, but because he was an amateur he could accept no prize money). Turning professional, he earned $100,000 to $200,000 a year in purses and hundreds of thousands more in endorsements and public relations. As Bud Collins, the writer and broadcaster, said, "He has impact well beyond the game."

His strokes are whippy and often spectacular, but he lacks concentration and seldom wins the key tournaments. Robert Screen, the tennis coach at Hampton Institute, said he lacked the killer attitude. "He has fought so long for acceptance that it's impossible for him to look at his opponent as his enemy."

He has often been criticized for passiveness in racial matters. Clark Graebner, once a ranked player, said, "He could have had it any way he wanted. He did speak out a little, but he took the money." But, Graebner added, "ultimately, he may do more for blacks that way." Rosemary Casals, a ranking women's player, was more critical. "He wasn't hungry enough. Everything was handed to him. He isn't really black. He's mostly white. He lives white and he gets paid by whites."

He answered those arguments by saying, "Anyone can speak out on racial issues in America. That's nothing new. I spoke out on South Africa when

nobody else was doing it. Why is everybody after me to speak out on everything? Nobody asks Walt Frazier to speak out on anything. Walt has earned his right not to be there, and so have I."

Race and his erratic performance weighed him down. "I've had a monkey on my back," he said. "I know the public expects me to be a winner. They expect the real Arthur Ashe to surface. They don't understand why he hasn't. Look, I'll probably never know what the hell the real Arthur Ashe is. I never brought out the real me. . . . The way I live my life, I'll probably never become Number One."

Atkinson, Theodore Francis (1916–   )

Few jockeys have enjoyed more success than Ted Atkinson, and fewer still have enjoyed his reputation for honesty and integrity.

Writer Pat Lynch described him as "an uncorruptible thread in the sport's frequently sordid tapestry." The 5-foot-2-inch, 105-pound Atkinson rode 3,795 winners in 23,661 races and his horses earned over $17 million during his 22-year career (1937–59). When he injured his sacroiliac and was unable to walk upright, he retired to become a racing official and later the chief steward in Illinois. His physician, Dr. Alexander Kaye, said, "He could not give his best, and that is the only way he rides."

Born in Canada and raised in upstate New York, he was a proud competitor. "The two-dollar public adored him because he rode every race all out, as if it were a $100,000 classic," Joe Val said. "He's in there trying every yard," wrote Joe Palmer, "and while he cannot come in ahead of the horse, he can be depended upon to get as much out of his mounts as heredity and the trainer have put in."

He was known for a degree of refinement unusual in racing circles. The New York *Journal American* referred to him as "the thoroughbred." Arthur Daley called him "a class guy." He was also diligent. "He is not a natural rider such as Eddie Arcaro," Roger Kahn observed. "His success came gradually and only because he applied himself to his trade with an impressive degree of scholarship."

Among fellow jockeys he earned the name The Professor because he was intelligent and articulate, but the public called him The Slasher because he often used his whip. He disliked the latter nickname. "I never drew blood on a horse in my life," he said in self-defense. "I was merely trying to impress upon the horse the urgency of the situation."

He took his share of harassment from losing bettors, but he was undisturbed. "If you ride a lot, you're going to ride a lot of losers and get a lot of abuse. But you're going to ride a lot of winners, too, so it's simply a question of keeping your sense of proportion." After retiring he continued living the racing life. "I grit my teeth and feel as if I'm riding myself when I see the horses closing in the stretch."

Auerbach, Arnold

(1917–   )

Red Auerbach was the most successful coach in professional basketball history. His 20 years as a pro coach (1946–66) spanned the Washington Capitols (three seasons), the Tri-Cities (one season) and the Boston Celtics (16 seasons). His Celtics won nine National Basketball Association championships in ten seasons with such players as Bill Russell, Bob Cousy, Bill Sharman, Tom Heinsohn, John Havlicek, Sam Jones and K. C. Jones. He is the only coach in NBA history with 1,000 victories (his lifetime record was 1,037–548). After retiring from coaching he became general manager and president of the Celtics.

As a player at George Washington University he was better remembered for enthusiasm than skill. As a pro coach he was cocky, brash and volatile, and he always lighted a cigar when victory appeared certain. "The cigar is a sign of relaxation," he once said. "The cigarette is a sign of tension."

He demanded 100 percent from his players. "If they play for me," he said, "they're ready to play or they're gone. I don't bawl a man out in public. I don't give him a serious fine. If he's that kind of trouble, I got to get rid of him anyway." At the same time, he knew the relative importance of coach and players. "The thing I've got to watch is being carried away with my own importance," he once said.

He was forever badgering referees. Rival coach Fred Schaus said, "He intimidates the officials. He's got that baiting of his down to a science. . . . He gets away with twice as much as anyone else." "He was a consummate actor during games," wrote Mac Davis. "He was thrown out of more games by officials than any other coach."

Everyone had a different explanation for his success. "He comprehends better than most men that winning is its own reward," Irv Goodman wrote. Tom Heinsohn, who played for him, said, "The reason he's so successful is that he's always the boss." Bill Russell, a Celtic star and his successor as Celtic coach, said, "In order to be successful, you've got to believe in yourself, which is commonly known as egotism. He's an egotist, just like me. He has his successes and his failures. He keeps his failures to a minimum." Mel Counts, who also played for him, confessed, "I like him, but I don't understand him."

He was always in control of himself, even when he harangued officials. He believed that basketball was a game of high emotion. "In my house," he said, "I don't go around yelling, blowing my top, losing my temper. Home is a different world, a different game."

He acknowledged he was not an easy man to be friendly with. "I'm not a hail fellow well met. I'm a good friend and a good enemy. You mellow with age. Once I was younger, tougher, meaner."

Baer, Maximilian Adelbert (1909–1959)

The New York Times said of Max Baer, "He clowned his way into the heavyweight championship . . . and he was still laughing when he lost it a year later. . . . He had everything a champion needed except the disposition to attend to business."

He was a big man (6 feet 3 inches and 220 pounds), a handsome playboy who fought professionally from 1929 to 1941. In 1934 he won the world title by knocking down Primo Carnera 11

times in 11 rounds. (When their feet tangled and both fell to the floor, he said to Carnera, "The last one up is a sissy.") The following year, failing to train seriously, he lost the title to Jimmy Braddock. Months later he was knocked out in four rounds by young Joe Louis, who said, "The man took more punishment than anybody I ever fought."

His punch was a bludgeon, a result, he said, of swinging a meat ax in his father's butcher shop. In 1930 Frankie Campbell died from a Baer knockout punch. In 1932 Baer knocked out Ernie Schaaf, and five months later, after losing to Carnera, Schaaf died.

During and after his boxing career he performed in movies, on radio, television, stage and in nightclubs. His chauffeured limousine often took him and his "social secretaries" to nightclubs. Minutes after he knocked out Max Schmeling he stood under a shower, a bottle of beer in one hand and a cigarette in the other.

The critics agreed that Baer's attitude was his undoing. "Nature endowed him with a magnificent body and all the physical requisites of a great champion, but he lacked the mental poise," Nat Fleischer wrote. "He could have been a great fighter for a long time, but training bored him," Joe Williams added. Arthur Daley said, "He should have been the greatest heavyweight champion, but he never bothered to learn his trade properly." But his flamboyant manner gave boxing a new zest. Grantland Rice called him "the New Deal for bored fight fans."

"He was a man difficult to dislike," Jack Sher recalled. "He chattered and charmed his way into the hearts of even the hard-bitten sports crowd—the writers, the managers, even the disgruntled bettors who often dropped a double sawbuck because of his clowning in the ring. . . . Exhibitionism ran riot in the man."

Baer himself said, "They say I'm my own worst enemy. Maybe I am, but imagine all the people who envy me. . . . I've got a million-dollar body and a ten-cent brain. . . . When I made it, I spent it, and sometimes I spent it faster than I made it. . . . I got no regrets. I was never meant to be a fighter."

rides in easy rhythm with his mount, so that, as trainer Jimmy Jones said, "Horses give so willingly for him." *Life* magazine called him "the icy rider with the gentle hands" and spoke of "his own gentle, personal style."

Eddie Arcaro called him a sit-still rider. "The horses seem to want to run for him," Arcaro said. "He doesn't flop all over a horse," Willie Shoemaker said of his riding technique. "He's calm and relaxed, and he seems to put this across to the horse he's riding." Racing people liked to say that he could ride with a glass of water on his back.

He shows his love of horses in many ways. He never abuses his mounts. "What is the sense of hitting a tired horse?" Baeza asked. "If he is doing his best for you, what will it serve you to keep on hitting him? . . . They are just like human beings. What is the point of beating them to death?"

Baeza, Braulio (1940–   )

At the age of eight he was galloping horses in Panama, where his father and grandfather had been jockeys. He was a jockey himself at the age of 15, and by 17 he was the best in Panama. He started riding in the United States in 1960, and by the end of 1974 he had won 2,875 races and over $31 million in purses.

Braulio Baeza (pronounced "Brow-oo-lee-oh Bah-AY-zuh"), at 5 feet 4½ inches and 112 pounds, is fragile-looking, wiry and regal. Temperamentally he is impassive, shy and aloof, and he has almond eyes that contribute to his Oriental, elegant look. "He is as serene as the face of Buddha," wrote Paul Lynch. He talks little but is unfailingly courteous.

"It is his relation to a horse, physical and otherwise, that forms the basis for the general esteem in which he is held at the track," Frank Graham, Jr., wrote. He has an ideal build for a jockey, and he

A statuesque Braulio Baeza poses atop Graustark after one of his victories.

32

Banks, Ernest (1931–   )

He played 19 years (1953–71) and 2,528 games (a club record) for the Chicago Cubs, hit 512 home runs and won the National League's most-valuable-player award in 1958 and 1959. He did it all with a sunny disposition. He was ever smiling, ever cheerful, a Little Mary Sunshine, a baseball flower child.

Onetime Cub manager Stan Hack said of Banks, "He's so calm and businesslike when he comes back to the bench, you couldn't tell whether he'd hit a homer or struck out." Banks had his own thoughts on his even temper. "The only person I ever get mad at is myself," he said. "I don't mind when a pitcher dusts me off or an umpire calls a close one against me. They've got a job to do. My job is to stand up there and keep swinging."

And how he swung! William Barry Furlong wrote, "He has revolutionized slugging, turning it from a free-swinging feast for big men into an art that can be—and is—now practiced by men of slight build." Clyde McCullough, a Cub teammate, agreed, saying, "He swings a bat like Joe Louis used

to throw a punch—short and sweet."

Ernie Banks, who came to love baseball so much, started reluctantly. When he was ten, his father, once a semi-pro catcher, bought him a $2.98 glove. The young Banks wasn't interested, and his father had to give him ten-cent bribes to get him to play catch. Yet he took to baseball, and at 17 he was barnstorming for $5 a game. The Cubs later bought him from the Kansas City Monarchs of the Negro American League, and in 1953, without having played in the minor leagues, he became the first black to play for the Cubs.

He played shortstop most of his career, then moved to first base because of fielding problems and an arthritic left knee. Even in his final seasons, Lee Greene wrote, "He hustled like a rookie trying to hang onto his job." "He was built like a letter opener, comported himself like a man applying for a loan and relished his work," Mark Kram wrote. "The only thing he disliked about playing two games was that he could not play three."

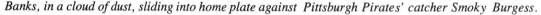

Banks, in a cloud of dust, sliding into home plate against Pittsburgh Pirates' catcher Smoky Burgess.

Bannister, Roger Gilbert (1929–   )

On May 6, 1954, Roger Bannister, a tall, angular, 25-year-old English medical student, achieved one of the most widely acclaimed feats in the annals of sport. He became the first man to run a mile faster than four minutes, an accomplishment that hardly evokes interest today but at that time was a milestone. "Long after the record is gone," *The New York Times* observed, "his name will live."

Bannister's memorable mile came at the Iffley Road track in Oxford, England, before a crowd of 1,000, mostly Oxford University students. That morning he worked in London, then took a train to Oxford, lunched with friends, walked by himself to relax and went to the track. The wind rose, and he feared his record attempt would be ruined. But he decided to run, recalling later that "There are some moments in life when one is really alone. That was such a moment. . . . I had reached my peak physically and psychologically. There would never be another day like it."

With two friends setting the pace, he won in 3 minutes 59.4 seconds, a world record. Seven weeks later John Landy of Australia ran 3:58.0. Seven weeks after that, Bannister defeated Landy in the British Commonwealth Games in 3:58.8. He resumed his medical studies and, soon after, his track career ended. "The day I qualified as a doctor, I stopped running," Bannister said.

He became a consulting neurologist and unpaid chairman of the British Sports Council, which developed British sports participation and facilities. He wrote in *The New York Times*, "Sport is a natural, worthwhile and enjoyable form of human expression and eminently deserves support in its own right and for its own sake." Witty, charming and philosophical, Bannister once mused, "Sport is not the main aim in life. Yet to achieve perfection in one thing, however small, makes it possible to face uncertainty in the more difficult problems of life. . . . Records should be servants, not the masters, of the athletes. . . . The four-minute mile had become rather like an Everest, a challenge to the human spirit. Now it is merely a physical, or at any rate a physiological, problem."

He remained a hero in Britain. He jogged once a week, clad in a sweatsuit and tennis sneakers, in London's Hyde Park, but few people saw him. "One must remember," he said, "that at eight o'clock on a Saturday morning, most people are in bed." He remained a celebrity at home, too, but with some confusion. "For a time," he said, "my wife thought I had run four miles in one minute."

Winning the mile at the 1954 British Commonwealth Games ahead of John Landy, who seven weeks before broke Bannister's world record for the event.

Baugh, Samuel Adrian
(1914–   )

He was lean and leathery and raw-boned. "He looked," wrote Jack Zanger, "as frail as an old picket fence." But Slingin' Sammy Baugh was a National Football League quarterback for 16 years, for many years the longest pro career of any player. "He is to passing," wrote Kevin Roberts, "what Lindbergh was to the airplane."

Baugh played tailback for Texas Christian from 1934 to 1936. He then entered the pros, playing for the Washington Redskins from 1937 to 1952. He led the league six years in passing, gaining 21,886 yards in the air, while leading in punting average for five years with a 45.1-yard career average. In 1943 Baugh led the league with 11 interceptions. In those days players were often on the field for the full 60 minutes.

Starting with the Redskins for $8,000 a year (the team's next highest salary was $2,750), he was earning $20,000 when he retired. He was a single-wing tailback, often blocking and carrying the ball, until the Redskins adopted the T formation in 1944. He was elected to the College Football Hall of Fame in 1951 and to the Pro Football Hall of Fame in 1963.

Sports Illustrated said of his contribution to the sport, "Above all, he gave to pro football a radical concept that he had learned from his college coach at Texas Christian, Dutch Meyer—namely, that the forward pass could be more than just a surprise weapon or a desperation tactic. Sammy Baugh made the pass a routine scrimmage play." Arthur Daley wrote that "he revolutionized football and altered all previous strategic concepts." Bill Rives said that Baugh reduced the forward pass to a simple element of offensive strategy. "In his worst games . . . he was as good as most quarterbacks on their best days," Roger Treat, the football historian, recalled.

In the 1950s and 1960s Baugh was a head and assistant coach for various colleges (Hardin-Simmons, Oklahoma State and Tulsa) and pro teams (New York Titans, Houston Oilers and Detroit Lions). Curley Johnson, who played for him on the Titans, said, "They respected him for his football ability and his honesty. If he told you it was going to rain at eight o'clock the next morning, you knew it would."

Baugh thoroughly enjoyed football. "Most men played pro football in those days because they liked football," he said. "It was more fun than it is now. . . . All there is to quarterbacking is to call the right play at the right time. . . . Except for having to live in the big city, the whole thing was wonderful."

Baylor, Elgin Gay

(1934–   )

Fred Schaus, his coach, called Elgin Baylor "the greatest cornerman ever to play pro basketball." Arthur Daley wrote that he was so slick, so smooth and so effortless that he didn't appear to command the attention that whirled around such teammates as Wilt Chamberlain and Jerry West. West himself said, "I guess the best way to put it is that he is the kind of guy that when he's not around, you know he's not around."

A 6-foot-5-inch forward, Baylor was fluid, cool and thoroughly professional. He played one year at the College of Idaho (on a football scholarship) and three years at Seattle University, where he made All-America in 1957 and 1958. He went on to 14 pro seasons, all with the Lakers in Minneapolis and then in Los Angeles. He retired as the third-highest scorer in National Basketball Association history, with 23,149 points, an average of 27.4 per game, and as the sixth leading rebounder (those ahead of him stood 6-9 or taller). He made all-pro ten times.

Writer Jim Murray characterized Baylor as "proud, sensitive, suspicious and generally aloof." Frank Deford wrote that "Were Elgin Baylor an animal, he would be a satin tiger. On and off the court, he glides with a regal mien." And Bill Libby wrote, "He appears above criticism. . . If he kicked his mother on the court, the fans would boo her, the press would give her bad notices and someone would start a collection and have his toe bronzed."

Bad knees plagued Baylor during the last half of his career. He had a torn left kneecap, stretched tendons in the right knee and calcium deposits in both knees. His courage and drive prompted the admiration of many people who saw him play. "It's like watching Citation run on spavined legs," Chick Hearn, the Laker broadcaster, commented. Carl Braun, a rival player, summed up the general feeling when he said, "You keep wondering how a man can get so much out of himself."

After ten years as a pro, Baylor still enjoyed his sport. "Pro basketball is still fun. The traveling, the schedule, the crazy hours never have bothered me. I

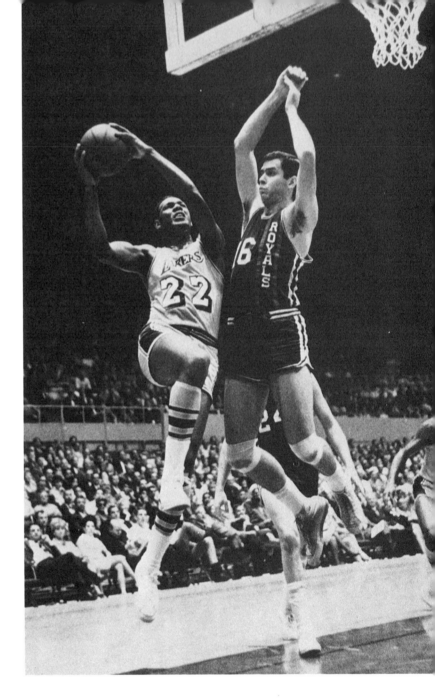

Baylor drives and shoots past the Cincinnati Royals' Jerry Lucas.

hear players younger than I am saying they can't get up for games anymore. I don't know what they're talking about. The day I decide to retire, it probably will be because I've had a whole season where I could not shake a succession of lingering injuries." When he did retire at 37 for just that reason, he said, "I do not want to prolong my career when I cannot maintain the standards I established for myself."

Beard, Ralph Milton, Jr.

(1927–   )

Few college basketball players enjoyed greater success and acclaim than Ralph Beard. His professional career promised to provide similar success until he was indicted in a point-shaving scandal and his world came tumbling down.

He was a 5-foot-10½-inch guard, wiry, fast, quick, clever and full of nervous energy. Ed Fitzgerald wrote, ''He looks like a bigger Mickey Rooney without the freckles.'' Another writer said, ''He simply runs his opposition to exhaustion.''

He was an All-American boy in high school (as was his younger brother Frank, who became a leading professional golfer). He won letters in basketball, baseball, football and track. But basketball was his first love. ''I started shooting baskets when I was just a baby,'' he said. ''My mother claims the first thing I used for a goal was my little old pottie.''

In four seasons (1945–49) at the University of Kentucky his teams posted a 130-10 won-lost record and won four Southeastern Conference titles, two NCAA championships and one National Invitation Tournament final. He was a three-time All-American and a star of the 1948 United States Olympic champions.

In 1949 he and four teammates turned pro together and formed the Indianapolis Olympians, in which they were all part owners. The glory ended in 1951, when he and two others were arrested and accused of accepting bribes from gamblers to win a 1949 game by less than the point spread (actually, they lost the game, and the gamblers still won their bets). Beard pleaded guilty and was sentenced to three years probation. His basketball team dissolved and he lost an investment worth $100,000.

As *Sport* magazine said, ''When exposure came, it almost destroyed him. His wife, finding it difficult to adjust to the pressures, divorced him. He couldn't get a good job and he was afraid to ask for one. . . . His Kentucky uniform, retired and put on display . . . had been thrown away. His picture . . . had been taken down.''

He became bitter. He pictured Adolph Rupp, the Kentucky coach, as an unscrupulous man with his own ties to gamblers. He sold automobiles and drugs before being drafted into the Army, where he played basketball and baseball. ''You just can't do a thing all your life and love it and then suddenly have it stop,'' he said. ''Sure, I want to play again.'' He did play for a year in the Eastern League, a high minor league, for $50 a game. ''It was enough,'' he said, ''just to play again.''

Bednarik, Charles Phillip
(1925–   )

Chuck Bednarik was a throwback to the days of old. He measured 6 feet 3 inches and 230 pounds, with a 17½-inch neck and a 36-inch sleeve. He was a tough, bruising, violent football player, a pro's pro. One observer said, "He knew the way the game is played. He had no apologies and his fellows demanded none." Joe Kuharich called him "the meanest man in pro football." Coach Weeb Ewbank said, "We figure the best percentage is not to run his way."

After high school he enlisted in the Air Force and flew 30 combat missions over Europe as a B-24 waist gunner. Then he entered the University of Pennsylvania and played four seasons (1945–48) as center. He was twice All-American and became the first lineman to win the Maxwell Award as the nation's outstanding college player.

In 1949 he joined the Philadelphia Eagles, played center and became the National Football League's rookie of the year. The following season he switched to linebacker and was all-pro for seven straight

years. When the Eagles won the NFL title in 1960, he played both offense and defense in most games. In the championship game he played 58 minutes. He was 35 years old, the oldest man on the Eagles, and he was the only man in the league playing both ways. It was his idea. "Football is mostly mind over matter," he said. "You get high, you get hopped up by winning and you keep going. . . . All I want is to go down in the books as a good, clean, honest-to-God football player. . . . You separated the men from the boys, and then you had football."

In 1962, when Chuck Bednarik, age 37, finished the last game of his career, his dirty uniform was quickly retrieved and sent to the Pro Football Hall of Fame. In 1967 he was admitted to this pro-football shrine. He was voted into the College Football Hall of Fame in 1969.

A character who often played tricks on the English language, Bednarik became a colorful and entertaining speaker and disc jockey. Once, when asked if he wrote his own scripts, he said, "No, but I'm catching on real fast. I'm getting so I can add some libs."

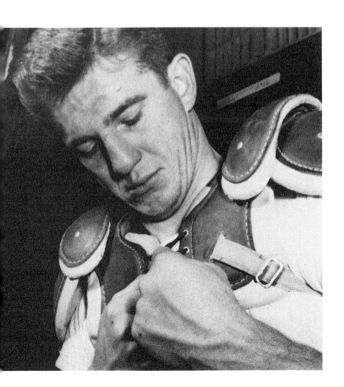

and $105,000 for five years, unbelievable money at the time. They got a bargain.

An adoring public called him Le Gros Bill (Big Bill). He was big at 6 feet 3 inches and 205 pounds. He was graceful, fast, clever—but too mild. "If he had the meanness of Gordie Howe, he'd be the greatest player by miles," Bob Pulford once commented. But he was rugged, too. As Bill Ezinicki said after crashing into him, "It was like running into the side of a big oak tree."

He was also a gentleman and a willing teammate. Canadien Yvan Cournoyer said, "It is like going to school for me to play with him." His coach, Hector (Toe) Blake, said he had never heard anyone say a bad word about him, a rare claim in the tough world of professional hockey. John Ferguson called him "the classiest guy I've ever met," while Arthur Daley compared his charm to that of Charles Boyer.

Recalling his early days, Beliveau said, "When I came up here, people thought that every time I would touch the puck I would score a goal." He kept the same style for 20 years, and it was a winning one. "If you make the NHL," he said, "it's because your style brought you there. When you are getting close to 40, there is only one way to play this game, and that is to play it for today. . . . I only hope I have made a contribution to a great game."

Beliveau, Jean Marc
(1931–   )

Jean Beliveau was so good a hockey player that few people appreciated him fully. Perhaps, as James A. Burchard wrote, "He made hockey look too easy." Larry Fox wrote that everything he did was taken for granted.

He did almost everything. In 20 seasons (between 1950 and 1971) with the Montreal Canadiens he scored 507 goals, 712 assists and 1,219 points in 1,125 National Hockey League games. He was an all-star ten times, he won two most-valuable-player awards and he helped the Canadiens win ten Stanley Cups.

He was so good as an amateur that the Canadiens bought the entire Quebec Senior League just to acquire him. Then they signed him for a $20,000 bonus

Bell, de Benneville (1895–1959)

"Bert Bell made pro football the major sport it is today, gave it stability, refinement and national stature," Joe Williams wrote of this former National Football League commissioner. Writer Al Hirshberg described him as "the most powerful commissioner on the American sporting scene. While his brother commissioners carefully fit their behavior to the rules, he fits the rules to his behavior."

Commissioner of the NFL from 1946 until his death in 1959, he was a small, roundish, noisy man with high blood pressure. He looked, wrote Jack Orr, "like an average Mickey Rooney." W. C. Heinz once wrote that his gravel voice "takes on the sound qualities of a circular power saw."

He came from a wealthy family from Philadelphia's fashionable Main Line. He was a 155-pound quarterback at the University of Pennsylvania and spent ten years as backfield coach there and at Temple University. In 1932 he and Lud Wray bought the Frankford Yellow Jackets for $2,500 and renamed them the Philadelphia Eagles. In three years the team lost 21 of 31 games and $80,000. His partners dropped out, and he became owner, coach and ticket seller. When the team was sold at auction he bought it back for $4,500. In 1940 he sold out and became half owner of the Pittsburgh Steelers. In 1946, when he became commissioner, he sold that interest.

Milton Gross wrote that, unlike other commissioners, "he never pretended an indifference or ignorance to the hard and seamy facts of life." He established the policy of television blackouts of home games and fought off Congressional attacks on that policy. He defended the league against attacks on the reserve clause and kept a close watch on pro-football gambling. He said he tried to make sure that every club owner "loves the game more than he loves money."

During his reign pro football reached new heights of popularity and financial stability. Attendance rose from 1,732,000 in 1946 to 3,140,000 in 1959 (it exceeded ten million in the 1970s). Everyone liked the man, though he was, *Sport* magazine said, "an absolute bull in the pro-football china shop." Arthur Daley wrote that he kept a kid glove on his iron fist

Commissioner Bert Bell presiding over the National Football League draft.

and that the owners loved him. Art Rooney, one of those owners, said, "I know where his heart is—whatever's good for our game." *The Sporting News* agreed, saying, "he had a sure instinct for the league's best interests."

In 1959, at Franklin Field, Philadelphia, where he had played as a collegian, he watched a game between the Eagles and Steelers, his old teams. A minute before the final gun he suffered a heart attack and died. As Red Smith wrote, "It was almost as though he were allowed to choose the time and place."

and runs batted in. At 25 his salary was $115,000 a year.

Johnny Bench has all the attributes. Sparky Anderson, his manager, said, ''It's almost pitiful that one man should have so much talent.'' Dave Bristol, Anderson's predecessor, said, ''He is so intelligent, far above average, and conscientious that it hurts him to have to be told about a shortcoming.'' Al Michaels, who broadcast Reds' games, said, ''All players make outs most of the time, but when Bench makes an out, you're almost disillusioned.''

Physically, Bench is imposing. John Devaney described him as being ''as powerfully compact as a heap of concrete.'' His right arm, wrote Roy Blount, Jr., ''is about the size of a good healthy leg.'' When he throws to second base, said Tommy Helms, ''it stings you.''

Bench, a perfectionist, is never fully satisfied with his achievements. ''There comes a time,'' he said, ''when you realize you are not going to do everything. But you want to do so much. . . . The fans can't expect any more from me than I expect from myself.''

Bench, Johnny Lee (1947–   )

Never in the history of baseball did a catcher so young show so much promise and live up to it.

In 1965, at the age of 17, Johnny Bench was drafted by the Cincinnati Reds. He signed for a $14,000 bonus and played for Tampa, where Yogi Berra saw him and said, ''He can do it all now.'' In 1966, at Peninsula, he was so good that his uniform was retired, a rarity in the low minor leagues where profits seldom allow such sentimentality. In 1967, at Buffalo, he was voted minor-league player of the year. In August 1967 he was brought up to the Reds and became first-string catcher at 19.

In 1968, his first full major-league season, he was National League rookie of the year. He batted cleanup for the heaviest-hitting team in baseball, caught 154 games for a rookie record and became the first rookie to win the Golden Glove as the major league's best defensive catcher. In 1969 Ted Williams autographed a baseball for him and wrote: ''To Johnny Bench, a Hall of Famer for sure.'' In 1970 and 1972 he led the National League in home runs

Berg, Patricia Jane (1918–)

In the early years of women's professional golf, Patty Berg was the game's greatest asset, an intense, immensely talented player and a warm, gracious person who made friends for herself and her sport.

A chunky redhead at 5 feet 2 inches and 140 pounds, with freckles and strong hands, she hardly looked the part of a champion. ''Here is a puffy little gnome of a woman who trudges the fairway looking more like a resolute middle-aged housewife on her way to a YWCA calisthenics class than she does a remarkable athlete,'' said fellow pro Betty Hicks. ''But when she grasps a golf club, the butterfly emerges from the cocoon. The greatest shots in women's golf have come off the faces of Patty Berg's clubs.''

She excelled in all sports. As a child in Minneapolis she played quarterback for her brother's neighborhood football team (one teammate was Bud Wilkinson). Runner-up for the national girls' speed-skating title at age 15, she took up golf the same year. Her first round was 122, but in only two years she was runner-up for the United States amateur title.

In 1940, having won more than 40 amateur tournaments, she became a professional, mainly to give clinics. The women's pro golf tour then offered few tournaments and little prize money, but she helped build it. Three times she was chosen woman athlete of the year by the Associated Press. She won 83 tournaments during her career, including every important one, and in one tourney posted a remarkable score of 64 for 18 holes.

One sportswriter compared her to the leading political figure of her time. ''On the course, she is Winston Churchill,'' Barbara Heilman wrote, ''shaped like him, doughty, peering out from under a visored cap set at Sir Winston's angle, requiring his exact lift of the chin to see out from under it at all.'' Herbert Warren Wind, describing her wonderful gift for hitting golf shots, was reminded of the great male golfers. ''She can handle a club with her fingers like no one since Walter Hagen. Her mannerisms at address and as she rocks into delivering the shot are highly reminiscent of Gene Sarazen. She . . . expresses her full personality as she plays each shot.''

In each shot, too, she expressed her appreciation of the game. ''Don't tell me that golf isn't one of the best relaxations in a world that has everybody's nerves drawn taut. I try to stay as relaxed as I can and not to worry. This is the life I chose. I have to think it's wonderful.''

Berra and son in the New York Mets' dugout during the former all-star catcher's coaching years.

Berra, Lawrence Peter (1925–   )

There are divergent stereotypes of Yogi Berra the baseball player. He was either a moody, suspicious, ugly, dumb clown or a joyous, witty, shrewd, sagacious man. ("This is Mr. Berra, which is my assistant manager," Casey Stengel used to say when Berra played under him.)

Like many stereotypes, there was some truth to each, for the real Yogi Berra was a complex person. As Stengel insisted, Berra had an instinct for baseball, but little beyond the world of sports interested him. "What he has to know he learns," said his wife, Carmen.

He learned baseball well enough to play on 14 American League pennant-winning teams in 18 sea-

sons (1946–63) with the New York Yankees. He played 2,116 games for the Yankees, mostly as a catcher, and posted a lifetime average of .285. In 1965, when he was a coach for the New York Mets, he played in four games.

A left-handed batter and a dangerous line-drive hitter, Berra was also an infamous bad-ball hitter. "Sure," said Hal Newhouser, "but I defy anyone to throw him a good pitch." He won three most-valuable-player awards, and in 1971 he was voted into the Baseball Hall of Fame.

He was dumpy, with thick shoulders, short legs and no neck. "He is shaped," wrote Roger Kahn, "like an inverted milk bottle." When Moe Berg, a

Princeton graduate, linguist, wit and former major-league catcher, first saw him, Berra was swinging by his arms from the dugout roof. There are two versions of Berg's comment: "Who discovered him—Frank Buck?" and "Who discovered him—Darwin?"

And then there were the Yogi Berra stories, most of which had him saying right things with wrong words:

"Nobody goes to that restaurant anymore. It's too crowded"; "My hat size? You mean now or when I'm in condition?"; "Bill Dickey is learning me his experience"; "You can observe a lot by watching"; "If you can't imitate him, don't copy him"; "If you're not hitting, swing at strikes"; "I'm not apprehensive, just scared"; "We lost the pennant because we made too many wrong mistakes"; and on Yogi Berra Night: "I want to thank everyone who made this night necessary."

Many Yogi Berra stories were exaggerations or inventions, some by Joe Garagiola, his boyhood pal in St. Louis who became a major-league catcher and, as a broadcaster, a major-league wit. At first Yogi disliked the stories because he considered them demeaning. He felt the same about his boyhood nickname of Yogi, and for years he signed autographs "Larry Berra." He didn't know what to make of Yogi Bear, the animated television hero named for him. Later, a mature Yogi Berra said of his fellow players, "I like it when they get on me. . . . I figure if they didn't like me, they wouldn't holler."

"They made a lot of fun out of him reading comic books," Casey Stengel recalled. "I wish that all ballplayers I ever had did nothing worse off the field than read comic books." As Toots Shor put it, "When a man earns over $50,000 a year, he ain't dumb." Berra himself said, "I know what some people think. Let them think what they want . . . but I'm no dope."

He was certainly no dope as a manager, but one failing cost him his job in 1964. He had been a Yankee player the year before. Now he was manager, and he had difficulty controlling former teammates who enjoyed drinking and late-hour fun. Several non-drinking players, including Bobby Richardson and Tony Kubek, complained to man-agement in what Maury Allen called the Malted Milk Rebellion. The Yankees won the pennant but Berra was fired.

From 1965 to 1972 he was a Mets coach. When Gil Hodges died during 1972 spring training Berra became manager. He was wiser now—always gentle and patient, never negative or in panic, an eternal optimist. In 1973, with the Mets staggering and Berra's job at stake, they won 20 of their last 28 games to take the National League Eastern title, beat the Cincinnati Reds in five games for the National League pennant and then took the Oakland A's to seven games in the World Series. As Casey Stengel said, "There's nothing dumb about Mr. Berra."

Mickey Mantle (No. 7) and Bill Skowron (No. 14) greet Berra after his first home run of the 1961 season.

Berwanger, John Jacob
(1915–   )

Jay Berwanger played halfback for the University of Chicago football team from 1933 to 1935. He ran, passed, punted, kicked off, kicked extra points, blocked, tackled, caught passes, called the plays and played 60 minutes a game. He was also the team captain.

In three years with a mediocre team he rushed for 1,839 yards and scored 22 touchdowns. He was named All-American in 1934 and 1935 and won the 1935 Heisman Trophy as the nation's outstanding college player. In those days, one of the All-America teams, *Liberty* magazine's, was actually an all-opponents teams picked by players. One year he became the leading vote-getter when 104 of 107 opposing players named him the best halfback they had faced that season.

In 1936 he was the first player selected in the first National Football League draft, but he declined, not wanting to play pro ball. In 1954 he was elected to the College Football Hall of Fame, and the Football Writers Association voted him to the modern all-time All-America in 1969.

In a memorable game in 1935 his punts kept powerful Ohio State at bay in the first half, and his tackling in the secondary kept Ohio State from breaking away early in the second half. In the third quarter he ran 85 yards for a touchdown through the entire Ohio State team. Ohio State won, 20-13, but its coach, Francis Schmidt, called Berwanger "the best back an Ohio State team has faced since Red Grange."

Christy Walsh, the football historian, called him "a defensive backfield all by himself," and Bob Zuppke said he was the best all-round backfield man in college football. "There's nothing he can't do, and most of what he does he does superlatively well," Russ Needham once said. Red Barber, who broadcast games for many years, called him "the greatest college player I ever saw."

In 1939, four years after his last game, Chicago defeated only Wabash and Oberlin and lost by such scores as 85-0 to Michigan, 61-0 to Ohio State, 61-0 to Harvard, 47-0 to Virginia and 46-0 to Illinois. Chicago, unwilling to pay the price of big-time football, dropped the sport after that, and Berwanger, after wartime service in the Navy, became a part-time intramural football coach.

Alfred Wright wrote, "He was nearly the only real football player Chicago had at the time. He not only could do everything that had to be done on the field, he had to." Clark Shaughnessy, the Chicago coach, put it another way. "Berwanger's all I've got," he said the day before a game. "If we do anything, he'll do it." Berwanger did it, as usual.

Bikila, Abebe (1932–1973)

Abebe Bikila of Ethiopia was the only man to win two successive Olympic marathons. He was the idol of his nation, perhaps second only to Emperor Haile Selassie. Jon Hendershott wrote, "He really was the catalyst of the African revolution in track. He was the first Olympic champion from that huge reservoir of seemingly endless talent."

He was a slight, impassive man, wiry, thin-legged, strong, graceful. He ran with an easy stride, his face gaunt and grim. Off the track, he walked with the erect carriage of the military officer he was.

In 1960, an obscure runner listed on Olympic entries as Bikila Abebe, he ran the marathon barefoot over the stones of the Appian Way and crossed the finish line in Rome in 2 hours 15 minutes 16.2 seconds, an Olympic record. In 1964, 40 days after an appendectomy, he won the Olympic marathon in Tokyo, wearing shoes, in 2:12:11.2, the fastest ever run at that time. He brushed aside the attendants ready to wrap him in blankets, ran to the infield, did calisthenics and jogged for a while. Soon after, the second-place finisher entered the stadium. Ron Clarke called it "the greatest performance ever in track and field."

In 1968, at the age of 36, he tried for a third Olympic title. This time, in Mexico City, he suffered a fractured left fibula and dropped out after ten miles. When he returned home he was promoted to captain in the Emperor's Imperial Bodyguard. Promotions followed every Olympics, prompting him to say, "My life was enriched by the Olympics in that way."

The following year his auto overturned and he was paralyzed from the neck down. He regained the use of his upper body, but he was confined to a wheelchair. He said later, "Men of success meet with tragedy. It was the will of God that I won the Olympics and it was the will of God that I had my accident. I was overjoyed when I won the marathon twice. But I accepted those victories as I accept this tragedy. I have no choice. I have to accept both circumstances as facts of life and live happily."

In 1972 William Johnson wrote, "He will have a seat of honor at the Munich Olympics, but it will be a sad and futile tribute of the type that healthy men pay to the cripples whose still, gleaming wheels line the sidelines at athletic contests."

Bikila died in 1973, at age 41, of a cerebral hemorrhage and a stroke. Among the 60,000 to 70,000 people at his funeral was Ethiopia's other national hero, Emperor Haile Selassie.

Barefoot Abebe Bikila crosses the finish line in record time at the 1960 Olympic marathon in Rome.

Blanchard, Felix Anthony, Jr. (1924–   )

Doc Blanchard and Glenn Davis, born 15 days apart, formed the most celebrated backfield pair in college football annals. For three seasons (1944–46) they played for an undefeated Army team. George Trevor

Blanchard running for his second of three touchdowns as Army defeated Navy, 32-13, in 1945.

of the New York *Sun* christened them Mr. Inside and Mr. Outside.

Blanchard was Mr. Inside, the fullback. He weighed 208 pounds, and his thighs were so hard that Leo Novak, the Army track coach, said, "If he pulled a muscle, he wouldn't even know it." "He is the only man who runs his own interference," Herman Hickman, another coach, said.

When Blanchard was a University of North Carolina freshman in 1941, Glenn Thistlewaite said, "I've seen all the great fullbacks, including Nagurski, but this boy will be the greatest." There were other favorable comparisons with the great Minnesota fullback. Steve Owen said he was as good as Nagurski, "only he has more finesse," while Fritz Crisler claimed he had just as much power and was faster. Clark Shaughnessy and Jack Lavelle called him the best player they had ever seen.

He was so strong that he put the shot almost 52 feet the first year he tried it. He was so fast that he ran 100 yards in ten seconds in a track meet. He was not much of a student (296th in a class of 310), partly because he was so easy-going and fun-loving. Glenn Davis said, "He took everything in stride. About the only time anyone knew he was worked up about something was when he talked or kicked in his sleep."

He was named All-American three times, and in 1945 he won the Heisman Trophy and Maxwell Award as the nation's outstanding college football player and the Sullivan Award (no football player had won it before) as America's leading amateur athlete. After college he became an Air Force pilot. In 1959 he bravely stayed with his flaming plane rather than let it crash into a heavily populated London suburb, and in 1968 he left Vietnam after flying 113 combat missions as a fighter-bomber pilot.

He remained a great football hero and may have been, as Notre Dame coach Ed McKeever insisted, "Superman in the flesh."

Brown, James Nathaniel (1936–   )

Statistically and artistically, he was the most impressive running back in professional-football history. Dick Modzelewski, who spent years trying to tackle him, said, "He's the best fullback God ever made."

In nine seasons (1957–65) with the Cleveland Browns he led the National Football League in rushing eight times (he failed only in 1962, when he played the entire season with a badly sprained left wrist). He retired as the all-time leader in carries (2,359), rushing yardage (12,312), touchdowns rushing (106) and total touchdowns (126). NFL players voted him player of the year three times.

Jim Brown was a man to behold, a magnificent physical specimen of 6 feet 2 inches and 228 pounds, with wide shoulders tapering to a 32-inch waist. Murray Olderman called him "a study in rippling, burnished bronze." He looked menacing and claimed it was easier for him to look mean than happy. "I got that mean thing in me," he said.

He was tough and dedicated. He never missed a game because of injury. "You never know if he's hurt," explained Morrie Kono, the Browns' equipment manager. "He doesn't complain. The guy was a Spartan the day he showed up."

He was a smart runner with slashing power and exciting outside speed. All-pro safetyman Larry Wilson recalled that "He would let you take a shot at him, and he seemed to have that instinct to move or to use your force to let him move in another direction." Ray Nitschke, an all-pro linebacker, said, "He knew where he was going and how he was going to get there."

His success was not accidental. "I always made it a business to use my head before my body," said the articulate Brown. "I looked upon playing football like a businessman might. The game was my business. My body and my mind were my assets, and injuries were my liabilities."

In high school in Manhasset, New York, he won 13 letters in five sports and was all-state in football,

basketball and track. As a senior he averaged 14.9 yards per carry in football and 38 points per game in basketball. Casey Stengel tried to persuade him to play baseball for the New York Yankee chain.

At Syracuse University he was All-American in football and lacrosse. Once, while warming up for a lacrosse game, he passed by the track and won the

Jim Brown rushing for three touchdowns in his last college game, the 1957 Cotton Bowl between Syracuse and Texas Christian.

He earned $75,000 a year. Success made him dapper, increasingly arrogant and independent. After the 1965 season he quit football at the peak of his career to become a movie actor. He had previously made one movie, and in 1966 he completed *The Dirty Dozen,* which made him a star and a box-office attraction.

Why did he quit football? "It wasn't a question of whether I could play three more years or five more years," he said. "Taking a realistic look at my life and my ambitions, at the things I wanted to achieve, it was time for a change. . . . I got out before I ever had to be like so many guys I've seen—sitting hunched over on the bench, all scarred and banged up, watching some hot young kid out there in their place."

He became a black activist and founded the National Negro Industrial and Economic Union. He openly criticized many aspects of pro football, especially black-white relationships, and said, "The white man has forced me to be prejudiced against him." He led a turbulent private life.

In 1971, the first year he was eligible, he was elected to the Pro Football Hall of Fame. At the induction ceremony, wearing a white knit jumpsuit, he received a standing ovation. He told the audience, "You have heard some bad things about Jimmy Brown. But the arrogant, bad Jimmy Brown can be humble when he is given true love."

high jump. The first time he played golf he shot in the low 80s. The first time he bowled he rolled several 200 games. He was, John Devaney wrote, "probably the finest all-around athlete since Jim Thorpe."

He was an immediate star in pro football. Ed Modzelewski, the Browns' fullback when Jim Brown arrived, said, "When we all saw what he had, I felt just like the guy who played behind Babe Ruth." The only way to tackle him, said Sam Huff, an enemy linebacker, was to "grab hold, hang on and wait for help." "You had to give each guy in the line an ax," said defensive tackle Alex Karras. Defensive back Henry Carr said he ran "like he has a halo over his head saying you can't touch."

One thing he seldom did was block. "My job," he would say, "is running with the ball." Blanton Collier, who coached Cleveland during Brown's last years, had no objection, saying, "You can't ask a thoroughbred to pull a milk wagon."

Brown, Paul E. (1908–)

He is one of pro football's most successful (and most experienced) coaches, dapper and suave, but he can also be cold, grim, forceful, even obsessed.

Jack Newcombe wrote, "He achieves strict discipline without playing the martinet, although many people who don't know him think of him as the hard-minded, unemotional, success-mad type." Bob Johnson, who plays center for his Cincinnati Bengals, said, "He is a man of the true American spirit. He believes that if you do your job you'll be paid accordingly. . . . He looks you in the eye, tells you what to do and that's it." Otto Graham, his great quarterback of a generation ago, acknowledged that Brown had done a great deal for him. "Most important, he taught me that if you want to be successful, you've got to dedicate yourself and concentrate entirely upon it."

It was a lesson he impressed upon all his teams. He was a 154-pound quarterback at Miami University of Ohio. He coached high-school football for 11 years (with a won-lost-tied record of 96-9-3) and went on to three seasons at Ohio State (18-8-1), two at the Great Lakes Naval Training Station (15-5-2) and 17 years with the Cleveland Browns, first in the All-American Football Conference and later in the National Football League (167-53-9).

He founded the Browns, and they took his name. He gave them brown uniforms, brown typewriter ribbons, brown everything. He even dressed in brown. His teams won ten division titles in a row, 11 in all, and seven league titles. But he was fired after the 1962 season because Cleveland's owner and players felt his thinking had become rigid. "I've always wanted to play for a coach I feel like going out and dying for," Jim Brown, his star fullback, said. "Paul Brown is not that coach."

For five years he played golf, bridge and gin rummy, traveled all over the world and collected $80,000 a year from the Browns. But "after a while," he said, "it began to seem pointless. It was terrible." Tex Maule wrote that "The years he was away from football were years in purgatory." In 1968 he returned as part owner, general manager and coach of the Bengals, a new expansion team, and by 1970 he had them in the playoffs.

Football, including coaching, has always been a team effort for him. "It's great to coach a team that's fighting for its life, kids that are exuberant and have this real joy of playing. . . . What an individual does as an individual is not important. It's what he does for the team." Brown waited out his years away from football. "Bitter people bore me. They say football passed me by, and I say that time has the answer for everything."

Otto Graham welcomes Brown, his former boss and mentor, into the Pro Football Hall of Fame.

Brumel, Valery (1942–)

For a five-year period Valery Brumel of the Soviet Union dominated the high jump as no man had before or since. He broke the world record five times, a centimeter at a time—7 feet 4¼ inches and 7–4⅝ in 1961, 7–5 and 7–5½ in 1962, 7–5¾ in 1963. His 7–5 record jump came at Palo Alto, California, in a United States–Soviet meet, and the

American crowd of 81,000 gave him a five-minute standing ovation. "I was filled with inexpressible joy," he said of the tribute.

He won the silver medal in the 1960 Olympics, the gold in 1964. By the end of 1962 he had made the six highest jumps of all time and 21 of the best 23. By the end of 1963 he had the ten highest jumps of all time and had cleared 7 feet 2 inches 43 times, compared with 15 times for all other jumpers combined.

He was handsome, with a sad, brooding face, dark hair and a high forehead. He was also exciting, graceful and quick, a showman who never watched his rivals jump. He was cocky, too. "Why should I be nervous when the bar is raised to 7–1 or 7–2?" he once asked. "These are practice heights for me."

He attributed his success to speed and strength, "the keys to high jumping." "The barbell and I are particular friends," he said, explaining his strength. Jim Tuppeny, an American coach, once said of his quickness, "With his speed, he is actually sailing."

He liked fast cars, fast motorcycles and fast living. They almost killed him. In 1965 he was thrown from a motorcycle that skidded out of control. His right leg suffered two simple fractures below the knee, his right ankle multiple fractures. The shinbones were pulverized. The attending surgeon said, "His foot hung by a thread," and an assisting physician described his leg as "a complete mess." He underwent surgery for five hours, almost losing the leg to gangrene. He ran a high temperature for three weeks and endured 28 more operations.

The leg was in a cast almost three years. Then he tried to exercise too soon, fell downstairs and needed six more operations. He trained lightly for three months, then tried jumping again and cleared 6–6¾ the first day. In 1969 he did 6–9⅛, not world class but remarkable under the circumstances.

"I'll never give up sports," he said. "It is my passion. It is my life. . . . I have made a comeback because of stubbornness. . . . I want to see how high I can jump. Every centimeter is a victory for me."

Brumel signals to the crowd after setting a world high-jump record of 7'5" in the 1962 U.S.–Soviet meet.

Brundage, Avery (1887–1975)

For years he was the most powerful man in amateur sports, perhaps in all sports. He was controversial, domineering, undiplomatic, misunderstood and single-minded to a fault. He waved the flag of amateurism, but, as Robert Lipsyte observed, "He expediently winked at the American educational system and the Socialist state-amateur system."

Even in his 80s he was imposing and erect as he walked four and a half miles daily between his Chicago home and office. In the 1912 Olympics he was fifth in the pentathlon and 14th in the decathlon (Jim Thorpe won both). He was president of the Amateur Athletic Union of the United States (1928–35), president of the U.S. Olympic Committee (1929–53) and vice-president (1945–52) and president (1952–72) of the International Olympic Committee. He became a millionaire in the construction business, and his collection of Oriental art was valued in the millions.

One writer called him "the Mother Superior for amateur athletes." "He is a self-made man," wrote William Johnson, "and his brand of ethics and his range of judgments have their roots in an impatience with anything that is not useful, negotiable or profitable." Red Smith called him "the greatest practicing patsy, or sitting duck, of the century . . . a rich and righteous anachronism." An associate said, "He lacks tact to a painful degree. If he did and said things with more diplomacy he'd get better results. He is a very domineering man." More sympathetically, *Sports Illustrated* called him a "defender of the faith. . . . He sleeps the sleep of the just."

"At one time or another I've been called a capitalist, a Communist, a Socialist, a Fascist and a lot of other things that are unprintable," Brundage said. "Kinder people have called me the last living amateur, and I'm proud of that. . . . Amateurism is a sort of religion. The Olympic movement is a twentieth-century religion. The Olympic movement today is perhaps the greatest social force in the world. It is a revolt against twentieth-century materialism—a devotion to the cause and not to the reward. . . . I'm a 110 percent American and an old-fashioned Republican. People like me haven't had anybody to vote for since Hoover and Coolidge."

Avery Brundage and wife, in Tokyo in May 1939, inspecting a model of the 1940 Summer Olympics grounds. The games were canceled by the outbreak of World War II months later.

Bryant, Paul William (1913–   )

In 30 years as a college football coach, his teams have won 242 games (no active coach has won more), lost 71 and tied 16. Everywhere he has coached—Maryland (1945), Kentucky (1946–53), Texas A&M (1954–57) and Alabama (since 1958)—he has turned losers into winners.

Bear Bryant is a popular sports figure, often controversial, sometimes grouchy. His face, wrote John Underwood, is "granite and ice and true grit." When George Blanda first saw him, he remarked, "This must be what God looks like." His teams are hard-working and highly motivated, but typically he understates his role.

"I don't have as much fun as I used to," he said, "because I'm not as close to the kids, not coaching as much. But still, today, tomorrow, when I walk out on that practice field, cold chills run up my back. A new day. And it's something I wouldn't swap for anything."

His football career started in Arkansas, where he earned his nickname by wrestling a bear for one minute (for $1). At the University of Alabama he played end (the other end was Don Hutson). After graduation he became an assistant coach at Alabama for $1,250 a year. Even now his salary, at his insistence, is less than $30,000 a year, but his many business interests, including television shows, meat packing, auto distribution and yarn-treating, have made him a millionaire.

He doubled the size of the Alabama stadium, built a fieldhouse and athletic dormitory (Paul W. Bryant Hall) and so successfully put Alabama football on a self-sustaining basis that football profits support the other sports. He has turned down many pro offers (when the Miami Dolphins could not get him, they hired Don Shula). He almost ran for governor of Alabama but changed his mind. "Football has been my life," he reasoned. "I control our football program, and if I do my job I know we're going to win. I couldn't control the levers in that polling booth."

He has coached such players as George Blanda, Ken Stabler, John David Crow, Babe Parilli, Bob Gain and Joe Namath, whom he called "the best athlete I've ever seen." The night before Gain, once a hell-raiser at Kentucky, went into combat in Korea, he wrote his old coach, "I love you tonight for what I used to hate you for." Lee Roy Jordan, who played linebacker for him at Alabama, said, "People get the idea he chews your tail for losing. It's himself he blames."

Why did he take the blame? "Football has never been just a game to me," he said. "I knew it from the time it got me out of Moro Bottom, Arkansas, and this is one of the things that motivated me, the fear of going back to plowing and driving those mules and chopping cotton for fifty cents a day."

Bear Bryant and one of his famous protégés, Joe Namath, after Alabama's Orange Bowl victory in 1962.

Budge, John Donald (1915–   )

If the measure of a man can be gleaned from the admiration of contemporaries and rivals, then Don Budge belongs at the top. Sidney Wood remembered that "Playing tennis against him was like playing against a concrete wall. There was nothing to attack. There was no weakness. When he was in his prime, no player, past or present, could have beaten him."

"He was devastating," said Bobby Riggs. "He could blow you off the court." Julius D. Heldman, like Wood and Riggs a contemporary player, recalled that "He never allowed his opponent to get his teeth in the match. . . . His unfortunate victim had the feeling of complete helplessness."

Don Budge, this all-powerful tennis player, was a gaunt, angular, six-foot redhead with freckles. He worked hard to perfect his game, but Al Laney found one shortcoming. "It is strange," he wrote, "that so great a player with so fine a game is yet so little graceful compared with the other great ones."

Though his overall game may have lacked grace, his backhand did not. He hit it with a heavy rolling stroke that had power, elegance and flair. It was the most celebrated stroke in tennis and Allison Danzig considered it "probably the most potent backhand the world has seen."

He took up tennis at 15, and a week later he was the California boys champion. He won the United States and Wimbledon titles in 1937, and the following year he became the first player, male or female, to achieve the grand slam (the United States, Wimbledon, French and Australian titles the same year). After the French final Pablo Casals, an avid and admiring spectator, invited Budge to his home to play for him and reciprocate for the enjoyment he derived from the match. For two hours the master tennis player listened in rapture to the master cellist.

In 1937 he played Baron Gottfried von Cramm of Germany in one of the most famous of all tennis matches. It was the deciding match of the Davis Cup interzone final, and Budge won in five spectacular sets. At the end Von Cramm told him, "That was absolutely the finest match I have ever played in my life!" They embraced and, recalled Budge, "I think we both wanted to cry."

After his grand-slam triumph he turned professional and dominated pro tennis until World War II.

Crowds loved him and his aggressive game. They also respected him because he was a gentleman who seldom questioned linesmen's calls. He always stayed close to tennis, fighting for open competition and a uniform playing surface.

He once expressed his confidence this way: "When a player arrives at a tournament, one of the first things he does is look at the draw. I made up my mind never to look at a draw under the premise that if I were good enough to win a tournament, I was good enough to beat anyone."

Butkus, Richard John (1942–)

He was the toughest, meanest, fiercest and best middle linebacker football has known. Dave Anderson called him the standard of violence against whom all the other middle linebackers in the National Football League were measured.

Dick Butkus was 6 feet 3 inches and 245 pounds of muscle. At the University of Illinois he was twice All-American. In nine years (1965–73) with the Chicago Bears he was all-pro seven times. He retired because an injured right knee forced him to hobble in pain. "It hurt so much," he said, "I had tears in my eyes." When he retired he was earning $115,000 a year, an astounding sum for a linebacker and one of the highest in football.

On the field he was a terror. Rival quarterback Bart Starr said, "He will rattle your brains when he tackles you." "He is so physical he can put the fear of God in you," said Greg Landry, another quarterback. Scout Joe Walton claimed he played the middle "like a piranha." Bob DeMarco, a rival center who had to block him, thought he was more like a mule. "He works himself up to such a competitive pitch," said teammate Mike Ditka, "that the day of a game he won't answer a direct question. He'll grunt."

He was a rough player in a rough game. He was once penalized four times in a game for personal fouls, and on one occasion he put his fingers in the eyes of Charlie Sanders, a rival player (Sanders laughingly called him "just a maladjusted kid"). He was accused of biting another player but denied it with the retort, "I'm a football player, not a gourmet." Ed Flanagan, an opposing center, called him "foul-mouthed and insulting on the field." Charley Winner, a rival coach, didn't understand "why a player of his caliber has to do things like that."

Teammates and rivals called him The Animal, a nickname he did not like but did not discourage. "I guess people think the Bears keep me in a cage and let me out only on Sunday afternoons," he said. "Nobody thinks I can talk, much less write my name."

He did not pretend to be an intellectual. "Ever since I was in the eighth grade," he said, "I've been nuts about this game. I love to hit and love to win. It has to be that way. You can never let yourself be embarrassed. I always keep in mind that any game could be my last. You never know in this business. I wouldn't ever want my last game to be a stinker."

Button, Richard Totten
(1929–   )

Dick Button, handsome, elegant and athletic, has been a dominant figure in figure skating for more than a quarter-century. In the post-World War II years he was the world's best skater and the one responsible for the trend to athletic figure skating. In recent years his enthusiasm as a television announcer of figure-skating competition has made it one of the major attractions among televised sports.

His skating was exquisite. "He is, without any doubt, the finest artist in sports," wrote Joe Williams, "far ahead of his time." Fred Katz said he was one of the most glamorous figures in sports history. Gus Lussi, his coach, said he was the perfect athlete to work with "because nothing short of perfection will satisfy him. . . . His style is so precise, so well balanced and polished that he makes the most difficult feats look simple. Some people say he is too mechanical. . . . But his technique is letter-perfect."

When he was five years old he announced that he would be a priest or a figure skater. When told that he had to be a Roman Catholic to be a priest, he decided to be a skater. When he was 12 a club pro dismissed his aspirations. "He'll never make a skater. Never. Not in a million years. He's too fat, for one thing, and he lacks coordination."

The pro guessed wrong. Dick Button became a 5-foot-10-inch, 175-pound model of coordination, winning seven straight (1946–52) United States and five straight (1948–52) world championships. He won the 1948 Olympic championship with jumps and spins no one else could do (which was not surprising, since he had invented them). In 1952, when he was a student at Harvard, the college allowed him to go to the Olympics only if he took his books and studied. He studied and he won. Harvard honored him as its outstanding senior athlete-scholar, and he became the first figure skater to win the Sullivan Award as America's outstanding amateur athlete.

He graduated with honors and became a lawyer and businessman. He skated professionally, eventually in his own shows. He skated before standing-room crowds in a 1949 Holiday on Ice tour in the Soviet Union, and *Pravda* reported that "The cordial reception melted the ice of the cold war."

As a commentator on television, he is exciting and candid. Jack Gould, former *New York Times* TV critic, called his style "an enormously encouraging innovation in sportscasting, a tactful but realistic analysis as opposed to the bland gee-whizzism of most television sports reporters."

He was scrupulously honest. After a near fall in the 1952 Olympics he was asked if it was due to a flaw in the ice. "The ice is never bad," he said. "Only the skater is."

Campanella, Roy (1921–   )

Tom Meany once wrote that Roy Campanella looked like "an oversized beer keg." Frank Graham, Jr., called him a "phrase-making exuberant fat man looked on as a friend by every kid, an endless source of comical stories and sensible observations by writ-

ers, and a wise old mother hen by his teammates." Ed Linn called him the Good Humor Man.

Roy Campanella was a catcher of infinite ability. He could handle pitchers, he could pick off runners with his peculiar snap throw and he could hit with power. In his ten seasons (1948–57) and 1,215 games with the Brooklyn Dodgers, he batted .276 and they won five pennants. Three times he was voted most valuable player in the National League. His major-league career started late because organized baseball barred blacks in his youth, and it ended early because of an automobile accident. In 1969 he was voted into the Baseball Hall of Fame.

At 15 he joined the Baltimore Elite Giants of the Negro National League for $60 a month. He played up to 275 games a year, once catching an afternoon double-header in Cincinnati and a twilight-night double-header in Middletown, Ohio, the same day.

In 1946, when Jackie Robinson became the first black to play in modern organized baseball, Roy Campanella, son of a white Italian father and a black mother, joined Nashua, New Hampshire, a Class B team, for $185 a month. In 1947 he played for Montreal, another farm club. He made the Dodgers the following year, then was farmed out and brought back. He celebrated his return with nine hits in his first 12 at bats and was in the major leagues to stay.

"What am I going to do when I'm through?" he once asked. "I'm not going to be through. They may be ready to take me, but I'm not going."

On January 28, 1958, at 3:34 A.M., he did go. His car skidded on an icy curve, bounced off a telephone pole and overturned. His neck was broken and his spinal cord severed. He was paralyzed and never walked again. Yet he persevered. "I'm not living with any regrets of what might have been," he said. "I always tell myself I feel good. When you're a pro you have pride, and I never lost that. . . . I don't have anything to kick about. I've had some pretty good days."

Campanella with the National League's most-valuable-player award for the 1951 season.

Carnera, Primo (1906–1967)

Primo Carnera was a lumbering giant from Italy. At 6 feet 5¾ inches and 260 pounds, he should have been a superb fighter. He did become heavyweight champion, but he could hardly fight. Almost every bout was fixed by the gangsters who owned him.

Paul Gallico wrote, "Never in all his life was he anything more than a freak and a fourth-rater at prizefighting. . . . His entire record, with a few exceptions, must be thrown out as one gigantic falsehood . . . a helpless lamb among wolves who used him until there was nothing more left to use, until the last possible penny had been squeezed from his big carcass, and then abandoned him."

Perhaps, as Nat Fleischer wrote, "He did not have the temperament, the killer instinct so necessary in a real champion." "All he had was his massive size, a webwork of varicose veins and a wide, friendly, snaggled-tooth smile," Joe Williams wrote. Ed Linn called him "a muscle-bound glandular case with a glass jaw and a velvet punch." "He looked big enough and powerful enough to slay an elephant with one punch," wrote Arthur Daley, but "he couldn't dent a cream puff."

He was a circus strongman when a French promoter discovered him in 1928. Two years later he was fighting in the United States. In 1933 he knocked out Jack Sharkey in six rounds for the title. In 1934, in a fight that couldn't be fixed, he lost the title to Max Baer, who knocked him down 11 times in 11 rounds. After the fight he cried. Years later he became a professional wrestler.

He was the subject of Budd Schulberg's stinging novel *The Harder They Fall*. "It is all true," he admitted, "but I wish he had come to me. I would tell him so much more."

The gangsters left him penniless and paralyzed in a hospital bed and moved *The New York Times* to comment, "Rarely has anyone been victimized as thoroughly by criminal elements." He said years later, "I believe that life has a way of evening things up. Where are the men who did that to me? They were either killed or put in jail or became little better than beggars and panhandlers. All that money! What good did it do them?"

Primo Carnera knocked out by Max Baer in the 11th round of their 1934 title fight.

Carter, Donald James (1926–   )

Don Carter, the most famous bowler in history, is a quiet, unemotional, icy competitor, even-tempered but stubborn, well liked by colleagues and adored by the public despite his lack of color. "He is the

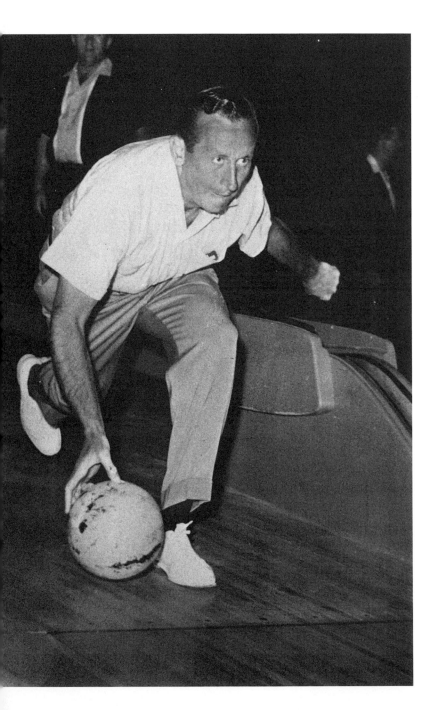

champion, the spokesman and the status symbol of America's most flourishing sport," Barry Gottehrer once wrote.

For all his success, Don Carter is better known for his odd, almost amateurish way of rolling a ball down the lane. His shoulders hunched, his right elbow crooked, his body in a crouch, he shuffles on tiptoes and releases the ball with a speed more reminiscent of the Tuesday-night bowler than a seasoned professional. The crooked elbow came from his childhood, when he was afraid he would drop the ball. He stayed with his style because, as he said, "It's the only way I've ever been comfortable."

Victor Kalman claimed his accuracy came from his style. "What he has done," Kalman wrote, "is develop, step by step, a method of bowling which reduces the margin of human error." For Ned Day, a leading bowler of an earlier generation, Carter "proves it's not necessary to copy a stylist. Just perfect a form that's comfortable for you and that you can repeat each time."

He was a baseball, football and basketball star in high school and a pitcher, infielder and outfielder in the Class D Tobacco State League. When his weight dropped from 180 to 140 he discovered that he could no longer hit or throw a curve, so he abandoned baseball and turned to bowling.

During a nine-year period (1953–62) he was bowler of the year six times, winner of the world invitation tournament five times and the All-Star tournament four times. He has bowled 13 perfect games. In 1959 he became the first president of the Professional Bowlers Association and guided the tour toward big-money status. Though purse money was small in his day, he earned a fortune from endorsements, clinics, slacks, shorts, bowling gloves and instruction books and from two thriving bowling establishments he owned.

"At first I bowled to make my arm stronger, and I found myself getting better and better," he said. "When I started, I bowled because I loved the game. There just wasn't any kind of money in it then. Now, I still love to bowl." His words included a bit of advice: "I never keep score. I just go for strikes. It's the strikes that win the tournaments."

Casper, William Earl, Jr.
(1931–   )

His onetime flabbiness, his exotic diet and his bland personality have overshadowed the true picture of Billy Casper the golfer. He is simply one of the great golfers of his day, consistent week to week, year to year.

When he started playing the pro tour in 1955 he had a hot temper. He learned to control it and in the next two decades won more than 50 tournaments, including two U.S. Opens and one Masters. During five years in the 1960s he had the best scoring average on the tour. In one streak he finished in the money in 100 consecutive tournaments.

Casper is known for his exceptional putting, which prompted Jack Nicklaus to comment, "He hits those eight-foot putts with one hand and reaches for the hole with the other." Ben Hogan was more caustic. "Casper," Hogan once told him, "if you couldn't putt, I'd be buying hot dogs from you at the tenth tee."

He is shy, impassive, conservative and inconspicuous. One writer, rephrasing a line created for Sarah Bernhardt, quipped, "An empty car drew up at the clubhouse and Billy Casper stepped out."

His golf game is like his personality—conservative, steady and intelligent. Yet, as Herbert Warren Wind wrote, "There is a lot of bulldog in him." "His inner drive and self-discipline would make even Vince Lombardi appear a bit of a softie," sportswriter Robert F. Jones said. "He is a saint with the instincts of a savage, or maybe vice versa. . . . He is so austere in his personal life that by contrast a Franciscan monk looks like a swinger."

He stands 5 feet 11 inches and in recent years weighs 185 pounds. But in his younger days he was an overweight 220-pounder who suffered from backaches, sinus problems and other ailments. An allergist discovered that, among other things, he was allergic to plastics, foam rubber, pork, lamb, eggs, chocolate, wheat, citrus fruits and certain fertilizers. He went on a diet of organically grown fruits and vegetables and such exotic meats as elk, moose, whale, bear, deer, buffalo and hippopotamus. His odd diet led sportswriter Jim Murray to say, "He has

Casper sinks a crucial putt to tie Gene Littler for the 1970 Masters tournament. Casper won the 18-hole playoff.

an Indian shoot breakfast for him," but he lost weight and felt great.

"When you come right down to it," Casper once said, "there are only four interests in my life—religion, family, golf and fishing, in that order. . . . Golf is the ultimate free agent's game. Each muscle must work in perfect harmony, under the control of a mind clear of self-doubt." Control was the key. "I believe in playing percentage golf. . . . If I try to gamble when I don't think I should, it's almost for sure that I'll blow it."

Chadwick, Florence May (1918–   )

Except for Gertrude Ederle, no Channel swimmer achieved more success and received more acclaim than Florence Chadwick.

Johnny Weissmuller called her "the greatest woman swimmer of all time—maybe of either sex—and it's time she got credit for it." Al Stump wrote, "Not since Gertrude Ederle . . . had anyone come along capable of pumping color into an essentially dull sport." When President Dwight D. Eisenhower greeted a group of athletes visiting the White House, he spotted her and said, "I'd know you anywhere." Gypsy Rose Lee called her "the most beautiful woman in sports."

At six, in San Diego, she swam her first race and finished last. At seven she swam another race and finished next to last. She had an excuse: She had stopped in mid-race to retrieve her chewing gum. At 13 she finished second to Eleanor Holm in a national backstroke final, but the distance was too short. In 1945 she turned professional by swimming in a bit role in the movie *Bathing Beauty*. The star was her former teammate on the Los Angeles Athletic Club, Esther Williams.

In 1950 she became famous by swimming the English Channel from France to England 71 minutes faster than Gertrude Ederle's 1926 record. In 1951 she became the first woman to swim the Channel the tougher way, England to France. In 1953 she swam the Channel, the Gibraltar Strait, the Bosporus and the Dardanelles. In 1955 she swam the Channel, England to France, in 13 hours 55 minutes, a record for women and men.

Then she tried the Irish Sea. In 1957, only two and a half miles from land, she was dragged from the water unconscious, and her heart beat irregularly 24 hours after. In 1960, in 56-degree water and covered with six pounds of grease to keep the body heat in, she tried again and quit seven miles short. Her body temperature at the end was 90 degrees, the lowest ever recorded for a Channel swimmer. That was her last race.

Her success brought her celebrity status. Television and newspapers covered every stroke of her big swims. She endorsed vitamins, jewelry and swimsuits, caps and goggles. A dissenting Los Angeles columnist wrote, "What do her swims prove except that she's got water on the brain? . . . She belongs on the entertainment page."

But she thoroughly enjoyed her sport. "Life seems so much simpler swimming," she said. "The experience must be similar to that of a flyer above the clouds by himself. I am also in my own little world out there. . . . If I had the chance to relive my life, I would do it all again because it is trying to do what you badly want to do that counts."

Florence Chadwick after one of her English Channel swims in the early 1950s.

Chamberlain, Wilton Norman (1936–)

Many people agreed with Ronald L. Mendell's appraisal that "He is the most dominant force in basketball." Wilt Chamberlain, rarely known for modesty, was among them. "I think my impact on basketball is going to be everlasting," he said. It will also be wrapped in controversy because Wilt Chamberlain, as good as he was, never seemed to satisfy the public.

One writer put the matter squarely when he said that whatever Chamberlain did was at once too much and not enough. A teammate thought the trouble was that "he is so close to perfection, he's always being compared to the perfect." "On any given night he can play basketball better than anyone alive," wrote Myron Cope. "And yet he has seldom been on a winning team. This contradiction is the center of his story."

He played 14 seasons (1959–73) at center for the Philadelphia Warriors, San Francisco Warriors, Philadelphia 76ers and Los Angeles Lakers. Two of those teams—the 1966–67 76ers and 1971–72 Lakers—won championships. The other teams did not, and he was often blamed.

He was called selfish and lazy. An NBA official once said, "That's a multimillion-dollar property out there trying his best to devaluate the dollar." But Bill Russell, his archrival for most of his pro career, thought he had been the victim of an "informal conspiracy." "He got tricked," said the Celtic center. "Most fans and writers emphasized points, so he went out and got points. . . . Then they said rebound, so he went out and got the most rebounds. . . . In his mind he has done everything required of a player because he had led in all the categories that they had told him about. And he still could not win."

He was a winner as a youth in Philadelphia. When he started high school he stood 6 feet 11 inches and weighed 202 pounds. His lankiness inspired a nickname he disliked—Wilt the Stilt—but it stuck. He played two years at the University of Kansas and one year for the Harlem Globetrotters. Then came the NBA, by which time he had grown to 7-1 1/16 and 275 pounds. He was awesome and became self-conscious about his size.

"What is it with people, anyway?" he once

Chamberlain extends to his awesome length in a shot against the Cincinnati Royals.

asked. "They see someone extra big and somehow all the politeness is off. They seem to think nothing of just grabbing me or walking right up and breaking into a conversation. When I'm eating, they just stand there and watch me eat. I think they regard somebody unusual as public property."

He is the National Basketball Association's all-time leader in scoring (31,419 points) and rebounding (23,924). He averaged 50.4 points per game in one season (1961–62), scored 100 points in one game (in 1962) and pulled down 55 rebounds in another (in 1960), all records. He was all-pro seven times and the NBA's most valuable player four times. He led the league 11 years in rebounding, nine in field-goal accuracy and seven straight in scoring.

He was physically imposing and intimidating. Rules were changed (wider free-throw lanes, no offensive goal-tending) to slow him, but they seldom did. His scoring lessened only because his coaches thought it would help their teams win. "In the later years of his career his game changed," wrote Zander Hollander, "and as his proficiency on defense increased . . . so did the records of the teams he played for." Wilt didn't agree. "I think it's pretty ridiculous to ask the greatest scorer in the game to give up scoring," he said. "You play the game to score points, but when a player scores a lot of points, they call him selfish."

His salary for his final NBA season (1972–73) was $450,000. During the 1973–74 season he coached the new San Diego team of the American Basketball Association (a court barred him from playing, ruling that he owed the Lakers an option year). His San Diego contract gave him $600,000 a year for three years plus part ownership. He continued to live in his million-dollar bachelor mansion in the Los Angeles suburbs and often missed practice.

He quit as a coach and player after one season. He said he was tired of the long seasons and wanted to travel, produce movies, play volleyball and coach his women's track team. He no longer wanted to be a target. "Everybody pulls for David," he once said. "Nobody roots for Goliath."

"Basketball burns you out," he said after retiring. "If you're smart, you'll save your money and be ready to retire at any time because your career can end as fast as the snap of a finger." He thought he accomplished things in basketball that no man might equal. "I've done more with my sport than any man ever," he said. "It's made me rich and famous." What, then, was the answer to the contradiction of which Myron Cope wrote? "I have been blamed for the failures of others," he said.

Coach Wilt Chamberlain studies his team, the San Diego Conquistadors, from the sidelines.

Chi Cheng (1944–   )

For two years Chi Cheng enjoyed the most overwhelming success of any woman in track and field annals. But then excruciatingly painful thigh injuries halted a career that had hardly begun.

Chi Cheng was born in Taiwan and represented her native land in the 1960, 1964 and 1968 Olympics, winning a bronze medal in the hurdles in 1968. Vince Reel, an American coaching in Taiwan, discovered her in 1962 and convinced Taiwanese officials to send her to the United States, where she would receive better training.

Her success astonished even herself and Reel. She became a world celebrity, a statuesque, willowy woman (5 feet 7¾ inches and 138 pounds), effervescent yet shy. She learned to speak English and was graduated from California Poly at Pomona with a straight-A average. Reel goaded her to excellence. "You want to see me suffer," she once told him. "You have no heart. You are mean." Reel denied the charge, saying, "She knows she can overhaul anybody, so sometimes she takes it a little too easy." She admitted as much. "My problem is that I am very lazy," she said.

In 1969 she won 70 of 71 races. In 1971 she won 63 of 63, set world records for 100 yards (10.0 seconds), 200 meters (22.4), 220 yards (22.7) and the 100-meter hurdles (12.8). She tied the world record for 100 meters (11.0), missed the world record (52.4) for 440 yards by a tenth of a second and won three American titles indoors and two outdoors. European sports editors voted her the year's outstanding athlete, male or female, in any sport. In both years the international panel of *Women's Track and Field World,* a monthly magazine, voted her the athlete of the year in women's track, an honor that was a source of pride and embarrassment to Reel, who was editor of the magazine and in 1970 had become her husband.

In 1971 pain developed in her left thigh. Cortisone, other drugs and acupuncture failed to help, and in 1972 she underwent surgery in Taiwan to remove a 14-inch sliver of stiffened muscle. A 12-inch strip was removed from her right thigh in a similar operation in 1973.

She tried to run again, but the pain kept returning. Dr. Jerome Bornstein said, "You are simply an athlete who has to compete with pain. . . . It is simply a choice of standing the pain or ceasing to compete." "I feel I've reached only half my potential," she said sadly. "I would hate myself if I stopped now. . . . Why do I run? It is written that people climb mountains because they are there. It is something like that for me with running. I do it for sheer joy."

Clancy, Francis Michael
(1903–)

True magazine called him "a rowdy hockey player and a rowdier wit." Andy O'Brien thought he was endowed with a great touch of the dramatic, almost always garnished with humor. Jim Primeau wrote, "There was something about the driving, inspiring way he used to play the game that made the referees overlook his phrasing."

A colorful hockey player with a colorful vocabulary, King Clancy was aggressive, brash, cocky, refreshing and a darling of the home crowd. He was fast and agile. He had to be; when he broke into the National Hockey League at the age of 18, he stood 5 feet 7 inches and weighed only 127 pounds. His mashed nose and gnarled face were testimony to his frequent fights on the ice. He seldom won.

"He was a fox terrier among defenders," Trent Frayne wrote. "The only tricks he didn't learn . . . were the ones he invented himself. . . . He yapped and scrapped and inspired his mates with his absolute antipathy for defeat." Charlie Conacher, a teammate, recalled one incident: "Three times during a single fight at Toronto, I yanked the little guy from under a pile of battling players and put him on top."

Despite his size he played defense for nine years with the Ottawa Senators and seven with the Toronto Maple Leafs. He started at $800 a year and finished at $7,200, a fancy salary in 1936. But he played only two games that final season. "The time to quit," he once said, "is when it's no longer fun." His legs had given out and it was no longer fun.

He coached the Montreal Maroons and later the Maple Leafs. He spent 11 years as an NHL referee and prompted Dick Irvin to call him the best referee he had ever seen. Later he became assistant general manager and vice-president of the Maple Leafs. He told young players, "Hockey is a brutal, fighting game. You've got to have courage and a great deal of stamina to make the NHL today."

Clark, James

(1936–1968)

Jim Clark had a quality peculiar to outstanding athletes. He was so good and made his work look so easy that many people failed to appreciate his talents. As Anthony Pritchard wrote, "Although he would drive really hard when the pressure was on, his style was so smooth, so precise, so consistent that he was a rather disappointing driver for the ordinary spectator to watch." People in the business knew better. Many called him a driving genius.

Jim Clark was a Scot, slender, dark-haired, shy and modest, yet smooth and charming. His wit sparkled with a Scottish brogue. He liked his privacy and never showed emotion. "Few people know him well," Bill Libby wrote. "He does not give much of himself to anyone. He is not married because he believes marriage and raising a family do not mix with racing."

He started racing in 1956 and drove in his first grand prix in 1960. He scored his first grand-prix victory in 1962 and in 1963 won seven of the ten grand-prix races and the world driving championship. He captured another world title (and six of the ten grands prix) in 1965 and won America's premier race, the Indianapolis 500, as well. David Lazenby of the Lotus team, his chief mechanic, said of the Indianapolis victory, "He did it instinctively, the way some people play the piano."

He once said he was only relaxed when he was behind a wheel. "I don't drive a car, really," he explained. "I put myself through a corner. The car happens to be under me and I'm controlling it, yes, but I'm part of the car and it's part of me."

He was always in command of himself. "You have to control your emotions," he once said. "If you let them go, you'd be a menace to yourself and to others. If you allow yourself to feel enthusiasm or pressure or anything else, you will make mistakes."

A mechanical error worried him more than his own mistakes. In his autobiography, *Jim Clark at the Wheel,* he wrote, "The one thing a driver fears is a mechanical fault in his car, something which is not under his control. You never doubt your own ability. But when there is any doubt about what the car is

A triumphant Jim Clark six months before his death.

going to do, it really unnerves you." It also unnerved his friends, and they urged him to retire. "You can't," he said. "Racing is like smoking. It gets into your blood and you have to carry on."

He carried on, but not for long. In April 1968, in an unimportant Formula Two race at Hockenheim, West Germany, he was driving at 175 miles an hour when his car veered sideways and smashed into a tree. Jim Clark was dead at age 32.

Clarke, Ron (1937–   )

Ron Clarke was an Australian distance runner, a nice guy who finished first except in the big races. He ran more often and broke more world records than any other modern distance runner. Yet he never won a gold medal in the Olympics or the British Commonwealth Games. "Upon that omission," wrote Kenny Moore, "he has been sternly judged."

From 1963 to his retirement in 1970 he ran 313 races, from a half mile to the marathon. He won 202 of them, mostly the hard way—by running in front from the start. He set 17 world records at distances from two miles to 20,000 meters (about 12.4 miles). In a ten-month span—December 1964 to October 1965—he broke 12 world records for seven distances. In 1966 Emil Zatopek, who had won three gold medals in the 1952 Olympics, gave him his 10,000-meter medal and said, "Not out of friendship but because you deserve it."

At one time he trained three times a day—morning, afternoon and evening—a total of 22 miles. Yet he worked full time as a corporation accountant, successfully combining running, business and family. "Athletics has been good to me," he said when he retired, "but it is the little things I have missed, like putting the kids to bed."

Some observers pointed to his temperament in explaining Clarke's failures in big races. Noel Carrick wrote, "He had been called a 'clock runner' who lacks the killer instinct . . . at his best only when running for the record book. . . . But he loves running in the traditional way of the gentleman amateur athlete—for the enjoyment of the race and to win if possible." "No emotions," Derek Clayton concluded. "The man couldn't lift himself in the important competitions. . . . The Olympics or a club race, it was all the same to him." Percy Cerutty, the Australian coach, said, "He had no real mental drive. When he came up against men with spirit, he let them beat him."

Sports Illustrated called him "a non-hero in Australia, the enigma who never won a gold." On that subject he once said, "The Australian behavior toward losers is far from healthy. If youngsters are taught that losing is a disgrace, and they're not sure they can win, they will be reluctant to even try. And not trying is the real disgrace." Replying to the critics, he asked, "What is this so-called killer instinct? . . . I do not have to hate an opponent to win a race, for I believe that if you feel this way about an opponent, all you want is for him to lose, not for yourself to win. . . . I loved testing myself more than I feared being beaten."

Clemente, Roberto Walker
(1934–1972)

In 18 years (1955–72) as a Pittsburgh Pirates outfielder, Roberto Clemente became a superb all-round baseball player. He made exactly 3,000 hits, with a .317 lifetime average, and won four National League batting titles, even though he swung at bad balls ("I go to the plate to hit, not to walk," he once said). His fielding was superb, and his throwing arm was the best of his day.

The Puerto Rican athlete was conscientious, serious, sincere, intelligent and outspoken. "You never had to guess where you stood with him," said Bill Mazeroski, a teammate for 17 years. "He wears his emotions on his thin skin," wrote Arnold Hano. Clemente worried about his public reputation and was bitter because he felt he never received the recognition he deserved. "You never give me credit," he once said to a writer. Joe L. Brown, the Pirates' general manager, agreed that "His value was never fully appreciated."

He played softball until he was 17. He then turned to baseball, and the Brooklyn Dodgers signed him. He played for their Montreal farm team and was drafted by the Pirates for $4,000 when he was left unprotected. Later he said, "I did not even know where Pittsburgh was."

He endured all types of injuries and illnesses—shoulder, arm, elbow, hand, back, ankles, thigh, curved spine, floating disk, tension headaches, malaria and more. Most people dismissed his physical complaints because he had a deserved reputation as a hypochondriac. But he played baseball intensely. "He does everything on the field with the outward appearance that it will be absolutely his last physical act," Jack Hernon wrote. Howard Cohn commented, "He swings at the plate as though he were lashing out at a man who had slurred his person and his race."

Humanitarianism led to Clemente's death. When an earthquake devastated Nicaragua, he formed a committee in Puerto Rico to obtain relief supplies for the victims. The supplies were loaded onto an old, overloaded and uninspected cargo plane. Clemente's wife begged him not to fly on it, but he

said he had to go, that he was needed. On December 31, 1972, the plane took off and soon crashed. All aboard, including Clemente, were killed. Thousands of Puerto Ricans, to whom Clemente was a national hero, crowded to the beach near the crash site, not knowing how else to express their grief.

Within months, after the five-year waiting period had been waived, Roberto Clemente was voted into the Baseball Hall of Fame. Yet he remained a mystery. As Steve Blass, a teammate, said, "He was the most decent man I ever met, yet somehow no one seemed to understand him."

Cobb, Tyrus Raymond

(1886–1961)

To most people, including many who hated him, Ty Cobb, the Georgia Peach, was the greatest baseball player ever. He was also courageous, daring, cruel, sadistic, angry and hot-tempered, almost possessed by his desire to win.

"Ty Cobb," wrote Herschel Nissenson, "lived for the edge." His heroes in history were Napoleon and Julius Caesar. He intimidated anyone he could, sliding into bases with spikes high (and the spikes had just been sharpened). "When he was in his prime," said Hughie Jennings, his manager for 14 years, "he had half the American League scared stiff." He fought with opponents, umpires, fans, even teammates. As Josh Greenfeld wrote, "It is a historic irony of our national sport that the very best baseball player who ever lived was widely and passionately hated." Jack Sher wrote that he was "the most hated and the most feared player of his or any other era."

As a minor leaguer, he complained when his roommate, Nap Rucker, beat him to the bathtub. "Do you want to be first today?" Rucker asked. Cobb replied, "I mean that I've got to be first all the time—first in everything." As an 18-year-old major-league rookie, he once shouted at a teammate, "Get out of my way. I'm a better ballplayer now than you'll ever be."

"Few people in sports," wrote Fred Katz, "ever have been as widely disliked as Cobb." Few ever achieved what Cobb did, either. He was an American League outfielder for 22 years (1905–26) with the Detroit Tigers and for two (1927–28) with the Philadelphia Athletics. He remains the all-time leader in batting average (.367), hits (4,191), runs scored (2,244) and stolen bases (892), and before Henry Aaron overtook him in 1974 he also led in games played (3,033) and at bats (11,429).

Batting left-handed, he led the American League 12 times in batting, nine years in a row. In the 14 seasons starting in 1909, he batted successively .377, .385, .420, .410, .390, .368, .369, .371, .383, .382, .384, .334, .389 and .401. As Ray Schalk, a Hall of Fame catcher, said, "It was hard to believe the things you actually saw him do." He was also player-manager for six years (1921–26) with the Tigers, and he had good success with a mediocre team.

In 1936, when the first voting was held for the Baseball Hall of Fame, Cobb led with 222 votes on 226 ballots. When the Hall was opened in 1939, the first memento formally hung was a pair of Cobb's baseball shoes. The spikes were sharp.

Success did not come to Cobb without work. To keep his legs in shape he wore heavy boots while hunting in winter and leaded shoes in spring training.

Cobb sliding into third base on Jimmy Austin.

He practiced bunting and sliding by the hour. He was the first to swing extra bats to loosen his muscles before going to bat.

Off the diamond Cobb was a different man. He was bashful and not an egotist. He often stammered and stuttered in public, but he had social grace. Most of his friends were from outside baseball, and he preferred to talk about anything but the game. While playing in Detroit he met auto executives who advised him on buying stocks, and he became a millionaire before retirement. Later, he built a medical center honoring his father, established scholarship funds and gave generously to many charities. When he died he left an estate of close to $12 million, mostly in General Motors stock.

Throughout his career Cobb tried to rectify his image. "I have been roughed up in print possibly more than any man who ever played at sport. . . . In legend, I am a sadistic, slashing, swashbuckling despot who waged war in the guise of sport. The truth is that I believe, and always have believed, that no man, in any walk of life, can attain success who holds in his heart malice, spite or bitterness toward his opponent. But I did retaliate. If any player took unfair advantage of me, my first thought was to strike back as quickly and effectively as I could. . . .

"Don't let anyone tell you I was a dirty player. When you're on those basepaths, you've got to protect yourself. . . . I had sharp spikes on my shoes. If the baseman stood where he had no business to be and got hurt, that was his fault. . . . I was their enemy. If any player had learned I could be scared, I would have lasted two years in the league, not 24."

Cobb seemed to agree with Fred Lieb, who wrote, "He played under the law of survival of the fittest," and with H. G. Salsinger, who wrote, "He was the greatest competitor the sport has known and probably the worst loser."

Cobb never doubted himself. A year before his death he was asked what he thought he could hit against modern pitchers. "I guess about .300," he replied. "Is that all?" "Well, you must remember that I'm 73."

Cobb, a daring base runner, rounds third and heads for home.

Cochrane, Gordon Stanley (1903–1962)

His mother called him Gordon, his colleagues called him Mike and the public called him Mickey. He was one of baseball's most celebrated catchers, a leader and a fighter, exciting, aggressive and high strung.

He caught nine years (1925–33) for the Philadelphia Athletics and four (1934–37) for the Detroit Tigers, batting .320 in 1,482 games. From 1929 to

1931, when the Athletics won three consecutive pennants, he batted .331, .357 and .349. In addition to his batting prowess he was an excellent catcher and in 1947 was voted into the Baseball Hall of Fame.

At Boston University, Cochrane boxed, ran track and played baseball, football and basketball. He also played the saxophone in a local dance band. He was so promising when he turned pro that the Athletics bought Portland of the Pacific Coast League just to get him.

In one 1928 game, in which the Athletics were losing to the New York Yankees, he stormed back to the dugout one inning, threw down his chest protector and yelled, ''You yellow-bellied ———, you're quitting like the yellow dogs you are.'' Cochrane grabbed his bat, went to the plate and singled. Then Al Simmons did the same, as did Jimmy Foxx and Bing Miller. The Athletics won the game, regained their pride and started winning again.

''He is a man as rugged in mind and heart as in the body,'' Frank Graham once wrote about Cochrane. ''When he has lost a fight,'' wrote John Kieran, ''he . . . prefers to regard it as unfinished business until he can get to bat again.'' Red Smith compared his temperament to that of the relentlessly combative Ty Cobb.

Cochrane was sold to the Tigers for $100,000 and another player in December 1933, when the Athletics were desperately in need of money. He became the Tigers' player-manager in 1934 and led them to pennants in 1934 and 1935. But he worried and couldn't sleep and had a nervous breakdown in 1936. The next season a pitch by Bump Hadley of the Yankees hit him near the right temple, fractured his skull and ended his playing career. In 1938 he was fired as manager.

''Lots of kids wanted to be a big-league player,'' Cochrane once recalled. ''But even as a kid, I wanted to be a manager. . . . Maybe I just had to be boss.'' He became the boss, but, as Jack Newcombe wrote, ''He was one of baseball's angry men. . . . His rage to win . . . nearly destroyed him.''

Collins, Edward Trowbridge, Sr. (1887–1951)

Ty Cobb and Connie Mack described Eddie Collins as the greatest second baseman of all time. Frankie Frisch called him "the greatest infielder I ever saw," and Babe Ruth said he was "as smart a ballplayer as there ever was."

His statistics were overwhelming. He played 25 years, an American League record, for the Philadelphia Athletics (1906–14, when he was part of the famous $100,000 Infield, and from 1927–30) and for the Chicago White Sox (1915–26). He made 3,311 hits and batted .333 in 2,826 games. Twice he stole six bases in one game, and only Cobb and Lou Brock stole more in a lifetime. He led American League second basemen in fielding nine times.

"He could do anything," said Cobb, "hit, field, run bases, play brainy baseball. I guess he was the smartest baseball player of them all. . . . The tougher the situation, the better he'd be." Other players nicknamed him Cocky.

In 1925 and 1926 he was playing manager of the White Sox. When Miller Huggins died in 1929, the New York Yankees wanted Collins to succeed him as manager, but Collins declined because Mack said he would become manager of the Athletics when Mack retired (Mack managed until 1950, when he was 87). When Collins had an opportunity to become vice-president and general manager of the Boston Red Sox in 1933, Mack insisted that he accept it.

Collins did, and he helped the Red Sox build one of baseball's better farm systems. "He suffers from an inability to sit still," wrote Jack Sher. "He is as fast a thinker . . . as he was in uniform." He turned over the general manager's job to Joe Cronin in 1947 because of failing health, but he remained in the front office until his death.

He had been a baseball player and 140-pound quarterback at Columbia University. His father wanted him to be a lawyer, while he thought of becoming a doctor. "I could have been a doctor, lawyer or teacher," he said, "but I became a professional baseball player and never regretted it."

Eddie Collins, the second baseman, during his years with the Chicago White Sox.

Conacher, Lionel Pretoria (1902–1954)

In a 1950 poll, Lionel Conacher was voted Canada's greatest all-round athlete of the first half century.

And even this accolade may not have done him justice.

His athletic versatility was astounding. For 12 years (1925–37) he was a defenseman and later coach in the National Hockey League. He played professional football for the Toronto Argonauts, and Bob Zuppke, the Illinois coach, called him "the finest punter I've ever seen." He played baseball for the Toronto Maple Leafs of the International League, soccer for Toronto Scottish and lacrosse in the Ottawa Senior League. In track he ran the 100-yard dash in ten seconds.

He was also Canada's amateur light-heavyweight boxing champion and once boxed a four-round exhibition with Jack Dempsey when Dempsey was world champion. He won Canadian or provincial titles in boxing, wrestling, swimming, diving and track and was the best player on teams that won titles in baseball, football and hockey. He became a Member of Parliament, and in a softball game between Parliament and the press he hit a triple and suffered a fatal heart attack.

He was a sturdy man, 6 feet tall and almost 200 pounds. He had his nose broken eight times and endured more than 600 stitches, but as Margaret Scott wrote, "He was always able to make his own exit from a playing field, a distinction few athletes can claim." In a 1936 hockey game he fought an opposing player on the ice and chased him up a ramp and into the lobby. The player was his brother Charlie.

He was the eldest of a family of five boys and five girls. Brothers Charlie and Roy played in the National Hockey League but as Frank Graham wrote, Lionel was "the greatest of the Conachers." Dave Trotter, who played hockey with and against him, said he never knew a man so strong. "With one arm, he could pin you against the boards and, I suppose, if he wanted to, could have thrown you into the seats."

"I was the first in the family to take up sports," Conacher once said. "When I was a skinny kid of 13, weighing less than 100 pounds, I decided to go out for school football. It was a radical departure from family tradition, and my parents were not enthusiastic about it." Years later, they, too, became enthusiastic.

Connolly, Maureen (1934–1969)

Everything happened early for Maureen Connolly. At 14 she was the United States girls' tennis champion, the youngest in history. At 16, she was the national women's champion, the second youngest in history. At 19 a horseback-riding accident ended her career. At 34 stomach cancer ended her life.

She was a wholesome, bubbly bobby-soxer from San Diego. On the tennis court she belted the ball relentlessly. "Helen Wills was my model," she said. "I tried to develop a baseline game like hers." Vinnie Richards wrote, "She hits her forehand harder and better than any other woman in history." Allison Danzig said, "She pummels a ball harder than any woman since Helen Wills."

Between 1951 and 1954 she won three U.S. and three Wimbledon titles, was three times ranked No. 1 in the world, made a grand slam of the world's four major titles in one year (1953) and was three times voted woman athlete of the year by the Associated Press. She lost only four matches in three years. In the 1952 AP poll for woman of the year she finished third behind Queen Elizabeth of England and Mamie Eisenhower. Yet she was so modest, her mother said, "When she was winning in the East, she didn't mail me as much as one newspaper clipping."

In 1954 the horse she was riding (a gift from San Diego admirers) shied into a concrete-mixer truck. Her right leg was broken and never healed properly. She married Norman Brinker, an Olympic equestrian rider, and she taught tennis. "I can teach adequately enough," she said. "I can hit the ball to my pupils and, if it comes back to me, I can hit it. . . . But if the ball is out of reach, I have to let it go."

She became discouraged when she realized she would never play tournament tennis again. "I just don't enjoy tennis any more," she said. "I've lost that old spark. . . . If I can't play like I used to, there's no sense in going on."

It was a shame, for as Al Laney wrote, "There was no telling how good she might have become." "Her character and temperament remained durable and unruffled in all circumstances," Duncan Macauley recalled. Her coach, Eleanor (Teach) Tennant, said she had no aversion to rigid training, and Ann Haydon Jones, an English player, remembered her tremendous zest for life.

Maureen Connolly, winner at Wimbledon in 1953, the year she achieved the grand slam of tennis.

The young Maureen Connolly, known as Little Mo, remained cheerful. "I always seem to have a wonderful time. And even though tennis is a big part of my life, it isn't everything, really. I love tennis, sure. But I feel that if it keeps me from sleeping or eating or having fun, it isn't worth it. I'd give it up."

Connors, James Scott (1952–   )

He is the world's best tennis player at the age of 23, having won more tournaments and more money and also more animosity than any rival. He is temperamental, brash, grating, often unpleasant and immature. His outbursts on the court are like those of his good friend Ilie Nastase. "Nasty taught me all the stuff," he said, "like how to act like a fool on the court."

Connors also can be charming, but seldom in the eyes of fellow players. Tom Okker said he was a child and Arthur Ashe accused him of "working at gamesmanship." Ron Laver, a mild man, chided, "He probably thinks he's the next best thing to 7-Up." Stan Smith said politely, "He does things that annoy a lot of the guys."

One of his annoying traits is that he doesn't seem to care what others say. "I'm cocky and confident and maybe I'm bullheaded sometimes," he said, "but I think I have some humility. I know what the others say, but I'm not that obnoxious. I am not a punk. I've got broad shoulders and I can pack a punch. Most of these guys are windbags, anyway. If they ever try anything on me, I'll be over the net fast."

Much of the criticism stems from his independence. He refuses to play for the United States Davis Cup team, partly because of personality conflicts between Cup officials and his manager, Bill Riordan. He refuses to belong to the Association of Tennis Professionals, the players' union, and for much of the year, instead of playing against the best professionals on the World Championship Tennis circuit, he competes on the United States Lawn Tennis Association's circuit against lesser players for less prize money. People have called it the Mickey Mouse Circuit, but it doesn't upset him. "My definition of best is Wimbledon and Forest Hills," he said. "Play there and see who wins and he's the champion." As Riordan said, "He's his own man and that's the way he's going to stay."

The way he plays tennis he can afford to go his own way. At 5 feet 10 inches and 155 pounds he does not look especially strong, and with his page-boy hair style he does not look especially tough. Yet he is tougher, stronger and better prepared physically and mentally than almost anyone he plays.

He is a left-hander who uses a two-handed backhand, a stroke seldom seen in men's tennis. He has unlimited energy on the court, and he likes to hit the ball on the run with slashing strokes. His ground strokes are sound, punishing and deep. His game is aggressive and unrelenting.

Opponents may not like him, but they respect his tennis. "Playing him is like fighting Joe Frazier," Dick Stockton said. "The guy's always coming at you. He never lets up." Bob Carmichael, an Australian, used to think he was just lucky. "But it's not that at all. He's bloody brilliant, he is."

He grew up in Belleville, Illinois, across the Mississippi River from St. Louis (his father operated the bridge between the two cities). His mother was a tennis pro, and he was three when she and his grandmother started teaching him to play. He became so good that they moved to California so he could be coached by the two Panchos—Segura and Gonzales.

He attended UCLA for one year, long enough to win the NCAA championship. In 1972 he turned pro and earned $90,000 in prize money. The following year he surprisingly won the U.S. pro championship and other tournaments. He shared the number-one spot in the USLTA rankings with Stan Smith, but Riordan, his outspoken manager, attacked the rankings as an "immoral, unethical fraud."

The 1974 rankings posed no problem. He won three of the four grand-slam tournaments—Wimbledon, Forest Hills and Australia. He was barred from the fourth major tournament, the French

championship, because he played in America's new World Team Tennis league (he sued everyone connected with the ban). For the year he earned close to $300,000 in prize money and $100,000 more for the four-month season of World Team Tennis—and he was ranked number one in the United States and in the world. His major setback of the year was his broken engagement to Chris Evert, the Wimbledon and U.S. women's champion. He began 1975 without setback in the tennis world, netting $100,000 for beating Rod Laver in a winner-take-all exhibition match.

He is, as Peter Ross Range wrote, "an irrepressible Peter Pan of a manchild." He has endured the travails of adulthood—criticism, envy, youthful folly, shattered romance and even an occasional defeat—and could still say, "Nothing's been bad in my life."

Corbett, James John (1866–1933)

James J. Corbett was one of the great heavyweight boxing champions and one of the great innovators. Dan Daniel said, ''The rise of Corbett remade boxing.'' Writer Jack Sher called him ''the father of scientific boxing'' and said he was the most powerful single influence in taking the fight game out of the hands of thugs and brutes.

He was a handsome and imposing man, slender, modest, engaging and a dandy dresser. He originated the counterpunch, the feint and fast footwork. He once fought 27 rounds with both hands broken, prompting one writer, W. O. McGeehan, to call him ''the most courageous fighter of them all.''

He won the title in 1892 by knocking out John L. Sullivan in 21 rounds at New Orleans. Sullivan was a heavy favorite and outweighed him, 212 pounds to 178. It was the first heavyweight title fight with padded gloves and fought under Marquis of Queensbury rules. The timekeeper was Bat Masterson. Corbett lost the title to Bob Fitzsimmons in 1897 and tried unsuccessfully to regain it from James J. Jeffries in 1900 and 1903.

Jeffries called him ''the cleverest man I ever fought. There isn't a fighter of any weight, living or dead, who could measure up to him as a boxer. Joe Louis wouldn't have been able to hit him in a week.'' But he never gained universal affection because, as Arthur Daley wrote, ''He had committed the equivalent of sacrilege by winning the title from John L. Sullivan, the idol of the multitudes.''

During and after his boxing career he was a stage actor of surprising talent, and he was known as Gentleman Jim. One critic wrote, ''We went to the play to scoff but remained to admire, for Mr. Corbett is really a very competent actor.'' He was highly regarded by fellow actors, who made him president of the Friars and a leader of the Lambs Club.

He wrote in the foreword to his autobiography, ''If I tell them the mistakes I made and the wrong, mean things I did, they'll believe the good ones.''

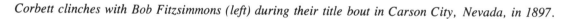

Corbett clinches with Bob Fitzsimmons (left) during their title bout in Carson City, Nevada, in 1897.

Counsilman, James Edward (1920–   )

Doc Counsilman is America's best-known and most successful swimming coach. He is also, wrote William F. Reed, "genius, coach, professor, scientist, author, physiologist, psychologist, psychoanalyst, nutritionist, businessman, photographer, anthropologist, gourmet, world traveler, comedian, metaphysician and all-round swimmer." His swimmers love him. "Anything Doc tells you is good," Charlie Hickcox said. Fred Southward said he had the know-how to get the full potential out of all his swimmers. "He lives swimming 24 hours a day, and not for himself but for the swimmer," George Breen said. "He knows how to handle his boys. He makes you enjoy it. He puts confidence in you. When Doc says something is so, it's so."

Counsilman was graduated 113th in a high-school class of 116. At Ohio State he was a national breaststroke champion, two-time captain and a thorn to Coach Mike Peppe. "He was probably the most disloyal kid I ever had," said Peppe. "We couldn't handle him. . . . He thought I was a lousy coach and he told the kids that."

He wrote his master's thesis at Illinois on the breaststroke and his doctoral thesis at Iowa on the crawl. In 1952 he became coach at Cortland (New York) State Teachers College and developed Breen, a former rower, into a world record-holder. He became coach at Indiana University in 1957 and led the Hoosiers to six straight NCAA team titles (1968–73). At Indiana his swimmers included Mark Spitz, Charlie Hickcox, Chet Jastremski, Mike Troy, Gary Hall, John Kinsella, and Jim Counsilman, Jr.

He warned his swimmers to expect "hurt, pain and agony," but he made practice fun with recorded rock music, jellybeans and games. His book *The Science of Swimming* sold more than 50,000 copies in six languages. Pools all over the world used the big workout clocks he made in his basement.

Kit Klingelhoffer described him as a master strategist who used physiology, psychology and mental attitude. A fellow coach said, "Most people don't understand him . . . but the people who do understand him include all his swimmers, and this is what counts." Rex Lardner said, "He is as good a coach as any in the world."

Counsilman explained his philosophy this way: "A coach needs to understand athletes . . . how he should handle them. . . . I don't think there should be an interchange. I think there should be a one-way pull . . . from the coach to the athlete. . . . You are the mature person, they aren't. . . . The way some coaches seem to feel, they think they're borrowing a boy's body."

Doc Counsilman and his latest superswimmer, Mark Spitz, at a 1972 meet.

Mrs. Court, relishing the last part of her 1970 grand slam, the U.S. Open championship.

Court, Margaret Smith

(1942–   )

She has won more important tennis championships than any other modern player, male or female. With her superb condition and power game, she plays more like a man than a woman. Rosemary Casals, a frequent opponent, described her as being "like a steamroller."

She has one glaring shortcoming, which Tony Kornheiser pinpointed: "She never had star quality." "She happened to be a Joe Frazier rather than a Muhammad Ali," wrote Barry Lorge. "She can only be what she is—a remarkably talented and accomplished athlete who is otherwise a plain, ordinary woman."

Margaret Court is tall (5 feet 10 inches), rangy, well-muscled and powerful. She lifts weights to build strength. "It's not too feminine, I suppose," she said, "but I can lift 150 pounds." As Maurice Brady wrote, "She built her strength on supreme athletic fitness."

She is also shy, bland and introverted. Grace Lichtenstein reported that when she mentioned to a tennis official that Mrs. Court lacked one of the most common mannerisms of women players—namely that she never talked to herself during a match—the official replied coolly, "What could she possibly think of to say?"

When she was 17 she won the national championship of her native Australia. By 1974 she had won 11 Australian, six United States, five French and three Wimbledon singles titles. In 1970 she scored a grand slam, winning these four major titles. In 1973, the year she lost to Bobby Riggs in a special "man vs. woman" match, she won $204,000 in tournaments.

Riggs beat her partly because she was nervous, a common failing. Virginia Wade, a contemporary player, told Riggs how to beat her: "You know you can equal her will. You know that if you really stand up to her, you will win."

She quit tennis in 1966 for 16 months. Tired of travel and the pressures of the tennis circuit, she opened a sports boutique in Perth. She also married Barry Court, a wool broker and yachtsman. She returned to the tour, leaving twice to have children. She travels on the tour with her husband and two children; in effect she takes her family to work.

Billie Jean King, a women's activist and rival champion, said, "She is Women's Lib in action, even though she doesn't seem to realize it. She earns the bread, and her husband babysits." To which she replied, "Billie Jean King and I are two different people. She's more outspoken. She just looks at everything different from me. I'm not Women's Lib. I'm just a wife and mother who plays tennis."

Cousy, Robert Joseph

(1928–   )

Bob Cousy was a one-of-a-kind basketball player, a 6-foot-1-inch playmaker with unusual peripheral vision, sleight of hand, ball-handling magic and ability to dribble and pass behind his back. "He could do more with a basketball—shoot, pass, dribble, anything—than anyone else I ever saw," Joe Lapchick said. Zander Hollander wrote, "It was Bob Cousy who made the game fun and attracted the crowds. He was the best ball handler and back-court man in the history of basketball."

He played four seasons for Holy Cross (1946–50) and made All-American. In the pros he played 13 years (1950–63) for the Boston Celtics and was their captain for 11 seasons. He made all-pro ten years in a row and led the league in assists eight straight years. When he retired he ranked first in all-time assists and third in points scored.

"By build, temperament and vision, he has been magnificently equipped to dazzle," Dave Anderson wrote. William Leggett wrote, "People in Boston have little doubt that while Dr. Naismith may have invented the game, Cousy made it as close to an art form as is possible." Walter Brown, owner of the Celtics, said Cousy "made professional basketball in Boston," and teammate Bill Russell, a later Celtics star, said, "The image of the Celtics is the image of Bob Cousy."

After retiring he coached Boston College (from 1963 to 1969) to a 117–34 record and three trips to the National Invitation Tournament. He hated the recruiting part of the job, saying, "You get a kid to come to your school by licking his boots. . . . When do you stop licking his boots?" From 1969 to 1974 he coached the professional Cincinnati Royals, who later became the Kansas City–Omaha Kings. He even played seven games for them at the age of 41, but ultimately he was unhappy. "I don't want to coach for a living anymore," he said late in his coaching career. "You don't have to be a shrink to see what's happening. Kids are much more complacent about sports than they used to be."

As Robert Lipsyte wrote, "He will be remembered . . . as the devoted, relentless, self-analytical, honorable magician who helped basketball into its current surge of popularity."

Crabbe, Clarence Linden (1908–   )

Buster Crabbe, one of the most successful swimmers of his day, became more famous as an actor. In 17 years in Hollywood he made almost 170 films and appeared in many television productions. He was usually the hero—Tarzan (he succeeded Johnny Weissmuller in the role), Buck Rogers, Captain Gallant or Flash Gordon.

Raised in Hawaii, he learned to swim at age five and starred in football, basketball and track as well as swimming. He set 16 world swimming records, mostly in the longer free-style races, and won 35 U. S. titles. He won a bronze medal in the 1928 Olympics and a gold medal in the 1932 Olympics. Afterward he swam professionally in the Water Follies, Aquaparade and Aquacade before becoming an actor.

With his broad shoulders and tapered waist Crabbe was quickly cast in he-man roles. Shirley Povich called him "a beautiful hunk of man." He was 43 when Philip Minoff wrote, "The splendidly-conditioned Crabbe is still not a fellow who's likely to get sand kicked in his face on the beach." During his early days in Hollywood, the New York *Herald Tribune* said, "His acting ability is limited," and *The New York Times* said sarcastically, "As an actor, he has a very deep chest." But later, Jack Gould wrote in the *Times* that "he obviously has been wasted in routine adventure films."

Crabbe had no illusions, saying, "I'm not an actor. I'm just a guy trying to make a living. . . . If worse comes to worse, I can always go back to combing the beach. . . . Those two Tarzan films were a real break for me because just before my first one I was making $12.50 a week as a stock clerk. Yet in a way they were a handicap, because after being tagged as a muscle guy, the only parts I could get were in Westerns or as a heavy in grade-B melodramas."

As a competitive swimmer he trained one or two hours a day and feared it was too much. He said, "If we had been forced to train the way they do now, I would have been a baseball player. But Roy Saari, with that flip turn he uses, would have licked me in my prime by 66 yards. . . . The youngsters who are competing today are better than we old-timers ever were."

Cronin, Joseph Edward
(1906–   )

Even if Joe Cronin hadn't married the boss's daughter he would have been a success. He was a major-league baseball player for 20 years and 2,124 games, a .300 hitter and perhaps the best shortstop ever in the American League. He managed major-league clubs for 15 years (1933–47), playing all but the two last seasons. Then he became vice-president and general manager of the Boston Red Sox (1947–59) and president of the American League (1959–73).

At 14 Joe Cronin was the junior tennis champion of San Francisco. He preferred baseball, and at 16 he was playing semi-pro ball for $10 a game (he gave half of the money to his mother). He was a clever fielder and bad hitter then. Later, he played for the Pittsburgh Pirates (1926–27), Washington Senators (1928–34) and the Boston Red Sox (1935–45). In 1933, at age 26, he became manager of the Senators. "When you're 26," he said later, "you don't think about being a manager." His 1933 team won the pennant, but the following season the Senators finished seventh.

That year Cronin married Mildred Robertson, the niece and adopted daughter of Clark Griffith, the Senators' owner. During the honeymoon Griffith traded his new son-in-law to the Red Sox as player-manager for $250,000 (a record price) and Lyn Lary. Cronin was player-manager until 1945, when he broke a leg sliding his 210-pound body into second base. He never played again. In 1956 he was voted into the Baseball Hall of Fame.

Sport magazine wrote that as Red Sox manager "he built the Dead Sox into the Red Sox." A young, immature Ted Williams conceded, "He understands me and knows how to handle me." Frank Graham said, "You have to admire him as a fighter." But, as Al Hirshberg wrote, "He still found it almost impossible to fire anyone and difficult to punish recalcitrants."

"There isn't a man in the game," Jack Sher wrote, "who will take as many chances, play as many hunches. . . . His players like that about him. When they play for him, they know they've been in a ball game." "You have to take chances," Cronin said. "I'd rather see a guy take a healthy cut at the ball and strike out than play it safe. . . . I don't like anything taken for granted in a ball game. It's a gamble and you shoot the works." To those who accused him of playing hunches too often, Cronin replied, "All managers play percentages. Hunches are just percentages read a little differently."

Ed Linn said of him, "Over the long run, he seems to have had an angel sitting on his back." Yet the angel wasn't always there. "Baseball is a game of disappointments," Cronin said. "The .300 hitter is a man who is only disappointed seven times out of ten."

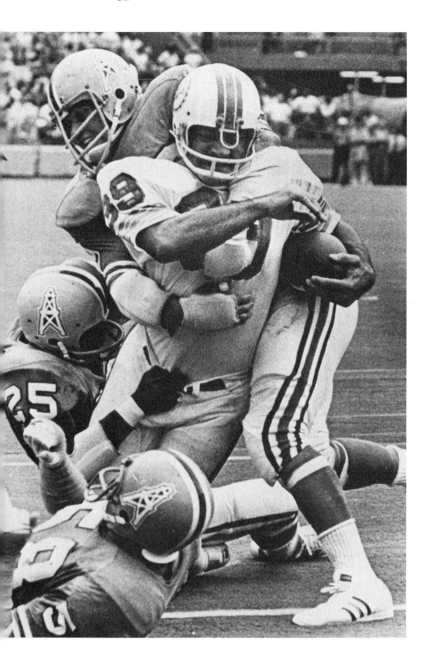

Csonka, Lawrence Richard

(1946–   )

Larry Csonka is the most feared power runner in pro football. He runs close to the ground and at defenders rather than around them.

"He likes to run where there's people," said Jim Kiick, a longtime teammate and friend. John Un-derwood wrote, "If foot-pounds at impact were measurable in football, it could well prove out that he hits harder than any back ever hit." He is known as Zonk, and his nickname indicates the kind of player he is—strong, violent and a hitter.

At 6 feet 3 inches and 235 well-muscled pounds, he looks the part. Off the field he is an Ohio farm boy, handsome, mild, witty, calm. Yet, he said, "I present the image of a brute, of knuckles dragging. I've had people hesitate to come up to me because they weren't sure what I'd do. I hate that. They don't know me."

At age 12 he was a 150-pounder playing every position. He did not do well at quarterback because, he said, "There was something about throwing the ball. I didn't want to turn it loose." An All-America running back at Syracuse University, he broke all the school rushing records set by Jim Brown, Ernie Davis, Jim Nance and his teammate, Floyd Little. He brushed off that achievement by saying, "I just carried the ball more."

He started his pro career in 1968, playing fullback for the Miami Dolphins. He led Miami to three straight American Football Conference titles (1971–73) and two Super Bowl victories (1973–74). In 1974 he signed with the Toronto Northmen (who became the Memphis Southmen) of the new World Football League. The three-year, almost $2 million contract starting in 1975 makes him one of the highest-paid players in any sport.

His aggressiveness led to severe headaches and two concussions, and he wore a special helmet with liquid and air compartments to absorb shock. Along the way he suffered ten broken noses. He did not complain; it was part of the job. "No matter what your style," he said, "you have to take a beating if you're a running back. If you're small and quick, it might catch up to you all at once, or if you're like me you might prefer to get it in regular doses. But sooner or later, the bill collector comes. It's all in the game. I'm no masochist, but I wouldn't want it any other way. I want to be physically involved. . . . The only thing that troubles me is that I won't be able to play forever."

Dancer, Stanley Franklin
(1927–   )

Stanley Dancer, the son of a dairy farmer, dropped out of school in the eighth grade. He grew into a wiry man of 5 feet 8 inches and 135 pounds, quiet, ageless, with the meek look of a hardware clerk or a bookkeeper. He also became, said the United States Trotting Association, "perhaps the best-known personality in the sport."

As an owner-trainer-driver of harness horses, he developed such pacers and trotters as Nevele Pride, Su Mac Lad and Albatross, all horses of the year, in addition to Cardigan Bay, Henry T. Adios, Noble Victory, Most Happy Fella and Super Bowl. In 1964 he became the first driver to win $1 million in purses in one year. From 1946 through 1974 he drove 2,996 winners and earned purse money exceeding $17 million.

His career started modestly. When he was 16 he borrowed $200 from his parents, bought a horse and drove it. He paid $75 for another horse that became a winner. In 1948 he started his stable with a nine-year-old, broken-down trotter named Candor. He bought the horse for $250, and his wife had to cash savings bonds to get the money. In those days he spent 18 hours a day with horses, training them in the morning and racing them at night.

Red Smith wrote of the young Dancer, "He doesn't look old enough to be allowed out for night racing." But, as William Leggett said, "His public acceptance came almost immediately in the big time in front of the largest crowds available and, more importantly, where the greatest amounts of money are bet." His wife, Rachel, saw in him "a quiet strength. He was shy, he was conservative, he was quiet, but he was a strong person."

He introduced an aggressive driving style, and he remained aggressive despite a numb right arm, a spinal condition that led to cervical disc surgery and a heart attack. "He scarcely knows how to slow down and savor his success," Pete Axthelm said. "At the height of his career, he remains vaguely uneasy, impatient and preoccupied. By some standards, he is a man who has almost everything, but he wants more. . . . His colleagues say he won't really be satisfied until somebody holds a series of races for

Stanley Dancer in the stretch with Albatross.

the greatest harness-racing horses in the world and finds that every one of them beds down in the Dancer stable."

Dancer discounted the risk in his work, saying, "There is nothing dangerous about harness racing. The worst crackup I ever had came in an auto accident. . . . You can never be sure of a horse until you test him for heart, in real competition." He said he never hit a horse. "The big thrill," he added, "is going all the way with a horse—that's breaking it, training it and driving it."

Dawkins, Peter Miller (1938–   )

As a college football player, Pete Dawkins was the best of his time. As an Army officer, as an inspiration, as a leader of men, he was better than the best.

He entered West Point in 1955 as a left-handed quarterback who had enjoyed great success in

Michigan private-school football. As a plebe he was hardly sensational. In his sophomore year he alternated between fourth-team and fifth-team halfback. As a junior he was a starter, and as a senior he became a legend.

In 1958 Pete Dawkins became the only cadet in West Point history to be captain of cadets, class president, football captain and a star man (in the upper 5 percent of his class academically) at the same time. (In 1903 Douglas MacArthur had been captain of cadets and a star man.) Dawkins also ranked tenth in a graduating class of 499, sang in the glee club and cadet choir, played six musical instruments and built hi-fi sets. He was an All-America halfback, winner of the Heisman Trophy and Maxwell Award as college player of the year, Phi Beta Kappa and a Rhodes Scholar.

Marshall Smith wrote, "If the authorities make book on future generals, he would be the surest bet since Robert E. Lee." Earl (Red) Blaik, the Army football coach, said, "I can practically prophesy that some day, if he stays in the Army, he will be Chief of Staff."

All sports came naturally to him. As a plebe he took up hockey, and in two years was the highest-scoring defenseman in the East. While studying in England on a Rhodes Scholarship, he took up rugby and played five weeks later for Oxford. He took up cricket and within weeks hit a boundary (the equivalent of a home run), prompting Alen Smith, the Oxford captain, to exclaim, "Jolly good, oh, say, jolly good." He began rowing and soon was competing.

By 1966 he was a frequently decorated captain advising the First Vietnamese Airborne Battalion. The next year he was made a major, in 1972 a lieutenant colonel. Tom Cahill, then the Army football coach, said of his impact on the cadets, "He personifies what they're supposed to be some day."

Frank Deford wrote, "He is locked into time. . . . He was the very essence of that time, a period that prized humility, respect and clean-cutness from a silent generation." But Dawkins disagreed. "Don't treat me like just another piece of nostalgia. You know, I don't live in the Fifties anymore, either."

Dean, Jerome Herman (1911–1974)

In 1930, in a spring exhibition game, 19-year-old Jerome Dean of the Houston minor-league team struck out one Chicago White Sox batter after another. "What's going on out there?" screamed Manager Donie Bush at his White Sox players. "You're letting that dizzy kid make a fool out of you."

Dizzy Dean, thus christened, lived up to his nickname. He was uninhibited, naïve, eccentric, colorful, glib, exciting, a drawling screwball with homespun humor, a fast mouth and an even faster fastball. Until a wrenched arm did him in, he pitched for the St. Louis Cardinals (1930, 1932–37) and the Chicago Cubs (1938–41). On a dare, he pitched the last game of the 1947 season for the St. Louis Browns. He had 150 victories, 83 defeats and a 3.04 earned-run average, and in 1953 he was voted into the Baseball Hall of Fame.

He was born Jay Hanna Dean, but when a boyhood friend died, he took his name. He was born on January 16 or January 22 or August 22 in Lucas, Arkansas; Holdenville, Oklahoma; or Bond, Mississippi. He gave different information to different writers, thinking he was helping them with exclusive stories.

In 1934 he won 30 games and his brother Paul won 19, and in the World Series against the Detroit Tigers they won two games each. His salary that year was $7,500. In the fourth game of the Series, when he was a pinch-runner, a thrown ball knocked him unconscious and he was rushed to a hospital. The next morning a newspaper headline shouted: "X-RAYS OF DEAN'S HEAD SHOW NOTHING."

Later, as a broadcaster, he became famous for mangling the English language ("He slud into third" . . . "The players are going to their respectable bases"). Teachers protested his use of "ain't," but, he said, "It was agreed that the teachers would learn them kids English and I would learn them baseball. . . . I only got as far as the second grade, and I didn't do so good in the first."

"He loved the sound of laughter," Jack Sher wrote, "and was big-hearted enough to want the whole world to enjoy him. . . . Wild horses couldn't have dragged him from the sheer physical joy of pitching, the pleasure of good company and ready ears."

"Baseball was never no work to me," Dean commented. "The reason I ain't pitching no more is that I had so much trouble with the right- and left-handed batters." Jack Newcombe wrote, "He was fortunate enough to come to the game when men showed an earthy zest for playing baseball for a living."

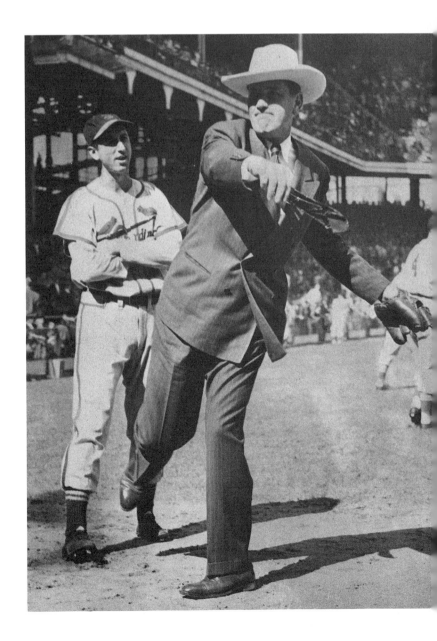

Dizzy Dean, with his famous ten-gallon hat, shows his old style at Ebbets Field, Brooklyn, in 1946.

Dempsey, William Harrison
(1895–   )

He was the world heavyweight boxing champion for seven years after World War I and probably the best-known boxer of his generation. He was, wrote Jack Sher, "the most loved and most hated prizefighter the ring has ever known, at once the most popular heavyweight champion of the world and the most despised."

He was despised while champion because he was so savage but became popular later because he was genuinely warm. Roger Kahn called him "a national monument" and wrote, "An age demanded an idol and Jack Dempsey arose."

In his prime he stood 6 feet 1 inch and weighed in the 180s or 190s. He was swarthy, angry, mean,

unshaven and violent. He hit below the belt, he hit after the bell, he hit while his opponent was climbing off the floor. "What do you want me to do," he asked, "write him a letter that I'm going to hit him?" He had intense black eyes, and when his man was down, one old-timer recalled, he hovered over him "like the Angel of Death."

He was loved and hated, affable and brutal, "the oddest mixture of humanity I've known," wrote Grantland Rice. "In the ring, he was a killer—a superhuman wild man. His teeth were frequently bared and his complete intent was an opponent's destruction. . . . Outside the ring, he is one of the gentlest men I know." Red Smith wrote, "He always comported himself like a champion."

Nat Fleischer described a typical Dempsey fight scene: "Blackly scowling, he would sit in his corner, glaring across at his antagonist, waiting for the bell. Once it sounded, he leaped to the fray like a hungry beast and habitually devoured his man with the unpitying fury of a jungle terror." Describing him watching Georges Carpentier being counted out, Irwin S. Cobb wrote, "His lips lift in a snarl until all his teeth show." Rex Lardner wrote, "He was certainly the most exciting, the most colorful, the most dynamic and the most savage. There was an immense fury coiled inside him waiting to be released." Roger Kahn wrote of "his unbelievable dedication to The Kill." "Whenever I went into the ring," Dempsey said, "I felt like the toughest guy in the world. . . . I just wanted to get that guy in front of me, belt the hell out of him before he'd belt the hell out of me."

He was born in the little mining town of Manassa, Montana (hence his nickname, the Manassa Mauler), the ninth of 11 children. He left home at 16 and for three years led the life of a hobo, riding freight cars and fighting in saloons.

One of his first real fights was against One Punch Hancock. When Dempsey knocked him out with one punch, Hancock's brother was so enraged that he challenged Dempsey, who knocked him out with two punches. His purse for the night: $2.50.

He fought from a crouch, with fast hands, fast feet and frightening power. He won the heavyweight title from Jess Willard in 1919, knocking him down seven times. He made five successful defenses, the

Dempsey knocked out of the ring by Luis Firpo in their celebrated 1923 fight.

last in 1923 against Luis Firpo in a brutal fight that saw Dempsey get knocked out of the ring.

He lost the title to Gene Tunney in 1926. When his wife asked him what had happened, he replied, "Honey, I just forgot to duck." After Tunney beat him again in the famous "long count" fight the following year, Dempsey more or less retired. "It was the greatest break I ever got," he said years later. "It was probably time I stopped fighting."

In 1940 he halfheartedly fought three times, but as Stewart Owen wrote, "It was like finding Sarah Bernhardt tap dancing in a burlesque show." In 81 fights from 1914 to 1940 he grossed $2.7 million, and he earned over a million more as a boxing and wrestling referee. Until 1935 only five fights had taken in $1 million or more at the box office, and he had fought in all five.

The public that had despised him when he fought idolized him after he left the ring, switching its hatred to Tunney for daring to defile its resurrected hero. In New York he presided over Jack Dempsey's Restaurant, first opposite the old Madison Square Garden and then a block away on Broadway. It had the best cheesecake in town, and it also had the hero of heroes seated by a front window, surrounded by boxing people and admirers who wanted to look at the great man and perhaps get an autograph or just a greeting.

He talked to everyone, especially the little old women from out of town who adored him. He called everyone Pal (like Babe Ruth, who called everyone Kid, he had a bad memory for names). He posed for photographs and was a soft touch for anyone who needed a dollar. He never forgot what a dollar had meant during his youth.

"The fight game is the toughest on earth," he said. "When I was a young fellow I was knocked down plenty. I wanted to stay down. I couldn't. I had to collect that two dollars for winning or go hungry. I had to get up. I was one of those hungry fighters. You could hit me on the chin with a sledgehammer for five dollars. When you haven't eaten for two days you'll understand."

Jack Dempsey in 1974.

Dillard, Harrison (1923–   )

He was the only man ever to win Olympic gold medals in both sprinting and hurdling. But the timing and the order of his medals were bizarre. Because he was primarily a hurdler, his sprint victory in the 1948 Olympics was as astounding as his failure to qualify for the hurdles that year. Red Smith wrote at that time, ''The chances are that he . . . will be a mighty mellow old gaffer before it happens again.''

Harrison Dillard had won 82 consecutive races until he took two second places in the 1948 national championships, one week before the United States Olympic trials. He made the Olympic team in the 100-meter dash. But in the 110-meter high-hurdles trials he hit hurdle after hurdle and failed to finish, an ignominious ending for a world record-holder.

But in the Olympics at London, he won the 100-meter dash in a major upset. His joyous coach, Eddie Finnigan, said, ''Fate is strange and wonderful. I'm going out to find a church somewhere.'' Dillard went into semi-retirement until 1952, when he made the Olympic team in the hurdles and, as expected, finally won the gold medal. ''Good things,'' he said, ''come to those who wait.''

Boyhood friends nicknamed him Bones because he was scrawny. In August 1936 the scrawny 13-year-old sat on a curb in Cleveland watching a parade for the home-town Olympic hero, Jesse Owens. ''I certainly was hit by the spark that afternoon,'' Dillard recalled. Later, Owens gave Dillard his Olympic shoes and changed the youngster's hurdling style.

When Harrison Dillard retired in 1956 he had won four Olympic gold medals (two in relays) and 14 AAU national indoor and outdoor titles. He had also swept the two AAU and two NCAA outdoor hurdles titles two years in a row. He had held every world hurdle record, indoors and out, and in 1955 he belatedly won the Sullivan Award as America's outstanding amateur athlete.

General George S. Patton, Jr., who saw Dillard win in an Armed Forces meet shortly after World War II, told him, ''Private, you are the best goddam athlete in the whole Army.'' Walter L. Johns, likening him to a champion race horse of his day, wrote, ''He's an Assault in the stretch.''

Dillard considered himself a hurdler, not a sprinter. ''I've always felt that sprinters, including me, are a dime a dozen,'' he said. ''That's just running. But when you combine running with the gymnastics ability required in the hurdles, you have a high art.''

Harrison Dillard (center) at the 1948 Olympics after tying the 100-meter-dash record.

DiMaggio, Joseph Paul
(1914–   )

He was perhaps the finest baseball player of his or any other day. He did everything well—hit for power, hit for average, throw, field and run—and as his contemporary, Dizzy Dean, said, "he did it all with class."

"He is a ballplayer without a flaw," wrote Jimmy Cannon, "a ballplayer of exceptional purity." Joe Cronin, who played and managed against him, said no one had his ability to produce in the clutch. Connie Mack, a major-league manager for half a century, called him "the greatest team player of all time." Joe McCarthy, his manager, said, "Of all the stars I've known, he needed the least coaching."

Joe DiMaggio had it all, and everyone knew it. In a 1969 poll of sportswriters and broadcasters he was voted the greatest living baseball player and the greatest center fielder in baseball history. He was placed in the all-time outfield with Babe Ruth and Ty Cobb.

He played center field for the New York Yankees from 1936 to 1951, except for three wartime years. In 1,736 games he batted .325 and hit 361 home runs. Three times he was the American League's most valuable player and twice its leading batter. More important, in his mind, was that in his 13 seasons the Yankees won ten pennants and nine World Series. In 1955 he was elected to the Baseball Hall of Fame.

He stood 6 feet 2 inches and weighed 195 pounds. He was modest, even-tempered and dignified. He was also moody and often depressed. He appeared aloof, but he was really shy. He was known as Joltin' Joe DiMaggio and the Yankee Clipper, the latter nickname after the stately sailing ships of the nineteenth century. As Jerry Izenberg wrote, "No sailing vessel ever moved with more effortless grace than DiMaggio in the field."

Of all his attributes, the most memorable was his grace. Casey Stengel, who managed him briefly, said, "He did everything so naturally that half the time he gave the impression that he wasn't trying. He had the greatest instinct of any ballplayer I ever saw. He made the rest of them look like plumbers." Tom Meany wrote that there was almost a nonchalance in his attitude but added, "It was only the mark of an athlete doing what comes naturally." Grantland Rice wrote, "If ever an athlete was meant for a sport, he was meant for baseball."

There was grace even in his retirement speech, which came after the 1951 season. "I feel that I have reached the stage where I can no longer produce for my ball club, my manager, my teammates and my fans the sort of baseball their loyalty to me deserves," he said. He seldom went to games after that, saying, "It isn't that I've lost interest in baseball—far from it. It's just that I can't look at a game I'm not in."

His baseball career started in 1932 in San Francisco, his home town. He was the eighth of nine children (brothers Dom and Vince also became major-league center fielders) of a Sicilian-born fisherman. At 17 he played the last three games of the Pacific Coast League season for the San Francisco Seals. At 18 he became a regular (San Francisco had to sell brother Vince to make room for him) and hit safely in 61 straight games. In 1934 the Yankees bought him despite his injured knee. They left him in San Francisco in 1935, and he batted .398.

Then came the Yankees. He set a major-league record in 1941 by batting safely in 56 straight games (after the streak was broken, he hit safely in 17 more games). Lefty Gomez, the Yankee pitcher, called it the greatest record in baseball. The streak almost ended when brother Dom of the Boston Red Sox pulled down a long drive. Joe said later, "I thought that while it might have been a great tribute to the integrity of baseball, it was kind of rubbing it in to be almost robbed of a record by your own brother, especially when he was coming over to my house for dinner the same night."

In 1949 he became baseball's first $100,000-a-year player. As his career was ending in 1951, Mickey Mantle and Willie Mays, the two best center fielders of the last quarter century, broke into the major leagues. "He was my hero," Mays said later. "I tried to do things like him, but you know only he could do them." He was Mantle's idol, too. "I think he was the greatest player ever," said DiMaggio's successor.

After retirement he was married briefly to Marilyn Monroe. He stayed in the public eye as a broadcaster and spring-training coach for the Yankees, and he looked after many business interests. At old-timers' games and celebrity golf tournaments he was always the center of attention. It continued to amaze him. "You'd be surprised," he said, "how many people remember me, considering how long I've been out of the game."

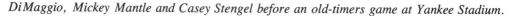

DiMaggio, Mickey Mantle and Casey Stengel before an old-timers game at Yankee Stadium.

Eckersall, Walter Herbert
(1886–1930)

Walter Eckersall may have been the greatest quarterback in college football history. He certainly was one of the smallest. When he entered the University of Chicago he weighed 138 pounds. By graduation he had built himself up to 144 pounds. He stood 5 feet 7 inches and wore lifts in his street shoes to look taller.

He went to Hyde Park School, down the street from the University of Chicago. In 1902 he led Hyde Park to a 105–0 victory over Brooklyn Poly for the national high-school championship. A 14-year-old boy named Knute Rockne crashed the gate and watched in fascination. He recalled that "Eckersall played prairie football. . . . He worked so quickly and so coolly that he made his offense bewildering."

From 1903 to 1906 Eckersall was the Chicago quarterback. He was named All-American his last three years, and his teams won 32 games, lost four and tied two. He could run, pass, punt and drop-kick (twice he drop-kicked five field goals in one game). He was a master strategist, inspiring and commanding when calling signals, and a vicious tackler. He was also gentle, modest and retiring. He was a 70-minute man (in those days teams played 35-minute halves) who never missed playing time because of injury.

Alexander M. Weyand wrote, "He was smart and shrewd and very fast." "He was a bad actor on the broken field," said Pudge Heffelfinger, "and it would never do to let him get away after catching a punt." Merrill (Babe) Meigs, a teammate, wrote, "He wasn't one of the greatest football players that ever lived. He was the greatest. I've been waiting 40 years to see his equal. I haven't yet. . . . He had the power to lift a whole team from mediocrity to the greatness of which he himself was capable."

His proudest possession was a diamond-studded watch. Instead of numbers, the face of the watch contained pictures of his Chicago teammates and Coach Amos Alonzo Stagg. The watch was presented by Chicago students and faculty members at the halftime of his final game. Donations toward the gift were limited to 25 cents per person.

Walter Eckersall, quarterback for the University of Chicago, in 1905.

Ederle, Gertrude (1907–)

When Gertrude Ederle was 19 years old she became the first woman to swim the English Channel. Paul Gallico called it "the greatest recorded athletic feat by a woman in the history of the world." He added, "She was the demonstration of those times that courage, training, willpower and indomitable spirit comprise the secret weapon against seemingly unconquerable obstacles . . . but she went through hell."

She was the daughter of a New York butcher, and she had, W. O. McGeehan wrote, "the simplicity of Shaw's Joan of Arc and the physique and many attributes of a male giant." Her amateur achievements included three medals in the 1924 Olympics, nine world free-style records and six national outdoor titles. In 1925 she turned professional and set out to swim the Channel, but she became seasick and quit.

On August 6, 1926, she tried again and made it. She swam from France to England in 14 hours 31 minutes, almost two and a half hours faster than any man in history had done. She succeeded despite wind, rain, storm, darkness and cold. With three miles to go and a storm raging, her father asked her if she wanted to quit. "What for?" she asked. Later, she said, "On the boat going back again, I thought, 'Did I swim all this way?'"

Covered in grease, Miss Ederle awaits the start of her Channel swim.

Miss Ederle with her mother at a New York welcome after becoming the first woman to swim the English Channel.

She returned home fondly regarded, Gay Talese wrote years later, as a "grease-smeared Venus." New York gave her a ticker-tape parade, and President Calvin Coolidge called her "America's best girl." She was inundated with stage, movie and other commercial offers worth hundreds of thousands of dollars. She spent two years in vaudeville at $2,000 a week.

Tragedy struck when at age 21 she went deaf and later hurt her spine. She was in a cast for four and a half years, and 19 neurologists said she would never walk again. Yet she did walk again and even swam in Billy Rose's Aquacade in the 1939 New York World's Fair. Later she repaired aircraft parts and taught deaf children to swim.

"I'm comfortable," she said, looking back. "I saved money. I've never been helped. . . . It doesn't matter if they've forgotten me. I haven't forgotten them. . . . It was worth it."

Elliott, Herbert James (1938–   )

Herb Elliott raced across the track scene, packed perhaps the greatest career of any miler into three years and then retired abruptly at age 22.

From 1958 to 1960 he never lost a mile race. He ran 17 sub-four-minute miles and recorded the two fastest miles and three fastest 1,500 meters to that time. In 1960, as a student at Cambridge University, he halfheartedly ran twice in May and never ran again. William Johnson wrote at that time that he was the most promising runner since Paavo Nurmi, but Roberto Quercetani wrote that he never reached his potential.

Herb Elliott came from western Australia. The lean, hawk-nosed youth ran his first mile (5 minutes 35 seconds) at 14. He was 17 when Percy Cerutty, the celebrated coach, told him, ''There's not a shadow of a doubt that within two years you will run a mile in four minutes.'' Two years later, toughened by Cerutty's rigid training methods, he ran a mile in 3:59.9. The next day he saved a girl from drowning.

In August 1958 he set two world records—3:54.5 for the mile and 3:36.0 for 1,500 meters. By the 1960 Olympics he was married and his enthusiasm for running had waned, but he won the 1,500-meter gold medal, breaking his world record. His time of 3:35.6 remained the record for nine years.

After that the thrill was gone. He recalled, ''I didn't realize what my goal was until I felt satisfied. I felt satisfied when I won an Olympic gold medal and broke a world record. Once that hunger had been satisfied, I lost interest altogether.''

Noel Carrick wrote of his ''almost brutal desire to mow down his opposition. . . . '' Cordner Nelson wrote, ''Few men are born with his natural ability. Still fewer punish themselves so hard in training. And nobody else ever had a greater will to win.''

His drive carried over to his nonathletic life. He said after retiring, ''I believe life falls into categories. When you are a youngish sort of bloke, as I still class myself, your career has to be developed to a level that makes you happy. I'm not happy by any means. There is a family to educate and a home to build and pay off. The first 15 or 20 years of married life must be a selfish sort of existence where job and family come first.''

Herb Elliott at London's White City Stadium, winning one of his last mile races.

Esposito, Phillip Anthony
(1942–   )

He is the dominant center in hockey, a big, burly man (6 feet 1 inch, 210 pounds) with hunched shoulders, a craggy face and a sullen look. "He plays center," Pete Axthelm wrote, "with little of the speed and shiftiness of an Henri Richard, the flair and defensive skill of a Dave Keon or the all-round brilliance of a Stan Mikita," but he has been the National Hockey League's most prolific scorer for many seasons.

Phil Esposito played his first four seasons (1963–67) for the Chicago Black Hawks, centering for Bobby Hull. The Black Hawks, considering him too slow, traded him to the Boston Bruins in 1967, and he has finished first or second in scoring every year since the trade. In the 1970–71 season he set NHL all-time single-season records for goals (76) and scoring points (152).

Bobby Orr, his teammate with the Bruins, recalled, "When he came to Boston, he came with a winning spirit that he brought from a winning club. He brought all of us together and made us believe we could win." Hal Laycoe, a rival coach, said, "When he has the puck, he dominates the game."

He has the puck often because he is on the ice 30 or 35 minutes of the 60-minute game, far more than most players. He likes to hover in the slot, the area in front of the enemy goal, and push in loose pucks. This style has given him a reputation as a garbage man. "Let them say what they want," he said. "I don't care if the puck goes in off my head." Gerry Desjardins, an enemy goalie, described him thus: "When he gets that puck in front of the cage, he is all arms and legs and looks like he is 12 feet wide."

He has great control of the puck, and a rival coach, Punch Imlach, explained why: "My guys stand around and watch him move the puck like they're mesmerized."

"I'm not a Bobby Hull, a Gordie Howe or a Bobby Orr," said Esposito. "I've never made people rise to their feet with spectacular plays. I just do my job. To tell you the truth, I wouldn't walk across the street to see myself play."

Teammates embrace Esposito in 1971 after he broke the NHL's single-season record for goals scored.

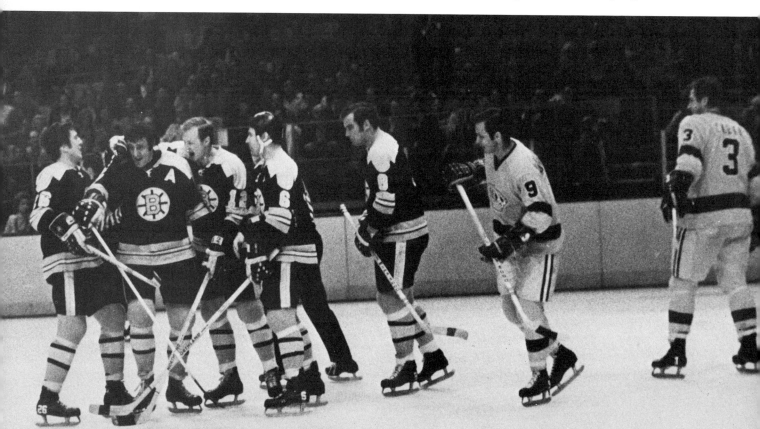

Etcheverry, Sam (1930–   )

He was the first exciting passer in Canadian football, solid, indestructible, ever the gambler, a national hero and an idol in Montreal even though he spoke French badly.

Sam Etcheverry, an American, played quarterback for the Montreal Alouettes from 1952 to 1960, never missing a game. He averaged more than two miles a year passing. Canadian Football League statistics show that he completed 1,630 of 2,829 passes for 25,582 yards and 174 touchdowns, and these figures do not include many unofficial statistics during his first two seasons.

At the University of Denver the 5-foot 11-inch, 190-pound quarterback wasn't impressive enough to interest any National Football League team. The Alouettes saw his name in a football yearbook and invited him to try out. "When I received their tryout contract," he said, "I gambled and made it."

His full contract had a no-trade clause, but after the 1960 season the Alouettes traded him to Hamilton (Ontario) anyway. Jake Gaudaur, now the CFL commissioner and then Hamilton's president and general manager, recalled, "When the trade was announced, people gathered in the streets in Montreal ready to lynch everybody, including me. When the cops found out who I was, they asked me to stay off the streets."

He left Canada in 1961 and 1962 to play for the St. Louis Cardinals of the NFL. A sore arm ended his career, and he returned to Montreal and became a stockbroker. He coached the Montreal Beavers in the short-lived Continental League and then the Alouettes. He won the Grey Cup in 1970, his first year, but was fired when his next two teams had losing seasons.

More than anyone else, he elevated pro football to a true national spectacle in Canada. "He had charisma that brought people in at the gate," Gaudaur recalled. "You couldn't buy a seat when he was there." Russ Jackson, a successor among great Canadian quarterbacks, said he was everything a quarterback should be. "When he was younger," added Jackson, "he was my type of quarterback. He ran more. Then he became a different type of quarterback—a classic passer." Gordon Walker, a CFL official, said Etcheverry always knew what he was doing, in and out of football.

Etcheverry preferred Canadian football to the American game. "The pro grind in the United States is murder," he said. "On the other hand, in Canada we work out only once a day. Practice is held in the evening, which means that the players can hold down regular outside jobs if they want. . . . I don't have any regrets about all those years in Montreal. They were nine wonderful years."

Etcheverry, playing for the St. Louis Cardinals, looks for a receiver downfield as Sam Williams (No. 88) closes in.

Evans, Charles, Jr. (1890–   )

Few people have had a greater impact on amateur golf than Chick Evans. He gave much to the game as a player and benefactor, and he stayed with it at an age at which most of his contemporaries had settled in rocking chairs.

He lived for years in a house bordering the Edgewater Country Club in Chicago, where he learned the game. Starting in 1907, he played in every U.S. Amateur tournament for half a century. In 1916, using only seven clubs, he won the U.S. Amateur and U.S. Open, a sweep never achieved before and achieved afterward only once (by Bobby Jones in 1930). He won 53 major tournaments, including the U.S. Amateur title in 1920.

In 1923 he lost a fortune in the stock market, and two years later he had a nervous breakdown. His game was never quite the same again, but his generosity was unchanged. He founded a scholarship fund that has sent thousands of caddies to college.

With his big, smooth swing, he had a crisp game from tee to green. "I have seen him plant a newspaper 160 or 170 yards away and pepper it with iron shots that rarely missed the target," Grantland Rice wrote. But, as Rice noted, his game had a major flaw: He couldn't putt.

"I've seen him miss shorties you could hole with a flick of your finger," Joe Williams wrote. Gardiner White, a golf contemporary, thought that more consistent putting, especially on short putts, would have won him several more national championships. Jerome Travers, an earlier U.S. Amateur champion, made the ultimate judgment on Evans' putting: He willed his putter to him.

In his mid-50s he shot in the low 70s and was still the Chicago champion. At age 68 he had a handicap of six. "I haven't won any kind of national senior tournament yet," he said, "but I have fun just the same."

Evans, Lee Edward (1947–   )

Coach Jim Terrill called him "the most competitive trackman in history." Dick Drake wrote, "He may go down in history, along with Tommie Smith, as the athlete who gave all athletes the courage to speak out on issues of individual rights and choice."

As a child, Lee Evans picked 250 pounds of cotton a day in the 100-degree heat of California's San Joaquin Valley. From 1966 to 1972 he was track and field's outstanding quarter-miler. He set world 400-meter records of 44.0 seconds in the 1968 U. S. Olympic trials and 43.8 in winning the gold medal at Mexico City. He won five national outdoor titles. From 1968 to 1972 he ran memorable indoor races against Martin McGrady, a world indoor record-holder. In 1973 he turned professional and was the leading money winner on the first year of the tour.

His running style was one to remember. Jim Scott wrote, "In his late surges, running low, his head snapping, his teeth bared, his body rolling, he looks for all the world like Groucho Marx sprinting after a shapely lass." Evans replied, "Lots of guys think they can beat me running because I'm not the best-looking out there. . . . Somehow, I manage to win."

He won, wrote Bert Nelson, because "he gets more out of his abilities than any other athlete I've seen." He also won because he trained harder than anyone else. Yet he was friendly, honest, refreshing, enthusiastic, shy, polite and, above all, proud.

His Olympic victory came after Tommie Smith and John Carlos had been thrown off the U.S. team for their Black Power demonstration on the victory stand. Evans was close to them, and Black Power advocates expected a similar demonstration by him. They did not get it. "I knew I was going to catch hell from whites and blacks no matter what I did," said Evans. "I'm not going to be the victim of anybody." Later he said of Mexico City, "It changed my life. It was a heavy learning experience. I was kind of naïve. I found out a lot about people. . . . I'm glad I went through it, but I'm glad it's behind me. . . . If I had to do it over again, I would do something more."

Once, when Evans lost, his son, Keith, then five, asked tearfully, "Daddy, why'd you let them beat you?" "Let them?" Evans recalled. "How do you tell a little boy you never let anybody beat you?" As Jerry Kirshenbaum wrote, "That episode is of historic importance because it is probably the only time Lee Evans has ever been called upon to defend his will to win."

Evans races to victory on the anchor leg of a 1,600-meter relay.

Evert, Christine Marie (1954–   )

She is the darling of international tennis, a pretty and pert Floridian whose success has been meteoric and relentless. At 16 she was a U.S. Open semi-finalist, at 17 the U.S. clay-court champion. She turned professional at age 18 and reached the Wimbledon and French finals. In 1974, age 19, she arrived at the top, winning the Wimbledon, French and Italian titles and earning more than $250,000 in prize money.

Grace Lichtenstein wrote, "She had seemingly billowed out of the Florida clay onto the glossy covers of national magazines fully grown like a Botticelli Venus—poised, pretty, famous and rich.

Men thought her adorable, little girls worshipped her, middle-aged mothers came up to her at tournaments and told her she had restored their faith in youth. She was Miss America Pie."

Chris Evert is slim (5 feet 6 inches, 110 pounds), poised, cool, reserved, immaculately dressed and groomed, always a lady. "Prim and proper in her blonde pony-tail and gold earrings, she resembles a poodle on parade," Dave Anderson wrote.

Her forehand and two-handed backhand are so consistent that they allow her to stay at the baseline and belt drive after deep drive almost to the point of boredom. "She will outstroke and outwait almost anybody else," wrote Peter Ross Range. Yet for rival Rosemary Casals, "What makes her tough is her mind . . . she doesn't know how to give up."

Other women players do not always like her, partly because of her quick success and partly because she plays only the tournaments she wants to play. "She is what she has to be, what the public wants—charming and gracious," wrote Tony Kornheiser. "She has traded friendship for public adoration."

Julie Heldman, a rival, thought that her coolness was deliberate, saying, "She's brighter than hell. She's created a good deal of her image. She really knows where it's at." Miss Evert said, "I don't show emotion, but it's there, believe me. If I smile and laugh out there, I'll lose concentration."

She was engaged to Jimmy Connors, the men's champion, but the engagement was broken because, she said, "We both chose our careers." She described herself as neither extroverted nor shy. "I like people. I like children. But I just can't go up and say, 'Hi, I'm Chris.' It isn't my personality."

Fangio, Juan Manuel (1911–   )

In 1948 he was driving a taxicab in Buenos Aires. Ten years later he had won the world driving championship five times and had become a millionaire.

In a world of young, slim, handsome, devil-may-care auto drivers, Juan Manuel Fangio was an anomaly. When he started big-time racing he was 38 years old, quiet, modest and mature, a stocky man with a middle-aged spread. He had won many races with inferior machinery in his native Argentina, but he hardly looked like a future hero of the European grand-prix circuit.

But looks were deceiving. In his first grand prix, in 1949, he drove a Maserati. He won world titles in 1951 in an Alfa-Romeo, in 1954 and 1955 in a Mercedes, in 1956 in a Ferrari and in 1957 in a Maserati. He was so gentle with his machines that he completed more than half his races—a rare feat. "Cars should be treated like women—gently," he once said. "The first basis of reaching the finish is not to press too hard, not to squeeze all that can be squeezed out of your machine."

Perhaps he didn't press too hard, but, as Frank Blunk wrote, "He could get every ounce of energy out of an engine." Anthony Pritchard wrote, "He combined speed, precision and a mastery of cornering technique with powers of tremendous endurance and a will to carry on to the finish regardless of the odds." Michael Frostick thought he was "probably the greatest racing driver of all time," and Phil Hill, a rival driver, called him "the one absolute of driving."

In 1958 he retired at age 47 at the peak of his career. "Champions, actors and dictators should always retire when they are at the top," he said. "But not many realize when they have reached the peak, and the road ahead can lead downward only. The exhilaration of racing a smooth-running car and the challenge of keeping in the lead had become drudgery. The joys of the first years became mere fatigue. My body is tired and my spirit as well.

"Never think of your car as a cold machine," he said, "but as a hot-blooded horse racing with the rider in one beautiful, harmonious unit. As for me now, the rider has grown older and more blasé than the horse."

Fangio rounding a turn in an Italian race.

Fangio surrounded by well-wishers after winning the Grand Prix of Europe at Rheims, France, in 1951.

Feller, Robert William Andrew
(1918–   )

At the age of 17 Bob Feller, an Iowa farm boy with a plowboy gait, graduated from semi-pro baseball to a mid-season exhibition game between the Cleveland Indians and the St. Louis Cardinals Gashouse Gang. In three innings he struck out eight Cardinals with a fastball that might have been the fastest of any

pitcher ever. In his first major-league start a month later he struck out 15 St. Louis Browns. A month after that, against the Philadelphia Athletics, he set an American League record by striking out 17 batters.

Thus started a spectacular career in which he won 266 games and lost 162, all for the Indians. He pitched from 1936 to 1956, but he missed almost four years at his peak because of wartime service in the Navy.

He struck out 18 batters in one game, the major-league record for 31 years, and compiled 348 strike-outs in one season, the major-league record for 19 years. He struck out 2,581 in his career and pitched three no-hitters and 11 one-hitters. He was elected to the Baseball Hall of Fame before he was 44.

In 1946 his fastball was timed at 98.6 miles per hour, and he said it would have been faster if he were warmed up. "Sure he's green," said Rogers Hornsby early in Feller's career, "but with a fastball like that, you can be so green that the cows chase you to the train." His curveball, said Joe DiMaggio, "was the best I've ever seen." Ed Fitzgerald wrote, "You find yourself crossing your fingers and hoping he's really hot, hoping he turns them all away hit-less, so you can go home and tell you saw him do it."

In 1947 his salary and bonuses totaled $87,000, breaking Babe Ruth's major-league record of $80,000. In good years he earned $150,000 from the Indians and outside activities—barnstorming, radio shows, newspaper columns, endorsements and an insurance business. He was the first baseball player to incorporate himself, and he was one of the first player representatives, a job that helped make him controversial. He could be narrow-minded and self-righteous and once prompted Gordon Cobbledick to write, "In some of his aspects he is not an attractive personality. . . . He has certain qualities that make it inevitable that . . . the wolves should yap at his heels."

His contribution to baseball was substantial. "He hasn't yet taken out of the game what he has put into it," Garry Schumacher, a long-time baseball execu-tive, once said. Feller thought differently, saying, "Baseball owes me nothing and I owe everything to baseball."

Filion, Herve (1940–   )

He is a fifth-grade dropout from the remote farm community of Angers, Quebec. He grew up around work horses and road horses because his family had no car. When his father started racing horses as a sidelight to help raise his ten children, Herve raced, too. At age 13 he won his first race, and he has never stopped winning.

In 1974 he drove the winners of 637 pacing and trotting races and earned purses totaling $3,431,366, both world records. He set the previous records (605 winners and $2,473,265) in 1972. By the end of 1974 he had won 5,147 races, a Western Hemisphere record, and purses totaling $15,776,184, the third highest in history. Many of his victories have been in claiming races with horses he trains, drives and often owns. One horseman said, "If he had Stanley Dancer's stock, he'd win a thousand races a year."

At 5 feet 6 inches and 145 pounds, he is stocky, dapper, charming and cocky. His earnings of $400,000 a year pay for a mod wardrobe, a $400 hairpiece and a big limousine with country-music tapes. He also owns a helicopter that allows him to

drive at one track in the afternoon and another at night, sometimes driving in 20 races a day.

"He has always pushed himself mercilessly," Murray Olderman wrote. Norman Dauplaise, a rival driver, said, "He never stops. He's like a machine." "I don't know where he gets the energy," a Yonkers Raceway official said. "He'll race night and day six days a week, and then he'll be looking for races in Delaware or Canada for Sunday. He digs it. He's really into driving. He loves to win."

Pete Axthelm saw another side of the man, writing, "He is neither a machine nor a humorless, puritanical worker nor a greedy Sammy Glick in a sulky. . . . For beneath those . . . silks lurks the soul of a true gambler, a man who has parlayed his abilities and his intense craving for action into a jackpot of record proportions."

Filion gave his own explanation of his success. "I'm as good as the next guy, no better," he said. "But maybe I work harder. The money's out there. You got to go out and get it. . . . If it wasn't for harness racing, I'd probably be carrying a lunch pail and working as a laborer on construction projects like my friends back home."

Fischer, Robert James (1943–   )

Bobby Fischer is, without doubt, the best chess player of today and perhaps any other day. He is also, without doubt, one of the most complex and unpleasant personalities in or out of sports.

Larry Evans, the American player who has been as close to him as anyone, said, "He is the most individualistic, intransigent, uncommunicative, uncooperative, solitary, self-contained and independent chess master of all time, the loneliest chess champion in the world." Yet Evans recognized that "his defiance of chess authorities and his demands for better playing conditions have raised the professional standards of the game."

"Men who play at the grandmaster level are almost, without exception, strange and unpleasant," D. Keith Mano wrote. "Fischer, best by acclaim, is certainly, also by acclaim, the strangest, the most unpleasant. . . . He resembles a device so specialized that all functions but the chess function have atrophied."

He is rashly temperamental and seldom displays positive emotions. Brad Darrach wrote, "I have rarely seen him register sympathy, invitation, acknowledgment, humor, tenderness, playfulness or love." Robert Cantwell thought he was socially evasive rather than hostile, "likely to greet even an old friend as if he were expecting a subpoena."

Bobby Fischer is lanky (6 feet 2 inches), pale, intent, brooding, contentious and electrifying. When he was six his sister taught him chess. At 13, when he became the youngest United States junior champion in history, he declared, "I'm going to win the world championship, hold it a couple of years, then take up something else and make a lot of money."

At 14 he was U.S. Open champion. The following year he won the first of his almost annual U.S. championships and became one of the world's 40 international grandmasters. In qualifying for the 1972 world championship series he won 20 consecutive games against some of the world's finest players, an amazing feat in a sport in which most games are drawn.

His world-championship series at Reykjavik, Iceland, with the defender, Boris Spassky of the Soviet Union, made front-page news around the world day after day. One reason was Fischer's antics. He refused to fly to Iceland until he received more money; he refused to play until television cameras were moved; for one game he refused to leave his hotel room (he lost by default). He almost flew home before the series ended.

He stayed and won, 12½ to 8½, becoming world champion. "Before the championship," wrote Curry Kirkpatrick, "he complained, bullied, threatened, boasted, bragged and politicked from hell to breakfast trying to gouge every possible advantage for himself. When play commenced, he had temper tantrums, abused his opponent, insulted officials and was rude to the media and spectators. When

Fischer at a 1970 match against Boris Spassky, the Soviet world champion.

he won, he made it plain that he succeeded because he was a superior chess player, not the representative of a superior institution or country.''

He earned $156,250 from the purse, but because of litigation he still had not received any of the money by 1975, and typically he refused to cooperate even with his lawyers. He secluded himself and refused to play in public. He resigned as world champion because he did not like new rules established for his first defense, but the international federation refused to accept the resignation. He did not blink even when Manila offered $5 million (62½ percent to the winner, 37½ percent to the loser) for a championship series.

No one could fully explain the man or his ways. He was certainly ''the ultimate chess player,'' as Dick Schaap, the writer, called him. Frank Brady, his biographer, called him ''an authentic phenomenon,'' and he certainly was that, too. *Sports Illustrated* may have come closest when it entitled an article on him ''A Mystery Wrapped in an Enigma.''

Perhaps, as Roy Blount, Jr., wrote, ''His whole life is based on the assumption that he is the most compelling figure in chess. . . . All the excuses for his behavior rest on the assumption that he is a genius, that he must be allowed to do things on his own terms because those terms produce unique and glorious chess.'' Burt Hochberg, editor of *Chess Life and Review*, accepted that theory. He wrote, ''No one can really know him who does not understand chess.''

Fischer saved his greatest fury for the Russians, saying, ''They don't look on me as a chess player who is trying to win the championship. They act as if I was a thief trying to steal something that belonged to them. . . . They're not great talents. . . . If they can win a match by drawing ten games in a row and then winning one, that is great chess in their book. They don't love the game. It's work, a job to them. It's a nine-to-five job.''

In 1970 he was asked who was the best player in the world. ''It is nice to be modest,'' he replied, ''but it would be stupid if I did not tell the truth. It is Fischer.''

In 1972, two weeks before meeting Spassky for the world championship in Reykjavik, Iceland, Fischer studies his opponent's book.

Fitzsimmons, James E.
(1874–1966)

On March 4, 1885, the day Grover Cleveland was inaugurated as President of the United States, ten-year-old Jimmy Fitzsimmons began walking horses after their workouts. In 1963, after a 78-year career in horse racing as a stable hand, exercise boy, jockey and trainer, he retired.

The three-quarters of a century had taken their toll. He was badly bent from spinal arthritis and said

sadly, "My head hangs so much, I can't see horses or people unless I'm sitting down." He did not have to get up at the usual hour of 4:30 A.M. any more, and sometimes he slept as late as 6:00 A.M. He apologized by saying, "I guess as a man gets older he gets lazier."

He had earned the right to sleep late. He trained such champion horses as Gallant Fox, Omaha, Johnstown, Nashua and Bold Ruler. During his long career the horses he trained won 2,275 races and purses exceeding $13 million. He earned $100,000 a year, having come a long way from the days when he rode horses for $1, fell on ice-covered tracks in below-zero cold and walked horses 15 miles between tracks.

He was a kindly, gracious man, warm, charming, gentle and beloved. His wonderful disposition earned him the name Sunny Jim. Racing people called him Mister Fitz, and he greeted everyone at the track, though he seldom remembered a name.

He had an instinctive feel for horses. "He knew all his life that the thoroughbred racehorse was the second most magnificent design in God's creation," Robert Riger wrote. Trainer Johnny Nerud said, "He has got the touch to make a billy goat run," and Eddie Arcaro, who rode many of his horses, said, "Mister Fitz is the greatest trainer who ever lived." To Arthur Daley he was "the greatest thoroughbred of all."

When he bet, it was usually $2, on rare occasions $5. He recalled that "Once I bet $100, and when the horse lost it almost killed me." The horse was Man o' War, and it was the only race he lost.

"No trainer can put anything into a horse that the good Lord hasn't put there already," said Fitzsimmons. "If you can bring out the best in any horse, you've done your job well. . . . No trainer ever made a bad horse good, but some trainers have made a good horse bad. Horses are like people. They're brave or cowardly, gentle or mean, willing or stubborn. Sometimes they're like children. That's when you should love them a lot."

At 86, Jim Fitzsimmons, the dean of American racehorse trainers, was still preparing mounts. He is shown with High Bid in 1960.

Fitzsimmons, Robert L.
(1862–1917)

Bob Fitzsimmons, at one time or another, held three world boxing titles. He invented the solar-plexus punch, a blow to the pit of the stomach that finished many opponents. James J. Corbett, whom Fitzsimmons defeated for the heavyweight crown, said, "For his weight and inches, he was the greatest fighter that ever drew on a glove."

He did not look the part. Rex Lardner wrote that he was "gangly, knock-kneed and walked with a shambling gait. He was freckle-faced, bald except for a fringe of pale reddish hair that circled his small head like a tonsure, and he had whitish skin that looked as though it had been decorated by a pointillist. After being in the sun, his skin became one huge freckle." John L. Sullivan called him "a fighting machine on stilts."

"As a figure of fighting manhood, he was grotesque, fantastic, incredible," Nat Fleischer wrote. "Outside the ropes, he was just an average person of no exceptional mental endowment, but in the ring he was a brilliant thinker, capable of making instant decisions."

He was born in England and raised in New Zealand, where he developed huge arms and shoulders as a blacksmith's apprentice. He won the middleweight title in 1891. In 1897, weighing only 156½ pounds, he won the heavyweight title by knocking out Corbett in 14 rounds with a left to the solar plexus. Bill Brandt called it "the most famous blow in the history of boxing."

Before leaving the ring Corbett demanded a rematch, saying he was entitled to another chance. Fitzsimmons replied that he was "through with the ring," but Corbett said, "If you don't fight me, I'll lick you every time we meet in the street." "If you ever lay a hand on me outside the prize ring, I'll kill you," Fitzsimmons said.

Fitzsimmons never fought Corbett again. He lost the heavyweight title to James J. Jeffries in 1899, won the light-heavyweight crown in 1903 and lost it two years later. He fought until 1914, when he was 52. He went into vaudeville, contracted double pneumonia and died at 55, a poor man.

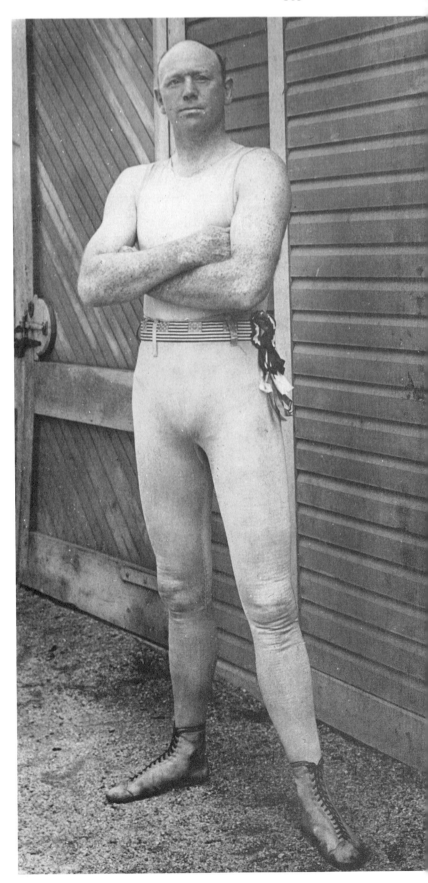

Miss Fleming at the 1968 Olympics at Grenoble, France.

Fleming, Peggy Gale (1948–   )

She is a portrait of beauty on ice, slim, black-haired, pale and pretty. Her smile is enigmatic and fragile, sweet and shy. She is the best-known and perhaps the most talented figure skater since Sonja Henie.

Her figure-skating style has been variously described as graceful, feminine, lyrical, expressive and technically fine. "She is a delicate lady," said Dick Button, an earlier champion famous for his athletic skating style. "She is not a fiery skater and she shouldn't be made to be."

Peggy Fleming was nine years old when she took up figure skating. Her father was a newspaper pressman, and he moved the family to Pasadena, California, and Colorado Springs, Colorado, so his daughter could train under the best coaches. She would be up at 5:00 A.M., practice from 6:00 A.M. to 11:00 A.M., take time out for school and then return to the ice from 5:00 to 8:00 P.M. Her high school in Colorado Springs had sired many figure-skating champions, and it arranged a classroom schedule that would allow her to train eight hours a day. People and schedules accommodated to her, but the drive was her own. "We have always let Peggy set her own alarm clock," said her mother, Doris Fleming. "That way, she had to do it herself. Nobody pushed her to skate."

She won the United States championship every year from 1964 to 1968 and the world championship from 1966 to 1968. She won the 1968 Olympic championship. Then she turned professional, becoming the feature attraction of the Ice Follies and appearing in television specials and commercials.

Her coach, Carlo Fassi, said, "She has an excellent disposition, which makes her forget a bad practice in ten minutes." But shrugging off a bad session was not always easy. "Sometimes I fight against being human," she said. "But in overcoming this, I learn, and that makes my life worthwhile. . . . Sometimes, when I practice my free-style routine off in a corner, I can see the other girls sort of watching me. . . . It makes you feel good to be champion."

At the same time she was happy when the day-in, day-out workouts for amateur competition ended.

Peggy Fleming at the national figure skating championships in 1968.

"This is really a hard sort of life," she said. "I really look forward to leading a life of my own. . . . I haven't devoted my whole life to skating. Some people just live for it. I've tried to be a normal American girl."

Foxx, James Emory (1907–1967)

During a major-league career that spanned 21 seasons, Jimmy Foxx was the greatest right-handed slugger of his day and perhaps the best multi-position man the game has known. He was also plagued by financial problems. As he put it, "I guess I was born to be broke."

Jimmy Foxx, nicknamed Double X, was a strapping man of 6 feet and 195 pounds. He was friendly,

but his bulging biceps scared people. His arms, wrote Stan Baumgartner, "looked like those of the village blacksmith." Jimmy Isaminger wrote, "He was so big at 14 that his high-school teacher was afraid to keep him after school for fear of talk."

He started as a catcher and alternated between first and third before settling down at first base. He played for the Philadelphia Athletics (1925–35), Boston Red Sox (1936–42), Chicago Cubs (1942 and 1944) and Philadelphia Phillies (1945). In 2,317 games he batted .325 and hit 534 home runs, second only to Babe Ruth until recent years. He hit 30 or more home runs a year for 12 straight years (a major-league record) and drove in 100 or more runs for 13 straight years. In 1932 he hit 58 home runs and had two others wiped out by rain. He was voted the American League's most valuable player three times in the 1930s. In 1951 he was voted into the Baseball Hall of Fame.

He joined the Athletics when he was 17. Lefty Gomez said, "He could hit me at midnight with the lights out." Though a star player, his salary was unexceptional. He never earned more than $32,500 in one season, and he lost much of his money in the Depression and almost $100,000 in a Florida golf-course venture when World War II broke out.

"He was a victim of constant check-grabbing, unfortunate investments and plain bad luck," Bob Broeg wrote. Arthur Daley recalled that "He was always a quick man with a buck." Joe Williams wrote, "It was almost as if he had a pathological dread of being called cheap." Ted Williams, a Red Sox teammate, told of another problem. "He never made any bones about his love for Scotch," said Williams. "He used to say he could drink 15 of those little bottles and not be affected."

In 1958 he declined an invitation to the Boston baseball writers dinner because he could not afford the plane fare. He said, "I had pride, but pride's not much good when you're broke." Job offers poured in and he worked at several jobs after that, but none lasted long. He was bitter, saying, "Baseball has no room for fellows who built up a lot of prestige as ballplayers." John Lardner wrote, "The only press agent Jimmy Foxx had was his bat."

He once said, "Baseball is hard work, but it isn't like taking out a dinner pail and working your eight hours. I must say, though, that the dinner-pail job will last longer."

Foyt, Anthony Joseph, Jr.
(1935–   )

A. J. Foyt can be affable, hot-tempered, intense, stubborn and impetuous—and all at once. Bloys Britt wrote that he could be taut as a banjo string under stress, a model in charm when things were going "according to Foyt." He is so intense, wrote John Riley, that "even when he smiles he looks mean."

Mario Andretti, his main auto-racing rival, said that Foyt had the greatest ability, but "he thinks himself such a superior being that he can't think of himself fighting with anyone. It's got to be a breeze or nothing." "His cars seem to challenge him," Bill Libby wrote, "and he drives them so hard they sometimes fall apart. He appears to drive right over his foes and charge away from them."

He is handsome and rugged (5 feet 11 inches, 185 pounds, a 47½-inch chest). He quit school in 11th grade to become a driver and became good enough to win the Indianapolis 500 (three times), the United States Auto Club season title (five times), the Pocono 500, Daytona 500, 24 Hours of Le Mans and many more. He has earned more prize money (more than $2.5 million) than any other driver in history, and he has earned at least as much in endorsements.

In addition to racing, he designs the Coyote racing chassis and owns oil wells in Louisiana, a Ford parts distributorship in Indianapolis and an auto agency and real estate in Houston, where he lives. "To be truthful, I don't know everything I do own," he said.

With all that, he still likes to race midget and sprint cars on rutted tracks for purses of a few hundred dollars. "What counts with him," Robert Daley wrote, "is not the money but the racing itself." Foyt said that he loved racing. "It's the only thing I've ever studied, the only thing I've ever really understood. . . . I just don't really have too much to drive for anymore except just for the glory.

"I'm very moody when we're not winning," he added. "I'm hard to get along with because there's certain things it takes, and until I'm proven wrong I just stick to the way I think it should be. . . . I've thought about dying many a time, but that's something you learn to live with regardless of what you're doing. I've had the devil scared out of me just driving down the highway, and I thought I was going to die."

Heat waves trail Foyt down the Indianapolis Speedway during a practice run for the 500.

Fraser, Dawn (1937–   )

She was a champion swimmer and a champion individualist. Dawn Fraser was a strapping Australian of 5 feet 8½ inches and 149 pounds. She was the only swimmer to win the same Olympic title (in her case, the 100-meter free-style) in three successive games (1956, 1960 and 1964). She won her final Olympic title at age 27. Her teammates, some only 14 years old, called her Granny.

She set 27 world records, including nine in a row in the 100-meter free-style. She won eight medals (six gold) in British Commonwealth Games and 23 Australian titles. She was the first woman to break one minute for the 100-meter and 110-yard free-styles, and she was always far ahead of the opposition.

She was a grownup in a world of child athletes. She went out three or four nights a week, always having a martini before dinner, and drank five or six beers at a party. She trained almost three hours a day but would skip a workout if she didn't feel like training. Yet she was so nervous that once she wore a warmup suit but forgot to put on a swimsuit underneath, and once she went to the starting block still wearing socks.

Sports Illustrated called her "the best woman swimmer in history. . . . She boldly and gaily dominated a sport that commonly verges on asceticism. . . . She loafed when she felt loafing was what she needed and she drank a beer when she was thirsty. . . . She provoked laughter in a sport that in recent years has forgotten how to laugh." Whitney Tower wrote, "Her greatness, while obviously the result of natural ability, is, according to her, just as much the result of her own refreshing philosophy on both training and competition." Pat Besford, a British writter, called her "an independently stormy petrel."

Her career ended abruptly when the staid Amateur Swimming Union of Australia suspended her in 1965 for ten years. The officials, who never liked her independence, refused to explain the suspension, but three incidents during the 1964 Olympics prompted it. She took part in the opening parade against orders, refused to wear the regulation swimsuit because she said it did not fit and swam the moat surrounding the Imperial Palace at midnight to steal a Japanese flag as a souvenir.

She had no regrets, saying, "I probably have a different mental approach to swimming than most people. I actually enjoy training most of the time. When I don't want to train, I don't. If it comes, it comes, and I don't force myself. . . . Many of our girls start competition at nine or ten, and when they lose interest at 15 or 16 it's often because they are driven too hard. I've always believed that the desire must come from within, not as the result of being driven."

Dawn Fraser and daughter, Dawn Lorraine, romp in the surf off Sydney, Australia, in 1972.

Frazier, Joseph (1944–   )

For three years he was the heavyweight boxing champion of the world, a burly (5 feet 11 inches, 205 pounds), aggressive, relentless fighter who withstood punishment so that he could get close enough to his opponent to deal out punishment.

He was born on a South Carolina farm, the youngest of 13 children. He was working in the fields when he was six, and at 15 he dropped out of high school and married. ''I wasn't learning,'' he recalled, ''and I was just taking up space. I guess I had the mind of a man early, and I mean about everything.''

He went to work in a Philadelphia slaughterhouse and took up boxing. When he returned from the 1964 Olympics with a gold medal and a broken thumb, he worked as a church janitor. He turned professional in 1965, and in 1970 he knocked out Jimmy Ellis for the heavyweight title. He outpointed Muhammad Ali in a memorable 1971 fight in which each earned $2.5 million (it was Ali's only defeat) and kept the title until George Foreman knocked him out in two rounds in 1973.

The way he slipped punches prompted his manager, Yank Durham, to say he was a big Henry Armstrong. But he never looked pretty in the ring. His fighting style suggested to Mark Kram ''a wild beast tangled in a thicket.'' Ali, his outspoken antagonist, said, ''He is not a great boxer. He is a great street fighter.''

Between fights he enjoys his $125,000 house, his motorcycle and eight cars and travels with his rock group, the Knockouts. Yet ''He is such a decent man,'' Eddie Futch, his trainer, said, ''money and fame haven't changed him. When he's with the sparring partners, he treats them as equals. When he walks into a room he drifts to a corner. You never feel the heavyweight champion has come barging in.''

''In my life, nothing ever came easy,'' said Frazier. ''But I like it that way. I like to work for what I get. . . . You can do anything you want to if you really put your heart and soul and mind into it.''

Frazier's left hook sends Muhammad Ali to the canvas in the 15th round of their 1971 title fight.

Frazier, Walter, Jr. (1945–   )

He has the fastest hands in the game and a cool demeanor, and he is the best defensive guard in professional basketball. He is handsome, unflappable and regal, a hero who, as Bill Russell said, "enjoys being a hero." Edwin Kiester, Jr., called his mutton-chop sideburns "the most magnificent bush of facial hair since President Chester A. Arthur."

Walt Frazier turned down football scholarships

(he played quarterback) at Indiana and Kansas to play basketball at Southern Illinois University. Since joining the New York Knickerbockers in 1967, he has led them to two National Basketball Association championships and has been an almost annual choice for the all-NBA and all-defensive teams.

He earns $300,000 a year for playing basketball and more from his basketball camp, liquor store and Walt Frazier Enterprises, a company he founded to

Walt Frazier keeps the ball away from four Boston Celtics during the 1974 NBA playoffs.

"Clyde" in typically mod attire.

He has artistry and hustle. Marv Albert, the Knick broadcaster, said of his quick hands, "He burrows into an opposing team and comes up with the ball so often he demoralizes the opponents." Bradley said he never saw anyone intimidate the opposition the way Frazier does. Bill Hosket, a former teammate, said, "He is the only man who can strip a car while it's going 40 miles per hour." Willis Reed, a teammate, said, "The ball belongs to him. He just lets us play with it once in a while."

Above all, he is cool. "Cool is a matter of self-preservation," he said. "Cool is reactions, reflexes and attitude. You got to feel out the situation. You can't be out of control." He is proud of his image. "The only thing about me that I'd want kids to identify with is that I'm my own man. Most guys are just basketball or football. Clyde is a title. It's different. It's a style. I dig it. . . . If I could start my life all over, I'd still want to be Walt Frazier. Clyde."

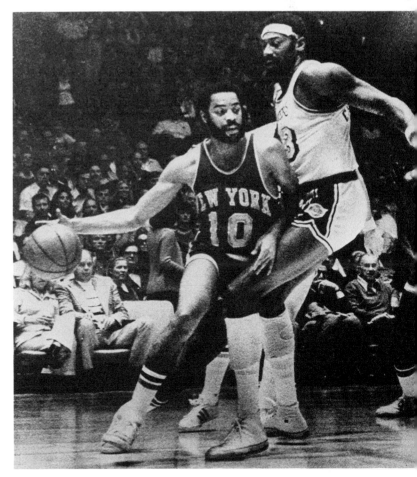

Frazier drives past Wilt Chamberlain for a score in the first game of the Knicks–Los Angeles Lakers NBA championship series in 1973.

negotiate contracts and endorsements for athletes. He endorses sneakers, shoes, clothes, furs, toothpaste and basketballs.

Early in his pro career, when he bought a $40 wide-brimmed hat of brown velour, he was given the nickname of Clyde, after Clyde Barrow, the bank robber celebrated in the movie *Bonnie and Clyde*. He still has the nickname, and he still dresses the part, replete with his mink coats.

His basketball style, like his dress, is elegant. Teammate Bill Bradley said that he is the only player he had ever seen who could be described as an artist, a man "who takes an artistic approach to the game."

Frisch, Frank Francis (1898–1973)

He may have been the best second baseman baseball has known. Frankie Frisch, the Fordham Flash, certainly was one of the game's memorable characters, a colorful, warm hustler with an outrageous and delicious sense of humor.

He joined the New York Giants fresh from Fordham University, where he was the captain of three teams. He played 19 seasons for the Giants (1919–26) and St. Louis Cardinals (1927–37), batting .316 in 2,311 games. He also managed the Cardinals (1933–38), Pittsburgh Pirates (1940–46) and Chicago Cubs (1949–51). Before and after the Chicago job he broadcast major-league games, and a generation remembered his high-pitched voice delivering his famous line: "Oh, those bases on balls." In 1947 he was elected to the Baseball Hall of Fame.

He baited umpires, managers and players, and they baited back. When Frisch once lost his cap running bases, as he often did, Umpire Beans Rear-

don asked, "How do you expect a round cap to stay on a square head?" Leo Durocher said, "I loved to get the Dutchman riled. He let go with a full fireworks display. It was like the Fourth of July."

When Casey Stengel, then managing a bad Boston Braves team, was struck by a taxicab, Frisch wired him, "Your attempt at suicide fully understandable. Deepest sympathy you didn't succeed." Stengel said years later, "Then there was Mr. Frisch, which went to a university and couldn't run fast, besides."

Frisch was "a remarkable study in contrasts, a hellcat in a baseball suit but a devotee of classical music," Joseph Durso wrote. He was a gentle, genial man whose house was surrounded by hedges, roses and an immaculate lawn. He often attended the Metropolitan Opera. He was a public speaker in great demand, and he kept his baseball humor in three loose-leafed notebooks.

In later years he decried batting helmets, spring-training comforts and other niceties that contributed to a country-club atmosphere. He said, "Rampaging, dictatorial managers have vanished with the bunny hug and the hip flask. Gone are the feuds, fines, profanity and fun. This is an era of love and kisses, of sciences and psychology."

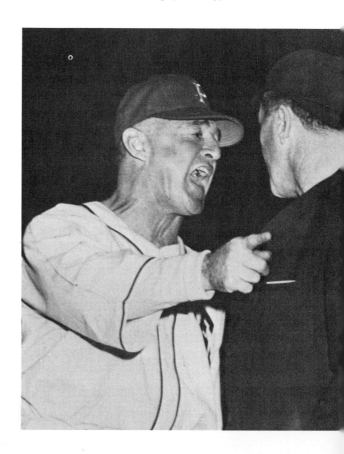

Gehrig, Henry Louis (1903–1941)

On June 1, 1925, Lou Gehrig pinch-hit for the New York Yankees. The next day, when Wally Pipp, the first baseman, complained of a headache, Lou Gehrig replaced him at first base. For almost 14 years, despite broken fingers, pulled muscles, lumbago and other ailments, he played every game until illness stopped him. Jack Sher wrote that he stayed in games "grinning crazily, like a macabre dancer in a grueling marathon." He played 2,130 consecutive games, the most glittering of all baseball records.

From 1923 to 1939 he played in 2,164 games for the Yankees, with a .340 batting average, 493 home runs and two American League most-valuable-player awards. Yet he was overshadowed first by Babe Ruth and then by Joe DiMaggio. He never complained because, as Max Kase wrote, "That would have fractured his sense of dignity."

"I'm not a headline guy," Gehrig said. "I'm just the guy who's in there every day, the fellow who follows Babe in the batting order. When Babe's turn at bat is over, whether he strikes out or belts a home run, the fans are still talking about him when I come up. If I stood on my head at the plate, nobody'd pay attention."

In 1938 his abilities slackened, and on May 2, 1939, he took himself out of the lineup. Soon after, he learned he was suffering from amyotrophic lateral sclerosis, a progressive and fatal type of paralysis that came to be known as Lou Gehrig's Disease.

The baseball writers waived the rules and voted him immediately into the Baseball Hall of Fame. The Yankees staged a day for him, and 61,808 spectators heard a tearful Gehrig say, "Today, I consider myself the luckiest man on the face of the earth." Babe Ruth, who had become estranged from Gehrig, threw his arms around him and cried. Two years later Lou Gehrig was dead.

"He was not the best ballplayer the Yankees ever had," Stanley Frank wrote. "Yet he was the most valuable player the Yankees ever had because he was the prime source of their greatest asset—an implicit confidence in themselves and every man on the club." Paul Krichell, the scout who had discovered him, said simply, "He was truly the Pride of the Yankees."

Babe Ruth embraces his former Yankee teammate on Lou Gehrig Day, the first baseman's farewell, in 1939.

Lou Gehrig's classic swing.

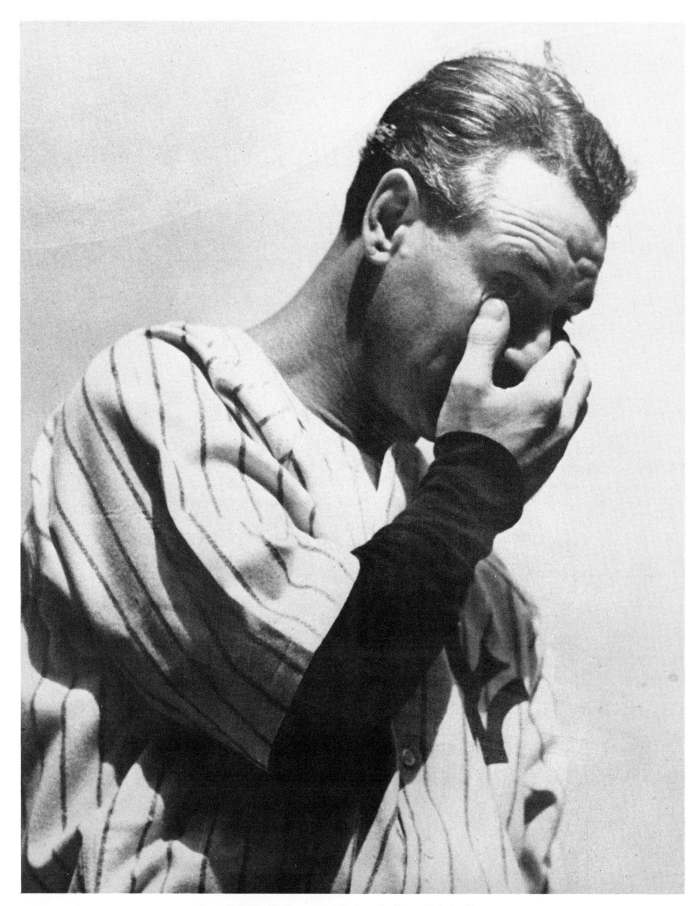

Lou Gehrig sheds a tear during the Lou Gehrig Day ceremony.

Gehringer, Charles Leonard
(1903–   )

Charlie Gehringer was one of the great second basemen, a mechanical man, a ballplayer's ballplayer, stylish, graceful, effortless, steady, poker-faced and silent. Leo Durocher said dryly, "One day, when he feels real talkative, he'll nod to you." He played 2,323 games for the Detroit Tigers from 1924 to 1942, batting .321 for his career and over .300 13 times in a 14-year stretch. In 1949 he was voted into the Baseball Hall of Fame.

Perhaps no other player with such skill received so little public acclaim. Bob Broeg called him "a craftsman so skilled and polished that it's doubtful the public ever appreciated fully how really great he was." H. G. Salsinger wrote, "Like Ty Cobb, he had the distinct qualities that are appreciated only by the skilled members of his profession." "His teammates got the headlines," Frank Graham wrote.

"All he got, save in rare instances, was the brush." Doc Cramer, a teammate, said, "You wind him up on opening day and forget him," while Satchel Paige remarked, "DiMaggio was good, but Gehringer was real good."

He might have been baseball's best two-strike batter ever. He seldom swung at the first pitch. He threw right-handed, but he batted and did almost everything else left-handed. In his mid-60s he was shooting 75 to 80 on the golf course.

He was vice-president and general manager of the Tigers from 1951 to 1953. Then he became a manufacturers' representative for automobile interior upholstery, and he earned much more than he did as a baseball player, when his highest salary was $35,000 a year. But he enjoyed baseball and had no regrets. "I was lucky. I came into the game when salaries were high and taxes were low. . . . If I were a kid again I'd like to do it all over again, the same way."

118

Geoffrion, Bernard André
(1931–   )

He is an imposing, sturdy, dimpled and dapper man who has played and coached hockey intently and relentlessly, saving nothing for the future. His dark good looks and his explosive temper made him one of the game's most colorful figures.

He is known as Boom Boom, or simply Boomer, because of his booming slap shot. He played 14 seasons for the Montreal Canadiens (1950–64), coached two seasons in the minor leagues and played two more for the New York Rangers. He then coached the Rangers for half a season, moved into the front office and then returned to coaching with the new Atlanta Flames.

In 883 National Hockey League games he scored 393 goals and 429 assists for 822 points. If he had not played the same position (right wing) as Maurice Richard and Gordie Howe, he would have made

more than three all-star teams in 16 years. His nose was broken nine times, and he once lost 14 teeth from one cross-check.

He combined power and versatility. Al Rollins, a rival goalie, recalled, "He once hit my pads with a shot just under the knees. It was so hard I thought my toes were paralyzed." And his stature on the ice had implications beyond sports. As Red Fisher wrote, "He carried the hopes and the message of French Canada with him wherever he went."

Coaching the Rangers almost killed him. He had lost half his stomach to an operation for ulcers, but his stomach troubles returned as coaching proved as agonizing as playing. "My Canadiens," he once said, "wouldn't lose the way the Rangers lost tonight."

He was a perfectionist whose health got in the way. "I was never what you would call a good skater," he recalled. "I had to work hard to skate and to play. . . . Only one thing worries me—my health. When I had my operation for ulcers, I thought all that was behind me. But sometimes I get up in the morning and I am so sick I think I am going to die. . . . My wife said I couldn't play every game 125 percent. This is my big problem. I want everything perfect. I know now it is impossible."

Glenn Hall, the Chicago Black Hawk goalie, stops shot by Geoffrion.

Gibson, Josh (1911–1947)

He may have been the hardest hitter ever in baseball, but Josh Gibson never received the opportunity to prove it in the major leagues. He was black, and blacks did not play in the majors until three months after his early death.

"He was the greatest hitter I ever pitched to," said Satchel Paige, "and I pitched to everybody—Williams, DiMaggio, Musial, Mays, Mantle." He was certainly the best hitter in the black leagues. Dodger catcher Roy Campanella said, "I couldn't carry his glove. Anything I could do he could do better." Dizzy Dean once said to him, "I wish you and Satchel Paige played with me on the Cardinals. Hell, we'd win the pennant by July 4 and go fishing until World Series time."

Josh Gibson was a catcher from 1930 to 1946, playing 15 years with the Homestead Grays and Pittsburgh Crawfords of the black leagues and two years in the Mexican League. He was 19 when the Grays called him out of the stands after their catcher split a finger. He hit 75 home runs that year, 67 the next, 84 in his biggest year and 623 in his career (his teams played 175 to 200 games a year). A special

committee elected him in 1972 to the Baseball Hall of Fame.

He was a strapping, graceful right-handed batter who hit tape-measure home runs. His baseball earnings were pitiful. In 1942 he held out for $1,000 a month plus $1 a day for meals. His highest pay was $1,200 a month.

By 1946 he had ballooned to 230 pounds and had begun to drink. Jackie Robinson had just joined Montreal, and Gibson was depressed because he was too old for the major leagues. "He was a frustrated man," said Bill Yancey. In January 1947 Josh Gibson died at age 35. "People say he died of a brain hemorrhage," Ted Page remarked. "I say he died of a broken heart."

Gibson, Robert (1935–)

Bob Gibson is one of the fastest and toughest pitchers of his day, angry and intimidating on the mound and in defending the black man in and out of baseball.

He has been called outspoken, aggressive, independent, articulate and thoughtful. Tim McCarver, who caught him, said he had "competitive fire that is unbelievable." Ron Fairly, a rival player, described his attitude: "I'm Bob Gibson, and if you don't know what that means, I'm going to teach you." Johnny Keane, his manager, maintained he was "an honest man, a decent man."

He is an honest pitcher, with an overpowering fastball that sometimes sinks and sometimes sails. He has good control, and no pitcher fields his position better. He joined the St. Louis Cardinals in 1959, and in 1974 he became the only man besides Walter Johnson to strike out 3,000 batters in a

The outspoken star with the Cy Young Award he won as the National League's best pitcher in 1970.

lifetime. In 1968, when he was named the National League's most valuable player and most valuable pitcher, he put together a 95-inning string in which he allowed only two runs and won 15 consecutive games, ten of them shutouts. He earns as much as $150,000 a year.

"It is impossible to talk about him without talking about race because race has forged the man," Fred Katz wrote. Gibson agreed, but he said his tone had softened. "Yeah, I've changed," he said, "but the guys who approach me have changed, too. They've changed their thoughts and ideas about what a black person is."

He also said, "If you can intimidate the batter, it's all the better for you. . . . When you intimidate someone they will take a back seat. Well, that's happened to the black man for 150 years. . . . The older I am, the more bitter I get. . . . I owe the public just one thing, a good performance. . . . I don't warm up easily to a lot of people. Why? Why should I?" Gibson played to win. "I can't stand losing. I never go into anything with the idea I might lose."

Gipp, George (1895–1920)

Never in the history of college football has one player been the subject of so many stories, some of them true, as George Gipp. He was the stuff of which heroes and legends are made. He was an athlete of almost unlimited talent, a man who could do many things better than his peers and make them like it.

There is fact among the fiction. George Gipp played fullback for four seasons (1917–20) at Notre Dame. He was big, strong, elusive, fast, brilliant and brash. He once drop-kicked a field goal 62 yards. He could run, pass, punt and play defense. He was a 60-minute player. The day he died, in 1920, he became Notre Dame's first All-America player. In 1951 he was voted into the College Football Hall of Fame.

As famous as he was then, he is more famous now. "He still is a legend to those who knew him well," Stanley Frank wrote. H. G. Salsinger wrote, "His punts will grow longer through the years, and so will his passes and runs." "He was a national celebrity," Jim Beach wrote, "regarded with the same awe as Woodrow Wilson, Black Jack Pershing and Douglas Fairbanks."

Toward the end of his senior season he played despite a sore throat and 102-degree temperature. A streptococcus infection attacked his throat, pneumonia set in and, 11 days before Christmas, George Gipp died. The next day an assistant coach said of Knute Rockne, the Notre Dame head coach, "It's the first time I've seen him break. Nobody can talk to him."

The best known of all George Gipp stories concerned what he did or did not say on his deathbed. Eight years later, in the 1928 Notre Dame–Army game, Notre Dame was being badly outplayed. At halftime in the Notre Dame dressing room, just before the team was to return to the field, Rockne told his players something that Gipp supposedly had told him as he was dying (in the movie *Knute Rockne — All American* Pat O'Brien played Rockne and Ronald Reagan played Gipp). Rockne said, "George Gipp told me, 'Some time, Rock, when the team's up against it, when things are wrong and the breaks are beating the boys, tell them to go in there and win just one for the Gipper. I don't know where I'll be then, Rock, but I'll know about it, and I'll be happy.' Boys, I'm convinced that this is the game George Gipp would want us to win for him."

Good Luck from Gipp

The Gipp remark may have been fictitious, but the Notre Dame players, tears in their eyes, stormed onto the field for the second half, scored two touchdowns, stopped Army on the one-yard line at the final gun and won, 12–6, a game Notre Dame won for the Gipper.

Jack Newcombe thought Rockne's story was more fancy than fact. "Such a romantic notion would have been completely out of character for a pool player and a gambler like Gipp," he wrote. "But it would have been natural for Rockne to use Gipp as an emotional prop in one of his pep talks. . . . The real Gipp was a remarkable young man whose interest in adult games gave him precious little time to devote to football."

Chet Grant wrote, "George appealed to Rockne as a reclamation project." A Notre Dame professor told the talented Gipp, "God blessed you with a remarkable intellect, but you are letting it lie fallow." Francis Wallace called him "a most peculiar kind of saint."

Football came easily to Gipp. "Like Jim Thorpe, he played at sports rather than worked at them," Alexander M. Weyand wrote. Jesse Harper, who coached him, said, "In one tough game . . . he made up three plays himself on the field and all three worked."

He was an avid gambler. Once, when Notre Dame was far ahead, he stood, hands on hips, as an opposing end raced by him and caught a long pass for a touchdown. "Why did you let him go?" asked Rockne. "Listen, Rock," he said, "I'd have laid you ten to one that that guy couldn't reach the ball." At halftime of another game he leaned against a dressing-room door smoking a cigarette. An angry Rockne said to him, "It looks to me as if this game is boring you. I presume you'd just as soon see Army win." He replied, "That's where you're wrong, Rock. I've got 500 smackers bet on us and I don't intend to lose it." Of course he scored two touchdowns in the second half. And of course Notre Dame won.

Al Stump wrote, "He was one of the most dazzling, dramatic, idolized athletes of all time . . . a national celebrity, but nobody knew him well." Frank Leahy, a latter-day Notre Dame coach, said, "He is still one of us, a very real part of our winning tradition. No, the Gipper didn't die." His coach, Knute Rockne, wrote a fitting epitaph: "A boy does well indeed who, so young, leaves the clean glory of a name behind."

Gola, Thomas Joseph (1933–   )

Tom Gola had two distinguishing characteristics as a basketball player—grace and unselfishness.

"The movements of his body on the basketball floor were made of the beauty that should have been choreographed and performed on a stage to music," Milton Gross once wrote. "It seemed a shame to waste them on bouncy-ball." Coach Forrest Anderson of Bradley University said, "He kills you even when he doesn't have the ball because he fakes so beautifully." Zander Hollander recalled that "his play was unspectacular, almost unnoticed, but he always scored the big basket, grabbed the vital rebound, set the tempo and pace of play for his team."

The 6-foot-6-inch Gola was a high-school All-American in Philadelphia. He played four seasons (1951–55) at La Salle, where he made All-America three times and led his teams to a 102–19 record and titles in the NIT (1952) and NCAA (1954) championships. He played professionally (1955–66) for the Philadelphia–San Francisco Warriors and New York Knickerbockers.

Ken Loeffler, who coached him at La Salle, said he had never seen a youngster with such poise. "It is his greatest asset. Nothing rattles him. He can do everything and do it well. . . . He is the greatest player I've ever seen, and I've seen them all, from the Original Celtics." Leonard Koppett wrote of his "self-sacrificing psychology." Eddie Gottlieb, who owned the Philadelphia Warriors, said, "The first year, he was so self-conscious about scoring, we actually had to tell him to shoot." Murray Olderman said of the unassuming Gola, "He always has regarded his athletic fame with somewhat amused detachment. His head size never got any bigger. His hunger for acclaim was subdued."

After retiring from pro ball Gola coached La Salle for two seasons (1968–70), sold insurance and served his neighborhood as a Pennsylvania legislator and Philadelphia as controller. He brushed off thoughts of coaching in the pros, saying he wouldn't last two games. "First, I'd have to throw out the whole system. I'd want guys who play both offense and defense, not just either one."

All-America Tom Gola dribbles toward the basket.

Pancho Gonzales after winning the U.S. title in 1949.

Gonzales, Richard Alonzo
(1928–   )

He was the dominant figure in tennis in the 1950s and much of the 1960s. He was powerful, fierce and angry, and so was his game. A hero from the wrong side of the tracks, he was an embarrassment to the proper country-club types who ran the game and felt it was theirs alone.

Pancho Gonzales had a memorable appearance, handsome and swarthy at 6 feet 3 inches and 185 pounds, with olive skin and jet-black hair. When he was seven, he drove his scooter into a police car, and it left a scar on his left cheek. Almost as prominent was his temper, which, wrote Ben Thomas, "stood out as blatantly as the scar on his face that always seemed a barometer of his anger."

He was born in the United States of Mexican-born parents. He was the oldest of seven children in a family where both parents worked, and he recalled, "We had few luxuries in our house, but we never went hungry."

When he was 12 his mother bought him a 50-cent racquet for Christmas. He played hooky from five high schools, finally dropped out and joined the Navy. When he finished his Navy hitch in January 1947 his father told him either to go back to school, get a job or get out of the house. He got out of the house, began playing the tennis tour and was quickly ranked 17th in the country. In 1948 he surprisingly won the U.S. championship. The following year he won it again.

Just before the start of the 1948 tournament he walked into the clubhouse bar in a T-shirt and ordered a beer. He was not served because, said the club officials, he was not properly dressed. After winning the title he entered the same clubhouse bar dressed in a T-shirt and again ordered a beer. This time he was served.

He was hard and lean, quick and graceful. Julius Heldman, a contemporary, called him "the most natural player who ever lived. . . . He made tennis look too easy." His serve was once clocked at 112 miles per hour, and his game was aggressive and relentless, always putting pressure on the opponent. Maurice Brady wrote, "The whole pattern of his game was of overwhelming strength."

Two weeks after he won the 1949 U.S. title he turned professional, and by 1954 he had established himself as the best in the world. For eight years, until he turned his attention to teaching tennis, he was unbeatable.

He can still be a terror on the court. At the age of 41 he crushed Arthur Ashe in three sets to win the Tournament of Champions at Las Vegas. At 42 he routed Rod Laver in a $10,000 winner-take-all match in New York. It was tougher than in his youth, he said, because "a set today seems like what a match used to be."

He struggled with Jack Kramer and other promoters to get the money he thought he was worth. He was never guilty of false modesty, and he usually was in full command of the situation. Bob Addie wrote, "He proved that an athlete who gives his last full measure of determination still is admired and applauded. He may have the mind of a scold, but he has the heart of a champion."

He had more than the mind of a scold. At times he was rude to everyone. "There's only one thing I owe people," he said, "and that's preparation. If I practice, stay in shape . . . then I can give my best, and that's what they're paying to see."

Though he was known for his quick temper and tenacious play, there was another side to him. "Built into the remarkable athlete's body is a happy-go-lucky disposition which is both a curse and a blessing," wrote Richard Phelan. "His extra-casual view of life and tennis can put him two sets down in a

crucial match and then, often but not always, save him by allowing him to win the next three. It has made his career a zigzag affair of boom and bust rather than the short, smooth ride that is common in tennis."

Tennis was always enjoyable for Gonzales. "I never felt I had to sacrifice or work because I enjoy tennis so much," he said. "To me, this is fun. . . . Once I'm on the court, I'm doing the thing I want to do, and I am very happy with my life."

He relished the individualism of tennis. "The true beauty of sports is to go beyond the idea of winning or losing. That's why I love tennis so much. It gives you the sense of total loneliness and self-reliance, a stage on which you can create your own beauty."

Gould, Shane
(1956–   )

For 24 months, from April 1971 to April 1973, Shane Gould of Australia was the world's most successful woman swimmer. Then, only 16 years old, she retired because, she said, "I would rather sit down and read a good book than spend all my spare time training to be a champion."

She was three years old when she learned to swim. At four she was climbing coconut trees in Fiji, where her father was an airline executive. When her family returned to Australia she became a champion swimmer. She was up at 4:20 in the morning and went to sleep at 7:30 at night. She was in the pool from 4:45 to 7:00 A.M. and 4:00 to 6:00 P.M., logging seven miles a day.

When she was barely 14 years old, in 1971, she broke four of the five world free-style records and tied the fifth (she broke that one in 1972). In the 1972 Olympics, at which the American girls wore T-shirts saying, "All That Glitters Is Not Gould," she won three gold medals, one silver and one bronze.

Slender, relaxed and poised, she was, as Murray Rose said, "more focused on what she's doing than any athlete I've ever seen." "Out of the pool, she has a Gidget-like personality," Selwyn Parker wrote. "Inside the pool or before a key race, she switches off and becomes the dedicated athlete." Forbes Carlile, her coach, said she had an innate capacity for endurance. Ron Gould, her father, said, "She never really needed any object of sublimation."

At 14 she said, "Breaking world records is more thrilling than going to parties and out with boys." At the same time, her mother, Shirley Gould, said, "By the time a girl is 18, she is usually looking for other satisfactions out of life."

Shane Gould did not wait until 18. She spent four months in California attending high school and won three titles in the AAU indoor championships. Then she became disillusioned with swimming. She discovered other sports and food, and her 5-foot-8-inch frame ballooned from 130 pounds to 154. In August 1973 the girl who once said "I am never bored in the water" retired from swimming.

The 15-year-old Australian holds up her stuffed kangaroo after setting a world record at the 1972 Olympics.

Graham, Otto Everett, Jr.
(1921–   )

Coach Paul Brown once said, "The test of a quarterback is where his team finishes. By that standard, Otto Graham was the best of all time."

Otto Graham played ten years (1946–55) for the Cleveland Browns—the first four in the old All-America Football Conference and the last six in the National Football League. The Browns won a conference title during each of those ten years and a league title during seven of the ten. He completed 1,464 of 2,626 passes for 23,584 yards and 174 touchdowns. Then he retired because of what he called "mental pressure." He was elected to the College Football Hall of Fame in 1956 and the Pro Football Hall of Fame in 1965.

During most of his pro career his plays were sent in from the bench. "Paul Brown maintains that a quarterback gets stereotyped in his calls, and that's right," he said. "His reasoning was sound, but he failed to realize that he himself had become stereotyped."

Dante Lavelli, his favorite pass receiver, remembered his split-second reactions. They were especially important because, as his center, Mike Scarry, said, his line didn't always give him all the protection he needed. "But he never complains," Scarry said. Brown, who coached him throughout his pro career, said, "He has a natural gift for throwing a pass that is straight, soft and easy to catch. He seems to pull the string on the ball and set it down right over the receiver's head."

He was a solid, strong quarterback at 6 feet 1 inch and 195 pounds. He was also confident, proud, outspoken and sometimes indiscreet. In high school he starred in three sports and played the violin, piano, French horn and cornet. At Northwestern University he was All-American in football (as a single-wing tailback) and basketball. After World War II he played pro basketball for the Rochester Royals.

After pro football he was athletic director and football coach at the United States Coast Guard Academy (1959–65) and later coach of the Washington Redskins (1966–68). In 1970 he returned to the Coast Guard Academy as athletic direc-

tor, and in 1974 he resumed coaching. His coaching job with the Redskins was short-lived because he was too easygoing. "The trouble with Otto," said Weeb Ewbank, a rival coach, "is that he frequently leads with his heart."

"I was born with good coordination," Graham once said, "but I worked for everything else I ever got out of sports. There is no shortcut to success. It takes practice. Too many kids like to think that because they have natural ability they're going to be stars. But it doesn't work that way unless they're willing to work hard to polish the skills God gave them."

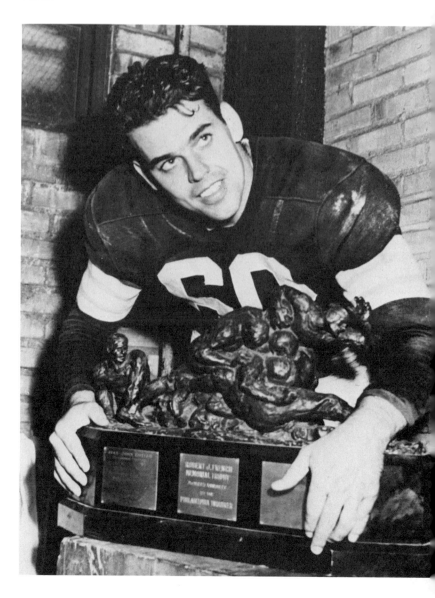

The Cleveland Browns' star quarterback poses with the Robert J. French Memorial Trophy.

Grange, Harold Edward
(1903–   )

He was called Red (for the color of his hair), the Wheaton Iceman (for his summer job of hauling big blocks of ice in his home town) and the Galloping Ghost (for his artful running style). He was the most famous of all college football players and perhaps, as Bronko Nagurski insisted, the best ever.

Grange brought excitement and respectability to football at a time when it needed both. Grantland Rice said that he had more influence on college and professional football than any other player. "He is three or four men and a horse rolled into one," Damon Runyon once said. "He is Jack Dempsey, Babe Ruth, Al Jolson, Paavo Nurmi and Man o' War."

Red Grange was a star from the start. He scored 74 touchdowns and won 16 letters at Wheaton (Illinois) High School. At the University of Illinois he was varsity halfback for two years and quarterback in his final season. He was All-American all three years. The student newspaper of the University of Michigan, a rival school, once wrote, "All he can do is run," to which Bob Zuppke, the Illinois coach, replied, "All Galli-Curci can do is sing."

He was a wiry six-footer, with all the requisites of a great ball-carrier—grace, balance, speed and a wonderful change of pace. He seemed to flow when he ran. "He would race from one sideline to the other, stopping and starting like a gust of wind," John Devaney wrote. "What made him great," said W. C. Heinz, "was his instinctive ability to size up a field and plot a run the way a great general can map not only a battle but a whole campaign."

His most memorable game was played in 1924 against an unbeaten and powerful Michigan team. A capacity crowd of 66,609 turned out for the dedication of Illinois' Memorial Stadium. Michigan kicked off, and he ran the kick back 95 yards for a touchdown. When Michigan punted after getting nowhere on its first offensive series, he ran 67 yards on the first play for another touchdown. With the game less than seven minutes old, he ran 54 yards for his third score. Only 12 minutes into the game, he ran 44 yards for his fourth touchdown of the day.

He turned to his quarterback and said, "I'm so tired, I can hardly stand up. Better get me out of here." After a rest and a five-minute ovation, he returned to the game, ran 13 yards for a fifth touchdown and passed 20 yards for a sixth as Illinois won, 39-14. He had carried the ball 15 times for 212 yards and completed six passes for 64 yards, all in 41 minutes.

The day after his final college game he signed a professional contract guaranteeing him $100,000 for 17 games. He became the first pro superstar, drawing capacity crowds everywhere. In three years he made almost $1 million, mostly from playing. He became an idol, and pro football became a serious business. "No man exerted a more profound influence over the destiny of the National Football League," Murray Olderman wrote. "He showed that people who had no college alumni affiliation would come to see grown men play football. And he showed them a flair that would keep them coming."

He played for the Chicago Bears in 1925, the New York Yankees in a maverick league in 1926 and in the NFL in 1927 and returned to the Bears from 1929 to 1934. (A knee injury forced him to sit out the 1928 season.) He was named all-pro four times. In January 1935, playing for the Bears against an all-star team in Los Angeles, he broke away, only to have a 230-pound guard tackle him from behind. "When you're in the open and they catch you from behind like that, it's time to quit," he said. It was his last game.

He became a charter member of the College Football Hall of Fame (1951) and the Pro Football Hall of Fame (1963), and he remained in the public eye as a radio and television broadcaster. And though, as Allison Danzig wrote, "his blue jersey, adorned with the mystic orange numerals 77, became as famous as Joseph's coat," he never let the legend get ahead of him.

"I thought, and still do, that they built me up out of all proportion," he said. "I could carry a football well, but I've met hundreds of people who could do their thing better than I. I mean engineers and writers, scientists, doctors." He moved to Florida, where, he said, "My neighbors know I played football a long time ago for some small Midwestern college, so I let it go at that."

Red Grange, playing for the New York Yankees, gains ground against the Wilson Wildcats at Yankee Stadium.

Graziano, Rocky (1921–)

Rocky Graziano, the Rock, was a champion middleweight fighter, a rough, tough, furious slugger who in later years became a beloved American character—a kid from the wrong side of the tracks who made good.

He was born Thomas Rocco Barbella on Manhattan's tough lower East Side. He spent six of his first 20 years in reform school and served ten months in an Army stockade for punching a captain and later going AWOL. He became a professional fighter in 1942 and during the next six years had three memorable middleweight title fights with Tony Zale. He was knocked out by Zale in six rounds in their first bout in 1946, but he won the title from Zale the following year with a sixth-round knockout in 120-degree heat and with one eye closed and the other almost closed. In 1948 Zale regained the crown, knocking out Graziano in three rounds.

He was a volatile, colorful fighter with a stinging punch. "When the Rock hits them, it stays with them," his manager, Irving Cohen, once said. The years Graziano spent on the streets of a New York ghetto influenced his style. "He admits he didn't care how he won," Rex Lardner wrote. "He rabbit-punched, he hit out of clinches, he hit fighters on the way down . . . and he hit after the bell. . . . He charged across the ring, threw his arms back, lunged forward and swung."

He was a Dead End Kid who mangled the English language, but his autobiography, *Somebody Up There Likes Me*, became a best seller and was made into a movie (Paul Newman played the lead). He became a celebrity, appearing on television as a comedian and actor and making commercials.

"I think I must have been born with too much energy," Graziano said. "I always had to do something, couldn't sit still. . . . I been in jail all my life. . . . I never amounted to nothing until I started fighting. . . . I'm legitimate and I'm doing all right and it's a free country and I'm glad I'm living in it."

Graziano struts around his downed opponent, Freddie (Red) Cochrane, in a 1945 fight.

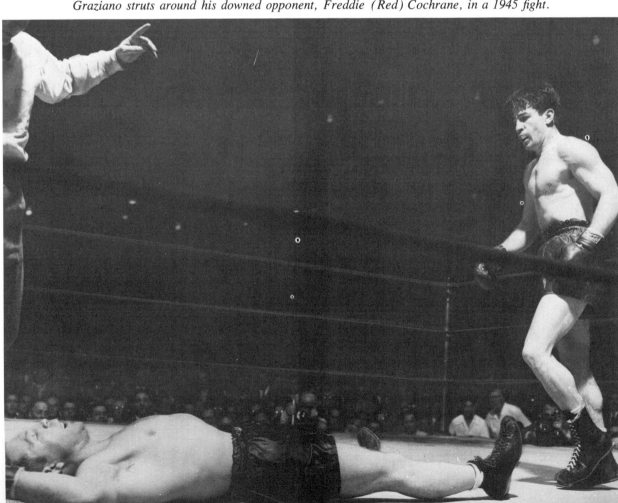

Greenberg, Henry Benjamin
(1911–   )

Arthur Daley wrote of Hank Greenberg, "The sport has had few more inept ballplayers than he and few who were greater." He has been described as "a slow, heavy-limbed giant," "as clumsy as he was big" and a "purely self-made star." His high-school coach, Irwin Dickstein, said, "He never played games, he worked at them."

Greenberg agreed. "I didn't have that much natural talent," he said. "I had to work extra hard to get where I got." Stanley Frank wrote, "He first despairs of reaching mediocrity, then promptly performs in a manner to make ordinary ballplayers look like so many mugs."

The work paid off. He pinch-hit in one game for the Detroit Tigers in 1930. He went on to play for the Tigers from 1933 to 1946 (except for four and a half years because of Army service during World War II) and for the Pittsburgh Pirates in 1947. He won most-valuable-player awards as a first baseman in 1935 and an outfielder in 1940. In 1,394 games he hit 331 home runs, 58 in the 1938 season. He had a lifetime batting average of .313 and a slugging average of .605.

Hank Greenberg crosses the plate after hitting a home run in the second game of the 1945 World Series.

The Pirates bought him from the Tigers and made him baseball's first $100,000-a-year player so he would teach Ralph Kiner, a budding star, the fine points of home-run hitting. He was a good teacher, but his body hurt. Stan Musial recalled, "His feet were killing him, and when he ran the bases he snorted like a broken-down racehorse."

He served as vice-president, general manager and farm director of the Cleveland Indians from 1948 to 1957. Later he spent several years as vice-president, general manager and part owner of the Chicago White Sox. While with the Indians he alienated many fans by firing Cleveland's popular manager, Lou Boudreau, after the 1950 season. Afterward he admitted, "My public-relations batting average is miserable."

"I probably would have been a wealthy man today," Groza said later. "The franchise was really paying off. . . . I sold my stock for $1,000, but it eventually could have been worth $100,000." Besides the money, he forfeited his athletic future. He had perhaps the brightest future in pro basketball of any of the players involved.

General Electric hired him as a planner, "not for what I've done or what I am," he said, "but for the job they expect me to do." He also did television broadcasting and ran the family tavern.

In 1959 Bellarmine College in Louisville chose him as basketball coach at $7,000 a year. His success as a coach and administrator led him into the American Basketball Association as business manager of the Kentucky Colonels and then general manager of the San Diego Conquistadors. "I was bound and determined to make a success of myself after this thing happened," he said. "There were a lot of people who had faith in me and I wanted to restore that faith. I'm proud that I've been able to come back. I realized I couldn't afford to make another mistake. I want other people to know that I didn't turn out to be a bum."

Groza, Alex John (1926–   )

Alex Groza's basketball career went from up to down to up. He was the first of the players convicted in the 1951 point-shaving scandals to return to college basketball.

He was a 6-foot-7-inch center for the University of Kentucky, a three-time All-American (1947–49) and an Olympic gold medalist (1948). He was a star and part owner of the Indianapolis Olympians, a new professional team, until 1951, when he was arrested for shaving points in a 1949 college game. He and Ralph Beard pleaded guilty. They escaped with three years of probation but were forced to sell their stock in the Olympians.

Gurney, Daniel Saxon
(1931–   )

The New York Times described him thusly: ''In the cockpit of his royal blue roadster, wearing a gleaming black helmet and white fireproof racing suit, he looks like a Hollywood version of a grand-prix driver—handsome, slick, terribly sophisticated.''

Dan Gurney, the race driver, lived up to the image. Tall and lean, blond and blue-eyed, like a boyish James Stewart, he was also witty, low-keyed, outgoing, bright and warm. As Bob Ottum wrote, ''He is the living assurance to every worried mom that hot rodders do not all grow up bad.''

In the 1947 Grand Prix of Belgium he became the first American in 46 years to win a world-championship race in an American car (the car was an Eagle he designed and built). He drove big cars at Indianapolis, stock cars at Daytona Beach and Riverside and sports cars and prototypes all over the world. Often he won. More often, especially in his early years, he failed to finish.

Mechanical trouble was often the reason. ''In a good car, he is an artist,'' Bill Libby wrote. ''The only rub is, his car usually breaks down.'' Phil Hill, a rival driver, thought it was more than that. ''I don't think he wants to win. He's a great driver, but something always goes wrong and it's not always just mechanical.'' Gurney was frustrated, but he disagreed with Hill, saying, ''You prepare for a race, work yourself up for a race, give everything, risk everything, get off to a winning start, then— bang—it's all over. . . . There's nothing you can do about it. If I abuse a car, I know it.''

He conceived the idea of a Lotus-Ford to run in the Indianapolis 500, convincing Lotus to build the chassis and Ford to develop the engine. He encouraged European grand-prix drivers to race at Indianapolis. When he retired as a driver he built Eagles for Indianapolis, grand-prix, Can-Am and Formula 5000 races.

He once described the danger of racing this way: ''Race driving is a form of brinksmanship. First, you use your judgment to determine where the brink is. Then you use your skill to approach the brink and stay at that point. It's sort of like balancing along a cliff. You can walk three or four feet from the cliff and have no problem, but someone closer to the edge can beat you. You need judgment to tell you where

the edge of the cliff is and skill to get there and stay within a given safety margin.''

Under those circumstances, did he enjoy racing? ''At times I enjoy it,'' he said. ''I'm aware of the danger all the time I'm driving, and I don't enjoy that. When Jim Ryun breaks the mile record, does he enjoy the actual running? He probably enjoys being the record-holder but not getting there. Well, that's how I feel. . . . I love racing. It's a cruel, bloody business, and it hasn't always treated me kindly, and I'm not sure it ever will, but it's my life.''

Hagen, Walter Charles
(1892–1969)

Walter Hagen may have been the world's greatest golfer. He certainly was the greatest golf character. He was a *bon vivant*, a lovable scoundrel, a showman, an elegant dresser, a master psychologist and a quick man with a buck. As Arthur Daley wrote, "He was the first golfer to earn a million from the sport and the first to spend it, too."

When he started as a golf pro, the going wage was $50 a week at best, and the pro was a country-club hireling who used the servants' entrance but never the dining room or the bar. Hagen changed all that. For a British Open, he was driven to the clubhouse front door in a chauffeured Rolls-Royce complete with footman. He stepped through the front door, and no one was bold enough to object. From then on the golf pro was a first-class citizen. As Arnold Palmer said to him at a 1967 testimonial dinner, "If it were not for you, this dinner would be downstairs in the pro shop and not in the ballroom."

Gene Sarazen said that Hagen made professional golf what it is. John Lardner wrote that he raised the living standards and promoted the independence of all professional athletes more than anyone else.

He always enjoyed himself. He spent many evenings on the town, invariably turning up late on the first tee and sometimes sporting dress clothes. Jimmy Breslin wrote, "He was a potentate, not an athlete. He went through life with a white silk shirt and with two hours of sleep." Chick Evans, a contemporary champion, said, "He is in golf to live, not to make a living."

And how he lived! Once, when he won $3,000 in Canada, he threw a party that cost more than his winnings. He always had a glass in hand and a few hidden around the room. He was quick to pick up a check, quick to spend and quick to tip lavishly. When he won his first British Open, he gave the entire prize money of $500 to his caddie.

He ranked with Bobby Jones, an amateur, as the leading golfer of the 1920s. In 1926, in a special 72-hole match, he routed Jones, 11 and 10. He received a purse of $7,600, the largest in golf history

The straw-hatted gallery at the 1919 United States Open as Hagen prepares to sink his putt.

at that time, and spent $800 of that money for a set of diamond-and-platinum cuff links for Jones.

He played exciting golf, often spraying tee shots. But, as Ben Hogan said, "He had the greatest mental approach to golf of any player I ever knew." He also knew how and when to use psychology. In the 1926 Professional Golfers' Association final against Leo Diegel, after conceding six-foot and eight-foot putts on early holes, he refused to concede a 25-inch putt near the end of the match. Diegel searched for a hidden slope, but there was none and he missed the putt. He also lost the match. The next year, in the PGA final against Joe Turnesa, after partying all night, he arrived 30 minutes late and conceded putts on the first three holes. On the 35th hole Turnesa faced a short putt. Hagen conceded nothing this time. Turnesa missed the putt and Hagen won the match.

From 1914 to 1929 he won five PGA titles (four in a row), five Western Opens, four British Opens, two United States Opens—more than 75 tournaments in all. Then he retired because, he said, "I can't stand the thought of possibly shooting an 80."

An adoring public missed him. As Alden Whitman wrote, "He captivated the public imagination as much for his resplendent personality as for his prowess with mashie and putter." Fred Corcoran, a prominent golf official and long-time friend, explained part of his allure, saying, "He lived the life lesser men dream about as they plod back and forth every day between their offices and the subway. . . . He broke 11 of the Ten Commandments."

In later years he seldom played golf, and his life became more restrained. But he always remembered to enjoy. His philosophy was summed up in a sign on his wall:

"DON'T HURRY. DON'T WORRY. YOU'RE HERE ONLY A SHORT TIME, SO BE SURE TO SMELL THE FLOWERS."

He was a philosopher on the golf course, too. "There's no such thing as a perfect round of golf," he said. "It's normal to make three or four bad shots a round. When you make a bad shot, forget it. . . . The trouble with most golfers is this: They may have perfect swings, but they have no philosophy. So they get nowhere. They can do well enough until they blow a shot or two. Then they are through for the day. When I start a round of golf, I expect to miss some shots." He rarely missed.

Halas, George Stanley (1895–)

George Halas spent nearly 50 years in the National Football League as a player and coach. At one point he served the Chicago Bears simultaneously as right end, coach, president, co-owner (later, full owner), promoter, office manager, ticket seller and publicity director.

He was a self-made man, stubborn, loyal, hard-working, paternalistic and parsimonious. *Sports Illustrated* called him "the last Puritan." His integrity was unquestionable, but his temperament was not always so. "He is a wonderful old man," wrote Dick Young, "with the outstanding trait of a lot of wonderful old men. If he doesn't get his way, he acts like a little boy." William Barry Furlong wrote, "He has all the warmth of breaking bones, a personality as daring as twin beds. . . . He smiles as though it hurts."

At the University of Illinois, Halas was a football end, basketball captain and baseball outfielder. He started in professional sports as right fielder for the New York Yankees during the 1919 season, but a hip injury ended that career, and the next year the Yankees had a new right-fielder, Babe Ruth.

He played football in 1919 for the Hammond (Indiana) Pros, an independent team, and in 1920 for the Decatur (Illinois) Staleys of the new American Professional Football League. In 1922 the league became the National Football League, and Halas, player and part owner, moved the team to Chicago and changed its name to the Chicago Staleys and then the Chicago Bears.

Halas played until 1929. He coached the team in that period (1920–29) and during three additional ten-year stretches—1933–42, 1946–55 and 1958–67. Under his leadership his team won 320 games (only one other NFL coach had won as many as 200) and six titles. His players included Red Grange, Bronko Nagurski, Sid Luckman, Bulldog Turner, Gale Sayers and Dick Butkus, all present or future Hall of Famers. In 1963 he became a charter member of the Pro Football Hall of Fame.

He made many football innovations. He was the first to hold daily practice, study game films of opponents, use public-address announcers, broadcast games on radio, put assistant coaches high in the stands during a game, adopt a team song and form an alumni association. He reigned like a despot. He was truly Papa Bear.

Halas exchanges congratulations with the team's mascot after the Bears won the NFL title in 1963.

Harmon, Thomas Dudley (1919–)

Tom Harmon of Michigan was the most famous college football player of his day. He won the Heisman Trophy and the Maxwell Award as the nation's outstanding college player in 1940 and made All-America two years. Playing wingback and single-wing tailback, he ran for 33 touchdowns, passed for 16 and broke Red Grange's Big Ten records.

The comparison with Grange was inevitable. Amos Alonzo Stagg, the retired coach, claimed he was superior to Grange in all areas except running. Fielding H. Yost, the old Michigan coach, was reminded of Willie Heston. H.G. Salsinger wrote, "He is one of the few who has come up in the last four decades who can be called truly great without abusing a much-abused adjective."

His athletic brilliance was not an unmitigated blessing, however. Stardom alienated him from teammates, and as Ed Fitzgerald wrote, "Jealousy and misunderstanding corroded his glory years and ate deep, ineradicable scars into his spirit." Cameron Shipp wrote, "He was afraid of the hero legend and did everything possible to kid it out of everybody's system."

During World War II he enlisted in the Army Air Corps, became a pilot and twice cheated death. In April 1943 his plane crashed in a storm, and he was lost in a Brazilian jungle for a week, the only survivor of a six-man crew. In November of that year he was shot down over China and hid 32 days behind Japanese lines before friendly Chinese guerrillas returned him to an American base.

He played two years for the Los Angeles Rams after the war, but combat leg burns from the war hampered his efficiency. He became one of America's leading sports broadcasters and married a former Hollywood actress named Elyse Knox. His only son, Mark, became starting quarterback at UCLA, and the proud father said, "I just hope he gets out of it what I did." Through the years he remained close to his college blocking back, Forest Evashevski, and was especially fond of Evashevski's youngest son, Thomas Harmon Evashevski.

Hartack, William John (1932–   )

Bill Hartack has always been an enigma. He is a jockey almost without peer, serious to a fault about his work, always giving the owner, trainer and bettor a run for their money. From 1952 to 1974 he rode 4,250 winners in 21,309 races, earning purses of $26,322,700. During four years he led all jockeys in victories, and twice he led in earnings.

Yet the Bill Hartack the public knows best is arrogant, sullen, graceless, bitter and highly emotional. He can be charming during television interviews, but he has alienated owners, trainers, fellow jockeys, jockey agents and, most of all, the press. He has antagonized so many racing people that this great jockey of the late 1950s and early 1960s was hustling for mounts by the late 1960s.

Jimmy Cannon called him "a curious kid who is exasperated by the small matters of his trade." Jack Mann wrote, "No incident is minor to him. There is, he said, one in every crowd, and one is too many."

In 1969 he won his fifth Kentucky Derby victory, equaling Eddie Arcaro's record. Yet after the race he hardly displayed the demeanor of a winner. Milton Gross wrote, "His petulance was autographed on his surly face," and Arthur Daley wrote, "He set a Derby record for rudeness."

Lenny Goodman, once his agent, said, "Sometimes he looks like he wants to fight the whole world. It's just that he has a bug in his head." Chick Lang, another of his many former agents, said, "It's his world, and the rest of us are supposed to live in it."

Hartack expressed a different attitude—that others should live outside his world, or at least not invade his privacy. "I know what I am. People who read about me don't, and who's responsible? I'm surely not. My work comes first. What people think of me comes second. I've done my best out on the race track—that's the important thing."

"All I ever asked newspapermen to do was to print the facts," he said of his vendetta with the press, "not the half-truths but the straight facts. When they do, they'll get a whole lot of cooperation out of me. . . . I don't have to talk to them because I don't give a damn and because my record speaks for itself. . . . There's no way in the world the press is going to educate the fans because they don't want to educate them. You think they care about the public? They care about themselves."

Hartack cared about winning and became even more difficult when he didn't win. "If I was an owner or trainer, you know who I'd want riding my horses? Me. Because I want my jockey, when he loses, to come back mad. I don't care who he's mad at. I want him to be mad."

Hartack, five-time Derby winner, studies the 1974 field at Churchill Downs with Sir Tristram, his entry for the classic.

Haughton, William Robert
(1923–   )

Billy Haughton has made harness-racing history with his driving success alone. In 1963 he became the first North American to win 2,000 career races, and in 1973 he became the first to win 3,000. In 1974 he became the first driver anywhere in the world to win $20 million in career purses. By the end of 1974 his career record showed 3,925 victories.

But his greatest mark was made as an owner-trainer-driver on a scale never before known. He usually took 150 or more horses, mostly two-year-olds, to Florida for winter training. He supervised as many as 11 assistant trainers and 84 grooms and had to answer to 60 owners for whom he trained. "He operates the General Motors of trotting," Red Smith wrote. Haughton enjoyed it, saying, "You've got to buy yearlings and make them into racehorses yourself. That's the most stimulating part of this business."

Billy Haughton (pronounced "Hawton") was raised 36 miles from the Saratoga thoroughbred track and started as a 16-year-old jockey at county fairs. He opened a harness stable in 1947 with two horses. Eventually he trained and drove such champion horses as Rum Customer, Romulus Hanover,

Billy Haughton and Magnus Apollo.

Tar Heel, Laverne Hanover and Handle With Care. His industry, sincerity and intelligence won him universal respect in a backbiting business.

Henry King, Jr., a Yonkers Raceway official, said, "Once, I asked him if he ever gets tired. You know, of being around horses and that murderous routine of his. He just looked at me kind of quizzically, as if he really didn't understand how I could ask the question in the first place." Dorothy Haughton said of her husband, "I wonder sometimes how he can make it another day." Mark Kram wrote, "If there were no barn, no 18-hour day, he would be like a big balloon soon after being pricked with a pin."

Haughton's philosophy: "Take it easy on your horses. They last longer that way and eventually they do better. . . . No driver can win with a poor horse and most drivers will win behind the good ones." Though he has won more purse money than any other driver in harness-racing history, the money was essentially a by-product. "I don't think about money much. It doesn't make me feel particularly good. My satisfaction comes in winning a race."

Hayes, Robert Lee (1942–   )

In 1964 Bob Hayes won two Olympic gold medals and universal recognition as the World's Fastest Human. Then he embarked on a professional football career and became the most dangerous pass receiver in the game.

Bob Hayes setting a world record of 9.1 for the 100-yard dash at the 1963 AAU track and field championships.

At 5 feet 11 inches and 185 pounds, he is chunky, with a big upper body, muscular thighs and thin calves and ankles. He runs pigeon-toed, his shoulders rolling in a peculiar gait. "He rolled amid a tangle of arms and legs," wrote Arthur Daley, "but was the epitome of raw, unbridled power and speed." Jesse Owens, an earlier Olympic champion, said, "When he comes off the blocks, he looks like a guy catching a ball in back of the line of scrimmage and dodging people." To Will Bradbury he looked "like a runaway tank."

Dick Hill, his college coach, agreed that Hayes's style was unorthodox, but he didn't try to change it. "If you were a baseball manager," he said, "you wouldn't tell Stan Musial to come out of that ridiculous batting stance, would you? You wouldn't tell Tom Heinsohn that a basketball shot must be arched and not thrown like a line drive."

Hill's tolerance paid off. In 1963 the ungraceful Bob Hayes set a world record for 100 yards (9.1 seconds) that lasted for 11 years. In the 1964 Olympics he tied the 100-meter record of 10.0 and won the 400-meter relay for the United States by turning a two-meter deficit into a three-meter victory.

At Florida A & M he was a sprinter in track and a running back in football. He joined the Dallas Cowboys of the NFL in 1965 as a pass receiver, made all-pro and broke Cowboy all-time records for receiving, scoring and punt returns.

Raymond Berry, the great pass receiver who helped coach him, said Hayes could learn anything he could teach him. Cowboys coach Tom Landry said, "With his great speed and playability, he can control the defense and win games even without catching a pass. That's how much he disrupts things." Dan Reeves, a teammate, agreed. "If he never catches a pass, he's worth a couple of touchdowns a game."

As a man, he is friendly, gregarious and casual. Sonny Margolis, his lawyer, said, "He inwardly knows how to draw people to him." Hayes said, "I want people to believe in me. It makes me do what I have to do when I'm not sure I can do it. . . . Catching a game-winning touchdown is more of a thrill than winning gold medals. You play football for your team, not for yourself."

Hayes, Wayne Woodrow
(1913–   )

He can be warm and witty, and he is a student of philosophers and generals. But the Woody Hayes the public knows is tyrannical, cantankerous and physically intimidating to young players, photographers or anyone else who displeases him. His temper tantrums on the sidelines have made him famous beyond the football world.

He was head football coach at Denison College (1946–48), his alma mater, and Miami University of Ohio (1949–50) before becoming head coach at Ohio State. His teams have won three national championships, four Rose Bowls, ten Big Ten championships and more than 200 games (among active coaches only Bear Bryant has won more). They are known for a conservative offense best described as three yards and a cloud of dust.

He is a paunchy man with a moon face who paces the sidelines in shirt sleeves even in cold weather. "Being cold, like being determined to win, is just a state of mind," he said. His mind is obsessed with winning. He refused to slow down after a heart attack and quoted Napoleon's remark, "I'd rather die a winner than live a loser." He also denies periodic reports that he has mellowed. "I'm not mellow. I'm the same guy I've always been. . . . The minute I think I'm getting mellow, then I'm retiring. Who ever heard of a mellow winner?"

"To him, football is less a game than a twentieth-century torture device," wrote Roy Terrell, "and on his own private rack, on a hundred Saturday afternoons in the vast stadiums of the Midwest, he has been subjected to agonies that would make your hair look like Harpo Marx's. . . . Deprive him of victory and he would die . . . and so, until victory is assured, he dies."

So do his players—or almost. "If you get through his preseason two-a-day workouts, you get the feeling that you can handle most of the other things you are going to run into in life," said Bob Vogel, one of his star tackles. Bill Reed, once commissioner of the Big Ten, said Hayes reminded him of what Winston Churchill said about Field Marshal Montgomery—indomitable in defeat, insufferable in victory.

For Hayes, victory is everything. "I don't think it's possible to be too intent on winning," he said. "If we played for any other reason we would be totally dishonest. This country is built on winning and on that alone. Winning is still the most honorable thing a man can do."

Haynes, Marques Oreole
(1926–   )

For more than a quarter-century he has been acclaimed the world's greatest dribbler. He once said, "Dribbling is nothing more than bouncing the ball," but his dribbling is something special. He can dribble the ball three times a second, high and low, quick and slow, on his knees or sitting. He has played more than 5,000 games, perhaps more than anyone else in basketball history. He has dribbled a basketball at least a million times.

Marques Haynes is slim (6 feet and barely 160 pounds), mild, ever cheerful, a former Boy Scout and a gentleman. He says hello to everyone each time he sees him, even if he sees him a dozen times a day.

He has an ageless face, and for years he kept his age a secret. "If I say how old I am," he says, "it would disappoint a lot of people who insist they saw me play in the late 1920s and 1930s. It would disappoint the people who swear they went to college with me in the 1920s."

He learned to dribble when he was a boy, and he perfected his style at Langston (Oklahoma) College. In 1947 he signed with the Harlem Globetrotters, the famous all-black touring, clowning team that Frank Deford later described as "part show biz, part sporting event and part Jack Benny." The Globetrotters have played in 89 countries before Popes, Kings, Presidents and more than ten million spectators.

He started with the Globetrotters earning $250 a month. In 1953, earning $10,000 a year, he left to form a similar touring team, the Fabulous Magicians. He was founder, president, chief booking agent, road secretary, publicist, typist, bookkeeper, coach and No. 1 attraction.

In 1973 he returned to the Globetrotters. He had achieved financial security through real-estate holdings in Oklahoma, Texas and Las Vegas, an insurance agency and an embryonic clothing business. Frank Deford wrote, "The years of one-nighters seem to have made his life a gentle flowing river rather than the jagged rapids that experience usually imposes." Deford saw him as a link in the father-son relationship. "The fathers are especially anxious to bring their children to meet him. It is some kind of communion for the father and the child to know that the father saw him dribble in a Globetrotter uniform 25 years ago, just as the child did this night."

Heffelfinger, William Walter
(1867–1954)

Grantland Rice called Pudge Heffelfinger "the most amazing football player I have ever known." He was one of the best and most exciting linemen in football history.

He was a starting guard for Yale from 1888 to 1891 and All-American the last three years (the All-America team had not yet been created when he was a freshman). After graduating he became one of the first professionals, receiving $500 a game. He played football and helped prepare Yale teams until he was 65, when he played in a semi-pro benefit for disabled veterans. When he was 83 he said, "I know I was better at 45 than I was at 20, but I will have to admit that I slowed down a little when I was 65. Not much, but a little. . . . I would like just one more shot before I turn in my cleats."

When he left home-town Minneapolis for Yale, his father told him, "Walter, when you get to Yale, see to it they don't call you by that ridiculous nickname 'Pudge.'" But the name stuck. His Yale coach was Walter Camp, and the ends were 27-year-old Amos Alonzo Stagg and 150-pound Frank Hinkey, all, like Heffelfinger, now members of the College Football Hall of Fame. He was so dedicated that he lost four to five pounds every scrimmage and took six-mile cross-country hikes on Sundays.

He was known as a fearless man of strong convictions. He revolutionized line play as the first guard to pull out of the line and lead interference for the ball carrier. John D. McCallum wrote that he was possibly "the greatest guard football ever knew, certainly the most unique . . . more a brain man than a muscle man." His tremendous desire and enjoyment of the game led Joe Williams to write, "To him, football was something of a religion. He had got so much out of the game as an undergraduate that it just logically had to mean more to him than most of his contemporaries."

"A game that can keep you so young and vibrant and all steamed up is a precious thing," Heffelfinger said. "I stayed in the game because I loved football and body contact. . . . I played football for the same reason that other middle-aged men played golf and tennis. Those are strenuous games, but they lacked something I wanted—the fierce elation that comes from throwing your body across an opponent's knees and feeling him hit the turf with a solid crack."

144

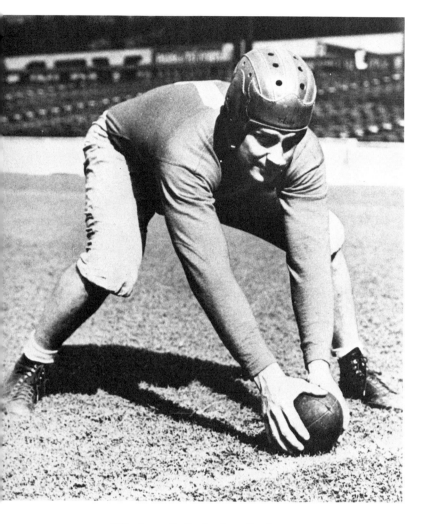

Mel Hein, New York Giant center, in 1939.

made all-pro eight straight years, and in 1938, when he was chosen as the National Football League's most valuable player, his salary was up to $275 a game. When he retired he was earning $5,000 a year, hardly a fortune but more than any other NFL lineman.

In his last three seasons he doubled as football coach and athletic director at Union College in Schenectady, New York. He worked there Monday through Friday, took a train to New York, worked out with the Giants on Saturday and played in Sunday's game. After retiring as a player he became an assistant coach for three pro teams and the University of Southern California. Later he was supervisor of officials for the American Football League (1966–69) and the NFL's American Football Conference (from 1970 until his retirement in 1974).

He played collegiate football from 1928 to 1930 at Washington State, where he was an All-America center. He was voted into the College Football Hall of Fame and the Pro Football Hall of Fame. His son, Mel Jr., became one of the first 16-foot pole vaulters. Football, the game of Mel Hein, Sr., had changed since his day. "The game is a lot different and a lot better now. The players are faster and bigger."

Hein, Melvin John (1909–   )

For 15 seasons (1931–45) Mel Hein played center for the New York Giants. Red Smith, Al Laney and Arthur Daley wrote that he was the finest center in football history. Wellington Mara, the owner of the Giants, called him the No. 1 player in the team's 50-year history, and Coach Steve Owen said, "In the 15 years he played for me, I don't think I had to teach him anything."

He had a lineman's size (6 feet 3 inches, 230 pounds), but he was mobile, fast, clean and durable, and he had great defensive instincts. He was the first center to lead running plays and the first to drop back to block for the passer. His worst injury was a broken nose on Pearl Harbor Day, at the end of his 11th pro season. Two weeks later he wore a nose guard in the playoffs.

In his second game as a rookie, earning $150 a game, he became a starter. Beginning in 1933, he

Mel Hein and pole-vaulting son, Mel, Jr.

Henie, Sonja (1912–1969)

As an amateur, Sonja Henie won every possible figure-skating honor. As a professional, wrote Ron Roach, "She gave the United States ice-skating fever," and she became a millionaire many times over from ice shows and movies.

She was the most famous figure skater ever, a chunky, charming Norwegian with blond hair, brown eyes and a round, dimpled face. She won three consecutive Olympic titles (1928, 1932 and 1936) and ten consecutive world championships (1927–1936). The 257 cups, medals, plaques and bowls in her trophy room were insured for $200,000 (her legs were insured for $260,000).

In late 1936 she joined a professional ice show and was billed as "Pavlova of the Silver Skates." Capacity crowds turned out everywhere to watch her Charleston and hula on ice, and eventually she owned her own show. As Joe Williams wrote, "When she turned pro, she became an entertainer of the first magnitude." Arthur Daley wrote that she was probably the shrewdest—and perhaps the richest—businesswoman since Hetty Green. Lew Diamond, her publicist, said, "The marvel of her skating is that she never makes an amateurish move. . . . She gives surpassing excellence. . . . Her perfection is so rare."

Her first movie, *One in a Million*, reportedly grossed $25 million, but the attraction was her skat-

ing, not her acting. "From the artistic viewpoint, she was just dandy as long as she stayed on skates," Thomas F. Moore wrote. A reviewer of *It's a Pleasure*, another of her films, wrote, "It doesn't fulfill the promise of the title."

She retired from acting and skating in the mid-1950s, and by then she had invested in real estate, liquor businesses, ice rinks, ice shows and art (her collection included five Gainsboroughs). A decade later she started skating again. As Eugen Mikeler, a former skating partner, said, "She should be an inspiration to all people to go out and be physically active. She has all this fame, all this money. She needs nothing. She could just sit at home and do nothing."

She once said, "Touring is exhausting work, even though it doesn't look like it. . . . Lots of people say to me, 'Why don't you retire?' and I answer, 'Why don't you leave me alone?' I love it."

Hirsch, Maximilian Justice
(1880–1969)

Max Hirsch was a rugged, weather-beaten man with a raspy voice. He was crafty, cunning and wily, and he had an eye for horseflesh. He spent 78 years at the race track, many with a felt hat slouched down to shade his eyes. When he died at the age of 88 he was America's leading trainer.

From 1909 to 1968 he trained 1,933 winners, and his horses earned $12,203,270 in purses. They included Assault ("The greatest horse I ever trained"), Bold Venture, Middleground, Grey Lag, Sarazen, High Gun and Better Self. They also included Sidereal, who scored the first victory of his career in 1921. Hirsch won $770,000 in bets on that race and never denied the popular rumor that $570,000 of the sum went to the gambler Arnold Rothstein.

He was riding quarter horses at Texas fairs at age ten. At 12 he stowed away in a boxcar carrying horses from Texas to Maryland and arrived without shoes and socks to find two feet of snow on the ground. He quickly became an exercise boy and jockey; for five years (from age 14 to 19) he rode thoroughbreds, winning 123 of his 1,117 races. Then he became a trainer. He saddled winners earlier than Sunny Jim Fitzsimmons. Three of the five Hirsch children became trainers, too.

He trained horses for 60 years and, as Charles Hatton wrote, "He never lost his skill." He lived in a cottage between two barns at Belmont Park, and every August, when the horses raced at Saratoga, his house there was always open to young trainers and other racing people for food and talk. "It is some measure of the man's class," the *Morning Telegraph* said, "that he inspired unswerving loyalty, both from his friends in all walks of life and from those who worked for him for most of their lives."

He was a gregarious man, generous with money and advice. Hambla Bauer wrote that "he was the softest touch on the race track."

"I've always had a damn good time," Hirsch said of horseracing. "I've always enjoyed myself. . . . Having young people around has kept me young." In his late 80s he was still active. "I've never given retirement a thought. Why should I retire? I feel fine, sleep good, eat well and have all my faculties."

Middleground gets sugar from trainer Hirsch after a close victory in the 1950 Kentucky Derby.

Hitchcock, Thomas, Jr.
(1900–1944)

Tommy Hitchcock was America's most celebrated polo player, an intense, aggressive, innovative and fearless man, a hero on and off the field of sport. He was, wrote Bill Corum, "the guy most of us hoped in our hearts we would some day be."

When the United States Army rejected him in World War I because he was only 17, he enlisted in France's famous Lafayette Escadrille and shot down his first German plane before he was 18. He was shot down behind German lines, but he escaped by leaping from a moving train. During World War II, as a lieutenant colonel in the Army Air Force, he crashed and died during a routine flight.

He came from a family of polo players. At three he was on horseback, at five on a polo pony, at 13 in his first polo tournament. By the time he was 20 he was an international polo star, and he enjoyed the game's highest rating (ten goals) 18 times in 19 years (1922–40).

"He was a legendary figure on a charging horse," Bill Brandt wrote, "the Babe Ruth of the ponies and the mallets. . . . He was the symbol of attack, attack, always attack . . . that's what sold him and polo to the man on the street." As Arthur Daley wrote, "The man had no fear . . . nearly every spill or collision he had was because someone neglected to give ground to him. He never gave ground to anyone."

Stanley Frank said, "He was, peculiarly and rather improbably, a product of democracy and his strenuous fight against the class distinction that governed the set into which he was born. . . . He was a tough, rich boy. . . . But few took harder swipes at vested privilege and arrogance." In his obituary *The New York Times* said, "He fired the American imagination more than any other polo player ever had." And, in an ultimate tribute, the *Times* added, "He never played a bad game in his life."

He was a banker, and he once said, "You can't play polo on air, so I pay more attention to business than you'd probably give me credit for. . . . One fault with polo players is that they talk too much polo and think too much polo. . . . Polo is exciting, but you can't compare it to flying in wartime. That was the best sport in the world."

Tommy Hitchcock in competition.

He was known as Bantam Ben because of his size (5 feet 6 inches, 137 pounds) and as the Iceman because he was cold, machinelike, seemingly without emotion. Even his friends could not get close to him. He seldom spoke to an opponent or caddie, and he always looked like a man at work. A friend said, "He looks at you like a landlord asking for next month's rent."

"He was a cold, detached artisan on the course," recalled Will Grimsley, "likened by some observers to an undertaker weaving a shroud of defeat for all his adversaries." Herbert Warren Wind thought that "As long as he remains a competitive golfer, he will probably never be so new or so mellow that the chip on his shoulder will entirely disappear. He seems to like it that way."

Gary Player recalled that in 1973 he was playing in a tournament in Brazil and was having a problem with his swing. He telephoned Hogan in Texas to ask his advice. Player said, "He asked me, 'Gary, who do you work for?' When I told him Dunlop, he

Hogan, William Benjamin
(1912–   )

He was the most successful, the most precise and the most feared golfer of his day. From 1946 to 1953, despite an automobile accident that almost killed him, he won the United States Open four times, the Professional Golfers' Association title twice, the Masters twice and the British Open once. In 1953 alone he won the Masters, U.S. Open and British Open, a feat as impressive as Bobby Jones's 1930 grand slam.

replied, 'Well, call Mr. Dunlop.' Then he hung up.'' Ben Crenshaw, a young pro, told a similar story. ''He asked me who I worked for,'' said Crenshaw. ''I said I worked for MacGregor. 'Why don't you call Mr. MacGregor?' he said.''

''I know a lot of people don't like me,'' Hogan once said. ''They say I'm selfish and hard, that I think only of golf. Maybe I do. But there's a reason. I know what it means to be hungry. I sold papers around the railroad station in Fort Worth when I was 12. I never intend to be hungry again, and I never intend for my wife, Valerie, to be hungry.''

He turned pro at 19, and for years he and his wife were hungry. Then he became a winner. ''He was not a man who played golf, he was absolute golf,'' Al Barkow wrote. ''He was *The Man* not only because of his great skill but because of the forbidding manner in which he ground down the opposition. To look at him was to shiver.''

His accuracy and energy were still deadly well into his 50s. Jimmy Demaret told a story, which may even be true: ''When he was out practicing two-irons the other day, he sent his caddie down the fairway. One of his shots hit his caddie in the shins and knocked him down. Before he could get up, Ben hit him twice more.''

He was fortunate to reach his 50s. In February 1949 a bus smashed into his car on a wet Texas highway. He suffered a fractured pelvis, collarbone, left ankle and a crushed rib, among other injuries. He almost died. Then, when he seemed to be recovering, blood clots threatened his life, and surgeons spent two hours tying off the main veins in his legs.

There were doubts whether he would walk again, let alone play golf. But in January 1950, only 11 months after the accident, he played in the Los Angeles Open and tied Sam Snead for first place before losing in a playoff. ''I kept looking over my shoulder,'' said Snead. ''The little man is coming.'' In June 1950, limping and in pain, the ''little man'' won the U.S. Open.

To this day his knees hurt, and he walks slowly and stiffly. Watching him climb the long, uphill 18th fairway at the Masters, writer Maury White said, ''There is a man whose feet hurt.''

But from tee to green, his game remains near perfection, though he seldom plays in tournaments. Only his putting lets him down. ''It's not the legs that go first,'' he said, ''it's the nerves.'' He once described his putting problem: ''It was like trying to roll a watermelon into a thimble.''

The younger pros revere him. Tom Weiskopf was so terrified the first practice round he played with him that he couldn't tee up the ball. Frank Beard, who idolized him, said, ''I think that one day, when he was in his 20s, he flat decided he was going to be the greatest golfer ever, and for the next 20 years he shut everything out of his life except golf. I don't think it was his natural way, but he put himself into a box, and nothing could penetrate that box.''

Hogan, in 1970, with a portrait of the golfer given to the U.S. Golf Association.

Holm, Eleanor Grace Theresa
(1913–   )

Eleanor Holm, daughter of a Brooklyn fire captain, was glamorous, photogenic, charming and fun-loving. She was also a great swimmer, but she was more celebrated for being ousted from the U.S. Olympic team en route to the 1936 Olympic Games in Berlin.

She had competed in the 1928 and 1932 Olympics. In 1928, at age 14, she finished fifth in the 100-meter backstroke in Amsterdam. "When she

went over, she wore white cotton socks. She came back wearing high heels and silk stockings," the New York *Journal-American* said. In 1932, when she was married to Art Jarrett and about to sing with his orchestra, she won an Olympic gold medal at Los Angeles.

By 1936 she was a Warner Brothers starlet who had set seven world records, won 29 U.S. titles and had not lost a backstroke race in seven years. On the ship taking the U.S. Olympic team to Berlin, she openly drank champagne and was dismissed from the team. She charged that 100 athletes had violated training rules aboard ship and said, "I train on champagne and cigarettes. If they start barring everyone who takes a drink, they won't have anybody left."

When she left for Berlin she had contracts to play theaters at $5,000 a week if she won. When she returned she got $8,500 a week instead. She became a professional swimmer, joining Billy Rose's Aquacade and, as Irv Goodman wrote, "Everyone came to see the beautiful swimmer who liked to train on champagne." Her fine wit and a flamboyant manner led one Broadway press agent to call her "a real laughing girl . . . a doll." She divorced Jarrett and in 1939 married Rose, who called her "my little champion."

But in 1954, with a sordid court case looming, she divorced Rose and moved to a Miami Beach condominium penthouse complete with French Provincial furniture, two Dalis and a Renoir ("Alimony, baby," she said). She became an interior decorator and took up golf (her best was 106). She also swam 50 laps a day in the condominium pool. She remained exuberant. "She speaks almost exclusively in italics and exclamation points," William Johnson wrote.

Looking back, she was happy with the way her life turned out. "I had been drinking champagne. If it had been whiskey or gin—well, all right. . . . It made me a star. It made me a glamour girl. Just another gold medal would never have done that."

Eleanor Holm and Pete Desjardins, an American Olympic diver, in 1928.

Holman, Nat (1896–   )

He was one of the most talented players in basketball, an innovator who contributed much to the sport, and one of the most celebrated and respected of coaches, even though his best team was involved in a point-shaving scandal. He was also a strange man—stodgy, aloof, slow to change his ways, often given to talking in platitudes.

Nat Holman cut an impressive figure—slim (5 feet 11 inches, 165 pounds) and distinguished-looking, with his hair slicked back, his shoes freshly shined and his voice deep and rich. He starred in four sports in high school and attended the Savage School of Physical Education, a two-year college in New York. Then, turning down a chance to pitch for the Cincinnati Reds, he started playing pro basketball for $5 a game.

He was the star of the Original Celtics, who from 1920 to 1928 won 720 of 795 games. "It was a great thrill playing in those games," he recalled. "With no backboard, we felt humiliated if we took a shot without getting in close, where we had a real chance to score. It required special skills that no other kind of game developed."

Joe Lapchick, a teammate and later a rival coach, said Holman was the brains of the Original Celtics. Zander Hollander wrote, "He improvised all sorts of individual moves that eventually became the foundation for 'New York basketball,' recognized the country over as connoting guile and finesse." Celtics games were a kind of clinic for college coaches who flocked to observe Holman's technique.

He coached at City College of New York for 37 seasons between 1920 and 1960. The tuition-free school had high entrance requirements and successful teams (his coaching record was 422–188). His best team won both the NCAA and National Invitation Tournament titles in 1950, but a year later it was disclosed that all five starters on the team had accepted bribes from gamblers to control the winning margin of games. Holman was crushed and compared the disclosure to a death in the family.

He was a man of conviction. Red Holzman, later coach of the New York Knickerbockers, was once his star player at City College. They did not get along, and he said he would be happy when Holzman had graduated. "But you wouldn't win without

him," said a fellow coach. "That wouldn't matter," he replied. "There's a right way and a wrong way to play this game, and I insist my way is right."

Hoppe, William Frederick
(1887–1959)

Willie Hoppe (pronounced "Hop-ee") was the finest all-round billiards player of all time. For 49 years—from 1904 to 1952—he ruled over billiards in a reign unparalleled in sports. He was a world champion in 18.1 balkline, 18.2 balkline and three-cushion billiards.

At the age of six, sitting on the edge of a billiards table in his father's barbershop in Cornwall-on-Hudson, New York, he was defeating adults. At ten he dropped out of fourth grade to tour, and at 13, playing straight billiards, he ran 2,000 points in a row. He won the first of his 51 world championships when he was 16 and his last at age 65. Then he retired.

He was a quiet, unassuming, courteous man, a sportsman and a gentleman. He was somewhat chunky and wore his hair plastered and parted down the middle. He took care of himself and his game, practicing four to five hours a day and sleeping nine or ten hours a night. He shunned reading and movies to protect his eyes.

In 59 years of competition he spent more than 100,000 hours at billiard tables, and his enthusiasm sometimes wavered. "I'll admit I've had my moments when I felt fed up," he said. "When that happened, I just forced myself to keep going. I like to win today as much as I did nearly 40 years ago."

People spoke of him in terms usually reserved for ballet dancers. A *New York Times* editorial cited his "delicate skill of wrist and arm." P. Hal Sims, a bridge and billiards expert, called his coordination "the greatest I have ever seen." Joe King was struck by his finesse. "He was not the overpowering slugger of his sport," King wrote. "He was the classicist, the artist. . . . His personality, his reputation, his impeccable play, his skill and gameness laid a shimmering fear on the table, but his nerves were never there. His rivals tried to beat him; he tried to beat the game."

Hoppe agreed, saying, "I never made a shot that I'm not positive I won't complete. Some of the star players step up to the table and wonder if they can make the shot. I never do. Maybe I'll decide on the wrong one. Maybe I'll miss, but I'm always sure I can make it."

Hornsby, Rogers (1896–1963)

''He was the greatest right-handed hitter who ever lived,'' said *Sport* magazine. ''And he knew it.''

Rogers Hornsby, baseball player and manager, was not a pleasant man. He was proud, aloof, tactless, outspoken, profane and sour. His players hated him because they could never satisfy him. Club owners and general managers hated him because he insulted and ignored them.

His playing record was spectacular. He was a second baseman who played 23 major-league seasons (1915–37), the first 12 for the St. Louis Cardinals. When the Cardinals won the 1926 World Series he demanded a three-year contract at $50,000 a year. The Cardinals offered $50,000 for one year or $40,000 a year for three years. When he refused both offers the Cardinals traded him to the New York Giants for Frankie Frisch, and their fans were furious.

In 2,259 games he compiled a lifetime batting average of .358, second only to Ty Cobb's .367. From 1921 to 1925 he batted .397, .401, .384, .424 (still the modern major-league season record) and .403. He led his league twice in home runs, seven times in batting and seven times in total bases. In 1942 he was voted into the Baseball Hall of Fame.

He was a loner who did not smoke or drink. His only vice was betting on horses. He avoided movies and reading to preserve his eyes. Miller Huggins, his first major-league manager, said, ''I don't know any more about him than the players do. I know this much, though. He'll show up every day in shape to play, which is more than I can say for some of the others.''

Between 1925 and 1953 he spent 13 years managing five clubs but winning only one pennant. As Frank Graham wrote of those days, ''To the Rajah, baseball was a battle won by the fittest. He was baffled by the resentment aroused in some of his players by his lack of warmth toward them.'' George Sisler, a contemporary player, did not resent that quality, saying, ''I liked the fact that you always knew where you stood with him.''

Hornsby insisted he was running a ball club and not conducting a popularity contest. ''I don't care what they think of me, just as long as they play ball for me the best they can. . . . They've written plenty of things about me, about how hard-boiled I am. Why, I'm the easiest guy to work for, if you give 100 percent. . . . You can't be independent and still keep a job as a major-league manager. But you can't keep the job long anyway, unless you own the club.''

He gave 100 percent and expected it of others. ''I live and sleep baseball,'' he said. ''I don't care about anything else, and I never did.''

Howe, Gordon (1928–)

As a youngster in Saskatchewan, he played hockey in 50-degree-below-zero temperatures. It paid off. At age 18 he reached the National Hockey League as a right wing for the Detroit Red Wings. When he retired because of an arthritic left wrist 25 years later, he held NHL records for seasons played, career games (1,687), goals (786), assists (1,023) and points (1,809). He won six scoring titles and six most-valuable-player awards, and he made the all-star team an unprecedented 21 times.

The Red Wings made him a vice-president but gave him little to do. He became bored, and when the World Hockey Association was formed, he and two sons, Mark and Marty, signed with the Houston Aeros. ''If I failed badly,'' he said, ''people would remember me more for trying to make a stupid comeback at 45 than for all the other things I did in hockey.''

He hardly failed. He led Houston to the WHA 1973–74 title, and he was voted the WHA's most valuable player. Mark was voted rookie of the year, and his proud father said, ''Having the boys with me

Superstars Bobby Hull (left) and Howe autograph sticks after the 1970 NHL all-star game.

is the best part.'' His wife, Colleen, said that the question had become ''Can Gordie Howe play with his grandsons, not just his sons?''

He is a solid 6 feet, 205 pounds, with a long size-17 neck, sloping shoulders and long arms. He was once shy and is still modest, but on the ice he is strong, tough and aggressive. His elbows have made the acquaintance of every opponent. His eyes blink from an injury suffered years ago. He has taken 300 stitches to close wounds. He recalled one good year when he had fewer than five stitches.

Jean Beliveau was a teammate of the great Maurice Richard, but he called Howe ''the best hockey player I have ever seen.'' Richard himself said Howe was a better all-round player. Bobby Hull said, ''I'd like to be half as good as Gordie.'' Bobby Orr and King Clancy used the same words in calling him ''the greatest player ever.''

He started with the Red Wings for $2,500 a year. At the end of his career with Detroit he earned $100,000 a year and more at Houston. He had come a long way to his $225,000 home in Houston and his investments in cattle, banks and apartment complexes. He remembered that during the first ten years of his marriage he needed a summer job to get by.

While son Mark (left rear) watches, Gordie Howe, the Houston Aeros' 45-year-old star, goes for the puck in a 1973 game.

Huff, Robert Lee (1934–   )

A 30-minute television show made Sam Huff and his job famous. The show was a 1959 documentary called "The Violent World of Sam Huff." The New York Giants linebacker was wired for sound, and for the first time the true sounds of pro football were heard by the public.

"Perhaps more than anything else," wrote Dave Anderson, "the voice of Sam Huff on this show made many fans aware of defense for the first time and particularly aware of the position of middle linebacker." Huff made $500 from the show, but it gave tremendous exposure to him and defensive football. "But it gave me some bad times, too," he recalled. "I got tagged by outsiders as a dirty player."

He was a 6-foot-1-inch 235-pounder, warm and friendly off the field but ferocious on it. He played for the Giants (1956–63) and Washington Redskins (1964–67 and 1969) and made all-pro two times. His duels with Jim Brown of the Cleveland Browns were classics. "Brown was such a great sport, such a nice guy, it was hard to play against him," Huff said. "I'd hit him my best shot and he'd say, 'Nice tackle, Big Sam,' and I'd think what a nice guy he is, and the next play he'd come flying."

Gene Ward wrote, "He isn't really dirty, just a bit mean at the edges. And he tends to overdramatize, like the villain in a wrestling show." Jack Newcombe wrote, "He has been one of the league's most virulent and emphatic tacklers." *Sport* magazine said, "He stands out as a symbol of pro football fury." William N. Wallace called him "the game's first identifiable defensive hero." Harland Svare said, "He plays every game. Not many guys can say that."

Sam Huff (his father coined the nickname) played tackle for West Virginia University but was overshadowed by the other tackle, Bruce Bosley. No one overshadowed him as a pro. "Football is rough," he said. "You have to hit the ball carriers hard. If you don't, they'll run right by you. . . . I play rough, but there is a difference between rough and dirty." Gene Ward agreed. "He isn't really dirty, just a bit mean at the edges."

Sam Huff of the Washington Redskins in 1969, his final season.

Huggins, Miller James (1880–1929)

Miller Huggins was a little man in a big man's world, a 5-foot-4-inch, 146-pound giant who became a major-league baseball player and an outstanding manager.

He was a lawyer before he turned to baseball. Playing second base from 1904 to 1916 for the Cincinnati Reds and St. Louis Cardinals, he was a distinguished fielder and leadoff man. He batted .265 but had little power. He managed the Cardinals, who were perennial losers, from 1913 to 1917 and the New York Yankees from 1918 to 1929.

He came to the Yankees at an opportune time. In 1920 the Yankees bought Babe Ruth from the Boston Red Sox, and under Huggins the Bronx Bombers won American League pennants in 1921, 1922 and 1923. They won three in a row again from 1926 to 1928. Years later Huggins was voted into the Baseball Hall of Fame.

Ruth was his greatest joy and his greatest problem. The Babe was a drinker and carouser, and like several teammates he was an independent soul who wanted no interference from a manager. Huggins and Ruth had many run-ins. Once, standing chin to chin, Ruth hollered at his manager, "I just wish you were 50 pounds heavier." Huggins hollered back, "It's lucky for you I'm not."

The Yankee manager with his star slugger, Babe Ruth, at spring training in 1929.

During the 1925 season Ruth's dissipations were affecting his hitting and fielding. But whenever Huggins was about to crack down, Ruth would hit one or two home runs and Huggins would ask, "How can I fine a guy like that?" Finally, in August, during a trip to St. Louis, Ruth failed to return to the hotel three nights in a row. Huggins fined him $5,000 and sent him back to New York with an indefinite suspension. Ruth was furious and threatened to quit but later apologized and tried to behave. As Arthur Daley wrote, "Huggins was the first to chop rambunctious Babe Ruth down to size."

When Westbrook Pegler wrote during the 1926 season, "The Yankees are a collection of individuals who are convinced their manager is a sap," Huggins pinned the story on the dressing-room bulletin board. The Yankees won the pennant that year and the next two years, and the 1927 Yankees were probably the best team in baseball history.

On September 20, 1929, Huggins walked into the ball park with an ugly red blotch under his left eye. He had a spreading infection of the skin called erysipelas, and he died five days later. Ruth wept at the funeral.

Huggins with Connie Mack, manager of the Philadelphia Athletics, in 1927.

Hull and Ralph Backstrom (14) do battle during a WHA contest between the Winnipeg Jets and Chicago Cougars.

Hull, Robert Marvin (1939–)

In his younger days he was the most exciting player in hockey. He was also the fastest (he was timed on skates at 29.7 miles per hour), and he packed the hardest, fastest shot in the game (clocked at 118.3 mph).

Rival goalies feared him. ''Even if you stop the shot, you are apt to get a bruise,'' said Gerry Desjardins. ''He's the only player I've ever faced who shot the puck so hard from the blue line that I actually lost sight of it,'' Doug Favell said. ''I mean I never saw the puck at all.'' (The blue line is 60 feet from the goal.)

He is solid and rugged, 5 feet 10 inches and 195 pounds, with a big chest and big biceps. His blond hair inspired the nickname of Golden Jet, but it is thin now despite hair transplants.

From 1957 to 1972 he played left wing for the Chicago Black Hawks. He scored 50 or more goals in five of his 15 seasons, a National Hockey League record at the time. In all he scored 604 goals in 1,036

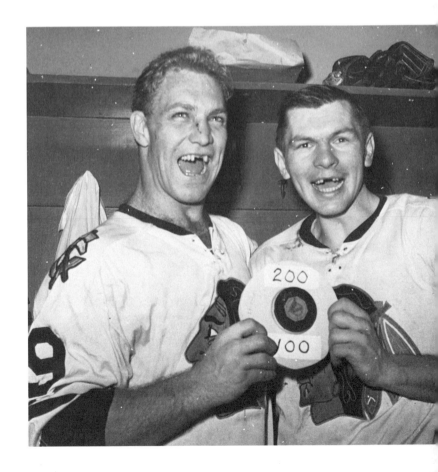

Hull (left) and Stan Mikita display their smiles.

games and might have broken Gordie Howe's lifetime mark of 786 goals had he stayed in the NHL. But the records didn't mean that much to him. "I just enjoy scoring goals," he said. "That's what I play hockey for—to score, for the kick out of scoring goals."

He became unhappy at Chicago because of annual salary fights and because he was being forced to play controlled rather than free-wheeling hockey. In 1973 he signed with the Winnipeg Jets of the new World Hockey Association for a $1 million advance against royalties, $250,000 a year for five years as player-coach and $100,000 a year for the next five years as coach or executive. The huge contract set off a bidding war between the leagues that sent salaries soaring for all players. "In a way it's sad," he said. "I spent 15 years in the NHL, and now I get my reward in another league."

Hutson, Donald Montgomery
(1913–   )

He was perhaps the finest end football has known—the most dangerous on offense and the best pass receiver in the history of the game. As Myron Cope wrote, "His agility and deft hands elevated pass catching to an art that nobody prior to his time had thought possible." John D. McCallum wrote, "He was almost beautiful in his faking . . . and the ease with which he gathered in the ball."

He was the first to perfect the fake in pass receiving. His coach, Curly Lambeau, recalled, "He would glide downfield, leaning forward as if to steady himself close to the ground. Then, as suddenly as you gulp or blink an eye, he'd feint one way and go the other, reach up like a dancer, gracefully squeeze the ball and leave the scene of the accident." Luke Johnsos, an opposing coach, said he was difficult to defend against because "half the time he didn't know himself where he was going."

He wore tiny shoulder pads and no hip pads, and he was willowy and swift at 6 feet 1 inch and 185 pounds. He was an All-American at the University of Alabama (1932–34), where the other end was Paul (Bear) Bryant. He played offensive end and defensive safety for the Green Bay Packers for 11 seasons (1935–45) and was all-pro nine seasons and the National Football League's most valuable player twice. He led the league eight years in receiving, eight in touchdowns and five in scoring and set an NFL record by catching passes in 95 consecutive games.

He started with the Packers at $175 a game (while most regulars earned $100), and his first reception was an 83-yard touchdown pass. In his final year he earned $15,000. He was a charter member of the College (1951) and Pro Football (1963) Halls of Fame.

He was so cool and quiet that his wife said, "The day we were married, he was so calm that you'd think he'd merely stepped into the church to get out of the rain." His mother said, "He wouldn't say two words in an A-bomb attack. He doesn't talk unless he has something to say." Hutson admitted he lacked color. "I was never very emotional about football," he said, "but I loved the game just the same."

The First 50 Years, the Story of the National Football League summarized Hutson's contribution to football: "During the age of ponderous and abrasive ground attacks, he brought the art of receiving to its full flower, striding through opponents with a swiftness and grace that changed the game. . . . He made it look easy."

Hutson (right) and teammate Dixie Howell, members of Alabama's 1935 Rose Bowl team, receive All-America certificates from Christy Walsh.

160

Iba, Henry Payne (1904–   )

He is Henry to his friends, Hank to the public, Mr. Iba to his players. He is a tall, stately, serious man, a highly successful basketball coach with a deliberate style of play that won games but in later years prompted criticism that he had fallen behind the times.

He was always in charge. He ran disciplined practices, saying, "I don't see any reason a basketball practice floor should be any different from a classroom. If you want to have a picnic, you should be somewhere else."

He coached four years at Maryville College in Missouri (1929–33), one at Colorado (1933–34) and 36 at Oklahoma State (1934–70). His teams produced a 767–338 won-lost record, two NCAA championships and 15 conference titles. He coached U.S. Olympic teams to gold medals in 1964 and 1968, but his strategy in the 1972 final with the Soviet Union ended in a controversial defeat.

After that final Coach Lefty Driesell of Maryland said, "The game we played is not representative of American basketball. We don't play that slowdown game anymore. Our game is fast break." Another coach said, "His coaching is anachronistic. . . . In recent years, he struck me as something of a reactionary in his concept of basketball. . . . Olympic players were prisoners of his methodical style and were hardly given a chance to express their individual abilities."

Robert L. Mendell described his philosophy as "Shoot only when necessary." Of the slowdown technique, Tom C. Brody wrote, "He invented it, polished it and displayed it . . . and a lot of teams have been playing it." "There isn't a pro coach in the business who wouldn't like to coach that style," Joe Lapchick said, "but who'd come out to watch it?"

Zander Hollander wrote that Iba's teams shot "only when there was nothing else to do with the ball." But Bob Burnes wrote that it was a misleading idea that his teams "stall with the ball, hold it and dare the other team to take it away. His players are constantly on the move and so is the ball."

Iba said he wasn't against shooting. "I'm against bad shooting," he said. "Our chief contention is that airtight defense will get you there more often than a high-geared offense. . . . I was taught that you should never let a boy get beaten badly, and that's why we use the system we do. . . . I want my boys to shoot. But glory be, make it a good shot."

Coach Iba instructs his Oklahoma Aggie basketball team from the bench.

Jackson, Joseph Jefferson (1887–1951)

Shoeless Joe Jackson was a superior baseball player. Ty Cobb called him "the finest natural hitter of all time." His .356 lifetime average was surpassed only by Cobb and Rogers Hornsby, and his batting stance was so good that Babe Ruth said he copied it.

From 1908 to 1920 he played outfield for the Philadelphia Athletics, Cleveland Naps and Chicago White Sox. His nickname originated in the minor leagues, when he played one game in stockings because his new shoes caused blisters. He could not read or write, and in later years he said he was amused that "all the big sports writers seemed to enjoy writing about me as an ignorant cotton-mill boy with nothing but lint where my brain ought to be."

After the 1920 season he and seven White Sox teammates were arrested and charged with accepting money to throw the 1919 World Series to the Cincinnati Reds (Cincinnati won the series, five games to three). Jackson, who was earning $4,500 a year, supposedly was promised $20,000 by gamblers but received only $5,000. The eight players were banned from baseball for life, though none was convicted in court (Jackson was acquitted in 1921).

His involvement in the Black Sox scandal cost him his otherwise assured place in the Baseball Hall of Fame. He never sought reinstatement and never asked to have his name cleared, though years after the scandal he insisted he knew nothing about it. "I played my heart out. . . . I made 13 hits, but they took one away from me. I handled 30 balls in the outfield and never made an error or allowed a man to take an extra base. I threw out five men at home." Official records show that he had only one assist.

Grantland Rice wrote after the infamous affair, "He sold out to thieving gamblers, who double-crossed him for peanuts. . . . He was dumb, ignorant and, in this case, crooked. But he was never crooked at heart." Arthur Daley later wrote, "It's pretty well agreed that he had been inveigled into the conspiracy."

Later, Jackson said, "Sure, I heard talk that there was something going on. I even had a fellow come to me one day and proposition me. . . . I started for him, but he ran out the door and I never saw him again. . . . I haven't been resentful at all. If baseball didn't care enough to see me get a square deal, then I wouldn't go out of my way to get back into it."

Ty Cobb recalled that he once was driving through Greenville, North Carolina, and knew that Jackson lived there. He found him working in a state liquor store. "He gave no sign of knowing me," Cobb remembered. "Finally, I said, 'Joe, can't you remember me? I'm Ty Cobb, your old friend.' 'Yes, I know, Ty,' he said. . . . I said, 'Why didn't you speak to me, come up and shake hands? I came by just to see you.' He said, 'I wasn't sure that you would speak to me. A lot of them haven't.' "

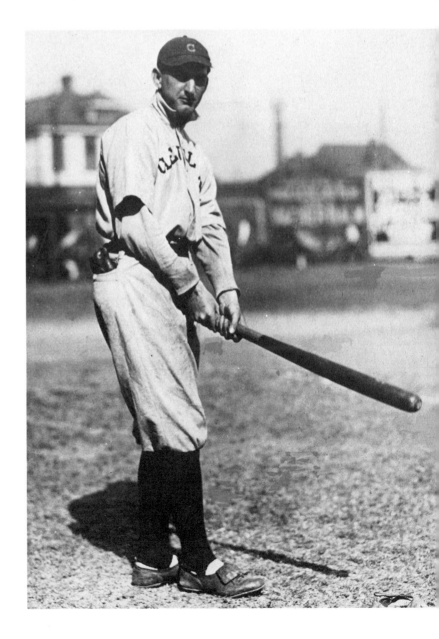

Jackson, Reginald Martinez
(1946–   )

Reggie Jackson jumps above the right-field fence to prevent a home run in a 1971 game against the California Angels.

He is a controversial figure, complex and unpredictable. He can be glib and charming, witty and spirited, or he can be sullen, evasive and quarrelsome. Roy Blount, Jr., wrote, ''He has the eagerly concerned, unsettled, open-eyed look of a man who will never be cynical, boring or fully aware of how he affects people.''

He has made his share of enemies. Stan Bahnsen, a rival pitcher, called him a prima donna. Dick Allen, the first baseman, said, ''Since he has never hit .300, I wonder how he can do all that talking.'' Bill North, a teammate with whom he had a locker-room fist fight, said Jackson was probably the most insecure person he knew. ''The more success he gets, the more insecure he gets, because he doesn't know how to accept his success. He's a very confused young man,'' said North.

He is one of four sons of Martinez Jackson, who owns the Jack the Tailor shop in Philadelphia. He has two older brothers—one a physician, the other a graduate of Harvard Law School. In 1966, after his sophomore year at Arizona State, he signed with the A's (then in Kansas City) for an $85,000 bonus and a new car. Later, between seasons, he returned to Arizona State and earned a degree in architecture.

When he talks about baseball he speaks of an exhilarating freedom. ''I'm in a cage now. I like to be left alone by people snatching at me, grabbing at me. . . . When I get that bat in my hands, people are paying attention. I'm alone then. I'm out of my cage. I'm free to move, to run, to go. I'm like an animal running through the woods.''

Almost from the day he broke into major-league baseball he has been a superstar, a left-handed-hitting outfielder with power and a perennial leader in home runs, runs scored, runs batted in and, less glowingly, in strikeouts (''I still need to learn the strike zone,'' he said).

Reggie Jackson has been an outspoken personality on the Oakland A's, generous, egotistical, emotional, confident, eager for recognition as a leader. Between his baseball salary and an investment company he co-owns, he earns more than a quarter-million dollars a year. He has an impressive physique (17-inch biceps, 27-inch thighs) and an impressive life-style—four cars and, a rarity for a bachelor, a $1.8 million life-insurance policy.

Jackson, Russell Stanley
(1936–   )

He played quarterback for the Ottawa Rough Riders of the Canadian Football League from 1958 to 1969 and was the best native Canadian in Canadian football. He won the Schenley Award as the CFL's most valuable player in 1963, 1966 and 1969, the first Canadian-born player to win that honor even once.

Russ Jackson was strong, muscular and durable at 6 feet and 195 pounds. He was also an intelligent man and a smart quarterback who could roll out and throw long, accurate passes. Gordon Walker, a CFL executive, said, "He is virtually a coach on the field."

He was virtually a one-man offense as well. He completed 1,326 of 2,530 passes for 24,593 yards and 185 touchdowns and ran 738 times for 5,045 yards and 54 touchdowns. When he retired he had played 195 consecutive games. "They were the great 12 years of my life," he said. "The challenge of playing quarterback was important, the idea of putting yourself against a defense. Something inside me insisted that I have such a chance. I had to perform and produce."

He graduated from McMaster University in Hamilton, Ontario, where he studied statistical mathematics. McMaster wanted to nominate him for a Rhodes Scholarship, but, as he said, "My whole life was built around sport and I wanted the opportunity to play professional football."

He got the opportunity and $4,500 a year to start. He finished at $40,000 plus bonus money. He then served as principal at two Ottawa high schools and color analyst for Canadian professional games on television. In 1975 he returned to Canadian football as head coach of the Toronto Argonauts. When he was offered a five-year contract at a salary estimated at $75,000 to $85,000 a year, his first reaction was "Why did they want me?"

Jack Gaudaur, the CFL commissioner, had an answer—pride. "He is native-born," said Gaudaur. "He didn't have high-school coaching and that good college training you get in the United States. The quarterback is paid the most money, and he gets credit when you win and abuse when you lose. But in his case, win or lose, I sense a certain pride because he is a Canadian who became such a great star in Canadian football."

Russ Jackson, the Ottawa quarterback, in action against the Toronto Argonauts in 1967.

Jacobs holds up a trophy after saddling his 3,000th winner on April 1, 1960.

Jacobs, Hirsch (1904–1970)

In 43 years as a trainer of thoroughbred horses Hirsch Jacobs saddled 3,569 winners, far more than any other trainer. "Forever is about the longest word there is," Bill Corum wrote, "but one is tempted to say that his record will stand forever."

While most other leading trainers worked with the best horses, he worked with some of the worst. Steve Cady wrote that horses that wouldn't run for anybody else ran and won for him. Howard Tuckner described his success this way: "He will buy an ugly colt that no one wants, ply it with mud, clay, Epsom salts, vinegar, compresses, aspirin, ice water and Dr. Spock-type psychology and watch it pay for its own oats."

He built a fortune on cheap, lame horses the rich didn't want. His most celebrated success was Stymie, a runty colt he claimed from King Ranch for $1,500. Stymie earned $918,485, a record at the time, and his earnings paid for Jacobs' 282-acre

breeding farm in Maryland.

He was a stocky, gentle man with a red face and red hair. He did not smoke or drink. He was born in New York City, one of ten children of an immigrant tailor. His first interest was pigeon racing, and he made enough money at it to quit his job as an assistant steamfitter and start training horses. The betting public loved him, wrote Joe Hirsch, because "He came from the people, and they identified with him. . . . He was a genius."

"You just got to use common sense and know when a horse feels like running," he once said. "They're like babies. You got to baby them and humor them, kid them along. . . . I don't feel good every morning, so why should a horse?"

For years, racing people have debated the relative importance of jockey and horse. "The horse is more important than the jockey," he said. "If I got the best horse, I'll take the third-best jockey."

Jeffries, James Jackson
(1875–1953)

James J. Jeffries had the look of an unbeatable heavyweight champion, and he was almost that. He

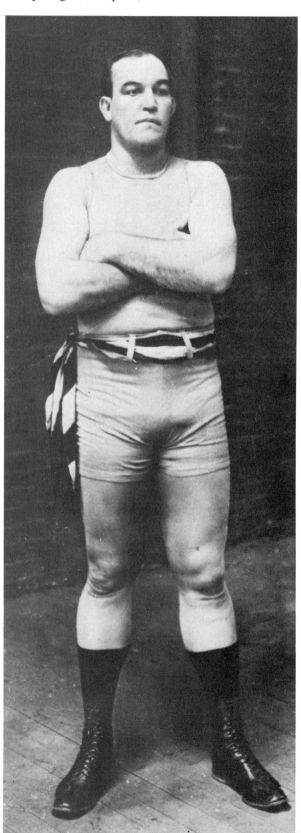

was a big man, 6 feet 2 inches and 220 pounds, with a 50-inch chest and a 31-inch waist. He was a workhorse in training, strong, powerful and willing, and when he fought in a crouch he was nearly impossible to hit.

Rex Lardner described him as "a muscular giant with arms like oak trees, a body rippling with sinew, a forest of hair on his chest and legs like the pillars of the Temple of Zeus." Lewis Burton wrote, "He was as great a natural athlete as ever lived—perhaps the greatest. . . . He earned the awe of his generation." His strength prompted James J. Corbett, an earlier champion, to say, "Nobody can ever hurt him, not even with an ax." He was Jack Dempsey's idol, and Dempsey used his crouch position.

He started fighting in 1896 and three years later unexpectedly knocked out Bob Fitzsimmons in 11 rounds to become heavyweight champion. From 1899 to 1904 he defended once a year. Lacking opposition and tired of training, he retired from boxing in 1905. Once he gave up the title he quickly ballooned to 320 pounds.

In 1910 he was talked into fighting Jack Johnson, who had become the first black heavyweight champion. Jeffries became the Great White Hope, and Jack London wrote, "Jeffries must now emerge from his alfalfa farm and remove the golden smile from Jack Johnson's face." The hope ended when Johnson knocked him out in 15 rounds in the only loss of Jeffries' career.

"His head and heart were right, but his hands and feet were not," Frank Gotch, the wrestling champion, said of that bout. *The New York Times* reported that friends said he aged ten years after that defeat, and he felt he had betrayed the white race. He earned $192,000 from the fight but later said the beating was not worth it.

Speaking of his days as Corbett's sparring partner, he said, "I gained $250 for four weeks' work and about $1 million worth of experience." He said he could beat Fitzsimmons every day of the week but said he hit too hard. "You give me headaches," he once told Fitzsimmons. Of his second fight with Tom Sharkey, he said, "It was the greatest combat ever waged in a ring between two human beings."

Johnson, John Arthur (1878–1946)

Jack Johnson was a great fighter who deserves fame for his boxing alone. But he is best remembered for his singular contribution to sports history: He was the first black heavyweight champion of the world (the second was Joe Louis).

He was a flamboyant, arrogant character and an irritant to white America. He knocked out Tommy Burns in 14 rounds in 1908 to win the heavyweight crown. He made five successful defenses, breaking off all of Stanley Ketchel's front teeth at the gums in one fight and knocking out Victor McLaglen in another, a defeat that helped convince McLaglen to give up boxing for acting.

In 1915, past his prime, dissipated and 37 years old, Johnson lost his title in 26 rounds to Jess Willard in Havana. A famous photograph showed Johnson on his back, being counted out while apparently shading his eyes from the sun. The pose led to suspicions of a fix, though the fight was probably honest.

He had a weakness for flashy cars, flashy clothes and flashy women. He had twice been married to white women, and in 1913 he was convicted under the Mann Act of transporting a white woman across state lines for immoral purposes. Sentenced to a year and a day in prison, he jumped bail and fled the country. He returned in 1920 and served his time.

"Few men in any field, of any color, were so arrogant as he," Rex Lardner wrote. "Few got so much pleasure out of flouting law and custom as he." Arthur Daley wrote, "He was a happy-go-lucky child of nature who had the people of all races down on him and hating him." He was the inspiration for *The Great White Hope*, a Pulitzer Prize-winning play (and later a movie) about his title defense with James J. Jeffries. In later years he told John Lardner, "When you write about me, remember that I was a man, a good one."

He became a boxing trainer and a vaudeville actor and even made a speech on sportsmanship to the Ku Klux Klan. He was killed in an auto accident and buried in Chicago, 200 feet from the grave of Bob Fitzsimmons, an earlier heavyweight champion. At his funeral the minister delivering the eulogy said, "If we hadn't had a Jack, we wouldn't have a Joe Louis now."

Johnson, Walter Perry
(1887–1946)

Walter Johnson may have been the best and fastest pitcher baseball has known. He may also have been the most saintly. He did not drink or smoke or swear. His favorite exclamation was "Goodness gracious!" and his only vice was casino for 25 cents a game. "He must have been as kind and as even-dispositioned a man ever to pull on a big-league uniform," wrote Bob Broeg. "He was a model for the growing American boy," wrote Dan Daniel.

Walter Johnson pitched his entire 21-year major-league career with one team, the Washington Senators. When he joined them in 1907, wrote Shirley Povich, "'he was everybody's country cousin, a big, handsome, modest hick." The Senators were always near bankruptcy and always near last place, but he won 416 games, an American League record, and posted an earned-run average of 2.17. He pitched 113 shutouts and struck out 3,508, both major-league records, and he pitched 531 games, the twentieth-century major-league record. In 1936 he became one of the five original members of the Baseball Hall of Fame.

In 1908 he shut out the New York Highlanders (later the Yankees) three times in four days—on a Friday, Saturday and Monday. There was no game on Sunday because of New York's blue laws. Grantland Rice wrote of that feat, "He was faster in the third game than he was in the first." His salary that season was $2,700.

In 1912 he won 16 straight games. In 1913 he had a 36-7 record and separate winning streaks of 10, 11 and 14 games, an earned-run average of 1.14, 12 shutouts, five one-hitters and an American League record of 56 straight scoreless innings. His salary that year was up to $12,000.

His teammates called him Barney after Barney Oldfield, not because of his fastball but because he loved to drive his Stutz at the then ungodly speed of 40 miles per hour. Grantland Rice nicknamed him

the Big Train because in those days trains were the fastest means of locomotion.

His speed was legendary. "Even though you knew a fastball was coming, it didn't help," Ty Cobb said. Umpire Billy Evans recalled that "On dark days, players used to hope the game would be over before they had to face him again." Ping Bodie, an opposing player, said simply, "You can't hit what you can't see." Al Schacht, a teammate, said Johnson was always afraid of hitting somebody. "He knew that with his speed it could be fatal." The cigar salesman who recommended him to the Senators told them, "He knows where he's throwing because if he didn't there would be dead bodies strewn all over Idaho."

He threw his fastball with a sweeping sidearm motion that put no pressure on his arm. He developed a mediocre curveball, but he could have used only his fastball and still have won.

In 1920 he pitched his only no-hitter, and it would have been a perfect game except for an error by Bucky Harris. The second baseman was dejected. "Goodness gracious, Bucky," Johnson said, "forget it." Once, in another game, when Johnson allowed the first two batters in the ninth inning to reach base, his shortstop and captain, George McBride, ran to the mound and told him to bear down. Johnson threw nine consecutive strikes to strike out the side. Then he found his shortstop and said, "Goodness gracious, McBride, I guess that will teach you to mind your own darn business."

Jack Zanger wrote of his "quixotic philosophy" about baseball and life. He quoted Johnson's words: "I just try to throw as hard as I can when I think I've got to throw as hard as I can. And sometimes I guess I don't throw quite hard enough."

Johnson last pitched in 1927. He managed the Senators (1929–32) and Cleveland Indians (1933–35), and though his teams did well, he had lost his patience and even became surly. Friends attributed the change to the death of his wife in 1930. After that shock, wrote Vincent X. Flaherty, "he was the loneliest man I ever knew."

Just before World War II he watched young Bob Feller pitch. "He's mighty fast," said Johnson. "He smokes the ball, goodness gracious." But was Feller as fast as the old Johnson? Modesty and honesty clashed in his mind. Honesty won. "No," said Walter Johnson, "he isn't as fast as I was."

Jones, Benjamin Allyn
(1882–1961)

Jimmy Jones said of his father, "He's the greatest horse trainer of them all. He was 78, but he lived 150 years." As Jack Hodgins, an old-time trainer, said, "He had the ability to look through a horse and see if there was anything worthwhile. There is maybe one in 10,000, that kind of man." John Partridge, a long-time colleague, said, "He knows horses. I think he talks to them."

Ben Jones spent 47 years with thoroughbred horses. He started as an owner-breeder-trainer on the Midwestern bush circuit, racing horses for $100 purses. He trained for Woolford Farm (1932–39) and Calumet Farm (1939–47) and built the Calumet empire. In 1947 he retired as Calumet trainer to become general manager of Calumet's 1,038-acre horse farm near Lexington, Kentucky. His son Jimmy became the new Calumet trainer, prompting

the father to say, "I can train three horses better than Jimmy, but Jimmy can train 50 better than me."

Plain Ben Jones was a burly man with a firm jaw. He trained the winners of 1,519 races, and his horses won $4,852,946 in purses. He trained six Kentucky Derby winners and two triple-crown champions (Whirlaway and Citation). In the 1940s and 1950s Calumet Farm led all other owners in annual earnings 11 times. "It's like running a grocery store," he joked. "I love to hear that cash register ring."

The public recognized his genius. "He could run Dobbin, the delivery horse, in the next Kentucky Derby and several million racing fans would confidently expect Dobbin to win," Hambla Bauer wrote. Other trainers recognized it, too. "I just watched what he did with his horses and tried to copy him," Johnny Nerud said.

"When I was a boy," Jones recalled, "I was crazy about horses and Holstein cows. I couldn't decide which I liked better. When I got big enough to help with the milking, I made up my mind right away. . . . What I learned about training I learned pretty much by myself. If you didn't learn, you didn't eat." At age 75 he found himself often working with young horses. "It's really something to watch them develop into stakes winners. Next year's horses and the hopes you have for them—that's what keeps you young."

Jones, David (1938–   )

According to Gale Sayers, Deacon Jones was the "finest defensive end in the National Football League." Merlin Olsen, who played next to him on the Los Angeles Rams' Fearsome Foursome, suspected there has never been a better football player. In a poll asking players who they would least like to run into, Jones won three years in a row, ahead of such players as Dick Butkus, Tommy Nobis, Bob Lilly and Carl Eller.

He is a big man—6 feet 5 inches and 270 pounds—and, in his prime, he was strong enough to break blocks, fast enough to overtake backs and quick enough to escape blockers trying to protect a passer. He has the graceful quickness of a halfback and is a daring open-field tackler.

He is one of eight children, six of whom went to college. He spent one year at Mississippi Vocational School and three at South Carolina State, where he played offensive end and defensive tackle. Though he weighed 230 pounds, he ran 100 yards in 9.7 seconds.

He was drafted by the Los Angeles Rams on the 14th round. As Don Freeman wrote, "He was unknown, unheralded and unpolished." Harland Svare, then a Rams assistant coach, recalled that he was green but showed great promise. "He had trouble with little things, like his stance. But he was very blessed physically, and he learned. Then, in time, his experience caught up with his ability."

Jones said he made good because "If I hadn't made it in pro football, where would I have gone?" He played for the Rams from 1961 to 1971, making all-pro six straight years (1964–69). In January 1972 the Rams traded him to the San Diego Chargers. He played for the Chargers, but he was bitter about the trade. "The Rams didn't treat me like a man," he said. "I was treated like a piece of machinery." In 1974 the Chargers traded him to the Washington Redskins.

He plays intelligently and hard. "When he gets rolling, he is awesome, like a railroad train plummeting downhill," wrote Bill Libby. "You would not want to get in his way." "Think of him the way you would think of Bill Russell," wrote Arnold Hano, "essentially a defensive player, yes, but a defensive player who makes the offense go."

"Quickness is the thing," Jones said. "A man

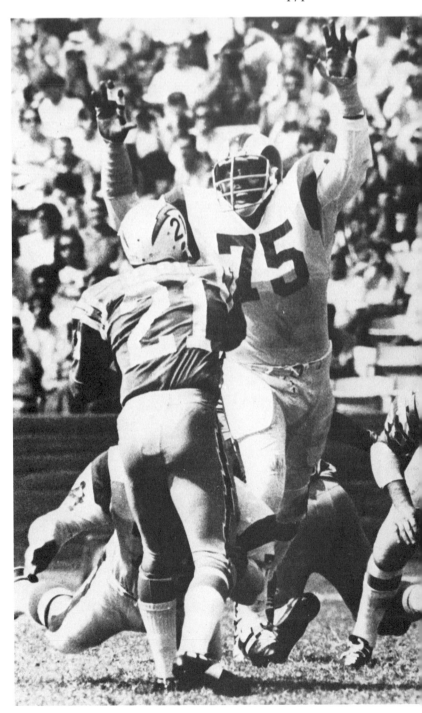

Deacon Jones puts a fierce rush on San Diego's quarterback, John Hadl.

comes at me full blast and he gets nothing but air. . . . I play for love, but mainly I play for money. There's a lot of things easier in this world than knocking heads with some guy who weighs 280 pounds."

Jones, Robert Tyre, Jr.
(1902–1971)

Bobby Jones was probably the most famous golfer of all time and probably the most successful, too. No one ever really knew how good he was because he quit the game at the age of 28, before it destroyed him.

"I loved to play golf," he said. "I played golf all the time. It wasn't the pressure of being tired of golf, but being tired of taking all that damn punishment in the tournaments. . . . Why should I punish myself over a golf tournament? Sometimes, I'd pass my mother and dad on the course, look at them and not even see them because I was so concentrated on the game. Afterward, it made a fellow feel a little silly."

Another time he described the pressures this way: "Playing around that golf course for four hours, you get so weighted down by the strain and the responsibility and the difficulty in concentrating that you just wish to goodness you could hit a careless shot—just hit the ball without thinking. And if you ever yield to that temptation, you'll always pay for it. So unless you're terribly keen to win, you just won't make yourself take that kind of punishment."

When he took the punishment he was superb. From 1923 to 1930 he won five United States Amateur titles, four U.S. Opens, three British Opens and one British Amateur. In 1930 he achieved the only grand slam in golf history by winning those four major championships (Lloyds of London had offered 50-to-1 odds against him). Then he retired from tournaments, partly because of the pressure of the game itself and partly to escape the pressure inadvertently caused by Atlanta friends who bet heavily on him whenever he played.

He was an intense man. As a youngster, he threw clubs and never won until he got his temper under control. Even as an adult he seethed inside, and he could not eat properly during a major tournament (he lived then mostly on dry toast and tea). He was brash, too. At age 18, playing Harry Vardon, the famous English pro, he dribbled a shot into a bunker, turned to Vardon in embarrassment and said, "Did you ever see a worse shot, Mr. Vardon?" "No," replied Vardon. It was the only word the Englishman spoke to Jones all day.

Off the course he was gracious, convivial and unspoiled. He was beloved in St. Andrews, Scotland, the cradle of golf. Once in 1936, when he sneaked into town to play a quiet round with friends, there were 5,000 townspeople at the first tee and 7,000 at the 18th. Years later he was made an honorary freeman of the Borough of St. Andrews, the first American so honored since Benjamin Franklin. Jones responded by saying, "I could take out of my life everything except my experiences at St. Andrews and I'd still have a rich, full life."

His rich, full life started in Atlanta, where he shot 90 for 18 holes at age ten, 80 at age 11 and 70 at age 12. He was handsome, chunky and apple-cheeked, strong enough to have ripped a pack of playing cards across the middle. Years later, however, a progressive disease of the spinal cord left him in a wheelchair. After golf he became a graduate engineer and practicing lawyer, soft-drink bottler, sporting-goods executive and a social leader in Atlanta. He was a founder of the famous Augusta (Georgia) National Golf Club and its even more famous tournament, the Masters.

British writer Bernard Darwin said of his game, "He thought it an act of incredible folly if not a positive crime to make a stroke that was not exactly as it ought to be made and as he knew he could make it." O. B. Keeler, the Atlanta writer who became his Boswell, said of the man that he had more character than any other champion in history. Another champion, Jack Nicklaus, said, "He is the only person I know, in or out of sports, who has the Churchillian quality of being larger than life and at the same time intensely human and intimate."

His close friend, Dwight D. Eisenhower, said, "Those who have been fortunate enough to know

him realize that his fame as a golfer is transcended by his inestimable qualities as a human being. . . . His gift to his friends is the warmth that comes from unselfishness, superb judgment, nobility of character, unwavering loyalty to principle."

Jones always kept his sport in perspective. "There are times when I feel that I know less about what I'm doing on a golf course than anyone else in the world. . . . Golf is like eating peanuts. You can play too much or too little. I've become reconciled to the fact that I'll never play as well as I used to. . . . First come my wife and children. Next comes my profession—the law. Finally, and never as a life in itself, comes golf."

After a four-year absence Jones returns to golf for the 1934 Masters paired with Paul Runyon (left).

Jones, Rufus Parnell (1933–   )

"No one matches him for sheer aggressiveness combined with a rare virtuosity of technique," said *Sport* magazine. Parnelli Jones was aggressive when he drove jalopies and stock cars in California in the 1950s and he is still aggressive 20 years later driving dune buggies on back-road courses in Baja California, though he has mellowed enough to say, "If I win, I win. If not, the world doesn't come to an end."

He is known as Parnelli because someone misspelled his middle name early in his career. He is a slender, baldish and tough man who chain-smokes cigarettes and chews cigars. He is, wrote Bob Ottum, "a man chiseled out of cold rock."

He drove that way, too. "When I started," he recalled, "I didn't know there was any other way to race but flat out. When I matured a little, I used to say to myself I would go out and take it easy, try to be around for a run at the finish. But as soon as the green flag fell, it was like my whole personality changed. I forgot everything and just raced like hell."

From 1961 to 1963 he won the national championship in sprint cars, one of the most grueling forms of racing. But his greatest fame came in the Indianapolis 500. In 1961 he was co-rookie of the year at Indy, and in 1962 he led until his brakes failed. He won in 1963 and finished second in 1965 when his car ran out of fuel. In 1967, driving the first Indy turbine car, he was leading when a 75-cent ball bearing failed with four laps remaining.

In spite of Jones's mechanical trouble in the 500, Rodger Ward, an Indy rival, said, "Some drivers are just right for some races and some tracks, and he is just right for the 500 at Indy. He has learned this track as few drivers have ever learned it."

He also learned to slow down. He quit the Indy circuit after the 1967 race and drove Mustangs in the Trans-Am series and an occasional stock car. He also had fun with dune buggies, but he devoted most of his time to his 17 businesses. He sold race cars and racing and street tires, he owned cars that twice won at Indy and he was president of the Ontario (California) Motor Speedway.

He was content with the life he had made for himself. "I lead a damn good life," he said. "I do anything and everything I want. If I should hurt myself badly or kill myself, I'd be all right because I had myself one old terrific time while I was at it."

Justice, Charles Ronald
(1924–   )

Charlie (Choo Choo) Justice was a college football hero at a time when one was needed—the years immediately after World War II. He was a friendly country boy from North Carolina who played tailback for the University of North Carolina from 1946 to 1949. He rushed for almost three miles, scored 39 touchdowns and passed for 25 and made All-America as a junior and senior. But more than a football player, he was a celebrity.

A song about him, "All the Way Choo Choo," sold 32,000 records in North Carolina. A Greensboro store sold 900 "Choo Choo Justice" T-shirts in an hour. Hundreds of babies were named for him. His mail was addressed "Choo Choo, N.C." In 1949, when a small-town high school in North Carolina asked its graduating class of 69 "Who was, or is, the greatest of all Americans?" five named Franklin D. Roosevelt, four General Dwight D. Eisenhower, two General Robert E. Lee and the other 58 named Choo Choo Justice. After his graduation the university's sports information director, Jack Williams, reported, "Everyone was in a state of mourning."

Speaking of his popularity, Orville Campbell, a friend, said, "He came along at a time when every little kid wanted to grow up to be somebody else, a

Choo Choo Justice gaining yardage against Rice University in the 1950 Cotton Bowl game.

football hero or even President. . . . Nobody captured the imagination of the American public the way he captured the imagination of the people of North Carolina." Kay Kyser, the band leader and a North Carolina native, said, "When they recruited him to play here, after his great football career in the Navy, it was a little like getting Clark Gable to appear in a local little-theater production. He was a star even before he got here. But he was just the opposite of a prima donna. It never got to him."

He played pro football for the Washington Redskins from 1950 to 1954 (except 1951), but injuries and his small size (5 feet 10 inches, 165 pounds) worked against him. He became a successful insurance man in North Carolina, and in 1961 he was voted into the College Football Hall of Fame.

"I just loved it all," he said of his college years. "I loved Carolina, the people here, and I loved football. . . . What I was was a football player, and that's all I ever wanted to be. I didn't even mind practice. Heck, I would have stayed out there all night if they'd let me."

Kahanamoku, Duke Paoa
(1890–1968)

Kahanamoku with Harold Lloyd, the movie comedian.

He was a sheriff and a stereotyped actor, but his fame rested on his swimming. He introduced techniques to the sport and dominated it for more than a decade.

Duke Kahanamoku was tall, strong and striking. He was supposedly of royal Hawaiian lineage. He won the 100-meter free-style in the 1912 Olympics, repeated the feat in 1920 (on his 30th birthday) and was second to 19-year-old Johnny Weissmuller in 1924. In 1932 he qualified as an alternate on the U.S. Olympic water-polo team after failing to make the Olympic swimming team. He was still swimming in competition when some of his contemporaries were grandfathers.

In 1911 he became the first swimmer to better one minute for the 100-yard free-style (his time was 56.0 seconds, and he later did 53.0). He set four world records at 100 yards and three at 100 meters. He pioneered the flutter kick (eight kicks to two arm strokes), which revolutionized swimming, and he introduced the surfboard to the mainland. Pat Besford wrote, ''He could plane on the surface of the water as no man of his size had ever done before.'' At the age of 57 he beat youngsters in a one-and-one-quarter mile race.

By that time he was sheriff of Honolulu. He served 13 terms without opposition and without arrests. His jet-black hair turned to snowy white, but until his final years he was erect and impressive. He played volleyball, swam and sailed almost daily. *The New York Times* called him ''Hawaii's best-known citizen.''

For years he appeared in movies. ''I played chiefs—Polynesian chiefs, Aztec chiefs, Indian chiefs, all kinds of chiefs,'' he said. Jim Murray wrote, ''Weissmuller got the girl, Duke got the horse.''

He was always easygoing, in and out of the water. ''We didn't train too vigorously in those early days,'' he recalled. ''I myself used what I call natural methods. I swam as far as I felt like and quit. . . . Stroking styles won't change, but sooner or later a stronger and better-trained boy will come along and rewrite the record book.''

Duke Kahanamoku at the 1920 Olympics.

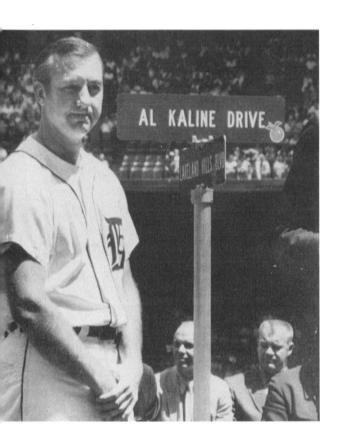

Kaline, Albert William
(1934–   )

In 1953 he graduated from a Baltimore high school, signed a $30,000 bonus-salary contract with the Detroit Tigers and became a major-league baseball player at age 18. Two years later he won the American League batting crown with a .340 average.

That was the making and unmaking of Al Kaline. Though he played 22 years, mostly in the outfield, and became the 12th major-leaguer to reach 3,000 lifetime hits, he never seemed to satisfy critics, including himself. Whatever he achieved was not enough. As Milton Gross wrote, "He is remembered for the heights he has never scaled."

The problem was that his sensational start created lofty expectations. "Fans think that anybody who wins the batting title at 20 should win it again four or five times," Jack Olsen wrote. "Kaline hasn't. Therefore, something must be wrong with him." "The worst thing that happened to me," Kaline said, "was the start I had. . . . Everybody said this guy's another Ty Cobb, another Joe DiMaggio. How much pressure can you take?"

Kaline honored at Tiger Stadium in 1970 after 18 years with Detroit.

He withstood considerable pressure and handled it by playing hard. Harold Rosenthal wrote, "He plays right field daily as though it was his last game as a college senior and his best girl was watching." Joe Falls said he had "an intense, almost fanatical desire to be the best player in baseball."

If he was not the best of his day, he was close to it. He was proficient at bat and in the field and could throw and run. He always kept in condition, and his lifetime batting average hovered around .300. He was clean-cut, steady but unspectacular, unassuming and taciturn. When the Tigers offered him a $100,000 contract for 1971, he declined, saying he didn't have a good enough season the year before. The next year, after a .294 season, he took the $100,000.

He was also modest. Once, after he had met Arnold Palmer at a golf tournament, he kept repeating on the way home, "Imagine that! I met Arnold Palmer today." His companion said, "Listen, Al, stop downrating yourself. What do you think Palmer's going to tell his kids? He's going to tell them he met Al Kaline today."

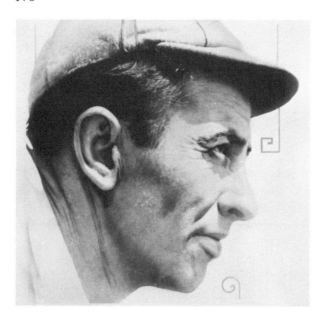

Keeler, William Henry
(1872–1923)

Willie Keeler is best remembered for saying, "I hit 'em where they ain't." According to another version, the full quote was "The way to hit is to keep your eye clear and hit 'em where they ain't." Another version of the Keeler legend claims he said neither.

He could have said anything about hitting and people would have listened. For in 19 seasons (1892–1910) as an outfielder with New York, Brooklyn and Baltimore of the National League and New York of the American League, he made 2,955 hits in 2,124 games and posted a lifetime batting average of .345. In each of his first 13 full seasons he batted over .300, and he made more than 200 hits in each of his first eight. In 1939 he was voted into the Baseball Hall of Fame.

He batted safely in the first 44 games of the 1897 season, the major-league record until Joe DiMaggio's 56-game streak in 1941. Keeler finished that season with 243 hits, 63 stolen bases and a batting average of .432.

His nickname was Wee Willie, and it was deserved; he was all of 5 feet 4½ inches and 140 pounds. He had an extraordinary batting eye, and he seldom struck out. He could bunt, he could hit high hoppers and beat them out and he could get hits on speed alone. He and John McGraw, a teammate on the celebrated Baltimore Orioles, perfected the hit-and-run play.

Honus Wagner said, "He was the master of all kinds of short-distance hitting." Charles (Kid) Nichols, an old-time pitcher, said he was the smartest hitter he ever faced. Allison Danzig and Joe Reichler wrote, "He was one of the cleverest men who ever stepped to the plate." Lee Allen and Tom Meany wrote, "The balls he hit seemed to have eyes, and there was no way to set the defense for him."

In verse in the New York *Herald*, Walter Trumbull summed up this classic ballplayer: "Wee Willie Keeler, smallest of them all, but in the height of manhood, you were mountains tall."

Wee Willie Keeler preparing to bunt.

Keifer, Adolph (1918–)

Adolph Keifer was America's most famous male backstroke swimmer, tall (6 feet 4 inches), handsome, blond and charming. His parents called him Sonny, but he did not look like a Sonny. Red Smith said he was ''a Van Johnson in pastel drawers . . . the greatest backstroke swimmer who ever lived.'' Arthur Daley called him ''a backstroke artist beyond compare.''

He broke his first world record when he was 15, and for more than ten years he held every backstroke record. He won the 100-meter backstroke in the 1936 Olympics, setting Olympic records in the trials and semifinal and a world record in the final. Then he swam 31 races in 39 days, winning them all and breaking 15 records. In the 1942 AAU indoor championships he set a world record for the 150-yard backstroke and equaled his American records for 50 and 100 yards.

During World War II he worked long hours as a lieutenant in charge of the swimming program for the entire Navy and revised the training program for 11,000 Navy swimming instructors. He had not swum a race in a year—and had not lost a race in almost ten years—when he was persuaded to compete against Harold Holiday, the fastest collegian. He led until he missed the last turn, and he lost by inches. Later he beat Holiday often.

He was an outstanding teacher. ''He doesn't get in there and say 'Do as I do,' '' Coach Ed Kennedy said. ''He has a gift for teaching men who know nothing about swimming and are afraid of the water to feel at home and learn the things that may one day save their lives.''

After the war he rejected Hollywood offers and began manufacturing swimming-pool equipment. His love for the sport never wavered. Once, when asked if he was tired after swimming so many years, he asked, ''How can anyone get tired swimming?''

When his sons, Dale and Jack, were three and one, Bob Kiphuth, the Yale coach, wrote to him, ''Inasmuch as you did not attend Yale, I hope your sons will.'' They did, and they became nationally ranked swimmers, but they weren't as good as their father. ''No one was,'' said Kiphuth.

Keifer (left) and Olympic teammates training for the 1936 games in Berlin.

Keino, Hezekiah Kipchoge
(1940–   )

Kipchoge Keino (pronounced "Kay-no") of Kenya is the most successful and probably the most gifted African distance runner ever. He is a national hero, and stadiums and babies have been christened with his name. He smiles often, but he is enigmatic and governed by moods. He is a showman who often throws off his cap at the start of the last lap, an almost sure signal that he is about to conquer.

Despite his moods and his flair for the histrionic, he is a straightforward, dedicated athlete. Norman Harris wrote, "His attitude at the start mark is 'May the best man win,' he is never resentful of the man who beats him, he is not nervous before races, he runs for his country rather than himself, he runs because he enjoys running. Trite, maybe, but that is how he expresses himself. Clearly, he is not such a mystery as some of us have thought him to be." Neil Allen agreed that "He is not some magical unbeatable man from the mountains."

Kip Keino started running early. When he was ten he came upon a leopard eating a goat, and he ran away quickly. Another time he was attacked by robbers, and he darted away. He ran his first race at 13, finished fourth to older boys and clutched his prize, a piece of soap. He ran a mile in 5 minutes 49 seconds at the age of 15, and at 19 he joined the police.

In 1965 he set world records for 3,000 and 5,000 meters and won a mile in London in 3:54.2. After that mile J. L. Manning wrote, "If a Nandi tribesman can drop out of a police station 7,000 feet up Mount Kenya, run a mile 'just to get up some speed' and miss the world's most sophisticated record by only six-tenths of a second because he does not 'understand lap times and all that sort of thing,' what next will come from the Dark Continent?"

Failure to understand lap times was only one shortcoming. He ran heats faster than he ran finals; he invariably set too fast a pace; he ran a three-mile and a six-mile the same day and did other things that shocked conventional track wisdom. He succeeded because of enthusiasm, conditioning and, as Cordner Nelson wrote, "his astonishing disregard for fatigue." "I just figure to run as hard as I can as fast as I can for as long as I can," Keino said.

In the 1968 Olympics he ran six races in eight days, trouncing Jim Ryun at 1,500 meters and running second at 5,000 meters. In the 1972 Olympics he won the steeplechase despite horrible form ("I am jumping like a horse," he complained) and ran second in the 1,500.

He once said, "An athlete has to be determined, has to have self-discipline, has to enjoy his practice and enjoy his competition, with no shortcut in anything, and not become big-headed, and then the way is open. You will win in anything." And he did.

Keino (right) and a Kenyan teammate, Ben Jipcho, at the 1968 Olympics.

Kelly, Leonard Patrick
(1927–   )

Red Kelly hardly fit the public image of the rough, tough hockey player. In many respects he remained a simple farm boy from rural Canada. As William Barry Furlong wrote, ''In what is probably the toughest professional sport in the world, he displays the demeanor and disposition of a small-town bank teller. . . . He is a throwback to the days of Frank Merriwell, when a man could be clean and honest and wholesome and not be ashamed of it, to the days when virtue in an athlete was an accepted fact.''

Red Kelly, soft-spoken, warm and boyish with his flaming red hair, was the highest-scoring defenseman in hockey history, with 823 points in 20 years in the National Hockey League. Starting in 1947, he played 12½ years for the Detroit Red Wings and led them to eight NHL and four Stanley Cup titles. While at Detroit he made the first or second all-star team eight years in a row. In 1960 he was traded to the Toronto Maple Leafs. Playing at center, he led them to four Stanley Cups and won his fourth Lady Byng Trophy for sportsmanship. He retired in 1967 and coached at Los Angeles, Pittsburgh and Toronto.

He was a picture player. One observer wrote of his ''velvet passing.'' Aloysius (Tod) Sloan, a team-

Red Kelly maneuvers around Al Arbour of Chicago.

mate, said, ''The fact that you know in advance that he isn't going to knock you into the seats or try to chop your head off with his stick doesn't make him any less effective. He's so good that rough play wouldn't make any difference.''

While playing for the Maple Leafs he served two terms as a Liberal member of the Canadian Parliament. Coach Punch Imlach of the Leafs said, ''The hockey season took no weight off him, but the political campaign took seven pounds.'' Kelly's intelligence and sincerity gave him the kind of public image that career politicians strive for.

Toward the end of his playing career Kelly said, ''I'd like to stay in hockey for a while and follow Casey Stengel's example. He obviously loves baseball, but he's financially independent of it. That's what I'd like to be with hockey. . . . My attaché case has 'RK' on the side. Now that I'm in Parliament, some people think I should use 'L' for Leonard now, but what the hey. I've been Red all my life, and I'm no different now than I was before.''

Ketchel floors Jack Johnson, the heavyweight champion, in their 1909 fight.

Ketchel, Stanley (1886–1910)

To call him a pugnacious fighter is an understatement. Rex Lardner said he was probably the greatest fighter, pound for pound, who ever lived. Arthur Daley described him in action: "He blazed across the fistic firmament as no other man ever had before or has since, one vivid, blinding flash—and then extinction."

Stanley Ketchel was born in Michigan as Stanislaus Kiecal. He was a handsome man with blond hair, broad shoulders and a deep chest. He liked fast living, with a special weakness for fast cars, women and candy. His electric quality prompted Dumb Dan Morgan, a boxing manager, to say, "He had the soul of a bouncer—but a bouncer who loved his work." After a knockout by him, Philadelphia Jack O'Brien said, "He is an example of tumultuous ferocity."

His punching ferocity earned him the nickname of the Michigan Assassin. He may have fought more than 250 unrecorded pro fights. Of the 61 in the record book, he won 49, all but three by knockouts.

He gained full recognition as world middleweight champion in February 1908, lost the title to Billy Papke in September and regained it by knocking him out in November. In a 1909 fight he knocked down Jack Johnson, the heavyweight champion. Whereupon, wrote Frank Graham, "Johnson leaped to his feet and knocked him cold with a single, terrible blow." One account of that bout claims two (or possibly four) of Ketchel's teeth were found imbedded in Johnson's right glove.

He never succumbed to modesty. He once fought all comers in a Montana theater for $20 a week and recalled, "I hit 'em so hard that they used to fall over the footlights and land in the people's laps." One afternoon he sent a telegram to his father saying, "I won the fight. Stanley." That night he won the fight.

He once said he would die before he was 30. He had overestimated. He was shot by a farmhand, and Wilson Mizner, the celebrated wit who managed him, said, "All they have to do is count over him and he'll get up." Mizner was wrong. John Lardner wrote, "Stanley Ketchel was 24 years old when he was shot and killed by the common-law husband of the lady who was cooking his breakfast."

Killy, Jean-Claude (1943–   )

For four years he was the best amateur skier in the world, and after a four-year retirement he returned as the best professional skier.

Jean-Claude Killy (pronounced ''Kee-lee'') is a French matinee idol—lean and strong at 5 feet 10 inches and 170 pounds, handsome, charming, a national hero. Lloyd Garrison wrote, ''He symbolizes the resurgence of Gaullist France on the world scene.'' One observer said, ''When he has a sore throat, France gargles.''

His family owns a hotel in the Alps, and he took up skiing at the age of three. He won a ski-jump event at six and at eight he was skiing better than his instructors. At 14 he was suspended from school for cutting classes to ski, and at 16, like other French male skiers, he quit school for good.

He won the European championship in 1965, two world titles in 1966, the World Cup in 1967 and 1968 and all three Olympic gold medals in 1968. ''Years from now,'' Dan Jenkins wrote, ''when the sport is better understood and more popular, his record may be regarded with all the misty-eyed reverence accorded a Babe Ruth summer.''

His Olympic triumphs were followed by charges that he had accepted many thousands of dollars worth of gifts and cash from commercial sources. The International Ski Federation threatened to take back his Olympic medals but never did, probably because under-the-table payments were a way of life

in amateur skiing. He admitted as much, saying, ''It is impossible to practice a sport as it was practiced 40 years before. Sport without money—that is a millionaire's concept. I am the first to say that if people had not helped me with my equipment, my trips, etc., I would never have become what I am.''

From 1968 to 1972 he made a fortune from endorsements, appearances and television commercials, but he skied only for fun. In the 1973–74 season, his commercial attractiveness diminishing, he emerged from retirement and won the world professional title. ''I decided,'' he said, ''that my clients would rather see me on a mountain than in a department store in Detroit.''

He never doubted himself. ''Nothing can shake my self-confidence,'' he said. ''When you reach a certain level, you never experience the slightest anxiety. I have never known physical fear because I started at age three on difficult slopes. Skiing to me is like breathing. When there's a bad accident, I think, 'Well, that's someone else, not me.' When I hurt myself, I look for the mistake I made. There's no apprehension.''

Jean-Claude Killy winning the men's slalom at the 1967 North American Alpine Championships on Cannon Mountain, New Hampshire.

King, Billie Jean Moffitt
(1943–   )

Billie Jean Moffitt was good at all sports, especially baseball (her brother, Randy, became a major-league pitcher). She took up tennis because she could see no future for a woman baseball player. Years later, Billie Jean Moffitt King has helped guarantee a future for women's athletics.

When she was young she played in shorts. Because she could not afford a tennis skirt, she was not allowed to join other junior players for a group picture. She never forgot. Even when she had become the best woman tennis player in the world she fought for the underdog, for the little man and woman and for women's equality in and out of tennis.

"She understood perfectly what the women's movement–tennis relationship was all about," Grace Lichtenstein wrote. "She was a jock who had spent her career discovering that she was a pioneer, that no one was yet ready to delete the terms for gender from the sports vocabulary, that women would still be second-class sports champions until they fought for the right to be classed in the same league as a Joe Namath or a Wilt Chamberlain." Robert Lipsyte said she was probably the most important sports hero in the country, "far more important to the national psyche than Mickey Mantle or a Joe Namath ever was, and she picked up where Muhammad Ali, who was narrower, left off."

At 5 feet 4½ inches and 130 pounds, she is stocky and strong. She wears glasses and displays a toothy grin, unbridled enthusiasm and a willingness to talk forever. She plays a serve-and-volley game like most of the male champions. "She isn't at all feminine," Tony Kornheiser wrote.

She is obsessed with winning. Anatole Broyard described her desire to win as ranging from "what sounds like pure, stubborn self-assertion to an almost Zenlike absorption in the game itself." Virginia Wade, a contemporary player, said that her will is so strong that "it's hard for me to impose mine on hers, not to be dominated by her." Frank Hammond, a tennis referee, said, "On the court, she's an evil, merciless bastard, totally ruthless. She'll do everything and anything within the rules to win."

She has won everything worth winning. At Wimbledon she captured five singles titles in eight years

(1966–73), along with nine women's doubles and four mixed doubles. At Forest Hills she won four United States titles in eight years (1967–74). In 1973, in a much-promoted and theatrical match seen by millions on national television, she beat 55-year-old Bobby Riggs and earned $100,000 plus another $200,000 from side benefits.

In 1971 she became the first woman athlete to earn $100,000 in prize money in one year (the total was $117,000). The following year she became the first to earn $200,000 in one year (the total was $290,000). Also in 1971 she had an abortion and talked about it publicly because, she said, "I believe women should have the choice over their futures."

Since 1965 she has been married to Larry King, a lawyer who is involved in many of her business

South Carolina fans cheer Mrs. King before match with Bobby Riggs.

ventures (World Team Tennis, magazine publishing, appearances, endorsements, etc.). But they maintain separate careers and seldom see each other. "The few moments we do have together are fantastic," she said. He once said he was "sick and tired of sharing her with the world" but added, "We have a lot of confidence in ourselves and in each other." She offers the view that "Marriage isn't a 50-50 proposition very often. It's more like 100-0 one moment and 0-100 the next."

She loves to talk about the beauty of tennis. "It is an art form that is capable of moving both the players and the audience . . . in emotional, almost sensual ways," she said, "a perfect combination of violent action taking place in an atmosphere of total tranquillity." She says that tennis has given her almost everything she has. "Oh, I know it's the toy part of the world and I'm not significant in any worldly fashion. But a long time ago I found this niche, and it has been right for me."

Of her image, she said, "Many people consider me a radical, but ten years from now my ideas will seem antiquated. . . . People are finding out athletes are not a bunch of Jack Armstrongs who neither smoke, drink nor have ideas."

Kiphuth, Robert John Herman
(1890–1967)

Bob Kiphuth, wrote Arthur Daley, "was a non-pedantic Mr. Chips . . . the most successful swimming coach the sport has ever known. He influenced for the better every man who came in contact with him."

Bob Kiphuth never went past high school. He arrived at Yale in 1914 as a physical-education instructor and in 1918 became swimming coach, though he knew nothing about the sport and learned it from books. Years later he wrote the books. When he retired in 1959 his Yale teams had won 528 dual meets and lost only 12. They had winning streaks of 65, 175, 63 and, unbroken at the end, 182. They won many AAU and NCAA titles.

He coached five U.S. Olympic teams and traveled to many countries to learn and coach. In 1963 President Lyndon B. Johnson presented him with the Medal of Freedom, America's highest civilian award. The citation read, "He has inspired generations of athletes with high ideals and achievements and sportsmanship."

Red Smith called him "a stocky, intense man of immeasurable vitality with a lip-smacking en-

Kiphuth with one of his best swimmers, Alan Ford.

thusiasm for life which has, almost incredibly, grown with every one of his 42 years on the job." "There was nothing of the natural athlete in him save physical coordination and stubborn Prussian determination, both inherited," Bill Ahern wrote. Gus Stager, who swam for and later coached Michigan, said, "He felt obliged to help any swimmer, even if he was on another team."

He had a booming voice and a great sense of humor. His best swimmers included Alan Ford, John Marshall, Jimmy McLane, Wayne Moore, Howie Johnson, Allan Stack and John Macionis. They were superbly fit because they endured three months of body-building exercises each fall before they were allowed in the water.

"We've never had a gimmick except the ability to roll up our sleeves, spit on our hands and convolute our brains a little," he said of his teams' success. "The swimming is only for fun. Studies are what count." But, he said, "Swimming can endow boys with the very qualities of discipline and competitiveness which will abet their post-graduate careers."

"To him, athletics was an integral part of learning," Yale president Kingman Brewster said, "and all learning was an exercise in self-fulfillment and self-discipline. Generations of students and athletes have outdone themselves because of the values he inspired and the standards he set."

Klem, William Joseph
(1874–1951)

Bill Klem, the Old Arbitrator, was baseball's most celebrated umpire, a short, lovable autocrat with a foghorn voice. Arthur Daley wrote, "He brought dignity and respect to his trade." "No one stood for the unimpeachable honesty of umpires more than he," Fred Lieb wrote. Ed Fitzgerald said, "He put the fear of God into the toughest ballplayers."

Bill Klem thought it significant that he was born on George Washington's birthday. He was a National League umpire from 1905 to 1940. Then, until his death, he was supervisor of National League umpires, with the job title of Chief of Staff. He picked it himself.

In 1902, when he was a semi-pro umpire, a famous American League umpire named Frank (Silk) O'Loughlin told him, "Umpiring is a lousy business. There's nothing in it but a lot of headaches." Klem refused to listen, and he found a way to cut down on the headaches. In his first week in the National League he had a run-in with John McGraw, the fiery manager of the New York Giants. "This will cost you your job, you busher," McGraw said. "If you can take my job away from me, I don't want it," Klem shot back.

In 1940, after working a game on a hot afternoon, Klem was heading for the dressing room when a woman asked, "Have a tough day, Pop?" At that moment he decided to retire. But it hurt, he said, because "baseball is not a game to me, it's a religion." In 1953 Bill Klem, umpire in the National League for 36 years and in the World Series for 18, was voted into the Baseball Hall of Fame.

He had been formal during working hours. "That will be enough, Mis-ter Frisch. . . . Did I hear you correctly, Mis-ter Durocher?" he would say. He was full of philosophy. When a young Pee Wee Reese looked back after Klem had called a strike on him, the umpire said, "Young man, don't blame me. It was the pitcher who fooled you."

"I never made a mistake," he once said. "Certainly, I must have called a strike a ball, and a ball a strike, but I never missed one in my heart, and if I didn't miss one there, how could I be wrong?"

Gilly Campbell, Chicago Cubs catcher, waves the ball in Klem's face to protest a safe call that brought in the winning run in this 1933 game.

Konrads, John (1942–)

At 5 feet 11 inches and 190 pounds, with a 44-inch chest, John Konrads looked like a circus strongman. Instead he was a champion swimmer.

He was natural, outgoing and charming. As president of his high-school student body, he wrote for his yearbook: "It is obvious that success can only be achieved through hard work, not only in studies but in sport and society."

He was born in Latvia during World War II (his name then was Jon), and moved with his family to Australia in 1949. The next year he contracted a mild case of polio and began swimming to strengthen his legs. At the age of 11, weighing 94 pounds and flabby, he paid $23.60 to train twice a day for six months under Coach Don Talbot.

He learned well. He won three gold medals in the 1958 Commonwealth Games, one gold and two bronze in the 1960 Olympics. He and his sister, Ilsa, two years younger, set 37 world free-style records between them. Of his 25 records, six were set in eight days. He studied international trade at the University of Southern California for two and a half years before returning to Australia to teach and coach swimming.

Sport magazine called the accomplishments of the two Konrads "one of the greatest testimonials to self-denial, perseverance and physical conditioning in the history of sports competition." Integrity was involved, too. When an American promoter wanted the youngsters to turn professional in 1958, their mother declined the offer, saying, "In their swimming, they have gained something money cannot buy."

Few swimmers trained as hard as the Konrads. John swam 1,500 miles a year in training, a huge volume in his day. Twice a week he worked out in the gymnasium, a typical workout consisting of perhaps 350 push-ups, 500 knee bends, 350 arm exercises and then an hour of pulling weights. But, as Don Talbot said, "Swimming is not a drudgery for them. It's a pleasure, and they love it. . . . No one is driving them. I'm not. Neither are their parents." John Konrads agreed. "I get tired of the suggestion that we are a couple of trained seals. Do we look unhappy, worn out, bullied or downtrodden? We are doing exactly what we want to do."

Korbut, Olga (1955–   )

At 4 feet 10 inches and 84 pounds, this lithe, long-legged elf with a boyish body, honey-blond hair in pigtails and a quick, extra-wide smile seems an unlikely Olympic champion. She is not even the best woman gymnast in her native Soviet Union, but she is the most famous woman athlete in the world.

She was the first woman to perform a back somersault on the balance beam and a half back somersault from the top bar to the bottom bar in the asymmetric (uneven parallel) bars, daring maneuvers that stunned spectators with their beauty and danger. When the International Gymnastics Federation considered banning both as too dangerous, she said, "If the ban is implemented, I see no place for me in the future of gymnastics. . . . It has always been considered that gymnasts have the right to determine their own style." In the end, the federation backed down.

She was unknown in the West until the 1972 Olympics, when she became a creation of television. She was 17 at Munich, just another member of the world's finest national team of women gymnasts. Television cameras at the Olympics focused on several women gymnasts, she among them. From the moment the cameras turned on her, she seemed to have a special quality. Then, losing concentration, she made two errors on the uneven parallel bars. She finished her routine, ran to the sidelines and cried, and the world cried with her.

The next day, with the cameras following every move of this newly discovered pixie, she was sensational. The crowd screamed with approval at her daring and booed the judges no matter how high they scored her. She won three gold medals and one silver, and she gave the world a new sport and a new heroine.

The American Broadcasting Company, which televised the Olympics to the United States, named her athlete of the year over Mark Spitz and his seven gold medals. She and her Soviet teammates performed in the United States three times in 18 months during 1973 and 1974. She was greeted by members of Olga Korbut Fan Clubs wearing Olga Korbut T-shirts. They were mostly teenage girls, and they welcomed her, wrote Gerald Eskenazi, "with the squeals of delight another generation reserved for Judy Garland."

There were keys to the city in New York and Olga Korbut Day in Chicago. She was overwhelmed by fan mail, much of it addressed simply to "Olga, Moscow." She continued to do well in competition but never as well as her teammate Ludmilla Turisheva, the Olympic and four-time world all-round champion. The dour Turisheva never seemed to understand the Olga Korbut phenomenon. Neither did the Soviet newspaper *Pravda*, which censured Korbut for encouraging a personality cult.

Censure or no, she remained the center of attention everywhere. Renald Knysh, her personal coach, said he was not interested in gold medals but rather how spectators reacted to her. They invariably reacted with resounding affection. After each performance, she would extend her arms to the spectators, demanding that they love her. The answer was always the same. They loved her. Martha Duffy wrote, "She shed energy on anyone who saw her."

She turned gymnastics from a select competition into a sport for many. Before the 1972 Olympics there were perhaps 15,000 women gymnasts in the United States. By 1974 there were 50,000. Marlene Bene, an official of the U.S. Gymnastics Federation, said, "She made gymnastics in the United States today. We must get 50 to 60 letters a day from girls wanting to know how to be another Olga Korbut."

In his book *Olga*, Justin Beecham wrote, "Her style was new and enchantedly captivating. Anyone who saw her recognized magic. . . . She has made a permanent impact on the world. She has managed to combine being first with being joyful. . . . To young people and old alike, she seems through her exuberance and her courage to embody the very best qualities of youth."

"My love is gymnastics," she said. "I will continue as long as my performance brings happiness to people. . . . For me, gymnastics is an expression of my innermost emotions, my response to the love and care with which I have always been surrounded in my life."

Koufax, Sanford (1935–   )

Sandy Koufax was the best pitcher of his day and, for the last half of his short career, perhaps the best pitcher of any day. He quit baseball when he was 30, at the peak of his pitching and earning ($135,000 a year) ability, because of a progressive arthritic condition that threatened the use of his left arm. Six years later he became the youngest player ever voted into the Baseball Hall of Fame.

He was handsome, intelligent, articulate and shy, a box-office attraction everywhere in the National League and the embodiment of all that was attractive in baseball and sports. As Milton Gross wrote, "In the age of the non-hero, when negative values loomed so large, he was a positive one."

Sandy Koufax never played in the minor leagues. He pitched for the Dodgers in his native Brooklyn and in Los Angeles from 1955 to 1966. In 12 seasons his record was 165-87, a .655 percentage, with an earned-run average of 2.76 and 2,396 strikeouts in 2,325 innings. But even those impressive figures fail to tell the full story because his 12-year career really consisted of two distinct six-year careers.

The young Sandy Koufax, like many young left-handed pitchers, was fast and wild. Buzzie Bavasi, the Dodger general manager, told him, "You've got one pitch—high." "Taking batting practice against him is like playing Russian roulette with five bullets," a Dodger teammate complained. Bob Broeg wrote, "He could throw a grape through a battleship, but he wanted to hear the guns roar."

He complained to Bavasi that he did not pitch often enough. Bavasi asked how he could get frequent assignments if he was so wild, and he responded by asking Bavasi how he could conquer the wildness unless he pitched more often. As Jack Olsen wrote, "He was caught up in the wild young pitcher's classical dilemma."

In a 1961 spring-training game against the Chicago White Sox, Koufax loaded the bases with none out. Norm Sherry, his catcher, walked to the mound and said, "If you get behind on a batter, don't throw your fastball. That's when you get real wild. Throw it easy." He took the advice, and it worked. "I'll never forget it," said Koufax. "Then and there I realized that there's no need to throw as hard as I can. I found out that if I take it easy and throw naturally, the ball goes just as fast."

Thus was born the new Sandy Koufax. During his first six seasons his record was 36-40. During the next six it was 129-47. He led the league three times in victories, four times in strikeouts and five straight seasons in earned-run average. He pitched no-hitters in four consecutive seasons (1962–65), the last being a perfect game. He was the National League's most valuable player in 1963 and the Cy Young Award winner as baseball's outstanding pitcher in 1963, 1965 and 1966. In 1965 he compiled a 26-8 record, a 2.04 earned-run average, 27 complete games, 336 innings and 382 strikeouts (the most to that time by any major-league pitcher in one year).

"He has the world in his left palm," Dick Young wrote. Allan Roth, the Dodger statistician, said, "It reached the point now where when anybody gets a hit off him, people turn to each other and say, 'Gee, I wonder what he did wrong.'" *Sports Illustrated* said prophetically, "He has money, a bronze Oldsmobile, an ear for Mendelssohn, a blazing fastball and a realization that none of it can last."

None of it did. He developed painful traumatic arthritis in his left elbow, which became as thick as his knee. He had to have it rubbed in red-hot red salve before he pitched. After a game, he would soak the arm in ice for 30 minutes, wearing a rubber sleeve to prevent frostbite. This procedure reduced swelling and slowed hemorrhaging, and cortisone injections and anti-inflammatory drugs helped, but the condition and pain progressively worsened. His arm got shorter and locked at an angle. Orthopedists warned that he might become crippled if he kept pitching.

Opponents refused to believe his condition was that serious. "No man with a bad elbow can throw like that," Roberto Clemente said. "Some sore arm," said Dick Sisler. "It's sore except between the first and ninth innings."

The condition was serious, and after a spectacular 1966 season (27-9, 1.73 earned-run average), he retired from baseball. "I don't regret for one minute the 12 years I've spent in baseball," he said. "But I could regret one season too many."

Dodger teammates mob Koufax after he became the first man in major-league history to pitch four no-hitters with this perfect game against the Chicago Cubs in 1965.

Kurland, Robert A. (1924–   )

Bob Kurland was the first seven-foot basketball player who was not disparaged as a goon. He lacked speed, but his size, seven feet and 225 pounds, did not hinder his quickness, agility, poise and sureness. He put his talents to good use in basketball and in track, where he competed in the high jump (clearing six feet), shot put and discus throw. Strangers always stared at him, and he said, "When you walk through a hotel lobby you can notice people watching to see if you're going to bang your head."

He played four seasons for Oklahoma A & M (now Oklahoma State), making All-America his last three years. In his last two seasons (1945–46) he led

his team to consecutive NCAA championships and was both times named the tournament's most valuable player.

"He made our type of game go," Henry Iba, his coach, said. "We knew he would get us the ball, so we never had to rush into a bad shot. . . . He's brilliant mentally." He was equally accomplished on offense and defense. W. C. Heinz called him "the biggest good player ever to work the backboards."

He was known as Foothills, and he was so fearsome under the backboards that opponents often held the ball rather than risk a blocked shot. As a result, Oklahoma A & M won games one season by 17-15 and 14-11. The rules committee combatted the problem by outlawing goal-tending, barring a defender from touching a ball in the air higher than the basket. It actually helped Kurland because he did not have to jump so much.

He worked hard to become good. "One afternoon he must have tried 600 hooks with his left hand," Iba recalled. "The first 100 didn't hit either the rim or the backboard. The next 100 didn't go in. After that, he started to connect. . . . He would skip rope by the hour. I guess he must have skipped rope across the country."

After college, he was besieged with professional offers. The New York Knickerbockers offered him $11,000 a year, huge money at the time. But he rejected the offer and went to work for the Phillips Petroleum Company, which sponsored an amateur basketball team and coveted Kurland's combination of athletic and academic ability (he was a Student Senate president and an "A" student). He played for the Phillips Oilers from 1946 to 1952 and led them in scoring each year. He won gold medals playing for the U. S. in the 1948 and 1952 Olympics. He started at Phillips stacking oil cans in a warehouse. Twenty years later he was president of a Phillips subsidiary.

"I may have had some doubts not going pro," he said, "but I don't now. . . . I don't have to worry about a job. I've got a good one. . . . There have never been any regrets."

Kurland hands trophy to Coach Henry Iba in 1946 after Oklahoma A & M won its second straight NCAA title.

Lajoie, Napoleon (1875–1959)

Larry Lajoie's grace on the baseball diamond inspired purple prose. George Trevor wrote, ''His batting and fielding might . . . be termed living poetry.'' ''Napoleon Lajoie was as smooth as Napoleon pastry and as sharp as Napoleon brandy,'' wrote Bob Broeg. One man said Lajoie was the only man he had ever seen ''who could chew scrap tobacco in such a way as to give a jaunty refinement to a habit vulgar and untidy in so many others.''

He played from 1896 to 1916 for Philadelphia of the National League and Philadelphia and Cleveland of the American League (in his honor Cleveland changed its nickname to the Naps). He also managed Cleveland from 1905 to 1909.

He was a line-drive hitter in a dead-ball era, and he made 3,251 hits and batted .339 in 2,475 games. He won four straight American League batting championships (1901–04), and his .422 season average in 1901 remains the American League record. Though he was not fast, he led American League second basemen six times in fielding. Fred Lieb wrote, ''No other player was in his class for making the hard ones look easy.'' In 1937 he became the first second baseman voted into the Baseball Hall of Fame.

He was a big man, handsome, well liked and mild. Once, when he was manager, a player argued with him and hit him over the head with a chair. He kept the player on the team, saying, ''He's a good player and we need him. That chair episode was just one of those things.''

Toward the end of the 1910 season he and Ty Cobb were competing for the American League batting title and the car that went with it. Cobb was leading and he sat out the last two games to protect his margin. On the final day, playing for Cleveland against St. Louis, Lajoie made eight hits in eight at bats, six on bunts against a third baseman who played deep on the orders of his manager, Jack O'Connor. No one proved that the almost universal hatred for Cobb and the almost universal liking for Lajoie had anything to do with it, but O'Connor was fired. Cobb won the batting title, .3848 to .3841, and both received cars. Lajoie said years later, ''I've always understood that the automobile I got ran a lot better than the one they gave to Ty.''

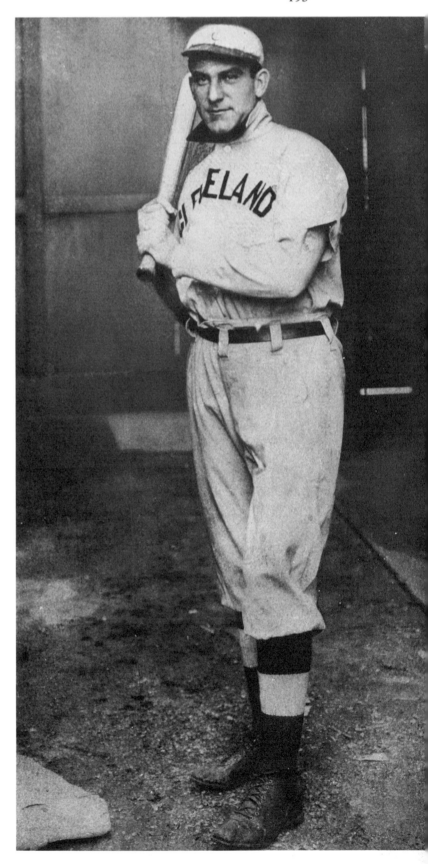

Landis, Kenesaw Mountain
(1866–1944)

When baseball's public image sank after the 1920 Black Sox scandal, the club owners agreed that they needed a czar to keep the game clean and restore public confidence. They chose Kenesaw Mountain Landis, a federal judge famous for having fined Standard Oil $29 million in a freight-rebate case (the Circuit Court of Appeals revoked the fine).

From 1920 until his death in 1944, Landis served as baseball's first commissioner. *Sport* magazine said, "For a quarter of a century, the incorruptible honesty of the gruff old dictator built a solid rock of public respect under the game that had been so dangerously shaken. . . . He ruled . . . with an iron hand." His memorial, Ed Fitzgerald wrote, was that baseball had become "synonymous with scrupulous honesty in the minds of the public." Arnold Hano wrote, "His pronouncements seemed to come from afar, from a height. Like a mountain, he seemed immortal."

He was named for a mountain—Kennesaw Mountain, where a Confederate cannonball struck his father. (He never knew why his name was spelled Kenesaw instead of Kennesaw.) He became a federal judge in 1905 and was flamboyant and, as one critic said, "startlingly conspicuous." Heywood Broun wrote, "His career typifies the heights to which dramatic talent may carry a man if only he has the foresight not to go on the stage."

When he became baseball commissioner he barred for life the eight Chicago White Sox players accused of throwing the 1919 World Series (the infamous Black Sox scandal). He once fined and suspended Babe Ruth for illegal barnstorming, and he fined Connie Mack for moving players around illegally. He freed Pete Reiser, Johnny Sain, Tommy Henrich and other youngsters illegally hidden in farm systems.

He had great power from which there was no appeal. He was, wrote various people, "baseball incarnate," "belligerently incorruptible," "an absolute despot," "the picture of rigid dignity." Yet he was small and frail, barely 100 pounds, with a long, frowning face, piercing eyes, sharp features and shaggy white hair.

Within a month of his death in 1944 he was voted into the Baseball Hall of Fame. As Bill Corum wrote, "He put baseball on a high pedestal and then climbed up there with it."

Baseball commissioner Kenesaw Mountain Landis at the Polo Grounds for the 1933 World Series.

Lapchick, Joseph Bohomiel
(1900–1970)

For 50 years Joe Lapchick was a winning basketball player and coach. He was warm but tough, gregarious, humble and universally loved. To Robert L. Mendell he was "revered and dedicated," to Mervin Hyman "intense and self-goading," to Warren Pack "a man who believes profoundly in truth and honor." As Leonard Koppett wrote, "He preached pride—pride in one's self, pride in accomplishment, pride in being a true professional who delivers all the effort he is paid for, pride in being able to win without gloating and to lose without whining."

He was the first of the mobile big men, a gangly 6-foot-5-inch center who could run all night. In the days when pro basketball consisted mainly of one-night stands in dance halls, he played from 1922 to 1935 for the Original Celtics, Cleveland Rosenblums and Kate Smith's Celtics.

When he was asked to coach St. John's University in Brooklyn, New York, in 1937, he wondered how, with only an 11th-grade education, he could relate to college students. He called his friend, Coach Clair Bee of Long Island University. "You're a coach, I'm not. How do you handle kids?" Lapchick asked. "The first thing you do is not let them call you Joe," Bee answered. "You're either Mr. Lapchick or you're Coach." "And then what?" "Then you're a coach."

He coached St. John's from 1937 to 1947, the New York Knickerbockers from 1947 to 1956 and St. John's from 1956 to mandatory retirement in 1965. His St. John's teams won four National Invitation Tournament titles, but he suffered from nervousness, stomach cramps and trips to the water cooler (someone once counted 24 trips in one half).

In a magazine story entitled "Each Game I Die," he wrote, "You die because you have so little control over what happens. This is a humiliating business. There are no geniuses in coaching. The players make the coach. The coach who thinks his teaching is more important than his talent is an idiot."

Lapchick gets an affectionate hazing in 1959 after his St. John's players won the third of their four NIT titles.

Laver, Rodney George
(1938–   )

Rod Laver of Australia is a small man (5 feet 8½ inches, 155 pounds), with red hair, freckles, a sharp nose and bandy legs. But he dominated men's tennis in the 1960s and early 1970s with a big game and wristy spin shots that led Bud Collins to write, "He never hit a ball straight in his life." He is left-handed, and his left forearm is so large—it is the same size as Rocky Marciano's—that his normal right forearm looks atrophied.

In 1962 he became the first male player since Don Budge in 1938 to win the grand slam—the Wimbledon, United States, French and Australian titles in the same year. He then turned professional and in 1969 became the only player to win two grand slams. In 1970 he became the first tennis player to win more than $200,000 in prize money in one year. In the first three months of 1971 he won $175,000, and he was the first tennis player to reach $1 million in career prize money. He has earned more from tennis camps and endorsements.

He reduced his tournament schedule sharply in 1973. "A lot of players make the mistake of really playing on for too long," he said. "If you play too long, you lose the desire to win." That desire never faded for Laver. Pancho Gonzales said he played every game as if he were behind 5-love. "And his concentration is so intense," Gonzales added. "It seems to come naturally to him. His mind is there all the time."

He is a shy man, honest, unaffected, gracious, proud and self-effacing. Dave Anderson wrote, "He lives, as he plays tennis, with an almost mechanical precision. There is no showboat in him." Alfred Wright wrote, "He was raised in the Harry Hopman school of Australian tennis where a small grunt is the only communication allowed between player and public." Al Silverman called him the "exemplary renaissance man of tennis."

Laver preferred the quiet way. "I talk to myself a little bit and throw a racquet occasionally," he said, "but I don't perform at the expense of winning. I never wanted to be the center of attention. . . . Open your mouth too often and what you probably will reveal is your ignorance."

Laver, in 1968, smiles with his third Wimbledon singles title and the first he won as a professional.

Leahy, Francis William
(1908–1973)

He was perhaps the most successful of all modern college football coaches. As head coach for two seasons (1939–40) at Boston College and 11 (1941–43 and 1946–53) at Notre Dame he had a won-lost-tied record of 107-13-9. Six Notre Dame teams were undefeated, four won national championships and one (in 1947) produced 42 professional players.

He was a large, ruggedly handsome man, scholarly, courteous and introverted. John D. McCallum said, "He had the ascetic features and the sad eyes of a parish priest." Jack Sher's first impression of Leahy was that no one could be so charming and gentlemanly without putting on an act. However, Sher wrote, "He is, actually, a very sincere man in everything he says and does. . . . But on a football field, his personality changes. He becomes grim, driving, serious and sarcastic."

He was an eternal pessimist. "No one," said one writer, "excelled him in the art of crying from hunger with a rib roast under each arm." He had a habit of talking, as Jack Orr remarked, "in polysyllabic, Pollyannaish prose." For example he once said, "A defeat at times is an asset. It may have countless other effects that will outweigh the disadvantages concomitant with defeat."

He played tackle for Knute Rockne's last Notre Dame teams. After college he became an assistant coach at Georgetown, Michigan State and Fordham. At Fordham he molded the Seven Blocks of Granite, among them Vince Lombardi. Then came a head-coaching career that ended at age 45 because of illness (spinal arthritis and a pancreas ailment). "I can't work 18 or 20 hours a day and bounce back as easily as I once did," he said.

As Ed Fitzgerald wrote, "He would like to believe that there are more important things in life than winning football games—and he goes around saying so eloquently—but he has never been able to bring himself to believe it." Leahy seemed to agree when he said, "I was so preoccupied with the game I often would sleep on my cot in my Notre Dame office and not get home for two or three days on the week of the game. Meanwhile, my children were growing up."

Leahy carried off the field by his Notre Dame team after the last game of its undefeated 1953 season.

200

Lee, Dr. Samuel (1920–)

Sammy Lee was 14 years old and had reached his full height of 5 feet 1¾ inches when he asked James Frederick Ryan, the great diving coach, to watch him. For four hours, the 6-feet-3½-inch, 270-pound Ryan criticized him, browbeat him and insulted him. Then Ryan turned to his friend Duke Kahanamoku and said, "See that half pint? I'm going to make him the world's greatest diver or break his back."

For eight months Ryan worked him in a sand pit without letting him into the water, and Sammy Lee was on the way to becoming the world's greatest diver. He became the first to repeat as Olympic champion (1948 and 1952) off the ten-meter platform. He also became a physician specializing in ear diseases and a round, gregarious good-will ambassador for his country and sport.

He was born in California of Korean-born parents. The family name was Rhee, and his father was a friend and distant cousin of Syngman Rhee, onetime President of Korea. When Sammy was in high school his father told him, "Anything is possible in America if you set your heart to it. But don't you be an athletic bum. Exercise your mind, too. The body grows old, but the mind stays young if you keep using it."

In high school in Los Angeles the youngster was one of two nonwhites and the first nonwhite president of the student body. He graduated at the top of his class. He was also a three-time California high-school diving champion, and his dives, wrote J. Campbell Bruce, "had the frenetic quality of a pinwheel."

He won two AAU titles in 1942 and retired. The following year he graduated from Occidental College and entered medical school. Later he entered the Army, dived again and won the AAU platform title in 1946. He won a gold medal in the 1948 Olympics and again retired. He emerged from retirement for the 1952 Olympics. He sent his wife ahead by ship before he qualified for the U.S. team and won another gold medal. In 1953, accepting the Sullivan Award as America's outstanding amateur athlete, he said, "I stand before you proudly but with humbleness, as a half-pint Oriental from Occidental."

He corresponded with divers all over the world and helped them all. "Diving is an art," he said. "I enjoy seeing others interpret it as well as they can. Where would medicine be today if the older men refused to teach the younger?"

Lenglen, Suzanne (1899–1938)

In 1974 an international panel of tennis writers overwhelmingly voted Suzanne Lenglen the outstanding woman player in tennis history. She was famous throughout the world, a prima donna who exicited the public with her presence, her temperament and her near flawless ability.

She dominated the women's tennis scene from 1919 to 1926. On the grass courts of Wimbledon she won six singles, six doubles and three mixed doubles titles in the All-England championships, the most prestigious in tennis. She also monopolized French tennis, winning six singles, six doubles and six mixed doubles titles on the clay courts of Roland Garros Stadium in Paris.

In the 1925 women's singles at Wimbledon she lost only five games. In the 1926 women's singles at Roland Garros, she lost only four games. Five times in her career she won tournaments without losing a game.

She was a plain girl—slim, supple, graceful, with the figure of a dancer. She had a long, crooked nose, irregular teeth and large feet and hands. But, as Al Laney once wrote, "For an ugly girl, she had more charm and vivacity than a hundred pretty girls." She had been a child star, and her mother was almost always at her side, with a little dog under mother's arm.

On the court she was perfection. As a later champion, Helen Hull Jacobs, wrote, "She played with the grace of a ballerina and the skill of a finished artist." A contemporary wrote of her game, "She was like a cat playing with a mouse."

From 1919 to her retirement in 1926 she lost only once, and the defeat was controversial. It happened in 1921, in the second round of the United States championship at Forest Hills, New York, against Mrs. Molla Bjurstedt Mallory, the defending champion (at that time the best players were not seeded). Miss Lenglen, trailing by 6-2, 1-0, complained of illness and defaulted. The American gallery considered her a quitter.

Miss Lenglen and Helen Wills, the American champion, after their celebrated match at the Carlton Club of Cannes in 1926. Miss Lenglen won, 6-3, 8-6.

Her scheduled audience with the queen was canceled, and she never played as an amateur again. C. C. (Cash and Carry) Pyle, a flamboyant American promoter, gave her a $50,000 guarantee to tour the United States later that year as a professional. Though she made more than $100,000 from the tour, she was not happy.

She played little tennis after that, devoting most of her time to a tennis school in Paris. At the age of 39 she died of pernicious anemia. The French government, which once had apologized to the British for Miss Lenglen's Wimbledon walkout, awarded her the Legion of Merit posthumously.

Her most celebrated match took place in 1926 in an unimportant tournament at the Carlton Club of Cannes. Her opponent was Helen Wills, at age 20 already a three-time United States champion (though Miss Lenglen preferred to call her "a sweet child"). It was their only meeting, and scalpers sold five-franc seats for 1,000 francs and people who could not buy seats watched from trees, fences and rooftops. Miss Lenglen won, 6-3, 8-6.

From the beginning she stood apart. Just after she won the 1920 Olympic championship in Antwerp, a gatekeeper stopped her and asked to see her ticket. She drew herself up haughtily and said in French, "I? I am the great Lenglen." The flustered gatekeeper apologized and begged her to enter.

Neither did her hauteur waver before the rigors of social protocol. During the summer of 1926 Queen Mary made a special trip to Wimbledon to watch Miss Lenglen play. Miss Lenglen kept the queen waiting half an hour and later quit the tournament.

Leonard, Benny (1896–1947)

Arthur Daley called Benny Leonard "the fighter with the hair-trigger brain and the hair-trigger reflexes, the consummate boxer and the deadly puncher." He was one of the great lightweights, a prizefighter with speed, strength and style.

One admirer said, "No one ever mussed his hair." Heywood Broun wrote, "No performer in any art has ever been more correct than Leonard. He follows closely all the best traditions of the past. His left-hand jab could stand without revision in any textbook. The manner in which he feints, ducks, sidesteps and hooks is unimpeachable. . . . He stands up straight like a gentleman and a champion."

He was born Benjamin Leiner on New York City's lower East Side, and he fought his first pro fight at the age of 15. He was world lightweight champion from 1917 to 1925, when he retired at the urging of his ill mother (he was 28). After losing a fortune in the stock-market crash, he fought briefly as a welterweight in 1931 and 1932. He became a leading referee, and he collapsed and died in a New York ring after refereeing a fight.

Frank Graham wrote that Leonard had everything—cleverness, a punch, speed, courage and stamina. Nat Fleischer, the boxing historian, ranked him second only to Joe Gans among lightweights. "I don't know whether I could have licked Gans or not, and neither does anybody else," Leonard said. "But if they have to dig up a dead one to lick me, I'm satisfied." Jack Britton, who fought him three times, thought Leonard was better than Gans. "Nobody who ever lived was as strong as this guy," he said.

"I've made more than a million dollars out of boxing," Leonard said. "But even if I'd never made a cent from it, I'd be thankful to the sport for what it's done for me. It's given me a strong body, a world of friends and what little education I've had. I'll be grateful to boxing for the rest of my life."

204

Lindsay, Robert Blake
Theodore (1925–   )

Terrible Ted Lindsay earned his nickname for his toughness, not for any lack of skill. Though he stood 5 feet 8 inches and weighed 163 pounds, he was the toughest hockey player of his day. As Marty Pavelich, a teammate, said, "He didn't back down from anybody."

"No man on skates was ever too big or too tough for him to challenge," wrote Zander Hollander. "He cut down some of the biggest, meanest men in the National Hockey League." He did that during 13 seasons (1944–57) with the Detroit Red Wings, helping them win eight NHL titles (seven in a row) and four Stanley Cups and earning nine all-star berths. At Detroit he was part of the famous Production Line with Gordie Howe and Sid Abel. Then he played three seasons for the Chicago Black Hawks, retired for three years and returned at age 39 for one more season at Detroit. In 17 seasons he scored 851 points in 1,068 games, took 1,808 minutes in penalties (still the all-time record) and had his wounds closed with 760 stitches.

He inflicted at least equal damage. Dave Anderson wrote, "He left behind a hundred-odd bruised or scarred opponents who had got in his way." Jack Adams, Detroit's general manager, called him "the greatest left wing of all time" but added that "when he goes out on the ice, nobody is his friend." Tim Cohane called him "a cagy playmaker," and Bill Durnan, a leading goalie of that era, said, "He comes in so fast on you, you don't know who it is."

Lindsay said meanness was a form of self-defense. "In this game, you have to be mean or you're going to get pushed around. I keep telling myself, 'Be mean! Be mean!' . . . I love hockey, but I can play it only one way—all out. . . . I never look for trouble. I just don't hide from it."

Lindsay shoots as Terry Sawchuk, the Toronto goalie, and Allan Stanley defend.

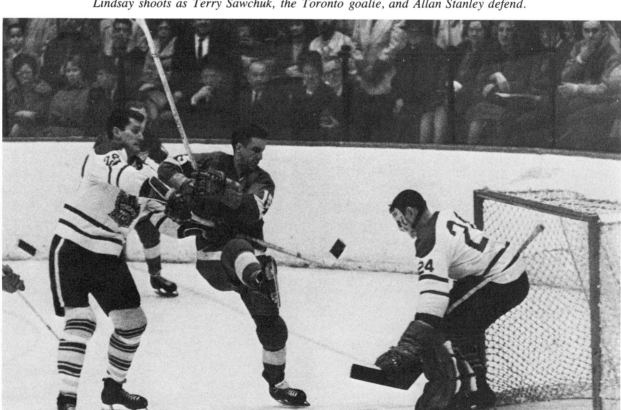

Liston, Charles (1932–1970)

Sonny Liston was a big, mean, intimidating brute who became heavyweight champion of the world. He had been a juvenile delinquent, an anti-labor strong-arm man and an armed robber who served two prison terms, and when he was champion his contract probably was owned by the underworld.

Writing in *The New York Times*, Steve Cady described him as a "hulking, menacing figure with size-13 fists and a baleful glare that intimidated many an opponent even before a bout started." *Esquire* called him "everybody's bad nigger." But, wrote Robert Lipsyte, "It must never be forgotten that he was a very good fighter and that the scorn he suffered toward the end was undeserved. He had been built up too large and so had too far to fall."

He was the 24th of 25 children. He could not read or write, and he often was in trouble.

He learned to box in prison, and as a professional from 1953 to 1970 he earned over $3.8 million in purses. He won the heavyweight title in 1962 by knocking out Floyd Patterson in the first round, and in 1963 he did it again.

In 1964 he fought a brash upstart named Cassius Clay (who later changed his name to Muhammad Ali). Liston predicted that "Cassius can't lick a Popsicle," but he lost the title to Clay when his injured shoulder kept him from coming out for the seventh round. In a return title bout in 1965 Clay knocked him out in the first round with a phantom right-hand punch that few people saw, and that prompted talk of the fight being fixed. "The most frightening figure on earth lost two fights to a boy," wrote Jack Olsen. "Suddenly, Sonny Liston was a bum, a stiff, a fake."

He fought sporadically after that, but as Gary Cartwright wrote, "No one in his right mind wants to fight Sonny Liston. He has less appeal than your average grown cobra." He was still semiactive when he died suddenly, under mysterious circumstances, at the age of 38 (some people insisted he was 44). Death was attributed to a heart attack.

"A boxing match is like a cowboy movie," he once said. "There's got to be good guys and there's got to be bad guys. That's what people pay for—to see the bad guys get beat. So I'm the bad guy. But I change things. I don't get beat. . . . Ever since I was born I've been fighting for my life."

Floyd Patterson goes down for the third and final time in his 1963 fight with Liston.

Vince Lombardi, age 21, one of the guards of Fordham University's celebrated line, the Seven Blocks of Granite.

years, but his success was unparalleled. In 1959 he became head coach and general manager of the Green Bay Packers. The Packers had not had a winning team for ten years, and in 1958 they were 1-10-1. There was little hope in the 194 bars that served the 70,000 inhabitants of Green Bay.

At the first meeting he told his players, "I have never been on a losing team, gentlemen, and I don't intend to start now." He didn't. His first Packer team won seven games and lost five. His second won a conference title. In the next seven years (1961–67) the Packers won five NFL titles and the first two Super Bowls.

Sam Huff, assistant coach of the Redskins, talks with Lombardi, the head coach.

Lombardi, Vincent Thomas
(1913–1970)

He was more than a football coach. He was a man who stood for basic values—hard work, fairness, honesty and dedication. The public was in awe of him. His players had mixed feelings about him, including fear.

Jerry Kramer, one of his star players, called him "a cruel, kind, tough, gentle, miserable, wonderful man whom I often hate and often love and always respect." Terence Cardinal Cooke said he was "a man of deep faith and firm hope." His wife, Marie, said, "He was kind of a mystery. He eludes you."

He coached football for 30 years. He was a head coach in the National Football League for only ten

In 1968 he retired as coach because of the pressures, but he stayed as general manager. He quickly learned that he could not get along without coaching. "I miss the fire on Sunday," he said.

He returned to the Sunday fire in 1969, joining the Washington Redskins for $100,000 a year as coach, general manager, executive vice-president and 5 percent owner. The Redskins had not had a winning season in 13 years, but his first season they were 7-5-2. A year later he was dead of cancer.

He had a smile memorable for the gap it showed between his front teeth. His laugh, a deep rumble, was reserved for friends. He was shy with strangers, and people who did not know him often considered him aloof.

Packer players liked to talk about his toughness. "When he says 'sit down,' I don't even bother to look for a chair," one said. Willie Davis said he made practice so difficult and so demanding that the game itself was fun. "He's fair," said Henry Jordan. "He treats all of us the same—like dogs."

There was respect, too. "When I came to him, I didn't have anything," Marv Fleming said. "He taught me how to be a winner." Bart Starr, speaking of his relationship with Lombardi, said, "He took a kid and made a man out of him." Red Smith wrote, "He was neither a saint nor a sadist but a human being who could sometimes seem to be one and sometimes the other. . . . He had the intelligence and drive and integrity to be, as his friend Wellington Mara suggests, President or Pope."

He had no fancy formulas for success. He taught simple football executed to perfection. He believed in giving 100 percent and knew how to get his players to give it. "If you cheat on the practice field, you'll cheat in the game," he liked to say. "And if you cheat in the game, you'll cheat the rest of your life. . . . Coaches who can outline plays on a blackboard are a dime a dozen. The ones who win get inside their players and motivate them." His best-known aphorism: "Winning isn't everything. It's the only thing."

At Fordham University he played guard on a famous line remembered as the Seven Blocks of Granite. He was the smallest block at 5 feet 8 inches and

170 pounds, but, as a teammate recalled, "He hit like 250." He was graduated *magna cum laude* in 1937 and hired by St. Cecilia's High School in Englewood, New Jersey, as assistant football coach and instructor in chemistry, physics, algebra and Latin. His salary was $1,700 a year. He became the head coach of football, baseball and basketball.

In 1947 he became an assistant football coach at Fordham, in 1949 assistant coach at Army and in 1954 assistant coach of the New York Giants. Then came the Packers and the Redskins, and he was a national hero. Virtue was rewarded. President Richard Nixon said in tribute, "He never asked more of any man than he asked of himself."

Alvin (Pete) Rozelle, the NFL commissioner, said after Lombardi's death, "Those who will miss Vince Lombardi the most are those who still had yet to play for him, who might have been taught by him, led by him and counseled by him."

Lombardi is carried from the field in 1961 after Green Bay won the NFL title.

Longden, John Eric (1907–)

In 40 years of riding thoroughbred horses, Johnny Longden won over six thousand races (the actual tally is 6,032 by most counts, though the *American Racing Manual* insists the number is 6,026) and earned purses exceeding $24.6 million. In 1956,

when he won for the 4,871st time, he became the all-time leader. He held that distinction until 1970, when Willie Shoemaker passed him.

He was born in England (he claimed in 1910, but most racing people agreed on 1907) and raised in Canada, where at age 14 he greased coal cars in mines for $2.50 a day. By the time he quit riding in 1966, at age 59, his interests in ranching, oil and land had made him a millionaire.

At 4 feet 10 inches, he was small even for a jockey, but he had a broad chest and a 15½-inch neck. His face looked like creased leather and his voice was high and squeaky. His body took an awful beating. At one time or another he broke both arms, both legs, both ankles, both feet, both collarbones, six ribs and his backbone. Rheumatoid arthritis left his hands gnarled and his knees aching. He won the Alberta Derby with a broken leg and the Butler Handicap with a broken foot.

Dr. Henry Schultz of San Francisco called him a "medical miracle." His son, Eric Longden, said, "He had to become a cripple before he'd quit. He can't walk 50 feet without having to sit down, the pain's so bad."

He withstood the pain. He rode Count Fleet to the triple crown in 1943, and he trained Majestic Prince, the Kentucky Derby winner in 1969. He even found an ideal exercise boy for Majestic Prince—62-year-old Johnny Longden.

Joe Fernandez, the Santa Anita announcer, said, "He can clean tack, muck out a stall, feed a horse, bandage a cut or walk out a hot horse better than anyone." Jim Murray wrote, "He is one of the few great jockeys who actually likes horses and enjoys riding them."

Speaking of her husband's debilitating injuries, Hazel Longden said, "He should have quit long ago, but there wasn't a way I could talk him into it." As Longden said, "I guess what it comes down to is that I just like to ride. . . . The writers, the fans, the track bosses had me washed up dozens of times. Well, they got their faith back. I took care of that. . . . Anybody who quits what he's doing while he's still able is going to get old pretty fast. . . . Once you get off horses, you're just a bowlegged little man walking around."

Louis, Joe (1914–)

From an Alabama sharecropper's shack without electricity or indoor plumbing, Joseph Louis Barrow, who became known as Joe Louis, rose to win the world heavyweight boxing championship. He held it longer than anyone else in history (11 years and eight months), earned over $4.6 million in the ring and kept not a nickel of it.

He was a strapping man of 6 feet 1½ inches and 200 to 210 pounds. He had speed and power and a jab that no rival forgot. "The first jab he nails you," said James J. Braddock, "you know what it's like. It's like someone jammed an electric bulb in your face and busted it." Red Smith called him a "shuffling predator."

He turned professional in 1934, earning $52 for his first fight and $54 for his next. He suffered his first pro defeat in 1936 when Max Schmeling knocked him out in 12 rounds. In 1937 he won the title from Braddock. The following year, in a return bout, he knocked out Schmeling in the first round. Writing of that fight, Bob Considine described Schmeling as "a man caught and mangled in the whirring claws of a mad and feverish machine."

From 1937 to 1942 he defended his title 21 times against what one writer christened the Bum of the Month Club. One victim, Jack Roper, said, "I zigged when I should have zagged." When Bob Pastor, another victim, said he would back-pedal from Louis, the champion said, "He can run, but he can't hide." Jimmy Cannon wrote, "In the days of his greatness, he inspired his straight men with a fear which caused them to fall in a clammy ecstasy as soon as the first punch grazed their chins."

When America went to war he gave the purse from one fight to the Navy Relief Fund and the purse from another to the Army Relief Fund. After one of those fights he assured the public that America would win the war "because we're on God's side." He joined the Army and fought perhaps 1,000 exhibitions around the world for more than five million soldiers.

After the war he made four more defenses. He retired as undefeated champion in 1950, but he owed

Max Schmeling hangs on the ropes after a smashing blow from Louis, who won the 1938 fight with a first-round knockout.

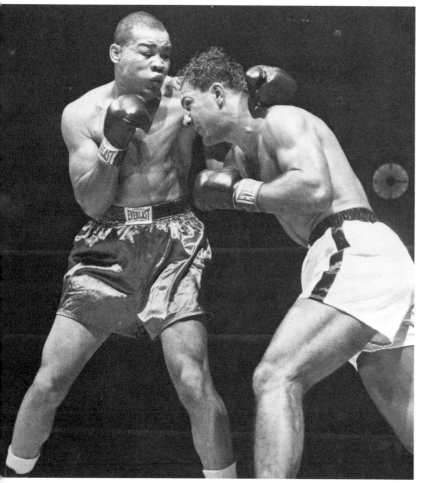

Louis battles Rocky Marciano in 1951. The Brown Bomber's comeback hopes were dashed by Marciano's eighth-round knockout.

The former heavyweight champion in 1972, in his new uniform as a Las Vegas casino greeter.

the government so much money in back taxes that he fought again. It wasn't the same. "My right hand don't leave me no more," he said. "I got to think to throw it now. When you're young, you see an opening and throw punches you can't even remember throwing."

In 1950, flabby and baldish, he lost to Ezzard Charles and announced he would never fight again. In 1951 he fought again and was knocked out by a young Rocky Marciano. "He was my idol," said Marciano. "I was very lucky that I didn't fight him ten years earlier."

That was his last fight. He refereed boxing and wrestling matches and wrestled briefly. He now works in Las Vegas as a casino greeter. To the public he is still the Brown Bomber, a great hero, a man loved by his generation.

Strangers slip money into his hands and make bets for him. He is fortunate that people have had such affection for him because for years he was always broke. He spent his boxing purses as fast as he collected them. He liked flashy clothes and cars and he had a knack for finding bad business investments.

"I took to having a good time with my winnings," he recalled, "and I had plenty of people to help me." Indeed, everyone knew he was an easy touch. "It's only money," he said. "And if they didn't need it, they wouldn't grab it."

In later years he used cocaine and was hospitalized for treatment. He also was hospitalized for what was called a "nervous disorder." Actually he had delusions that the Mafia was trying to kill him with poison gas. To thwart the threat, he once spread mayonnaise in the cracks of his hotel-room ceiling. In other hotels he carefully placed tape over the air ducts. Often he would build a makeshift tent in his bedroom and sleep fully clothed in the tent. "Here he was with his shoes and everything laying under his tent," said his wife, Martha. "It was the most pathetic thing in the world."

"For years, he had worn a halo not of his own making," said Barney Nagler, his biographer. "He was a great fighter, but he was just a human being outside the ring." As Dave Anderson wrote, "His life has been a tragedy, but somehow he is a tragedy to be revered."

Luckman, Sidney (1916–   )

He was the first great T-formation quarterback in modern football. He made the Chicago Bears the National Football League's dominant team in the 1940s, leading them to four NFL and five division championships.

Sid Luckman was a football genius whom Bob Zuppke, the former Illinois coach, called "the smartest player I ever saw, college or pro." Bob Snyder, his substitute and later a pro coach, said, "He can sit down and draw you every blocking assignment of the other ten Bears from each of the vast repertoire of plays the Bears used." In those days the Bears had 300 to 400 plays, each with perhaps ten variations.

George Halas, the owner and coach of the Bears, said he never called a wrong play during his 12 years on the field. "Having him at quarterback was like having another coach playing on the field," Halas said. "He was the greatest play-director I have ever seen. . . . He worked hard, stayed up nights studying and really learned the T. When others left the practice field, he stayed on."

Luckman was a solid 6 feet and 197 pounds, with curly black hair. He had a warm, gentle manner that proved, wrote Ed Fitzgerald, "that success could be achieved in even a rough-and-tumble game like pro football without requiring the sacrifice of the qualities of a gentleman."

He played single-wing tailback for Columbia University from 1936 to 1938, working his way through college by washing dishes and walls, delivering messages and babysitting. His teams seldom won, and he took weekly physical beatings (his nose was broken three times in college and five times with the Bears). Dan Parker wrote of his college days, "He was a jewel whose effulgence was dimmed by a bad setting."

He planned to enter the family trucking business after college, but Halas talked him into playing pro football and becoming a quarterback in his new T-formation. He played for the Bears from 1939 to 1950, completing 904 of 1,744 passes for 14,686 yards and 137 touchdowns. Five times he was all-pro, and he was voted into the College Football Hall of Fame in 1960 and the Pro Football Hall of Fame in 1965.

Of his introduction to pro football he said, "I was completely shocked by what I saw. It was the first

The Chicago star passing against the New York Giants.

time I'd seen the T-formation, and I didn't believe it could conceivably work, where you have no blocking in front of the ball carrier. Then, when I saw it in operation, I knew right there it was the most wonderful thing that could happen to me." After retiring, he served for years as an unpaid assistant coach with the Bears. Even after stepping down from that post, he said, "I have never really left the Bears."

Lujack, John (1925–   )

More outstanding quarterbacks have come from Notre Dame than from any other college, and the most celebrated of all Notre Dame quarterbacks was Johnny Lujack. He was a handsome matinee idol, quiet, cool, deliberate, enormously self-confident, a great leader.

As George Halas, his pro coach, said, "Completely stripped of all his amazing football skills, he is still indispensable for one thing—his poise." "You don't have to worry about a team with Lujack in charge," Coach Bernie Bierman of Minnesota said. "Just turn the reins over to him and relax." Ed Fitzgerald wrote, "He radiated confidence and class. He's a natural-born Big Man on Campus, and it doesn't make any difference that his current campus is the professional gridiron."

He was the Notre Dame quarterback in 1943, 1946 and 1947, with the two years out for wartime service in the Navy. His college teams won 26 games, lost one and tied one, and all three teams were national champions. In the famous 0-0 tie with

Lujack with the Heisman Trophy he was awarded as the nation's outstanding college football player of 1947.

Army in 1946, he made three open-field tackles on Arnold Tucker (all after Tucker had intercepted his passes) and one against Doc Blanchard that saved the game. Yet he said, "It was the worst game I ever played."

He won the Heisman Trophy as the outstanding college player in 1947, and he and 41 teammates went on to the National Football League. He signed with the Chicago Bears for four years at $18,750 a year and at first played defense. Then he succeeded Sid Luckman at quarterback and in a 1949 game against the Chicago Cardinals broke Sammy Baugh's one-game record by passing for 468 yards. The next year he was all-pro. But in 1951 his arm lost its power. After that season, at age 26, he retired as a player and for two years served as a Notre Dame assistant coach under Frank Leahy.

Leahy said, "He has everything it takes for success—brains, character and personality. He can make a million dollars if he wants to." He made his million, as an automobile dealer and television color announcer for college and pro football. Of the two games, he preferred the pros. "I would rather see one pro game than six played by top-ranking collegiate teams," he said. "The pros offer far more variety."

Luisetti, Angelo Enrico
(1916–   )

Hank Luisetti introduced the one-handed shot to basketball and revolutionized the game. Later he was chosen for the all-time All-America teams of the Helms Athletic Foundation and *Sport* magazine.

He was a slender 6-foot-3-inch forward, handsome and dark-haired. He came from Galileo High School in San Francisco, which also produced Joe DiMaggio and O. J. Simpson. In four years at Stanford University (1934–38) he made All-America three times and set all-time college records (since broken) of 50 points in one game and 1,596 career points.

In December 1936 Stanford invaded New York's Madison Square Garden, the citadel of basketball, to play Long Island University, which had won 43 straight games. Luisetti's one-handed shots, never seen before in the East, won the game and changed the sport. A Garden spectator said in mangled English, "It is the end of an area." Dick Friendlich wrote, "Two years after his appearance in the Garden, every school kid coming to an Eastern college was firing one-handed shots off his ears."

His shooting obscured his other talents. "He is an amazing marksman, a spectacular dribbler and an awfully clever passer," Nat Holman said. Joe Lapchick was impressed by his "uncanny ability to control the ball while going at top speed." Chuck Hyatt, his AAU coach, could not recall seeing him make a mistake. John Bunn, his Stanford coach, remembered him as "the perfect combination of everything needed for a top athlete."

After college he earned $10,000 for playing a basketball player in a Betty Grable movie. The AAU suspended him for a year for that breach of amateurism, but he later became an outstanding AAU player and coach and, years later, an automobile salesman and travel-agency executive.

"I guess we really didn't know what we were starting that night in Madison Square Garden," Luisetti recalled. "We had no idea that we would bring on a revolution. And I had no notion what that one game would mean to me." What did he think of today's shooting? "Shooting today is like throwing a penny in a wishing well. . . . Today's shooter takes off like a startled partridge, both feet off the floor, literally falling away from the basket."

214

New York Giants in mid-1902. The Giants were in last place at the time, and they were in last place in June 1932, when he stepped down, a sick old man. In between, his Giant teams won ten pennants and three World Series and finished in the first division in 27 of his last 29 full seasons.

He stood only 5 feet 7 inches, but he was tough, argumentative, hot-tempered and aggressive. He would do anything to win. He once said, "I'm an absolute czar. I order plays and they obey. If they don't, I fine them." One of his players, Travis Jackson, remembered that "When we were losing, his neck would swell up and his face would turn purple." Umpire Bill Klem said, "He was a man of great character, but he couldn't stand to lose a ball game."

He imposed strict rules on his players, but he was loyal and paid them well and booked them in first-class trains and hotels. He was called Little Napoleon (which was appropriate), Muggsy (which he hated) and Mr. McGraw (which suited him best). In 1937 he became the first manager to be voted into the Baseball Hall of Fame.

Grantland Rice said, "His very walk across the field in a hostile town was a challenge to the multitude." Jack Sher wrote, "He *was* the Giants, responsible for everything the name conveys— gigantic hate and terror, love and respect."

McGraw, John Joseph (1873–1934)

"He was the greatest of all managers," recalled Frank Graham. "He fashioned the most aggressive, the most exciting teams of his time. He could be charming or offensive, forgiving or vengeful, generous to his enemies, exasperating, even hateful, to his friends. . . . By his ruthlessness in battle, he made the Giants the most hated team on the road— and the most loved team at home."

From 1891 to 1906 John McGraw played 1,082 games, mostly at third base, for five major-league baseball teams. He batted .334, and he was, wrote Jack Sher, "a speedy, scrappy dynamo, the Eddie Stanky of his day."

After managing Baltimore teams in two leagues for two and a half seasons he became manager of the

McGraw (left) with Rogers Hornsby.

Mack, Connie (Cornelius Alexander McGillicuddy) (1862–1956)

Early in his playing career his name was shortened by a sportswriter so it could fit in a box score. His new name, Connie Mack, became one of the most famous in all baseball. He managed one team, the Philadelphia Athletics, for 50 years (1901–50), until he was 87. It helped that he owned the team, but he did win nine pennants and five World Series.

Red Smith wrote, "He was tough and warm and wonderful, kind and stubborn and courtly and unreasonable and generous and calculating and naïve and gentle and proud and humorous and demanding and unpredictable." He was soft-spoken when other managers were roughnecks. He called everyone Mr. and everyone called him Mr. Mack. He seldom smoked, drank, swore or spent money on his team.

"His players learned from him not only about baseball but how to live," Frank Graham wrote. He was, Al Horwits wrote, "a smart, shrewd man with vision and initiative." In later years, when the Athletics were always near last place, Harry Robert wrote, "He had no need to stage an expensive show because he had found that a cheap one drew just as well. . . . He could sell Philadelphia a shabby article of baseball because no matter how bad the Athletics might be, he could always count on the Phillies being worse."

He was a major-league catcher from 1886 to 1896 and a light hitter but smart. He was player-manager at Pittsburgh of the National League (1894–96) and Milwaukee of the Western League (1897–1900). When the American League was founded in 1901, he was awarded the Philadelphia franchise.

His first great team won pennants in 1910, 1911, 1913 and 1914, but he sold off his stars because the team won so often that fans stopped attending games. His next great team (including Lefty Grove, Mickey Cochrane, Jimmy Foxx, Jimmie Dykes and Al Simmons) won pennants in 1929, 1930 and 1931. He sold those stars, too, because the team needed cash during the Depression.

When he was in his 80s and still managing the Athletics, he said, "I'll stay in the game as long as my mind is clear. Besides, if I quit baseball, I would die in two weeks." In 1954, with the Athletics near bankruptcy, he sold the club. Fifteen months later, Connie Mack died at 93.

Connie Mack, Washington Nationals, 1887.

MacPhail, Leland Stanford
(1890–   )

As a baseball executive, red-haired Larry MacPhail was flamboyant, free-wheeling and abrasive, a showman and a bully who created turmoil wherever he went and whatever he did.

Gerald Holland asked, ''Who could be hauled off to jail for cop-fighting and turn up in the headlines again . . . as co-chairman of a drive to save the Baltimore Symphony Orchestra?'' With MacPhail, wrote Tom Meany, ''bizarre is orthodox.'' Bill Terry called him ''a brilliant screwball.'' And yet, wrote Arthur Daley, ''For the most part, he exploded in the right directions.''

At age 20 Larry MacPhail was a lawyer arguing his first case. He enlisted in World War I as a private and rose to captain. After the war he and seven other American officers tried to kidnap Kaiser Wilhelm from his refuge in the Netherlands (all he got was a souvenir ashtray).

He worked at many jobs before turning to baseball. Spending money freely, insulting some people and punching others, he revitalized three major-league franchises. As general manager of the Cincinnati Reds from 1934 to 1936 he introduced night baseball and air travel to the major leagues. As executive vice-president and then president of the Brooklyn Dodgers from 1938 to 1942, he hired (and frequently fired) Leo Durocher as manager and Red Barber as New York City's first play-by-play radio announcer.

In 1945, after he had served in World War II as an Army colonel, he, Dan Topping and Del Webb bought three baseball teams and their stadiums—the New York Yankees and Yankee Stadium, the Newark farm club and its ballpark and the Kansas City farm club and its stadium—all for $2.8 million. Topping and Webb put up the money, and MacPhail got one-third of the stock.

When he clashed with Joe McCarthy, McCarthy quit as manager. When the Yankees won the 1947 World Series, he rushed to the dressing-room celebration, punched a former Club Secretary in the eye, fired George Weiss as farm director and retired as president of the club. The next day he sold back his stock to the Yankees for $2 million and left baseball, never to return.

He bought a 1,000-acre estate in Maryland and raised cattle and thoroughbred horses. One son (Lee) became president of the American League and the other (Bill) was vice-president of sports for the Columbia Broadcasting System.

Gerald Holland wrote, ''He is what Walter Mitty dreamed of being: the man who could do anything, tell off the boss to his face, put over the big deal, take a punch at the cop, say the things at the time that most people don't think of until the next day.''

MacPhail, president of the New York Yankees, embracing Joe DiMaggio (left) and Joe Page after the Yankees won the 1947 World Series and MacPhail announced his retirement from baseball.

Mantle, Mickey Charles
(1931–   )

He was one of baseball's great players, a country boy who could hit the ball a mile and who could run in the field and on the bases when he was healthy. That was also the problem. He was seldom healthy. He played almost continually with pain, and fellow players marveled at his courage.

"When he is healthy," Maury Allen wrote, "he is 20 years old again, racing through the grass at Yankee Stadium, plucking off a fly, driving a baseball into the bleachers, lining a single to center field. . . . When he is ailing, he sulks, grows testy, dreams of ways to escape the agony of the ballfield. But where is there to go? . . . Retired and out of baseball, he's another rich Texan with a big house and some beautiful memories. Almost any middle-aged Texan can claim that."

Few baseball players could claim a record like his. He played for the New York Yankees, mostly in center field, from 1951 to 1968. In 2,401 games he hit 536 home runs and batted .298. He led the American League six times in runs, five in walks, four in home runs and four in slugging. Three times he was voted the league's most valuable player. In 1974, the first year he was eligible, he was voted into the Baseball Hall of Fame.

He was strapping at 5 feet 11½ inches and 195 pounds, a switch hitter with a hard swing who hit the ball record distances. One home run at Washington was measured at 565 feet. Another almost became the first fair ball hit out of Yankee Stadium.

A kick in the shin during his schoolboy football days in Oklahoma led to osteomyelitis, a rare, painful and debilitating bone disease. Along the way he underwent three operations on the knee and one on the shoulder. There were other physical ailments, too.

Joe Pepitone said, "Sometimes you feel tired and low. Then you think about him and what he must be going through with the pain and you say to yourself, 'If he can do it the way he feels and the way he must be hurting, then I can do it, too.' " Gene Woodling, another teammate, said, "Forget about baseball. Is this man going to be able to walk when he's 50 or 55?"

Mickey Mantle was a shy and retiring player, idolized by the public, distant to those he did not know and overwhelmed by New York. Larry Merchant wrote, "It took him 20 years to learn that his country-boy wit would go over in a big city." Dick Young called him "a man of moods who has the pride of a superstar. He is a very decent person." Young added, "He has heart, to a fault. He is, almost paradoxically, very trusting and very shy. People take advantage of his trust. They drive him to seclusion."

His father named him for Mickey Cochrane, the famous catcher. The youngster became a schoolboy star and signed with the Yankees for a bonus of $1,100, which paid off the family mortgage. In 1951 he was striking out too often, and the Yankees farmed him to Kansas City, then in the minor

Mickey Mantle, 21 years old, proudly points to the ball he hit 565 feet for a home run in 1953.

enough to play here. I'll never make it. I think I'll quit and go home with you.'' He was looking for sympathy, but he did not get it. His father said, ''Well, Mick, if that's all the guts you have, I think you better quit. You might as well go home right now.''

It was a bad moment. Mantle recalled, ''I never felt as ashamed as I did then, to hear my father sound disappointed in me, ashamed of me. . . . All he did was show me that I was acting scared and that you can't live scared. A year later, he was dead. . . . He didn't die scared, and he didn't live scared.''

Neither did the son. He became a winning player (the Yankees won 12 pennants in his first 14 seasons) and a rich player, earning $100,000 a year. He also became an inspiration. ''He made you bear down,'' Tony Kubek recalled. ''He made you concentrate.'' Bobby Murcer, a latter-day Yankee who benefitted from his coaching, said, ''He helps you just by being Mickey Mantle.''

Mantle takes a last look at his uniform in 1969, when he retired after 18 years with the Yankees.

leagues. He made only one hit (a bunt) in his first 22 at bats there. His father came to see him play, and the young Mantle was depressed.

''I'm not good enough to play in the major leagues,'' he told his father, ''and I'm not good

Marchetti, Gino John (1927–   )

Gino Marchetti set the style for the quick, mobile defensive ends of modern pro football. He was a vicious pass rusher, and at age 35 he could still run 40 yards in 4.9 seconds.

His father once told him, "When all those players run at you, get out of the way," but he never did. As *The First 50 Years, the Story of the National Football League* said, "He had strength and the meanness necessary to give and take the pounding of interior-line play. He used his hands and weight well, pushing and throwing and clubbing off linemen. But his major contribution was not to increase punishment but to add finesse, and it was this element of his ability that raised him above his peers."

After World War II service as a machine gunner in Europe, he returned home, formed a semi-pro football team and, four years after high school, entered the University of San Francisco. He played pro football for the Dallas Texans (1952) and Baltimore Colts (1953–64 and 1966). He made all-pro six times in his 14 years. When the Colts asked him to return in 1966 after a one-year retirement, he did, saying, "I'm not making a comeback. I'm doing them a favor. Everything I have I owe to them. The Colts treated me like a man, not a number."

Carroll Rosenbloom, the Colts' owner, encour-

Marchetti tackling Paul Flatley of the Minnesota Vikings.

aged him and two other players to go into business. They decided on a hamburger stand, but there was no money for a long-term lease. Rosenbloom co-signed, and that was the start of the Gino's chain that has made the players wealthy.

At his peak Marchetti stood 6 feet 4 inches and weighed 245 pounds. Gail Cogdill, a 195-pound opponent, said, "I bounce off him like a bird run into a windowpane." George Wilson, a rival coach, said he never repeated the same move and thought no one else had such imagination. For Bobby Layne, a rival quarterback, "He was the best defensive player I ever had to go against." In 1972, the first year he was eligible, he was voted into the Pro Football Hall of Fame.

He really loved the game. "I never had the feeling that football is a grind, something just for money," he said. "I never give up. Second effort counts a lot."

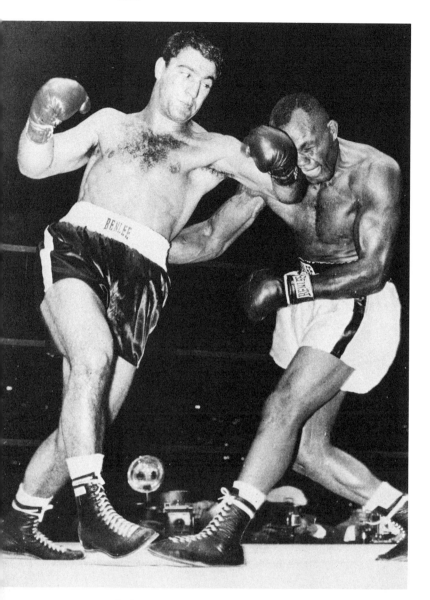

champion. After defending against Walcott, Roland LaStarza, Ezzard Charles (twice), Dan Cockell and Archie Moore, he retired in 1956 as undefeated champion. He had won every one of his 49 pro fights.

His purses grossed $1.7 million, but in four years he had seen his wife only 152 days. "My lonesome family convinced me that I should quit while I'm still in good shape," he said. "I was proud of being champion and I was determined never to get out of condition. So I boxed 250 rounds before the Ezzard Charles fight, 250 before each of the Walcott fights and 200 for the Dan Cockell fight. And every round, even in training, was a real battle."

He was, as Arthur Daley wrote, "a totally dedicated man, so single-minded of purpose that he subordinated himself to the monastic regimen." Red Smith wrote, "Probably there will be scornful things said and written about his punching power. Because he is known as the best one-punch hitter of them all, his antagonist is supposed to drop the first time he swings a glove."

Jersey Joe Walcott said, "He was a man of courage in the ring. Outside, he was kind and gentle." Abe J. Greene, a long-time boxing official, said, "He epitomized all the characteristics that true lovers of boxing held as their standards for the sport."

Marciano, Rocky (1923–1969)

He was a stocky man with short arms, a flat, high-pitched Boston accent and a gentle, pleasant and humble manner. He was plain, articulate and, as the years went by, immensely popular.

He was a good-enough catcher to get a tryout with the Chicago Cubs (his throwing arm was not major-league caliber). So Rocky Marciano, born Rocco Francis Marchegiano, became a fighter. In 1951 he knocked out an over-the-hill Joe Louis and hurt him so badly that for a week Louis couldn't raise his arms high enough to brush his teeth. In 1952 he knocked out Jersey Joe Walcott and became heavyweight

Marciano hangs up his gloves in 1956 and retires as undefeated heavyweight champion.

Marciano punches his way to a successful title defense against Ezzard Charles (left) in 1954.

Sport magazine called him "a man of character." Al Weill, his manager and not exactly a sentimentalist, said, "He was the sweetest man I ever knew. . . . He don't want to hurt nobody."

He resisted a comeback, saying, "I am the only heavyweight champion in the entire history of boxing who ever was undefeated when he retired. No one can ever beat that record. Never."

He did not live long enough to enjoy his retirement. He was flying in a private plane to a party to celebrate his 46th birthday when the plane crashed, killing all three aboard.

Mathewson, Christopher
(1880–1925)

Christy Mathewson was a real-life Frank Merriwell. He was handsome, dignified and popular. At Bucknell University he was a baseball, football and basketball star, honor student and class president and member of the glee club and two literary societies. As a major-league pitcher he was perhaps the best ever, and in 1936 he became one of the five charter members of the Baseball Hall of Fame.

He pitched for the New York Giants from 1900 to 1916 and one game for the Cincinnati Reds in 1916, winning 373 games (a National League record he shares with Grover Cleveland Alexander). He still ranks third in all-time major-league victories and shutouts (83) and fifth in earned-run average (2.13). He once needed only 67 pitches to win a nine-inning game, and for 12 straight years he won 22 or more games. In the 1905 World Series he pitched three shutouts against the Philadelphia Athletics—on a Monday, Thursday and Saturday. His best pitch was the fadeaway, a right-handed reverse curve similar to the left-handed screwball that Carl Hubbell made famous a generation later.

He was traded to the Reds in 1916 so he could become manager. He won the only game he pitched for them, but he labored so that he told his Cincinnati players, "If I ever go into the box again, I'll buy every one of you a suit of clothes." He managed the Reds until 1918, when he volunteered for the Army in the midst of the First World War. His lungs were seared by poison gas overseas, and he was stricken by tuberculosis, which caused his early death. Bob Broeg described his life as "sweet tragedy."

His manager with the Giants, John McGraw, called him the greatest pitcher who ever lived. Connie Mack said it was wonderful to watch him pitch—as long as he wasn't pitching against you. His control was so good that John (Chief) Meyers said, "You could sit in a rocking chair and catch him."

Grantland Rice wrote, "He handed the game a certain touch of class." W. O. McGeehan called him "the best loved of all ballplayers and the most popular athlete of all time." "As a player and a man," wrote Jack Sher, "he was to our national game what Washington and Lincoln were to our country."

Mathias, Robert Bruce (1930–)

At the age of 17, two months after graduating from high school and six weeks after competing in his first decathlon, Bob Mathias won the 1948 Olympic decathlon and became the youngest Olympic champion in track and field. Four years later and a senior at Stanford University, he won the 1952 decathlon. Soon after, he retired from track, unbeaten in one of the most challenging sports events.

He was truly an All-American boy. He was modest, clean-cut, self-confident and tenacious, but his road to success was not smooth. He high-jumped 4 feet 8 inches when he was ten, and at 12, in his first meet, he cleared 5-6. But by 14 he stood 5-10. He was growing too fast, and he became weak from anemia. His father, a physician, prescribed iron pills, liver pills and a daily nap, and he regained his strength.

His track coach at Tulare (California) High School wrote for a book on the decathlon, an almost masochistic ordeal involving ten track and field events in two days. In the spring of 1948 his coach started him on a training program aimed for the 1952 Olympics. In June he entered a regional meet, and though he had never competed in six of the ten events, he won. That qualified him for the national championships two weeks later, which he also won. That qualified him for the Olympics four weeks later and, at the age of 17 years, eight months and three weeks, he won that, too.

President Harry Truman welcomed him home. So did 200 marriage proposals. He went to prep school and Stanford. Then, in 1952, despite a pulled thigh muscle that shot stabbing pains through his back and side, he won the Olympic title again and set his third world decathlon record in three years.

His triumphs earned him roles in four movies (including the title part in *The Bob Mathias Story*) and a television series. He became a Congressman, and he owned summer camps for children.

Don Kowet wrote, "His two Olympic victories, before he reached the age of 22, make him the greatest decathlon champion ever. . . . Perhaps there has never been a more perfect blend of talent and temperament." Brutus Hamilton said, "He is not only the greatest athlete in the world, but he's also the greatest competitor."

Mathias with President Gerald Ford and Dennis Pringle, mayor of Clovis, California, during Mathias' 1974 reelection campaign.

Throwing the discus at the 1948 Olympics.

Randy Matson, shot-putter turned stockbroker, at work in his Houston office.

Matson, James Randel (1945–)

For almost a decade, Randy Matson put the shot farther than anyone else, past or present. Dave Maggard called him "the best athlete I've ever seen in any sport, pro or amateur." Bob Giegengack called him "the surest first-place winner anybody has in any event in any meet."

In the ninth grade he stood 6 feet 3 inches, in 10th grade 6-6. In his prime he was 6-6½ and weighed 260 to 272 pounds. For all his size and strength, he was quiet, humble and shy. To strangers he always said "Yes, sir" and "No, sir."

As a 19-year-old freshman at Texas A&M he won the silver medal at the 1964 Olympics. In 1968 he won the gold. He was the first man to put the shot 70 feet. He set world records of 67-11¼, 69-0¾ and 70-5¼ in a one-month span in 1965. In 1967 he raised the record to 71-5½.

He swept the NCAA shot-put and discus titles three years in a row (1965–67) and won four AAU national titles with the shot. By the start of 1971 he had made the 25 longest puts of all time and 52 of the best 53. In 1973 he turned pro, and in 1974 he was the best of the pros.

He played football in high school and only one year of college basketball, but he showed such promise that he was drafted by professional teams in both sports. Hank Foldberg, the Texas A&M athletic director, once said, "What a football player he would make. But I wouldn't dare issue him a football suit. If anything happened to him, this state wouldn't be big enough to hide me."

Payton Jordan described his putting style by saying, "His foot explodes, his calf explodes, his thigh explodes, his hip, his back, his shoulder, his triceps and right out to the very tips of his fingers. It's like a whole string of firecrackers going off." Pat Putnam cited another attribute, writing, "As long as there was his own world record to better, he always managed to get the adrenalin turned on in a meet."

Typically, he downplayed his sacrifices. "People say you must really be dedicated," he said, "but it doesn't seem that way to me. . . . Just working at throwing the shot can't make you very tired. . . . I've had lots of desire in trying to throw farther and win. . . . You have to feel winning is important. . . . It's kind of embarrassing to get beat."

Matson at the 1968 Olympics.

Mays, Willie Howard (1931–   )

For 22 seasons he was one of baseball's most dynamic and successful players. In his early years baseball was a joy. "He plays the game," said Walter Alston, "as if it's fun." In later years his body rebelled, and as Peter Schrag wrote, he was "defying time . . . defying age itself."

Willie Mays had all the skills. He could hit, run, throw and excite the public. His lifetime batting average was .302, and when he retired he ranked third among the all-time leaders in games played (2,992), third in home runs (660), third in runs (2,062), fourth in at bats (10,881), seventh in hits (3,283) and seventh in runs batted in (1,903).

These are only figures. The real Willie Mays was the unsophisticated youngster who joined the New York Giants as an outfielder in 1951 and couldn't wait to get home from a game to play stickball in the streets with neighborhood admirers. This was the Willie Mays whose cap kept falling off when he tore around the bases, who addressed teammates as "Say, Hey" because he could not remember names, who called his manager Mr. Leo.

Years later, the innocence of youth gone, some of the joy disappeared, too. He was often withdrawn, curt and unhappy. Roger Kahn wrote, "Once he was a boy of overwhelming enthusiasm. He has become a man of vigorous pride. . . . He stands up to time defiantly and with dignity." Dave Anderson wrote, "The carnival music of boyhood once seemed to be tinkling wherever he went. But now soft violins accompany him."

New Yorkers loved him, but when the Giants moved to San Francisco in 1958 the people did not take to him, perhaps because he was an alien hero. Instead they glorified a rookie named Orlando Cepeda. In 1962, when the Mets were created and the San Francisco Giants played in New York for the first time, the New York fans ignored Cepeda. When they glimpsed Mays for the first time, they screamed in delight. A New York writer turned to a San Fran-

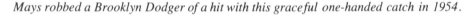

Mays robbed a Brooklyn Dodger of a hit with this graceful one-handed catch in 1954.

The ties with the carefree past were running out. "When I was a kid, it was all fun," he said. "But sometimes, when I get tired and with all that pressure, it gets to be work. I knew when I was 16 years old I never did want to work for a living."

He retired after the 1973 season. His contract with the Mets guaranteed him $50,000 a year for ten years as a coach, good-will ambassador or almost anything else he wanted to do. He acknowledged that "not playing is a comedown. . . . I didn't want to be a full-time coach. For me to play the number of years I did and go out there and coach at first base, that's like a statue."

He was anything but a statue. Leo Durocher, his first major-league manager, remembered, "He could do everything the day he joined the Giants, and the only other player who could do it all was Joe DiMaggio. . . . He never had to be taught a thing." Jesus Alou, a teammate, said, "It's wonderful seeing him all the time hustle, hustle. He taught me that's what baseball is all about." Roy Blount, Jr., wrote, "He has the air of that kid in a pickup game who has more ability and fire than the others and wishes intensely that they would come on and play right and raise the whole game to a level commensurate with his own gifts and appetites."

That was the public side. The private Willie Mays was different. His second wife, May Louise, said, "He's a private person. He's often told me, 'How can I tell you when I don't know what I'm thinking?'"

cisco colleague and said, "The big man just found out who the big man really is."

In 1972 he was near the end of his career when the Giants sold him and his $165,000 salary to the Mets. The idea, both teams said, was to take care of Willie—a paternalist attitude and phrase that smacked of antebellum dealings between plantation owners and slaves. In his first game for the Mets his home run beat the Giants, and Pete Hamill wrote, "It was as if some forgotten promise had been kept."

He played for the Mets, when he felt well enough, for the rest of the 1972 season and all of 1973. Tug McGraw, the spirit of the Mets, called him "the essence of the athletic spirit." Milton Gross described his performance as "an emotional experience" and wrote, "He is the tie that binds so many of us to our carefree days of the past."

Meyer, Deborah Elizabeth
(1952–   )

At five, Debbie Meyer learned to swim. At eight, she swam her first race. At 14, she set the first of her 15 world records. At 16, though she was ill much of the time with a stomach infection, she became the first swimmer to win three individual gold medals at one Olympic Games. At 19, the magic was gone, and she retired.

As Neil Amdur wrote, she worked long and hard for success. She credited her coach, Sherman Chavoor, with the lesson that swimming was "a sport of nerves and guts." He put her through tough workouts that revolutionized training theories. "In a sense, I guess you could say that I was one of the guinea pigs," she said. "But now that I look back on it and see that some of my records are still standing, I realize how far ahead of my time I must have been."

She stood 5 feet 7½ inches and weighed 127 pounds. She was unassuming, even self-effacing. For Pat Besford, the British writer, "she typified

Debbie Meyer holding two of her three Olympic gold medals. She gave the third to her coach, Sherman Chavoor.

everything American in looks, personality and swimming." Her smile could have been painted by Rembrandt, her apple cheeks by Franz Hals.

Some of her performances were astounding. Her world free-style records for women at 400 meters (4 minutes 24.5 seconds in 1968) and 1,500 meters (17:19.9 in 1969) would have won the 1956 Olympic gold medals for men. But her interest began to wane. "It's hard to motivate champions," Chavoor said. "What do you wave in front of a champion? The Olympics?" Her mother, Mrs. Betty Meyer, said, "She finds it harder to keep herself motivated."

She tried to renew interest in 1971 by filling her room with Olympic posters, but to no avail. Prior to the 1968 games she had swum 30,000 training miles in 11 years. For the 1972 games she would have to swim 13,000 yards of high-quality workouts every day.

In January 1972 she quit, saying, "It got to the point that I was starting to hate workouts. I just couldn't stand the thought of putting in all that time and effort without getting results. And I didn't want to go to the Olympics again unless I knew I had a chance to win."

Mikan, George Lawrence
(1924–   )

George Mikan grew up self-conscious and self-doubting. During his career he took a greater physical beating than perhaps any contemporary. Despite that, wrote Norman Katkov, "He was the gate attraction that procured major-league status for professional basketball."

Mikan leaps high for a hook-shot past Nat (Sweetwater) Clifton of the New York Knicks during the 1953 NBA playoffs.

At the age of eight he stood 5 feet 9 inches. He was 6 feet at age 11 and he grew to 6 feet 10 inches.

He wanted to go to Notre Dame, but Coach George Keogan rejected him as "hopelessly clumsy." Instead he went to DePaul University in Chicago, where he skipped rope, shadow-boxed and ran by the hour to overcome awkwardness. With his thick glasses and 245-pound bulk, he hardly looked like an athlete, but he made All-American three straight years (1944–46) and was twice named player of the year.

Even college teammates teased him about his size, especially with one jingle: "Mikan's girl is ten feet tall, she sleeps in the kitchen with her feet in the hall." Yet college and pro opponents found nothing funny about his bulk, especially his flying elbows. He took more than his share of punishment as a pro—breaking his left leg, his right leg, right foot, the arch of his left foot, his right wrist, nose, thumb and three fingers—plus 166 stitches.

He played for the Minneapolis Lakers from 1947 to 1956, leading his team to five titles in six years. He was all-pro his first six seasons and scoring champion three times. To counter his effectiveness under the basket, officials widened the free-throw lane, where he stood like a monument, from six feet to 12. The next year he scored 61 points in one game, and he retired with 11,764 points, a 22.6 average and many other lifetime records. He became a lawyer and, years later, the first commissioner of the American Basketball Association.

"He would have been a stickout anytime, anywhere and under any conditions," Red Auerbach said. A Madison Square Garden marquee once said simply: "Tonight George Mikan vs. Knicks."

As a youngster he loved music and felt he had enough talent to become a concert pianist. "But," he said, "I was foolish enough to let myself be laughed out of it." He remembered that as a youngster he used to stoop to make himself look shorter. "I became round-shouldered, ungainly and so filled with bitterness that my height nearly wrecked my life," he said. "Later, I found that a tall man didn't have to accept clumsiness. He could be well-coordinated and graceful if he was willing to try hard enough to improve himself."

Mikita shoots against Ken Dryden of the Montreal Canadiens in the third game of the 1973 Stanley Cup finals.

Mikita, Stanley (1940–   )

For his first six full seasons in the National Hockey League, Stan Mikita would fight any opponent at any time for any reason. He lost most of the fights, but he got away with fighting because he was good at everything else. Then he stopped fighting and became a superstar.

Jack Zanger wrote, "He once was the embodiment of the whole *Dirty Dozen* by himself." Denis DeJordy, a teammate, said there probably wasn't anyone in the league outside his own team who liked him when he was on the ice. But like him or not, they universally respect him. He was born in Czechoslovakia as Stanislas Gvoth. When he was eight the Communists took over, and he moved to Canada to live with an uncle named Mikita. There he took up hockey, and since 1958 he has played center for the Chicago Black Hawks. He has been an all-star eight times, scoring champion four times, most valuable player twice and winner of the Lady Byng Trophy for sportsmanship twice.

He is small (5 feet 9 inches and 165 pounds) and rugged and has narrow eyes. *Sport* magazine said he looked like a movie tough guy. He may be the best face-off man in history, and few players have done so many things so well. "He has such tremendous reflexes that he can change his mind in mid-stride when he's skating or shooting," Glenn Hall, a teammate, once commented. Bobby Hull, a teammate and fellow superstar, said there wasn't a smarter player in the NHL.

Mikita once explained his aggressive style. "I've heard of guys who came into this league with more ability than I had at the same stage, and guys would take two or three runs at them and they'd run the other way. They never stuck. They got chased out. I didn't want this to happen to me." His stature was constantly on the line. "I always had to prove myself. I always wanted to be the best. If I were a Ping-Pong player, I'd have to be the best in the world."

twice lowered his 110-meter record to 13.1. From 1970 to 1974 he lost only twice. In 1974, rejecting pro football because he could not get the money he wanted, he turned professional in track, went undefeated and set a world indoor record of 6.7 seconds for 60 yards.

He is soft-spoken and shy, and he smiles easily. Yet with all his success he has not always been happy. Before the Olympics, *Boys' Life* wrote of him, "He is . . . a vulnerable human being who suffers because the world he lives in is not always perfect, because people he considers friends are not always loyal, because the world makes great demands on him. He is not a loner, but much of the time he would rather be left alone."

Milburn does not enjoy being a celebrity. "Everybody pressures me," he has said. "Track is nothing but hassles. You run for your country and what do you get? Nobody says, 'Thanks, Rod.' They don't care."

Milburn, Rodney, Jr. (1950–   )

Joseph Valerio wrote, "Rod Milburn is part of a restless generation which seeks instant gratification." Gratification came quickly and often because Milburn won every possible high-hurdling honor and broke every possible record from 1970 to 1973.

As a Louisiana youngster, he was the fastest high-school hurdler in the country. At Southern University, where he combined speed and technique as no hurdler had done before, he won AAU, NCAA University Division, NCAA College Division and NAIA titles indoors and outdoors. He was the 1971 Pan-American champion, and he went to the 1972 Olympics as the strongest favorite in any track and field event. His winning time in the Olympics equaled the world record of 13.2 for 110 meters.

In the 120-yard high hurdles, he set a world record of 13.0 in 1971 and tied it in 1973. In July 1973 he

Milburn, named Louisiana's outstanding college athlete in 1973, with his award.

Miller, Delvin Glenn (1913–)

Jeremiah Tex wrote of Del Miller, "He is the finest all-round horseman that sulky racing has ever produced. . . . No man's career has yet encompassed every facet of the sport with such resounding success." Red Smith said it in a different way: "He is an authentic titan in his field."

Del Miller, baldish, easygoing and generous, made his mark in harness racing as a driver, trainer, owner, breeder, buyer, seller and track owner. When he had two horses in an important race, he let an assistant drive the better horse. When a rival needed advice, he gave it.

From 1939 to the end of 1974 he drove 1,775 winners and earned purses of $6,773,073. Others have more impressive figures, but he drove trotters and pacers only part time because he had so many other interests in the sport. He built and ran The Meadows, harness racing's first all-weather track, and Meadowlands Farm, a huge breeding operation, in the little village of Meadow Lands, Pennsylvania. And he dominated the sport with one horse.

Countess Adios (No. 7), with Del Miller in the sulky, winning the 1960 Cane Pace in record time.

The horse was Adios. Miller bought him in 1948 for $21,000 (of which he borrowed $15,000). Adios was then eight years old. He lived to age 25 and became the most famous and most productive sire of modern harness horses. Miller earned a million dollars with Adios, depreciated him, sold him for $500,000, paid a capital-gains tax on the sale and then bought back a one-third share in him for $166,000 and depreciated that, too.

"He is affable, he is shrewd, and it detracts nothing from his fame to say that he also is very lucky," Kenneth Rudeen wrote. "Adioses do not fall to unlucky men." Milton Gross wrote, "He is such a singularly successful money-making machine that he exemplifies harness racing's climb from the county-fair circuit to the capital-gains class."

Miller said, "When I started out in harness racing there were very few kids like me around. Most of the old-timers wouldn't teach you anything. You had to find out everything yourself. I made up my mind I'd be different if I got to be successful. . . . I don't get so much of a bang driving in races as I used to. When I get to the place where I go up to the gate and I'm getting nervous and scared, that's when I'll quit driving."

Miller, John Laurence (1947–)

He is an All-American boy with All-American looks—a slim (6 feet 2 inches, 170 pounds) figure and long blond hair. He is an elder of the Mormon Church and does not smoke, drink or swear.

Johnny Miller is also a professional golfer who became an almost instant success. And he did it on his terms. He seldom practices. He often skips major tournaments. "I keep everything in perspective," he said. "Maybe I am a little selfish in not playing as much, but that's the way I want it."

He wants his freedom. "I hate to feel we are like cattle," he once said, "with people shoving us around, telling us when to play and how many times we should play and how much money I can win."

While other pros are hitting a hundred practice shots, he may hit only three or four. "My game doesn't require a lot of maintenance," he said. ". . . My swing is grooved, for good or bad. . . . " His swing, said Jack Nicklaus, is "the best on the tour."

He started hitting golf balls at the age of five. In 1966 he signed up to caddie in the United States Open. Instead, he qualified to play and finished eighth, a heroic performance for a 19-year-old amateur. He didn't think so. He thought he should have won.

Seven years later, in 1973, he did win the U.S. Open with a final-round 63, the lowest score in the tournament's history. In 1974 he won eight times on the tour and set a one-year earnings record of $353,021. In 1975 he won the tour opener, the Phoenix Open, by 14 strokes and finished 24 under par for 72 holes. The next week he won the Tucson Open by nine strokes and finished 25 under par. In each tournament he shot a 61.

Jerry Heard, a fellow pro, said Miller is as good as Nicklaus, "maybe better." John S. Radosta wrote, "The mechanics of his game are flawless." Barry McDermott wrote, "The day may come when people discuss the Miller Attitude the same way they do the Vardon Grip."

The Miller Attitude is built on much confidence and little emotion. "When I'm standing over the ball," he said, "serenity is knowing my worst shot is going to be pretty good."

Miller before the final round of the 1973 Bob Hope Desert Classic. He finished behind Palmer and tied for second place with Nicklaus.

Moss, Stirling (1929–)

Few race drivers in history had the skill of Stirling Moss. Those who did became world champions. But Moss, Michael Frostick wrote, ''was certainly the most famous and most able driver never to be a champion.'' And, as Anthony Pritchard said, ''He was a far greater champion than many of the men who gained the title.''

The public and his rivals held him in awe. He was slim yet muscular at 5 feet 8 inches, attractive and popular. He was the best sports-car driver of his day and almost the best grand-prix driver, but for years he failed to win the big races because as an idealistic Englishman he insisted on driving British cars.

In 1955 grand-prix races he drove a Mercedes, in 1956 a Maserati, in 1957 and 1958 a Vanwall, and each year he finished second in the world-championship standing. In 1959 he drove a Cooper and a BRM, in 1960 and 1961 a Lotus, and each year he finished third. His racing career ended in 1962 when a crash the day after Easter left him unconscious for a month and partially paralyzed for six months.

He won 194 of 466 career races, and he finished 307 times among the top three. He earned $150,000 a year, Queen Elizabeth raised him to the Order of the British Empire, and women adored him. When he stopped racing he became active in many businesses involving the sport.

He remained a dynamo. Denis Jenkinson, a British auto writer who spent considerable time with him in and out of race cars, said, ''As a driver he was faultless. As a person, he could be tiresome. . . . He could never relax, take unnecessary time over a meal, read a book or listen to a symphony. He was always on the go.''

Despite his near-fatal accident, he never feared speed. ''A driver shouldn't be frightened of speed,'' he said. ''The things that frighten me are mainly things I don't understand. If one gets into a situation he's not sure he can handle, then one realizes he is out of his depth and is frightened. . . . To me, though, speed is exhilarating.''

His priorities, he said, were misguided. ''Jackie Stewart's premise was to win a race at the slowest possible speed,'' he said. ''My philosophy, which was wrong, was I'd rather lose a race driving at the fastest possible speed.''

Victory flowers surround Stirling Moss after he won the 1961 Monte Carlo Grand Prix.

Moss, an Englishman who usually drove only British cars, in a Lotus in an Italian race.

Marion Motley carries against the New York Giants.

Motley, Marion (1920–)

From 1946 to 1953, Marion Motley played fullback for the Cleveland Browns with a toughness that earned him a place in the Pro Football Hall of Fame. He stood 6 feet 1 inch and weighed 238 pounds. As a runner he was quick, explosive and hard-working. He ran for 4,720 yards (averaging 5.7 yards a carry) and 31 touchdowns, almost all by bulling his way up the middle. When he ran, wrote Myron Cope, he was "truly fearsome."

His other skill was pass blocking. He was the bodyguard on the field for Otto Graham, the great passer. Graham called him "the best fullback I ever saw . . . a better all-round player than Jimmy Brown." For Blanton Collier, a coach with the Browns, Motley was the best blocker, the best fullback and the greatest all-round football player he ever saw. Tony Adamle, a teammate, said, "He was one helluva unselfish player. Marion Motley never thought about Marion Motley—only the team."

It was all a struggle. He played one year at South Carolina State and three years at the University of Nevada, and he was no sensation. He was 26 when the Browns signed him, primarily as a roommate for Bill Willis, their first black player. There were few blacks in pro football at the time, and he took physical and verbal abuse from white opponents.

From 1950 on he had knee trouble, and he quit after the 1953 season. He made a comeback with the Pittsburgh Steelers in 1955 as a linebacker, a position he had played in his early years with the Browns when he was a 60-minute player. His knees did him in again. For all this, he earned $4,000 as a rookie, $12,000 a year at his peak.

After his playing days he wanted to coach, but few blacks were hired as coaches. He moved from one dreary job to another. In 1967 he coached a women's football team in Cleveland but said, "Coaching the girls' team isn't very satisfying."

He felt that the Browns had abandoned him. "The thing that burns me up is that the other ball clubs give their players a break when they're all through," he said. "But Cleveland didn't do anything for me. . . . I thought I should have gotten a job or something. I deserved a chance."

Musial, Stanley Frank (1920–   )

He was the National League's best hitter of his day, and his day lasted from 1941 to 1963. He was one of baseball's greatest players and one of its greatest human beings, a modest, simple man who knew what he was doing and loved it.

Everyone loved Stan Musial. His teammates once gave him a plaque that described him as "the perfect answer to a manager's prayer." Ed Linn said, "It is difficult to write about him without sounding as if you were delivering the nominating address at a Presidential convention."

He played outfield and first base for the St. Louis Cardinals. He had a lifetime batting average of .331, and at the age of 41 he was still batting .330. He won seven batting titles and three most-valuable-player awards during his 22 major-league seasons. Before Henry Aaron passed him, he ranked first in the major-league all-time standing in extra-base hits (1,377) and total bases (6,134), second in games (3,026) and at bats (10,972) and fourth in runs (1,949) and runs batted in (1,951). He still ranks second in hits (3,630) and doubles (725) and sixth in bases on balls (1,599). He was voted into the Baseball Hall of Fame in 1969, the first year he was eligible.

He was almost unstoppable at the plate. Before Willie Mays played against him for the first time,

Leo Durocher, Mays's manager, ran down the Cardinal batting order and told Mays how to play each batter. Mays reminded him that he had omitted the third man. "The third hitter," said Durocher, "is Stan Musial. There is no advice I can give you about him. He will show you why the first time he gets to bat."

He showed everyone, but he remained modest. "Some players can remember exactly what they hit in a certain game," Musial once said. "I'm not too good at that. I just enjoy playing ball. Sure, I like my hits as much as the next guy does, and I'd be kidding if I said I didn't get pleasure out of my records. But in a ball game, I'm mostly interested in winning."

He was never satisfied with his accomplishments. Frank Lane, once his general manager, said, "I could name a lot of hitters who get two hits and then lean back, satisfied that they've had a good day. With him, when he had two hits, you knew he was gunning for the third. And when he got that third hit, you knew damn well that he was hungrier than ever

for the fourth.''

His confidence never wavered. Jim Toomey, the Cardinals' public-relations director, told the story of a team plane ride. Thirty seconds after take-off, one engine quit. The players rushed to the windows to look at the dead propeller. Musial, sitting by a window, said with his usual giggle, ''I can see the headline now: 'Cardinal Plane Crashes; Musial Sole Survivor.''' Toomey said, ''This is what makes a .300 hitter—utter confidence under all conditions.''

He was a left-handed batter with a unique corkscrew batting stance. ''Musial at bat is a man with an angle,'' Jerry Izenberg wrote. ''He is studying as he stands there, and with proper concentration he can tell a fast ball from a curve when the pitch is still 30 feet out.'' Outside the Cardinals' park in St. Louis is a nine-foot statue of Musial in that peculiar batting stance. It cost $40,000, raised in nickels and dimes from an adoring public that knew him as Stan the Man.

It was not always so. In 1938 he started in the minor leagues as a left-handed pitcher with a fre-quently sore arm. In 1940, playing in the outfield between pitching starts, he tried for a shoestring catch, but his spikes caught in the grass and he landed on the point of his left shoulder. He could never pitch effectively again, and he became an outfielder. By the end of 1941 he was a major leaguer.

After retirement he stayed with the Cardinals as vice-president and sometimes general manager. He was chairman of the President's Council on Physical Fitness, a partner in a thriving St. Louis restaurant and a public hero.

During his long career he never lost his love of baseball. ''I know a lot of players dislike the life, the traveling,'' he said. ''I like it. I enjoy being a big-league ballplayer. Heck, everybody wanted to be a big-league player once, didn't they? I like it all, every part of it. . . . But I know you can't go on forever. It's tough for a ballplayer to get old. It's tough for anybody to get old, but a ballplayer has to grow old twice. . . . I've had my years and I've had my hits and I've had my thrills.''

Nagurski, Bronislau (1908–   )

Bronko Nagurski may have been the toughest football player ever. He stood 6 feet 2 inches and weighed 230 pounds. He had a heavy jaw, a barrel chest, legs like a tree trunk, a size-19½ collar and a ring size of 19½ (the largest ring Tiffany carries is a size 12). As a ball carrier, blocker and tackler, he was destructive. "No one better embodies the symbol of strength," Murray Olderman wrote.

"There probably has never been a football player stronger than Nagurski or any who could develop so much horsepower from a standing start," Pudge Heffelfinger said. Jimmy Gallagher wrote, "Those who were unlucky got in his way. Those who were lucky got out of it." Steve Owen said, "Tacklers to Nagurski are like flies on the flank of a horse—a nuisance but not serious." Ernie Nevers said, "Tackling him was like trying to tackle a freight train going downhill." "If you hit him above the ankles," Red Grange said, "you were likely to get killed." Grantland Rice said he was "the only man who ever lived who could lead his own interference."

Harry Newman, Benny Friedman and Johnny Dell Isola, all from the New York Giants, had special memories. "I tried to stop him in the open field," Newman said. "I hit him as hard as I could, and all it did was throw him off pace a little." Friedman recalled, "I was at safety when he broke through with only me between him and the goal. . . . It was like ordering a switchman to stop a locomotive with his bare hands." Dell Isola remembered once hitting him head on at the line of scrimmage. "It was the hardest tackle I ever made. I figured maybe he might have made a yard at most and I was congratulating myself pretty good. Then I heard the referee say, 'Second down and two.'"

Two New York tacklers struggle to bring down Nagurski during the 1934 championship game between the Giants and Bears.

Only his mother was unimpressed. "I don't understand," she said. "He was always the laziest boy in International Falls."

He was born to Ukrainian immigrants on the Canadian side of a lake that spans the border between Canada and the United States. He was raised on the other side, in International Falls, Minnesota. His first teacher could not understand his mother's pronunciation of Bronislau. To her, it sounded like Bronko, and his nickname was born.

He played mostly at tackle and some at fullback for the University of Minnesota from 1927 to 1929. As a junior he broke three ribs playing fullback in one game and played the entire next game at tackle. He played fullback and linebacker for the Chicago Bears from 1930 to 1937, never earning more than $5,000. When the Bears refused to pay him $6,000 in 1938, he retired. In 1943 he made a wartime comeback at tackle and helped the Bears win the NFL title. He was a charter member of the College (1951) and Pro Football (1963) Halls of Fame.

He wrestled professionally from 1933 to 1953 and refereed for ten years after that. "Wrestling wasn't fixed on the scale it is now," he said. "But I wish I hadn't done it. I wasted a lot of time." Dick Cullum said, "He's a humble person who humbly bypasses the opportunity to capture more wealth and glory for a summer's fishing with his sons."

Nagurski said that when he was young he never really thought about going into football. Years later he was happy he did, saying, "Football doesn't owe me a living. For the times, I made good money. . . . I still feel a lot of my injuries, especially on rainy days. . . . I think those people who missed out on the pioneer days missed out on a lot. I was a pioneer."

He also was and continues to be a legend. As Steve Gelman wrote, "He did so many unbelievable things in football that it is already hard to distinguish fact from fancy."

It was fact that one day, playing for the Bears, he ran 45 yards for the winning touchdown by smashing through most of the opposition, crashing into the goal post and ramming into a brick wall beyond the end zone. When he revived, he supposedly said, "That last guy hit me awful hard."

It was fiction that when Dr. Clarence Spears, the Minnesota coach, asked road directions from a youth behind a plow, the youngster (Nagurski, of course) picked up the plow and pointed. Herman Hickman often told that story without naming Nagurski as the hero. Hickman said that when he told the story to Nagurski and came to the punch line, with the youth picking up the plow, Nagurski asked seriously, "Without horses?"

Namath, Joseph William
(1943–   )

Few athletes received the publicity and experienced the pressure that surrounded Joe Namath before he played his first professional football game. He survived both and became such an accomplished and dynamic quarterback that he assured the survival of the American Football League and its eventual merger with the National Football League. He is a colorful, controversial figure who has become a celebrity off the football field as well as on it. Women want to love him or mother him. Most men envy his football ability and life style. Conservatives dismiss him as a new-generation rebel.

He grew up in the poor section of Beaver Falls, Pennsylvania, and was an indifferent student at the University of Alabama (where people called him Joe Willie). In a game in 1964, his senior year at Alabama, he suffered torn ligaments of the right knee, an injury that hampered his mobility and made his professional success even more impressive.

When Namath was drafted by the New York Jets of the AFL and the St. Louis Cardinals of the NFL, the rival leagues tried to outbid each other for college stars. The Jets' president was David A. (Sonny) Werblin, a highly successful show-business agent before he turned to football. Werblin saw the need for the star system and a young star, and he signed Namath for the highest contract ever negotiated until that time in professional team sports. The package, covering three years and an option for a fourth, totaled $427,000.

Soon after Namath signed, he underwent surgery on the right knee, the first of several operations on both knees. Bursitis developed in the left knee, which became more troublesome than the right. One day, when someone asked him, "How's the good knee?" he replied bitterly, "Which one is that?"

Playing with a heavy brace on the right knee, Namath became an instant star. In 1967, his third pro season, he passed for 4,007 yards, more than any other professional in history. In 1968 he passed the Jets to the AFL title and in January 1969 he led a 16-7 upset of the Baltimore Colts, the NFL champions, in the Super Bowl. The Jets had been 17-point underdogs, and no AFL team had won a Super Bowl, but the brash Namath had guaranteed publicly that the Jets would win. When they did, the AFL gained immediate parity with the NFL.

With his new glory Namath became an even greater target for opposing teams. At various times he suffered a separation of the left shoulder, fractures of the right cheekbone and the right wrist and torn ligaments in the left knee. Opponents raised kitties for the player who tackled Namath the most. As Ron Billingsley, a defensive end for the San Diego Chargers, said, "He is the best passer there is, so naturally you try harder against him than against any other quarterback."

Through it all, he remained his own man. He was his strongest critic. (After one game in which he suffered five interceptions, he said, "I ain't saying nothing except that I stink.") He lived in style on Manhattan's fashionable upper East Side in a penthouse with a six-inch-thick white llama rug. He wore long hair and, at various times, a Fu Manchu mustache, a beard and a mink coat. He starred in movies. In an era when others wore black football shoes, he wore white. He was honest, outspoken and often blunt.

When he thought he was right, he seldom budged. In June 1969 Alvin (Pete) Rozelle, the NFL commissioner, ordered him to sell his half interest in Bachelors III, a New York restaurant and bar, because patrons allegedly included organized-crime figures. Namath said he knew nothing about that, refused to sell and, at age 26, quit football. Six weeks later, after training camp had opened, he reluctantly sold his share and rejoined the Jets, but he called Rozelle's order "totally unfair."

"I like girls. I like Scotch. I like to relax," Namath once said. "And I believe in doing anything I like to do as long as it doesn't hurt me or anybody else."

While many idolized him, others disliked him and his life style. "I wouldn't like my son to be like that," a man once said. "He's not your son," a man close to the Jets replied. "His father likes him."

White-shoed and weak-kneed, Joe Namath runs for a score as three Buffalo Bills pursue.

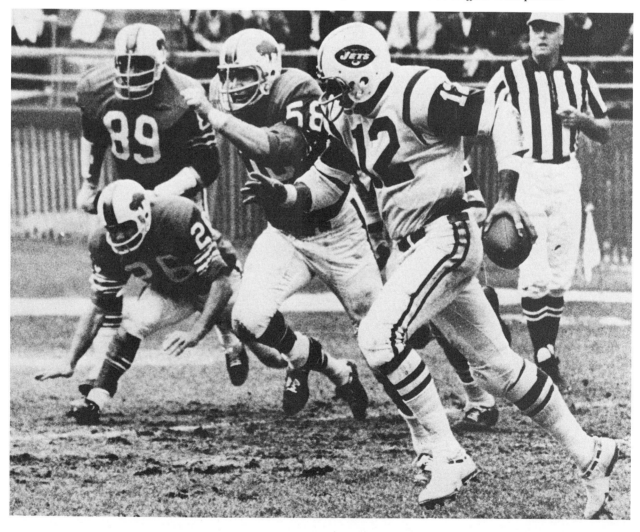

Nastase, Ilie (1946–   )

Off the tennis court he is a charming, delightful companion. On the court he is an ogre, a madman who can be obnoxious or cute while baiting opponents, haranguing and throwing balls and towels at officials or making indecent gestures to the crowd.

Ilie Nastase, logically known as Nasty, was a sickly, skinny, moody child in his native Rumania. He is now an officer in the Rumanian Army, but he does his only fighting on the tennis court. He won the United States Open championship in 1972 and the season-long Grand Prix in 1972 and 1973. His 1973 earnings exceeded $200,000.

Once, an angry and riled opponent, Clark Graebner, jumped over the net, grabbed him by the shirt and threatened to kill him. A few minutes later Nastase defaulted the match, saying that he was "physically terrified." Graebner, he said later, had "no sense of humor."

Wells Twombly wrote, "It is a question among his peers whether he has vast talent or if he is simply a supreme con artist who steals his opponent's concentration by consistently creating a furor." But Pancho Gonzales said the complainers "only bitch because he's winning." After losing to Nastase, Arthur Ashe said, "He is a great player, and when he brushes up on his court manners he'll be even better." Lance Tingay wrote of his "natural flair," Rex Bellamy of his "resourceful stroke play." Fred Stolle, a fellow pro, said, "He's quicker than anybody."

Curry Kirkpatrick insisted that Nastase was good for tennis, writing, "He is just the person needed to crush old molds, outsmart hoary conventions and even break the austere rules that have held the game back from that one crucial, giant step to total public acceptance and the big time. He is a nonpareil showman, an utterly exasperating gamesman, a pouting, crying genius with a racquet in his hands and a curse on his lips."

He seems to enjoy his antics but complained of his public image. "Why they talk me all the time?" he asked. "Why they listen me and nobody else and ask me behave? What is behave? Every player like this, not only me. We all nervous, all temperament, all crazy."

Nevers, Ernest Alonzo (1903–   )

Ernie Nevers was so good at so many things in so many sports that people often overlooked his singular quality. Bruce Lee called it "an unquenchable thirst for competition," and Benny Friedman described it as a flaming spirit "like a knight leading his troops to battle." To John D. McCallum, "He had the desire, instinct and inspired ability of a Viking of old."

At Stanford University he earned 11 letters in four sports. He was a thick-shouldered fullback and a 210-pound workhorse. He played for Stanford from 1923 to 1925, running, punting, blocking and tackling. In his junior year he broke his left ankle in a pre-season scrimmage. In November he returned to the field and broke the other ankle after three minutes of play. He built himself an artificial ankle joint, reported for practice four days before the Rose Bowl game and played the full 60 minutes. Murray Olderman wrote, "Some guys can't function with a torn hangnail. With him, it didn't matter if he was knocked silly. He came to play."

He played pro football for the Duluth Eskimos in 1926 and 1927 and missed the next season because of a broken neck. From 1929 to 1931 he was head coach and star fullback for the Chicago Cardinals. In 1929 he scored all 40 points in a 40-6 rout of the Chicago Bears, inspiring Knute Rockne to tell his Notre Dame players watching the game, "That, gentlemen, is how to play football." In 1931 he played every minute of all 19 games, though he was once knocked unconscious for two minutes (the game was delayed until he recovered). After he recovered he carried the ball 16 straight times for a touchdown.

He pitched for the St. Louis Browns for three years (1926–28) and played pro basketball in a league that preceded the National Basketball Association. But his true fame came from football. He was a charter member of the College (1951) and Pro Football (1963) Halls of Fame, and, as Walter Eckersall wrote, "He is about the best fullback who ever graced a gridiron." Pop Warner said, "He could do everything Jim Thorpe could do, and he always tried harder than Thorpe ever did." Jimmy Conzelman, a coach, said, "He was great in spite of the fact that he was always playing with lousy teams. He was able to lift them beyond their capacities."

Nicklaus, Jack William (1940–)

He has won more major championships and more money (in 1973 he passed $2 million) than any other golfer in history. But public acceptance and acclaim came slowly to Jack Nicklaus.

One reason was the gallery's love affair with the colorful Arnold Palmer, Nicklaus' rival for so many years. As Red Smith wrote in 1972, "When Nicklaus is on his game, he is the best golfer in the world. . . . Until this year, he was an upstart and an interloper, the crasher who had dared to expose Arnold Palmer as merely human."

Another reason was his appearance. For most of his career he was pudgy (5 feet 11½ inches, 205 to 210 pounds), unexciting (except for his golf) and not exactly a fashion plate. His wardrobe, wrote Buddy Martin, "contained all the color of a hospital ward." In 1970 he lost 20 pounds (and six inches off his hips) in three weeks, let his blond hair grow and put color in his clothing. Along with the new image, he was more relaxed and extroverted.

Jack Nicklaus, known as the Golden Bear, started playing golf at ten, when he shot 51 for nine holes (at the same age his son, Jack 2d, shot 81 for 18 holes). At 15 he qualified for the U.S. Amateur championship, at 16 he won the Ohio Open, and by 21 he had won the U.S. Amateur title twice. He started playing the pro tour in 1962 and in his first tournament earned $33.33.

Things soon improved. He has won at least one tournament a year since then. He led in tournament earnings six times between 1964 and 1973. He has won the Masters five times, the U.S. Open three times, the PGA championship three times, the British Open twice, the World Series of Golf four times and the Tournament of Champions four times.

He hits a ball with a power seldom seen in golf. As Morten Lund wrote, "He has the ability to pull that unbelievable shot when he needs it." Bobby Jones said, "He can keep on winning as long as he can remain inspired to play."

He picks his spots now, concentrating on the major championships. "People 20 years from now won't be impressed that I earned $250,000 playing golf in one year," he said. "But they might recall who won the most big ones. . . . Golf has been a great and rewarding thing in my life, but it's not everything and never will be."

Nicklaus holds up a check for $44,000, his purse for winning the 1974 Hawaiian Open.

Jack Nicklaus, one of the most powerful golfers of today, tees off at a 1974 tournament.

Nurmi, Paavo Johannes
(1897–1973)

Paavo Nurmi, the Flying Finn, was the world's most famous distance runner. He and Jesse Owens are the most celebrated runners of all time. ''His imprint on the track world was greater than any man's before or since,'' Cordner Nelson wrote. ''He, more than any man, raised track to the glory of a major sport.''

In the hero-worshipping Golden Era of Sports, the 1920s, Paavo Nurmi was one of the star attractions. In three successive Olympic Games—1920, 1924 and 1928—he won six individual gold medals and three team gold medals, more than any other track athlete in history.

The 1,500-meter and 5,000-meter finals in the 1924 Olympics were run 55 minutes apart. Nurmi won them both. He knew he could because, two weeks before, he ran the two distances 55 minutes apart and broke the world record for each. He was angry that Finnish officials did not let him defend his 10,000-meter title that year, and when the starting gun was fired he supposedly started running the 10,000 meters on a practice track and finished before the Olympic winner.

From 1921 to 1931 he broke 23 world outdoor records in 16 events ranging from 1,500 meters (just under a mile) to 20,000 meters (12.4 miles). His six-mile record stood for 18 years, his ten-mile record for 17 years. In 1925 he toured the United States for four months and won 66 of 68 indoor races. During the first 12 days he ran five races and broke seven indoor records. Alden Whitman wrote of that trip, ''His newspaper coverage was comparable to that of visiting royalty.''

There were rumors that Nurmi had demanded and received huge amounts of expense money from American promoters. Someone said, ''Nurmi has the lowest heartbeat and the highest asking price of any athlete in the world.'' Shortly before the 1932 Olympic Games, in which he planned to run the marathon, international track officials ruled him a professional, saying he had received excessive expense money in Germany in 1929. A tearful Nurmi said, ''If I did something wrong, why did they wait three years before taking action? Why turn on me

Nurmi winning the 1,500 meters at the 1924 Olympics.

246

Paavo Nurmi setting a world record for the six-mile run that lasted 18 years.

first. In later years he said, "I run for myself, not for Finland." When someone asked, "Not even in the Olympics?" he replied, "Not even then. Above all, not then. At the Olympics, Paavo Nurmi mattered more than ever."

He became a prosperous contractor and a recluse, a national figure on the level of Sibelius and Mannerheim. *The New York Times* said, "His countrymen thought him a sour fellow and miser, an impression he did little to dispel." But the people also revered and remembered him. At the 1952 Olympics in Helsinki, 73,000 spectators packed the stadium for the opening ceremonies, wondering who would have the honor of carrying the Olympic torch around the final lap. They looked down the road and saw a 55-year-old man running toward the stadium, the flaming torch held high. His flowing stride was unmistakable. He raced into the stadium and a thunderous roar went up. The electric scoreboard flashed his name in giant letters:

"NURMI."

Paavo Nurmi in 1964.

now and end my career when my heart bleeds to win the marathon?"

Paavo Nurmi began running at the age of nine, and as a boy he often raced the morning mail train. As Roberto Quercetani wrote, "He grew into a grave, unsmiling, silent man who fought his battles with extreme mental and physical discipline." With his high, long stride, his head held high and one hand against his chest, he was not a stylish runner, but he was efficient and methodical. Before his day distance runners dallied until the last lap or two, then sprinted. He was the first distance runner to plan his races scientifically. He often carried a stop watch in his hand to check his progress and threw it aside as he started the last lap.

At a dinner of Finnish-Americans he was asked to drink a toast to Finland. He said he never drank. "But this is for the honor of Finland," he was told. "Where is the honor of Finland if I lose my next race?" he replied. Yet he did not always put country

O'Brien, Joseph Cyril (1917–)

"In all of trotting today, with its emphasis on racing aged horses at the night pari-mutuel tracks, there are regrettably only a bare handful of superior trainers of colts," *Sports Illustrated* said. One of those handful, it said, was Joe O'Brien, a trainer-driver-owner from a famous harness-racing family in Alberton, Prince Edward Island. Ed Keller called him "Canada's greatest reinsman."

At the age of seven Joe O'Brien crawled onto a jog cart and took a horse onto a track for a training mile. From 1939 (when complete records started) to the end of 1974 he drove 3,586 winners and earned purses of $13,306,411. In 1972 he drove Steady Star to the fastest harness-racing mile in history—1 minute 52 seconds. He also drove Scott Frost and Fresh Yankee (both horses of the year), Flower Child and Armbro Flight.

He hardly looked the part. He is small and wiry (5 feet 6 inches and 140 pounds), gentle and soft-spoken, a man of few words (two of his favorite words are "My goodness"). "He has the sad, gentle manner of a guy who just heard you had a death in the family," someone once said. Trent Frayne wrote, "He bears all the swagger and exhibitionism of a kneeling monk."

With all that, winning became an obsession. "Every race he's in is the Hambletonian," Jim Har-

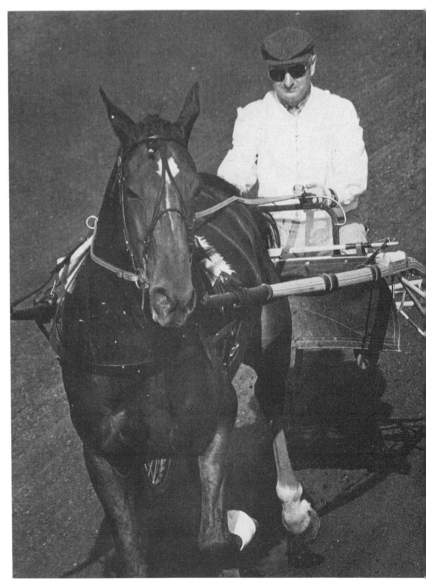

rison wrote. "He never contested an event that failed to draw from him every ounce of skill, every drop of energy, every measure of devotion to a cause that is his life—harness racing."

He made races exciting because he held back his horses until the finish. John Simpson, Sr., once said, "You're not going to flush him out until he's ready." O'Brien said of his driving finishes, "No matter which way you go, you're going to get beat a great many times, many more than you win. I'd rather get beat by waiting too long than by coming too early. . . . You will at least have saved your horse as long as possible." Of his sport he said, "There isn't any way a man's going to make it in harness racing unless he loves horses more than anything else in the world."

Oldfield, Berner Eli (1877–1946)

He was the first to drive an automobile a mile a minute and the first to drive two miles a minute. For years, when policemen flagged down speeding drivers, they invariably asked sarcastically, "Who do you think you are, Barney Oldfield?" Of the real Barney Oldfield, H. G. Salsinger wrote, "Long after his records were dwarfed by men with faster cars, his name remained as a synonym for speed and daring."

He was a big man, coarse, tough and virile, a braggart who looked the part with his red leather jacket and an unlighted black cigar always in his mouth. He always gave the customers a show, and in 16 years he earned half a million dollars in race cars, a huge sum at the time.

He was a professional bicycle racer until 1902, when two young car builders named Henry Ford and Tom Cooper persuaded him to drive a car they had just built (neither had the courage to drive it). He had never driven before, but he learned in a week.

"This chariot may kill me," he said before a race, "but they'll say afterward that I was going like hell when she took me over the bank." Cooper recalled, "He never looked around. He never shut off on the curves; he simply let the car go. He was about half a mile ahead at the end of the race." He covered the five miles in 5 minutes 28 seconds. Later he said, "Boy, I really thought I was flying."

In 1903 he drove the first sub-one-minute mile, averaging 60.4 miles an hour. In 1910, on the hard beach at Daytona Beach, Florida, he raised the world record to 131.724 mph. Even at age 55 he was planning an assault on the world record (then 253.96 mph) and thought he could do 300 mph with the right tires.

Brock Yates wrote, "He was a truly brilliant driver when he kept his mind on his work. . . . Throughout much of his career he contented himself with such foolishness as match races with airplanes and against local drivers on tank-town fairground circuits." His conduct so upset the American Automobile Association, which at the time supervised racing, that it suspended him for life four times.

"I didn't need to throw dice with death on the track to make a living," he said years later. "but racing gets into the blood." But he thought auto racing had outlived its usefulness, saying, "It has ceased to be racing and has become merely a morbid and brutal spectacle. Its carnage must end."

Barney Oldfield in 1917.

The Boston Bruin star skates behind Bobby Clarke of the Philadelphia Flyers during the 1974 Stanley Cup finals.

Orr, Robert Gordon (1948–   )

He was 12 years old when Boston Bruins officials first saw him. They were so impressed that they maneuvered to get his National Hockey League rights. They did, and even they were astounded by his success.

"He was a star from the moment they played the national anthem in the opening game of his rookie season," said Harry Sinden, who coached him. Scotty Bowman, a rival coach, said, "The Bruins started rebuilding the year he was born." Teammate Phil Esposito called him "the best player in the game," and Milt Schmidt, a former Bruins player and coach, called him "the greatest player there's ever been."

Bobby Orr has the All-American (actually All-Canadian) look. He is solid (5 feet 11 inches, 185 pounds) and handsome, with floppy hair and a shy smile. He does almost everything in hockey better than anyone else, starting with skating. John (Frosty) Forristall, assistant trainer of the Bruins, said, "He skates like he's afraid he'll be sent back to the minors. He takes chances like a rookie."

No defenseman has ever skated with his speed, agility and purpose. "I have found out," he said, "that you can save a lot of energy by being smart on the ice, by passing the puck more. Why crack through two defensemen yourself when you can pass the puck to a teammate, then sneak around behind the defenseman and get a return pass?"

Few defensemen have ever been as bold on defense as he has been from his days as an 18-year-old rookie. He was rookie of the year, and every season since he has won the Norris Trophy as the NHL's outstanding defenseman. For three straight seasons he won the Hart Trophy as the NHL's most valuable player. He became the first defenseman to win a scoring title, and beginning with his fourth season he has scored at least 100 points a season.

With all these accomplishments he is not content. "I know my mistakes," he said, "and I make plenty of them. They say practice makes perfect, and they're wrong. Practice'll make you better, but nothing'll make you perfect. At least, I'll never be. I do dumb things." Perhaps, but not often.

Ott, Melvin Thomas (1909–1958)

Sport magazine called Mel Ott "the monument that John McGraw left behind." He was a lasting monument who played 2,730 games in 22 seasons (1926–47) for the New York Giants, mostly in right field. When he retired he held National League career records for home runs (511), runs (1,859), runs batted in (1,860) and bases on balls (1,708, still the record).

The Giants signed him at the age of 16 for $400. McGraw, the fiery Giant manager, seated the youngster next to him on the bench and taught him baseball. He started as a catcher. When McGraw asked him if he had ever played the outfield the 17-year-old Ott replied, "Only when I was a kid, Mr. McGraw." He became an outfielder, and in

1928, just after his 19th birthday, he became a starter. In 1951, the first year he was eligible, he was voted into the Baseball Hall of Fame.

He was a left-handed batter who raised his right leg to knee height and then planted his right foot just before he swung. His style was different, but it worked. McGraw said he was the most natural hitter he ever saw.

He managed the Giants for seven unhappy seasons (1942–48). Al Stump described him "going through sheer hell, sitting on the bench as his athletes booted game after game away." He was too soft to be a manager, and he was the nice guy Leo Durocher referred to when he said, "Nice guys finish last." Ironically, when the Giants fired him in mid-1948, he was replaced by Durocher. He seemed relieved to give up managing, saying, "I never realized what a burden that manager's job was until I was rid of it."

Baseball and the public idolized him. He was, wrote Arthur Daley, "strictly big league—in personality, in character, in performance and in downright class." Stan Musial, a later Mel Ott, recalled, "When I was moving in on his records . . . he'd not only wish me well, but he'd actually encourage me to spur me on."

Ouimet, Francis D. (1893–1967)

In one week in 1913 Francis Ouimet (pronounced "Wee-met") changed the face of golf. As Herbert Warren Wind wrote, "He was the man who more than any other took golf out of the hands of the very rich and gave it to the whole people."

He was a modest, mild-mannered, warm gentleman. He was lanky (5 feet 11 inches and 133 pounds), the son of a gardener who lived across the road from The Country Club in Brookline, Massachusetts. He caddied there for 10 cents an hour plus tips, and in his spare time he learned to play golf (he played his first 18-hole round at age 13 and shot 84).

In 1913 the U. S. Open championship was held at The Country Club, and Ouimet entered the competition. In those days Britons dominated the sport, and the favorites in the Open were two celebrated British pros, Harry Vardon and Ted Ray. Neither had ever heard of Ouimet, an obscure 20-year-old amateur, but after the regulation 72 holes they found themselves tied with him for first place at 304.

The next day, in an 18-hole playoff, Ouimet won by shooting a 72 against Vardon's 77 and Ray's 78. He became the first amateur to win the Open, upsetting the best in the world. With typical candor he said, "I'm as much surprised and pleased as anyone here."

Henry Leach wrote that day, "No boy has ever done such a thing before and I cannot believe will ever do it again." *The New York Times* ran the story at the top of page one. As a *Times* sportswriter, Arthur Daley, later wrote, "Ouimet had become a folk hero overnight."

Speaking of the historic match, Ouimet later recalled, "We were on the first tee. Not a word had been spoken. It occurred to me that as an American playing two celebrated foreigners, I should say something, anything, for politeness' sake. I teed up my ball, turned to them and apologized: 'Gentlemen, I hope I don't play so badly that it will ruin your afternoon.' There was no response. How could they know I was shaking in my boots? More likely, they thought me a bit of a showoff. Anyway, we played in total silence."

Later, he won two United States Amateur championships, and from 1922 to 1949 he was a player or non-playing captain of every Walker Cup team. Ever conscious of his humble childhood, he set up a scholarship fund for caddies. He never turned professional, and he shunned public adulation. As Al Laney wrote, "He never attracts attention to himself if he can help it."

Owens, James Cleveland
(1913–   )

He was the best-known athlete in track and field history, and he is just as famous in retirement as in his glory days. As Jerry Liska wrote, "No athlete left a more wondrous imprint on a single sport."

He was the son of an Alabama sharecropper and he picked cotton as a youngster. When the family moved to Cleveland, a schoolteacher asked his name. "J.C.," he replied. The teacher thought he said, "Jesse," and the youngster had a new name.

He became a sprinter, slim and lithe at 163 pounds. He ran with fluid grace. His accomplishments came without starting blocks (sprinters simply dug starting holes) and over tracks primitive by modern standards.

He worked his way through Ohio State operating an elevator because he had no athletic scholarship. Just before the 1935 Big Ten championships he wrenched his back and had to be helped from the car that drove him to the track. He even needed help to remove his warm-up suit. He did not warm up before his events, but it hardly mattered. That afternoon he equaled the world record for the 100-yard dash (9.4 seconds), set a world record for the broad jump (26 feet 8¼ inches), set a world record for 220 yards (20.3) that also broke the record for 200 meters and set a world record for the 220-yard low hurdles (22.6) that also broke the 200-meter record. In 45 minutes he had established five world records and tied a sixth. Watching him compete, Kenneth L. (Tug) Wilson, the Big Ten commissioner, said, "He is a floating wonder, just like he had wings."

In the 1936 Olympics at Berlin he won four gold medals, broke two Olympic records, tied one and had a hand in a world relay record. Adolf Hitler did not congratulate him or any other American black athlete. Later, Owens said, "It was all right with me. I didn't go to Berlin to shake hands with him anyway." Of his four gold medals he said, "It opened doors for me and kept me alive over the years."

But not right away. When he returned from Berlin he became a playground janitor because he could find no better job. He raced against motorcycles and

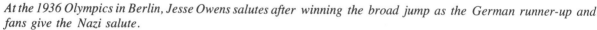

At the 1936 Olympics in Berlin, Jesse Owens salutes after winning the broad jump as the German runner-up and fans give the Nazi salute.

horses. "Sure, it bothered me," he said. "But at least it was an honest living. . . . I had to eat."

He finally made his mark as a public speaker. He still speaks two or three times a week, mostly to sales meetings and conventions, mostly to primarily white audiences, and earns over $75,000 a year. He has about five basic speeches, all praising the virtues of patriotism, clean living and fair play. He is a gregarious man, and his oratory is spellbinding and old-fashioned. His ringing voice reminded Jon Hendershott of a Sunday-morning preacher. William Johnson called him "a kind of all-round super combination of 19th-century spellbinder and 20th-century plastic P.R. man, full-time banquet guest, eternal glad-hander, evangelistic small-talker . . . what you might call a professional good example."

But not to everyone. During the 1968 Olympics, when he attempted to mediate with militant black athletes on behalf of the U.S. Olympic Committee, dissenters called him an Uncle Tom. He wrote one book decrying militancy and a later book saying his first book was wrong. Larry Merchant saw him as an ingratiating evangelist. "He had taken himself too seriously," he wrote, "which is to say that if they gave a gold medal to blowhards, he would win that, too." But he survived the controversial moments, and as Bill Bruns wrote, "If he has proved anything, it seems to be that criticism is transient and fame, if properly polished, can be enduring."

Blowhard or philosopher, this is part of the Jesse Owens gospel:

On the value of sport: "We all have dreams. But in order to make dreams into reality, it takes an awful lot of determination, dedication, self-discipline and effort. These things apply to everyday life. You learn not only the sport, but things like respect of others, ethics in life, how you are going to live, how you treat your fellow man, how you live with your fellow man."

On American black athletes who question the value of their gold medals: "Any black who strives to achieve in this country should think in terms of not only himself but also how he can reach down and grab another black child and pull him up to the top of the mountain where he is. This is what a gold medal does to you."

On dignity: "Regardless of his color, a man who becomes a recognized athlete has to learn to walk ten feet tall. But he must have his dignity off the athletic field."

Jesse Owens, a high-school student from Cleveland, breaking a record at an interscholastic meet in 1933.

Owens at the 1968 Olympics in Mexico City, where he attempted to mediate with black-power advocates.

Paige, Leroy Robert (1906–   )

He pitched 55 no-hitters and perhaps 2,500 games before ten million spectators, traveling almost a million miles to do it, so he may have been the busiest pitcher in baseball history. He was also one of the best, but he did not get a fair chance to prove it because baseball's Jim Crow traditions kept him out of the major leagues until he was old.

When he was carrying luggage in the railroad station of Mobile, Alabama, at the age of seven, he invented a contraption that allowed him to haul four satchels at once. From then on he was known as Satchel Paige, and the name became famous as he toured the country with black teams. He was the main attraction, which meant he had to pitch every day and year round—summers in the United States, winters in the Caribbean.

Pitching for Bismarck, North Dakota, in 1934, he started 29 games in one month. That season, he said, he won 104 of 105 games. "There never was a man on earth who pitched as much as me," he boasted. "Not even come close to it. . . . But the more I pitched, the stronger my arm would get."

He often faced major-league players in exhibition games, and he invariably left them gasping. In one game he outpitched Dizzy Dean, 1-0. In another he struck out Rogers Hornsby five times. Hack Wilson, one of the great sluggers, told him, "It looked like you were winding up with a baseball and throwing a pea." Umpire Bill Summers said, "His fast ball makes you blink." Joe DiMaggio called him "the best I ever faced. And the fastest."

Except for those interludes, his life meant low pay and heavy travel under dismal conditions. "Hell," he said, "we didn't know where we were staying one-half of the time, or what was in those old houses where we used to stay. We knew there was a lot of bed bugs around, I can tell you that, and we used to keep the light on all night. And you had to sleep on paper. That was really the onliest thing to scare 'em off. It was the rustling of the paper. Probably when you turned over it would scare them, see, and they would crawl off. Five or six, sometimes we stayed nine in a room. Sometimes, the whole club'd be in one room."

In 1948, with the major-league color barrier broken, Bill Veeck signed him for the Cleveland Indians. He was 42 years old, and *The Sporting News*, the respected baseball weekly, called the signing "a travesty on baseball."

The new major leaguer was tall (6 feet 3½ inches) and slim (180 pounds), with thin legs, a thin mustache, a low-keyed, easygoing manner and all kinds of pitches at all kinds of speeds. His first game attracted 72,000 spectators, and he won. More than 78,000 turned out for his third game, still the largest one-game crowd ever for a regular-season game.

these players, but Veeck, scorning what he called separate but equal facilities, saw to it that Paige was enshrined with the Ty Cobbs and Babe Ruths and other white stars.

And so the Satchel Paige legend was preserved. Gordon Cobbledick wrote, "I suspect he has lived so long with—and by—the legend that he isn't exactly sure where it leaves off and the man begins." But Paige had no doubts. "No telling how great I might have been," he said. "The players what was in the big leagues then, it wasn't no sweat for me to get them out. There weren't five homers hit off me in three years."

His advice to the next generation: "There ain't no man can avoid being born average. But there ain't no man got to be common."

He again pitched for the Indians in 1949 and joined the St. Louis Browns, then owned by Veeck, from 1951 to 1953. Afterward, he pitched in the minor leagues and barnstormed. In successive years he pitched three or four innings a day for 167 straight days each year. "The whole time, I never got a rubdown," he said. "I just used hot water."

In 1963, at age 57, he pitched two or three innings a day for 145 days. At age 59 he pitched one game for the Kansas City Athletics, yielding only one hit in three innings. At 61 he pitched one inning for the Atlanta Braves in an exhibition game against Richmond and struck out two. He spent that season as an Atlanta coach, sitting in a rocking chair in the bullpen with a nurse to massage his arm.

In 1971, despite a major-league won-lost record of 28-31, he was voted into the Baseball Hall of Fame in a new category created for players from the old Negro Leagues. A special wing was planned for

Satchel Paige admires his Hall of Fame plaque in 1971 after becoming the first player admitted from the old Negro Leagues.

became the first golf professional to reach $1 million in career earnings.

But the public's romance with Palmer, kindled by his golf-course heroics, was sealed by his personality—outgoing, honest, emotional, always willing to accept the challenge. At every stop, huge galleries of loyalists known as Arnie's Army tramp after him for 18 holes a day, sharing his little triumphs and defeats.

In his prime Palmer played the game every hacker wished he were brave enough and good enough to play. He always attacked the course. As the New York *Herald Tribune* said, "In all the time golf has been played, it is unlikely we have ever had a champion more bold who yet could calculate the chances so accurately and was so little afraid of taking them." *Sports Illustrated* spoke of Palmer "combining the boldness of a Brink's bandit with the fearless confidence of a man on a flying trapeze. . . . He doesn't play a golf course, he assaults it." Jerry

Palmer smiles a winning smile at the 1968 Kemper Open.

Palmer, Arnold Daniel (1929–)

From the 1950s to the mid-70s, when professional sports blossomed and the professional golf tour became an $8.5-million-a-year extravaganza, the golfer who has captivated the public the most is Arnold Palmer. He might have done it on his record alone—four victories in the Masters (1958, 1960, 1962 and 1964), two in the British Open (1961 and 1962), one in the United States Open (1960), a total of 61 in major American tournaments. In 1968 he

Barber, a fellow pro, said, "He goes right for the throat of a course and then he shakes it to death."

Herbert Warren Wind got to the heart of it when he wrote, "His ability to perform wonders is based on an honest conviction that they are not wonders at all." Palmer agreed. "Eighty percent of the time, there is a way out of trouble," he said. "You just have to know how to look for it. . . . Why hit a conservative shot? When you miss it, you are in just as much trouble as when you miss a bold one."

Arnold Palmer, the son of a greenskeeper and teaching pro in Latrobe, Pennsylvania, all but grew up on a golf course. He was swinging a club at five, and at seven he broke 100 for 18 holes. At nine he shot 45 for nine holes. In 1954, at age 25, he turned pro and earned only $2,050 in his first six months before starting to win. Mark McCormack, his business manager and lawyer, explained what set Palmer apart from his contemporaries: "Most touring pros come to hate golf courses, in part because it is the course that thwarts their ambitions. Palmer wants courses to fight back at him and considers them gallant opponents."

With McCormack managing his financial affairs, Palmer became a tycoon. His companies made golf clubs, golf balls and clothing. He owned all kinds of businesses—insurance, power tools, dry cleaning, laundry, maid service. In 1967 he sold some of them to the National Broadcasting Company for millions.

Palmer has the look of an athlete—broad shoulders, arms like a blacksmith, thick wrists, strong hands, thin waist, hips so narrow that he constantly hitches his trousers. His charm has entranced a nation. Even non-golfers identify with him. Dr. Ernest Dichter, head of the Institute of Motivational Research in New York, explained, "People see themselves winning through Palmer. He looks and acts like a regular guy, and at the same time he does the kinds of things others wish they could do. His expressiveness makes his spectators feel that they are part of his game. He looks as though he needs their help, and they respond."

The New York Times, talking of the same bond between Arnie and Arnie's Army, said, "When Palmer is happy, his face lights up. When Palmer is thinking, he frowns. When Palmer plays a bad shot, he scowls, and the world hates the ball that betrayed him. His emotions are never in doubt. He moves around the golf course like a caged tiger. He does what Everyman wants to do—he murders the ball."

Lester Patrick, manager of the New York Rangers, with his sons, players Lynn (left) and Muzz Patrick.

Patrick, Curtis Lester (1883–1960)

He spent 43 years in hockey, as a player, coach, manager, pioneer, innovator and organizer. He played 19 years and managed 33 in the major leagues, leading his teams to seven Stanley Cups. He and his brother Frank built Canada's first artificial ice rinks, and his innovations included blue lines, free movement for goalies and defensemen, numbering of players, farm systems, the modern playoff structure and substitution of entire lines.

As Arthur Mann wrote, "Practically every forward step taken by professional hockey between 1911 and 1925 can be traced to the keen brain of Frank Patrick and the practical knowledge of Lester." He and Frank founded the Pacific Coast League in 1911 and built all the rinks. They played on the Renfrew Millionaires, the first professional team, and Lester was paid the unheard-of salary of $3,000 for 12 games. Later he became coach and manager of the New York Rangers, where his players included his sons, Muzz and Lynn.

Lloyd McGowan wrote that he was never a martinet or taskmaster in running his teams. "Rather, he had a flare for showmanship. He liked the theatrical." His most theatrical moment came in the 1928 Stanley Cup finals between the Rangers and Montreal Maroons. Lorne Chabot, the Ranger goalie, was struck in the eye by a shot and carried off on a stretcher. In those days teams carried no substitute goalies, so 44-year-old Coach Patrick, far out of shape, put a baseball cap over his bushy white hair and played in the goal. The Rangers won the game in overtime.

"Hockey has a reputation for being a rough, tough game," he once said. "It is primarily a game of skill, but the crowd likes hard body contact and we have to give it to them. There are certain things you've got to do in professional sports to please the crowd." But he said that brains played a bigger part in hockey than they did in any other sport. "This is a game for smart fellows," he said.

Pelé (Edson Arantes do Nascimento) (1940–   )

The world's most popular sport is called soccer in the United States and football in most other countries, and the greatest of all soccer players, and probably the world's best-known athlete, is a Brazilian known as Pelé.

The soccer-playing world, and especially Brazil, adored him. Admirers mobbed him after every game and tried to tear off his jersey and shorts for souvenirs. He did not mind. "It happens all over the world," he said. "It's a pleasure for me. I always have a spare pair of pants underneath."

When he went to Biafra, the civil war there was suspended for two days. When he visited Khartoum and Algiers, political disputes there were interrupted. When he played his final international game, bullfights in Spain were canceled because the promoters knew everyone would stay home to watch him on television. Reversing protocol, Prince Philip of Britain left his seat to meet the soccer hero rather than wait for Pelé to come to him.

At 5 feet 8 inches and 160 pounds, he looks like an ordinary man. He does not smoke or drink, and he

lives simply. But he became so successful that he paid more taxes than any other Brazilian citizen. At his earnings peak he made $1.5 million a year—$700,000 for playing soccer and $800,000 from his many endorsement contracts (Pepsi-Cola, Puma soccer shoes, Café Pelé, etc.) and businesses. His business office had a staff of 20, including three lawyers.

His success came from unpromising beginnings. He was a poor student usually in trouble with the truant officer, and at the age of ten he quit school in the fourth grade. His father had been a good sandlot soccer player, earning $4.50 a game, and the son played well enough to be included in men's games. At 15 he was hired by the Santos Football Club on a trial basis for $75 a month. "I was scared of failing," he recalled, but he did not fail. Soon he was earning $600 a month, and at 16 he made the Santos first team. At first, said Luca, the Santos coach, "he was just an errand boy for the older players. He would buy soda for them, things like that. Then, before they knew it, they were looking up to him."

He led Santos to league championships in his first six seasons. He played more than 1,000 games for Santos, averaging a goal a game. He led Brazil to World Cup championships in 1958, 1962 and 1970 (the World Cup is contested every four years). When three Italian teams pooled $2 million in an effort to buy him from Santos, the President of Brazil blocked the sale by declaring him a national treasure.

"Almost every move he has ever made on a soccer field has been something very special," Pete Axthelm wrote. "He dribbles the ball as if it were attached to his feet by sensitive strings. He shoots harder and more accurately than anyone else in the game. When he rushes through the offensive zone toward a goal, he captures the imagination in a way that only the most dramatic of athletes can. He is one of those rare performers who can, for the moment, make all the patterns and tactics of a complex game seem unimportant."

His final international game, Brazil vs. Yugoslavia in 1971, was televised worldwide. At halftime he trotted around the field in tears, stripped off his shirt and waved it to the crowd of 130,000. He retired from Santos in 1974, and Julio Mazzei, the Santos trainer, said, "Now, people tell their little babies, 'Too bad. You will not see Pelé play.'"

Mazzei was wrong. In 1975, lured by a complex deal that made him the highest-paid team player in sports history, Pelé signed with the New York Cosmos of the North American Soccer League. He agreed to play about 100 games, including exhibitions, during three years and assist the Cosmos and their corporate owners, Warner Communications, in promotions and public relations. The gross value of his contracts was about $4.7 million. Pelé said he came out of retirement because he wanted to make soccer a major sport in America. "You can say now to the world," he said, "that soccer has finally arrived in the United States."

Despite those grandiose words, Pelé never forgot that he was a common man. "I appreciate the crowds around me, especially the kids," he said. "I know when I was growing up football was one of the few things I could enjoy. Seeing a top player was always a big thrill. Now I get a thrill myself by having the kids around me."

Luca was frequently asked if Pelé was the greatest player he ever coached. His stock answer: "He is the greatest player anyone has ever coached."

Pelé's farewell lap around the Rio de Janeiro stadium in 1971 after his last international game for Brazil.

Pep, Willie (1922–   )

Willie Pep may have been the fastest fighter ever. He was certainly one of the best. Angelo Dundee, who trained Muhammad Ali, among others, called Pep ''the greatest boxer I have ever seen.''

He was swarthy and skinny, with long arms, spindly legs and a lightning jab. He won his first 62 fights, the longest professional streak until then, and after losing his next fight he won 73 in a row. But even after he became featherweight champion he had little money, the result, he said, of ''fast women and slow horses, instead of the other way around.''

Until he started fighting he was William Guiglermo Papaleo. He turned pro in 1940. His largest purse in 1941 was $48. The following year he won the title and held it until 1948, when his memorable series of vicious title fights with Sandy Saddler began. Saddler won the first fight by a knockout, and Pep won a rematch on points in 1949. Saddler won in 1950 and 1951 on knockouts.

''What most people remember about Willie Pep,'' John Ross wrote, ''is that twice he sat on his stool and quit to Sandy Saddler, once while he was winning and again after he had engineered one of the roughest and dirtiest fights that has ever disgraced the game.'' Pep said that the fights were rough because ''he gets me so mad that I lose my head.''

He retired in 1959 but returned to the ring in 1965, broke and 42. Watching him fight in a 630-seat Masonic temple in Miami for $500, Phil Pepe wrote, ''He tried to recapture a forgotten and glorious past. He didn't quite make it.''

He was never the same after the fights with Saddler. Jimmy Cannon likened him to ''a hoofer, suddenly gone deaf, who loses the orchestra's beat.'' To Frank Graham, he had become ''a little old man.'' Yet Red Smith called him a marvel and wrote, ''Time cannot wither nor custom stale the little desperado's incomparable gifts. . . . He was Manolete and Michelangelo in the handy pocket-sized package, with a dash of Ponzi for seasoning.''

''I guess you'd like to know what happened to all the big money,'' Pep once said. ''So would I. . . . I've piled up so much scar tissue that I look like I'm wearing blinders. But boxing is my business. Only way I know to make so much fast.''

Willie Pep (left) takes a punch from Sandy Saddler in their 1949 title fight. Pep won by decision.

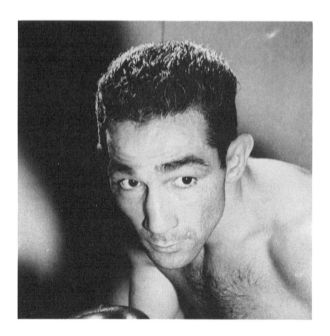

Pettit, Robert E. Lee, Jr.
(1932–   )

Zander Hollander thought he might have been the best front-court man ever to play professional basketball. Elgin Baylor said he was the best forward he had ever seen or played against. "He just kept coming at you," Baylor said, "no matter what the score." Ben Kerner, his only pro owner, said, "There may have been greater players, but none with greater desire and dedication." Phil Pepe said there was no greater competitor in the game.

When he started high school he was 5 feet 9 inches and 118 pounds. As a junior he stood 6-6 and he grew to 6-9. He weighed 200 pounds when he turned pro and 240 when he retired in 1965. He played center at Louisiana State, making All-America in 1953 and 1954, and played 11 years at forward for the Hawks in Milwaukee and St. Louis. He was the National Basketball Association's rookie of the year, an all-star ten times, twice most valuable player and twice scoring champion. Until Baylor bettered it, his lifetime total of 20,880 points was the NBA record. After basketball he turned to banking, insurance and real estate, all with success.

Bob Pettit was a handsome, easygoing gentleman, not fast but a smooth rebounder and shooter with a soft jump shot. He took physical beatings game after game, but they seldom stopped him. During the 1957 season he broke a hand, and a St. Louis newspaper ran a headline saying, "Pettit Out for Season." He missed only one game.

"As long as I play," Tom Heinsohn said, "I'll have memories of him leaning on my shoulders. There are ruts in them from his elbows." Ed Macauley said, "He always knows exactly what he wants to do and how to go about doing it." Bill Sharman said he was the best at knowing just the right time to shoot. Nat Holman said he would have made any of the great pro clubs of any era.

"As you go along in life and work hard," Pettit said, "you reach new plateaus of accomplishment. With each plateau you reach, the demands upon you become greater and your pride increases to meet the demands. You drive yourself harder than before. You can't afford negative thinking, so you always believe you'll win. You build an image of yourself that has nothing to do with ego—but it has to be satisfied."

Petty, Richard Lee (1937–)

Next to football, the sport that excites Southerners most is stock-car racing, fender-to-fender, bumper-to-bumper battles over high-banked tracks at speeds that sometimes exceed 200 miles an hour. The most successful driver in the annals of stock-car racing, financially and artistically, is Richard Petty.

Since 1958, when he was rookie of the year, he has won more than 160 major races of the National Association for Stock Car Auto Racing (NASCAR), twice as many as his nearest rival. In 1974 he won for the fifth time both the NASCAR season title (no one else had won it more than three times) and the richest and most important race on the NASCAR circuit, the Daytona 500 (no one else had won it more than twice). Robert F. Jones, writing in *Sports Illustrated*, called him "Jeb Stuart on wheels."

He is the chief breadwinner of Petty Enterprises, Inc., a company headed by his father, Lee Petty, a former driving champion. Richard is long and lean at 6 feet 2 inches, curly-haired and gracious, a small-town boy from North Carolina. He does not drink and he smokes only cigars. Invariably he wears extra-wide sunglasses.

He is universally known as Richard ("If my mother wanted to call me Dick," he said, "she would have named me Dick"). Once, when he held an open house, 15,000 people showed up. In 1973 the annual convention of the Richard Petty Fan Club (of which there were 6,500 paid-up members) attracted 300 members from 17 states.

Of his driving style, Kim Chapin wrote, "His primary goal is to establish a pace quick enough to stay near the leaders, yet slow enough to ensure that his car will indeed complete the race distance. As the saying goes, 'You can't win unless you finish,' and that is what he does best." Roy Blount, Jr., wrote, "One always thinks of him in terms of skill rather than old country death defiance."

In 1971 he became the first stock-car driver to earn $1 million in career purses, and he is closing in on his second million. He has seldom tried other types of racing, saying, "I have never had a reason to do anything else but stock-car racing. I'm making a good living and I don't see any reason to climb into something else. . . . We do some real racing. Those Indy cars are so delicate that they can't touch each other." His proudest feat? "I guess in still being alive."

Petty flashes a victory sign after winning a Texas race with an average speed of 144 mph.

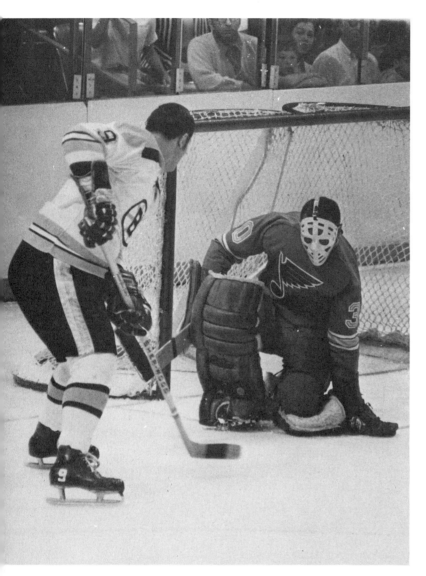

Goalie Jacques Plante of St. Louis stops shot by Boston's John Bucyk in the 1970 playoffs.

When he was 11 years old he earned 50 cents a game playing goal for a factory team in Shawinigan Falls, Quebec. He played 837 National Hockey League games from 1952 to 1973. From 1952 to 1963 he helped the Montreal Canadiens win six Stanley Cups (five in a row), earned six Vezina Trophies for goaltending (and shared a seventh with a teammate) and was named to the all-star team seven times. In late 1973 he moved to the new World Hockey Association, first as a coach-manager and then as a 45-year-old goalie.

In 1959, having received 150 stitches, two broken cheekbones, two broken noses and one broken jaw in his career, he wore an experimental plastic face mask in practice. When a puck ripped his nose in a game, requiring seven stitches and a 20-minute delay, he returned to the ice wearing his mask. He won that game and the next 11, and the mask stayed. Now, almost every goalie at every level of hockey wears one.

"My business is getting shot at," he once said. "When I stop shots, business is good. When I don't, business is bad. You must be born a goaltender, a man alone. . . . You don't have to be crazy to play goalie, but it helps. Every goal that goes in, I say that's my fault. I figure I should stop it even if they are impossible."

Plante, Jacques (1929–   )

For more than two decades Jacques Plante was probably the best goalie in hockey, certainly the most colorful. He was the first goalie to wear a protective mask, the first to rove far from the net after a loose puck. After a shutout, he would throw his arms high over his head. He might kiss the ice, blow kisses to the crowd or take a lap of honor.

Frank Selke said, "He has changed goaltending for the better, but I'm sure he could be an even better goalkeeper if he didn't let his showmanship get the better of him." Others thought he was good enough. "None of the other goalies can come near him," King Clancy said. "He makes the big saves the others don't." Charlie Halpin wrote, "With him, there is no second best."

Player, Gary Jim (1936–   )

Gary Player seems almost too good to be true. He worked hard to build himself and his golf game, preached and lived the good life and became a millionaire and an international celebrity.

He is a South African with a powerful, compact build (5 feet 8 inches and 150 pounds), black hair, good looks, meticulous grooming and, wrote Milton Gross, "forearms like Popeye." He is intense but gregarious, he does not drink or smoke and he is a physical-culture addict who can do 70 fingertip push-ups. He believes in health foods and devours dried fruits, honey, wheat germ and nuts. He used to eat so many bananas and raisins that growers had him on retainer. He often dresses entirely in black—"for added strength," he says.

When he was 14 he chose golf over rugby and cricket, two other sports at which he excelled. He turned pro in 1953 and began playing the pro tour in 1955. Through the years he has won three British Open titles, two PGA championships, two Masters titles, one United States Open, six Australian Opens, five Piccadilly world match-play titles and two World Series of Golf. When he won the U.S. Open in 1965 he gave away his entire purse—$20,000 to American junior golf and $5,000 to cancer research (his mother had died of cancer). He also gave his 16-year-old caddie $2,000.

Alfred Wright wrote, "The enjoyment that he gets from performing in public is immediately apparent on the golf course." Walter Bingham wrote, "Inside him somewhere, his desire to excel takes hold and does not let him collapse." "The more dedicated you are," Player said, "the more sacrifices you make, the more you appreciate winning a major championship."

He has often been challenged to defend South Africa's racial policies. "I am not a racist," he insisted. He has helped non-white golfers in South Africa and offered to play exhibitions in the United States to aid the United Negro College Fund (his offer was declined). Speaking of Player's difficult position, John Hildyard, a South African golf writer, said, "He says enough, he believes, to establish his right to compete in other countries, but if he says too much, he could be condemned in his own."

Player at the 1974 Masters tournament.

Reed, George Robert (1939–   )

He is the most prolific and the most durable running back in the history of professional football, American or Canadian. Since 1963 American-born George Reed has played fullback for the Saskatchewan Roughriders in the prairie city of Regina, and he once played 111 games in a row, a Canadian Football League record.

In his first 12 seasons he carried 2,920 times for 14,662 yards and 123 touchdowns, all CFL records that surpass Jim Brown's NFL records. Ron Lancaster, his quarterback, said, "We haven't been fair to him. We've asked him to do a lot of things you shouldn't ask one back to do." Russ Jackson, an opposing quarterback, said, "Like Jim Brown, he has the ability to carry the ball 25 or 30 times a game and not get hurt."

He always looks hurt because he gets up so slowly after each carry. But he is built like a weight lifter—5 feet 11 inches, 203 pounds. To accommodate his 29-inch thighs, he buys trousers with 40-inch waists and takes them in six inches. "His thighs give him a combination of quickness and power," said Earl Lunsford, a Canadian player and later executive. "He gets those legs into you good. If you hit him there, he has the power to run through you."

Football is only part of his life. He is Saskatchewan sales-promotion manager for Molson's Brewery, three-time president of his local PTA, coordinator of the local Special Olympics for retarded children, a fund-raiser for programs to fight multiple sclerosis and the first American and the first black president of the CFL Players Association. "He has a bad habit," said his wife, Angie. "He can't say no to anybody."

He played cornerback and rover at Washington State, but American pro teams lost interest when he broke an ankle in his junior year. Jake Gaudaur, the CFL commissioner, said, "That was our gain. He would have done what he has done in any league." Bud Grant, coach of the Minnesota Vikings and a former coach in Canada, agreed, saying, "He would have been a superstar here just as he is in Canada."

Reed, a quiet, thoughtful, honest man, said he had no regrets about staying in Canada rather than trying the National Football League. "I had no reason to go back but pride," he said, "and pride will just make you go hungry."

Richard, Joseph Henri Maurice
(1921–   )

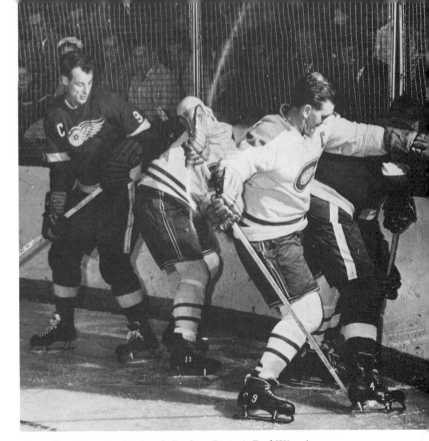

He was the most exciting, most explosive and most hot-tempered player in hockey. He was also the highest scorer of his day, adored by his public, feared and sometimes hated by opponents.

Maurice Richard, known as The Rocket for his speed on the ice, played right wing for 18 seasons (1942–60) for the Montreal Canadiens of the National Hockey League. In 978 regular-season games he scored 544 goals (a record at the time), 421 assists and 965 points. He made the first or second all-star team 14 times.

He was a solid 5 feet 11 inches and 190 pounds, with black hair, a fierce look and deep-set, menacing eyes that threatened rival goalies. "When he came flying toward you with the puck on his stick," Glenn Hall said, "his eyes were all lit up, flashing and gleaming like a pinball machine. He was terrifying." Another goalie, Don Simmons, said, "His eyes flash like the headlights of a big truck."

Every opposing team harassed him, and Roger Kahn wrote, "He is as anxious to fight as he is to score a goal." To that Richard said, "That fiery spirit of mine has been my weakness as well as my strength. If it has driven me to success it has also kept me in hot water throughout most of my career. . . . But too often, the rough stuff which caused me to blow up has been completely overlooked."

As a youngster injuries almost stopped him before he had started. In his first minor-league game he broke an ankle and missed the season. The next year he broke a wrist and missed the season. "I began asking myself whether this was worth all the pain and frustration," he recalled.

He overcame it all, became a huge success and, late in his career, played on the same line with his brother Henri (who was called The Pocket Rocket). Nine months after he retired he was voted into the Hockey Hall of Fame, and he became a Montreal businessman with interests in television, oil and fishing lines, among others.

"I am not a smooth player in the classic tradition of Jean Beliveau or my little brother Henri," he once said. "I do not have the skills of Gordie Howe. . . . Hockey must remain for me just what it was when I was a child skating on the Back River near home— the most urgent thing in my life."

Canadien Maurice Richard checks a Detroit Red Wing in a scramble for the puck as Detroit's Gordie Howe (No. 9) prepares to move in.

Richard grins at the Stanley Cup trophy in 1958 after the Canadiens beat the Boston Bruins.

In high school he smoked and drank and belonged to a teen-age gang whose other members wound up in reform school or prison. He was spared because, he said, "The Lord spoke to me at the time of my greatest need, and I listened." At the age of 20 he became an ordained minister in the Church of the Brethren. In later years he earned $125,000 a year—$75,000 from television commercials and appearances for Wheaties and $50,000 for inspirational speeches on the lecture and banquet circuit. *Sports Illustrated* described his message as a homily for "diligence, perseverance, goodness and the Breakfast of Champions . . . packaged in his own golden glow of fitness, verve and enthusiasm." Myron Cope, describing his oratorical style, wrote that with his "bobbing and weaving, his forehead glistening with perspiration, he is Rocky Marciano on the attack against Archie Moore. He is Bart Starr on fourth down." Of Richards' non-fiction book, *The Heart of a Champion*, Cope wrote, "Not only do his athletes remember to say their prayers, they advance into battle enduring torturous injuries. . . . Page after page, crippled athletes come forward wincing until the reader begins to believe that he is a spectator at a giant, agonizing Olympic Games that somehow has been awarded to Lourdes."

Sports taught Richards to set high goals. "You learn to give yourself to a cause greater than yourself," he said, "something that will lift you outside your own ego and complexes. . . . I owe my athletic achievements to the power of the Lord."

Richards, Rev. Robert Eugene
(1926–   )

During a decade that spanned the 1940s and 1950s, Bob Richards was the world's leading pole vaulter. Years later he became even more famous as the television voice of Wheaties, the breakfast cereal.

He finished third in the 1948 Olympics and won gold medals in the 1952 and 1956 games, becoming the only two-time pole-vault winner in Olympic history. From 1948 to 1957 he won the national outdoor championship nine times and the indoor championship eight times. He also won three national decathlon titles and one national all-round championship. Using old-fashioned metal—as opposed to today's fiberglass—poles, he cleared 15 feet 126 times, with his best performances 15 feet 6 inches indoors and 15-5 outdoors.

Rickard, George Lewis
(1870–1929)

Tex Rickard was, according to *Sports Illustrated*, "America's greatest and most colorful sports promoter." Nat Fleischer called him "one of the greatest showmen who ever coaxed the dollars out of an easily excited public. . . . It was the combination of Tex Rickard and Jack Dempsey, promoter and star, that registered Dempsey as the ring's greatest money-maker." "For an out-and-out gambler," W. O. McGeehan wrote, "he probably was the greatest success of the age."

He was born in Missouri next to the farm where the mother of Jesse and Frank James lived, and shooting was common there. "I never had a boyhood in the sense that the ordinary boy does today," he once said. "Circumstances forced me into cutting out my own way at a time when most boys are out flying kites."

He made $60,000 in the Klondike gold rush, invested it in an Alaskan gambling hall and lost it all. He went to Nome with $35, opened a saloon, made $500,000 and lost most of it in bad gold claims. He moved to Nevada, opened a hotel and gambling hall and started promoting fights to publicize the town.

Eventually he promoted fights all over the country, including boxing's first million-dollar gate, the 1921 Dempsey–Georges Carpentier match in Jersey City, which grossed over $1.7 million, and the first $2 million gate, the 1927 Chicago rematch between Gene Tunney and Dempsey, which took in over $2.6 million. His Dempsey fights (against Tunney twice, Carpentier, Luis Angel Firpo, Jess Willard and others) grossed $10 million. He built and became president of a new Madison Square Garden in New York.

Rex Lardner wrote, "He had going for him, in the classic time of the con, the mark and the hustler, an immense respect for his word. If he said a deal was set, it was set." Jack Hurley recalled that his word was the only contract he needed with him. Dempsey said, "His eyes were his bond." He was, as Charles Samuels, his biographer, wrote, "a very shrewd man . . . brash, imaginative, always on the lookout for a new fast deal."

When he died at age 59, his body was placed in a $15,000, 2,200-pound solid bronze casket in the center of Madison Square Garden. Fifteen thousand people filed past, and 10,000 attended the funeral at the Garden. Dan Parker wrote, "If he could have sat up . . . he would have exclaimed, 'Gosh, I never seed nothing like it.'"

Tex Rickard (seated) with Luis Firpo, one of the many boxers whose fights he promoted.

Rickey, Wesley Branch
(1881–1965)

Branch Rickey, wrote Fred Lieb, "left a more emphatic mark on baseball than any other man in this century." Arthur Mann called him "the most original mind, the best organizer and the shrewdest horse-trader . . . baseball has ever produced."

For 59 years Branch Rickey served major-league baseball as player, manager and executive. He developed the farm system and broke the color line. He forced the major leagues to expand by becoming president, in 1959, of the Continental League, a projected third major league that never materialized.

He played 119 major-league games between 1905 and 1914, mostly as a catcher. In 1907, catching with a sore arm, he allowed 13 stolen bases in one game. He managed the St. Louis Browns (1913–15) and St. Louis Cardinals (1919–25), never finishing higher than third.

He was vice-president of the Browns in 1916, vice-president or president of the Cardinals from 1917 to 1920 and vice-president of the Cardinals from 1925 to 1942. During these years he created baseball's first and most successful farm system, built the Gashouse Gang and led the Cardinals to six pennants and four World Series. He was vice-president of the Brooklyn Dodgers in 1942 and president from 1943 to 1950, winning two pennants and

building the team that won four more after he left. From 1951 to 1955 he served the Pittsburgh Pirates as general manager at $100,000 a year, and from 1956 to 1959 he was board chairman. In his 80s, he returned to the Cardinals as a consultant.

He was a religious, God-fearing man who never played on Sunday and went to the ballpark on Sunday only three times in his career. He had a booming voice, and he loved to talk and preach. He was shrewd and intellectual, a practical visionary one writer called "a road-company William Jennings Bryan." Red Smith wrote, "To say he has the finest mind ever brought to the game of baseball is to damn with the faintest of praise, like describing Isaac Stern as a lively fiddler." "He is a man of many facets," wrote Tom Meany, "all turned on."

In 1946 he signed Jackie Robinson to a farm-club contract, and in 1947 he made Robinson the first black man in major-league baseball. Rickey said later, "I have never intended to be a crusader. I hope I won't be regarded as one." Larry MacPhail did not see him as one. "Rickey was not kidding anybody in baseball with all that bunk about his conscience," MacPhail said. "Churchill must have had Rickey in mind when he said [of Sir Stafford Cripps], 'There, but for the grace of God, goes God.' "

Branch Rickey (right), retiring president of the Brooklyn Dodgers, congratulates his successor, Walter O'Malley, in 1950.

Riggs, Robert Larimore
(1918–   )

In his prime he was the best amateur tennis player in the world and then the best professional. A generation later he returned to notoriety as a buffoon who played two nationally televised matches against women, made a fortune from endorsements, commercials and hustling and enjoyed antagonizing much of womankind with unbridled male chauvinism.

In his youth and in middle age Bobby Riggs was a man apart. His tennis game had little power, but he was fast, clever and all desire. As Paul Metzler wrote, "He never lacked self-confidence. He made his own contribution to tennis, though probably the game could not hold too many like him at any one time." Julius D. Heldman, who played him, said, "He was undoubtedly the cagiest player of all time and was a superb gamesman as well. . . . To beat him, you simply had to outhit him. Nobody could outsteady or outthink him. No one could outpsych him." Billy Talbert, another former star, agreed, calling him "a player with no real weakness—and no real strength, either, except the all-important one: he got the ball into the court. He returned everything."

He was Wimbledon champion in 1939, United States champion in 1939 and 1941. Then he turned pro and won four world professional championships before quitting the tour in 1949. He married the heiress to a photography fortune and joined the business, but he hated the life of a corporation executive. "I never thought of my wife's money as half mine," he said. "The millions weren't mine. The $100 I won on the golf course was. That was a challenge, and I won it on my own."

The marriage broke up, and he spent most of his time hustling. He played tennis wearing roller skates or an eyepatch, a raincoat or a dress or carrying a suitcase, a bucket of water, an umbrella or a dog on a leash, always for a bet and almost always winning. He hustled in golf, table tennis, backgammon, dice, poker and on and on. He would bet on anything.

"What I live for," he said, "is the game, the matching of wits. . . . People misunderstand the mentality of a hustler. It doesn't matter how well you do things, it's how you negotiate handicaps. I found out long ago to always gamble up, play rich guys and knock 'em in. It's no fun playing guys who go broke if they lose. . . . As long as you understand the term, to be a hustler is no disgrace."

His ultimate hustles came in 1973. He was 55 years old, short (5 feet 8 inches), with glasses, bad vision, a squeaky voice, a hairpiece and tinted hair. He walked like a duck, and, in his words, he had "one foot in the grave."

He also had an idea he thought would make money—playing tennis against young women pros.

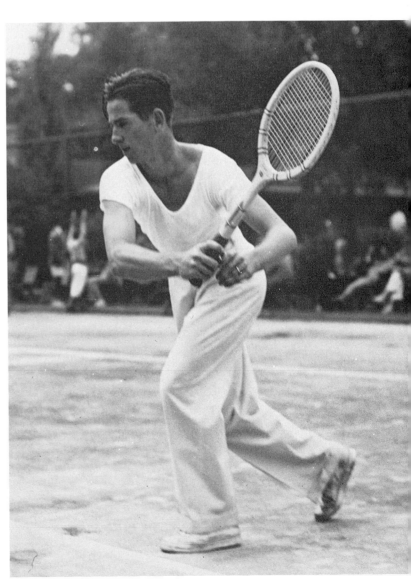

Bobby Riggs, age 18, at the National Clay Court championships in 1936.

Riggs, in 1973, with some of the vitamins he took daily in preparation for his challenge match with Margaret Court.

On Mother's Day he played 30-year-old Margaret Court of Australia, at that time the most successful woman pro in the world. When they took the court Riggs, ever the showman, handed her a dozen roses. She was shaken by the carnival atmosphere and she choked. He won, 6-2, 6-1, and collected $12,500.

The big money came three months later when he played 29-year-old Billie Jean King, another ranking woman player and Women's Lib advocate. This time there was a $100,000 winner-take-all purse plus

at least $100,000 each from television rights. They played in a circuslike atmosphere in the Houston Astrodome before 30,000 spectators. Mrs. King beat him, 6-4, 6-3, 6-3, but he had won, too. As Curry Kirkpatrick wrote, "He pulled off the finest pure hustle in the modern history of American sport."

The profits were just starting. He became in great demand for commercials, appearances and social tennis, all of which brought in money. He declined to play on the Grand Masters tour with such old-timers as Pancho Gonzales, Pancho Segura and Frank Sedgman. Instead he tried unsuccessfully to play in women's tournaments, even offering to wear a dress.

He needed attention and notoriety. "I'm on the go all the time doing something," he said, "but I love it. I don't do it for the money. I do it for the fun of it, the excitement, to keep busy and stay active. . . . What I really am is just an old broken-down tennis bum trying to hang around a little longer and have some fun."

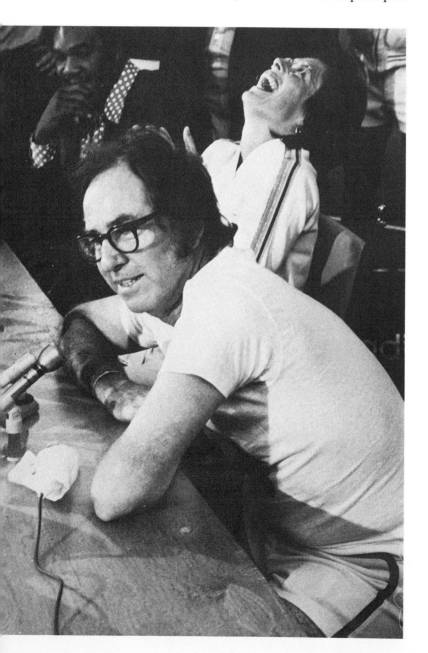

Billie Jean King laughs at a Bobby Riggs male-chauvinist remark during a news conference on the eve of their "battle of the sexes."

Robertson, Oscar Palmer
(1938–   )

Coach Phog Allen called him "the greatest basketball player of all time for a fellow his size." Coach Red Auerbach said no one came close to him. Paul Hemphill wrote, "In his prime, there was no way to stop him from doing anything he wanted to do."

Oscar Robertson, known as the Big O, stood 6 feet 5 inches tall and weighed 220 pounds. Off the court he was quiet and introverted, and Ira Berkow, his biographer, said "He's so aloof that nobody knows him." William Barry Furlong, the writer, called him "articulate but not quite candid."

He played guard fluidly, smoothly, seemingly without effort. He controlled his games. Eddie Gottlieb, a long-time owner of pro teams, said, "In his prime, when he had the ball and the game was close, he could take it over in the last two or three minutes." Phil Berger wrote, "He had the most prepossessing talents for the game but an autocratic tendency in regard to the ball." Jim Schottelkotte wrote that his Cincinnati Royals coaches hated the fact that he controlled the ball.

He made All-America twice in high school and three times at the University of Cincinnati, where he was also three-time player of the year and three-time

national scoring champion. His collegiate scoring average of 33.8 points per game broke the all-time record at that time.

He played 14 seasons (1960–74) in the National Basketball Association—ten with the Cincinnati Royals and the last four with the Milwaukee Bucks. The Royals traded him because Coach Bob Cousy preferred mediocre team play to superior one-on-one play, so he went to the Bucks and helped them become winners. He made the first all-pro team in his first nine seasons and retired as the NBA's all-time leader in assists and free throws and second in scoring to Wilt Chamberlain.

Sam Goldaper called him "pro basketball's most complete player." Coach Joe Lapchick once said, "There's never been one like him." Robertson appreciated these tributes, saying, "I've done the best I could. I've accomplished everything I could have hoped for."

Robertson, playing for Milwaukee, lays the ball up as Lou Hudson of Atlanta defends.

Robinson, Brooks Calbert, Jr.
(1937–   )

He started in the minor leagues as a second baseman, but because he did not have the range or the arm for second base, he was made a third baseman. And thus was a hero born.

Since 1955 he has been playing third base for the Baltimore Orioles. He is a consistent hitter and a slow runner. As a fielder he is, by common consent, the best third baseman in baseball history, a human vacuum cleaner. He is sure to be enshrined in the Baseball Hall of Fame. His glove is already on display there.

Ed Linn wrote, "He is undoubtedly the only player in history—choose your position—to whom the spectacular play is routine. It is not a question of whether he is going to make the play; it's only a question of whether he's going to have the opportunity to make it." Umpire Ed Hurley said, "He plays third base like he came down from a higher league."

From 1960 to 1972 he led American League third basemen in fielding ten times. From 1960 to 1974 he averaged 157 games a year (a team plays 162). He is the major-league all-time leader among third basemen in games played, fielding percentage, putouts, assists and double plays. He has played in every All-Star Game since 1960. His sensational fielding plays in the 1970 and 1971 World Series were shown over and over on television.

His personality is as mild as his fielding is splashy. Mark Kram wrote, "He is charmingly bland, a Musialian figure in Baltimore; a truly gifted performer and a species of player baseball presses to its bloodless heart. . . . But a certain force, a third-rail quality, never surfaced. He is not sure what leadership means, anyway. . . . He seems to take a secret pride, like a big-city evangelist, in his way with people. . . . He always manages to be earnestly dull."

Even his wife, Connie, marvels at his temperament. "He's so patient," she says. "He's never moody, never sulks. I tell him, one of these days he's going to explode because he must be keeping it all inside."

He insists he is perfectly happy. "As long as I play ball," he said, "I think I'll enjoy it. I've never wanted to do anything else. If you look at all those people who are doing something not because it's the thing they do best or that they want to do most, it's fantastic to be able to do what you do best and love most. If that isn't what happiness is, then I don't know."

Robinson robs Johnny Bench of a hit with this spectacular catch in the 1970 World Series.

Robinson, Frank (1935–   )

In his first 19 seasons as a major-league outfielder, Frank Robinson collected 2,900 hits, 574 home runs and a .295 batting average. Nine times he batted

above .300, and four times he led his league in slugging. Yet, he will be remembered more as major-league baseball's first black manager. And he will be remembered for his struggle to reach that plane.

A year before his appointment he said, "They make excuses. . . . They tell me I haven't managed in the minors even though I have five years managing winters in Puerto Rico. They tell me people wouldn't come to watch a team with a black manager. That's nonsense. . . . Baseball owners are prejudiced. They are almost all bigots. Only when I see a black manager will my opinion change."

He plays baseball to win at any cost. He plays hard. He leans far over the plate, daring the pitcher to hit him, and the pitcher often does. He has five-inch scars on both elbows from opponents' spikes. "Whatever he did, he did 100 percent," teammate Brooks Robinson said. "He played when he was hurt, when he shouldn't have played. He never saved himself, and I think these things rubbed off."

He played outfield for the Cincinnati Reds (1956–65), the Orioles (1966–71), Los Angeles Dodgers (1972) and California Angels (1973–74). When the Angels sold him to the Cleveland Indians in September 1974, he was a designated hitter. Three weeks after the sale and 27 years after Jackie Robinson became the first black player in the major leagues, Frank Robinson became the first black manager. The Indians gave him a one-year contract as playing manager at $175,000, his 1974 salary as a player.

He had been a leader since his years with the Reds. He lived high in those days and, as Mark Kram wrote, he was "broodingly distant, a chronic dissident." He had matured by the time he joined the Orioles, where he inspired by example.

When he was named manager, one thing was on his mind. "In my heart," he said, "I don't think I was hired because I was black. I hope not. I think I've been hired because of my ability." The Indians did not agree fully. Ted Bonda, their executive vice-president, said, "We needed somebody to wake up the city. We felt we had to generate excitement." At least they picked a man who could do it.

Frank Robinson after he was named manager of the Cleveland Indians in 1974. Phil Seghi is at rear. The former outfielder is the first black manager in the major leagues.

Robinson, Jack Roosevelt
(1919–1972)

If Jackie Robinson had been the first black man to play major-league baseball and nothing more, he would have been assured a place in history. But he was far more than a passive symbol. He was fiery, aggressive, angry and often abrasive. He played baseball as if it were warfare.

In a sense, all of Jackie Robinson's life was warfare. His father was a Georgia sharecropper, his grandfather a slave. Though raised in Pasadena, California, and a star in four sports at UCLA, he suffered racial discrimination. In the Army, where he became an officer in World War II, he was arrested for refusing to move to the back of a Southern bus.

Before the postwar era there had never been a black player in modern times in the major leagues of America's three leading team sports—baseball, football and basketball. Pro football's first modern black would be Deacon Dan Towler of the Los Angeles Rams and pro basketball's would be Chuck Cooper of the Boston Celtics, both in 1950. The doors were opened because baseball had broken the color line in 1947.

The man who smashed the barrier was Jackie Robinson. The man who made it possible was Branch Rickey, once an undistinguished player and manager but later a front-office genius with the St.

Robinson as a rookie with the Brooklyn Dodgers in 1947.

Louis Cardinals and Brooklyn Dodgers. In 1946, as vice-president and general manager of the Dodgers, he sensed that America was ready for black major-league players. He also knew there was a gigantic untapped market of black players.

Rickey also realized that the first black player would have to be a strong, bright man who could survive the racial invective sure to come from the bigots of white America. He chose Robinson and had him play in 1946 for Montreal, the Dodgers' most important farm club. In 1947 Rickey promoted Robinson to the Dodgers and prepared him for the reception awaiting the first black major-leaguer.

The reception indeed was rough. Fred (Dixie) Walker, a popular outfielder reared in the South, was one of several Dodgers who resented a black teammate. He asked to be traded, and after the season he got his wish. When the St. Louis Cardinals threatened to strike if Robinson played against them, Baseball Commissioner Albert B. (Happy) Chandler warned them to expect severe penalties, and the strike never came. Spectators, opponents and even teammates tormented Robinson. He survived it all and won the respect though not always the affection of the baseball and outside worlds.

Robinson signs his 1949 major-league contract as Branch Rickey watches.

Robinson slides home safely, scoring from first on an error by the New York Giants in this 1951 game. Pee Wee Reese (No. 1) scored moments before.

He played ten years for the Dodgers, mostly at second base. He was the most exciting base runner of his time and a line-drive hitter with a lifetime batting average of .311. In 1962 he was elected to the Baseball Hall of Fame.

His post-baseball life was tragic. His son, Jackie, Jr., after overcoming a drug habit, was killed in an auto accident. Robinson himself was still frustrated by racial injustices—"I remain a black in a white world," he said—and he berated baseball for failing to appoint a black manager. He had high blood pressure, heart trouble, diabetes and blindness in one eye. He became feeble, and on October 24, 1972, he died at age 53.

A few months before, Roger Kahn had written a book telling how unkind the years had been to Robinson and his old teammates. The book was *The Boys of Summer*, a title inspired by the words of Dylan Thomas, "I see the boys of summer in their ruin." There was ruin in Jackie Robinson's life. There was glory and history, too.

Jackie Robinson in 1972.

Robinson, Sugar Ray (1920–)

He was the world welterweight champion, five times the middleweight champion and almost the light-heavyweight champion. He was, as almost every boxing writer has written, pound for pound the greatest fighter of all time.

He was slim, smooth and handsome. Phil Pepe wrote, "He moved like a ballet dancer and he hit like a sledge hammer." Charles Morey described his repertoire of punches: "His left jaw was a straight stab. He was a master of the feint. His right cross came as though shot from a cannon. His left hook was a jawbreaker. His combinations were classic in their speed and accuracy. His ring brain was a veritable computer. And he had a searing will to win." A manager once said, "When he fights, every boxer in the country should pay his way in to see how it's done."

He was born Walker Smith, Jr. When he was 15 and too young to get an AAU boxing card, he borrowed one from a friend named Ray Robinson and kept the name. A few years later, when a writer named Jack Case remarked, "That's a sweet boy you have there," George Gainford, his manager, replied, "Sweet as sugar."

Thus was born Sugar Ray Robinson, a professional boxer for a quarter-century (1940–65), an exciting, flamboyant man adored by the public and often hated by promoters when he failed to show up for fights. He traveled with an entourage that included a barber, valet, chauffeur, secretary and golf pro. He once owned several blocks of Harlem real estate and many New York businesses. Roger Kahn, the writer, described him as "emperor of his own little world," and Jimmy Breslin wrote that he was "egotistical, hard to reach in conversation, but possessing rare color and individuality." Barney Nagler called him "a remarkable man, admirable in some respects, dislikable in others."

He lost most of his money, and he turned to dancing in nightclubs and acting in movies and television. He fought until he was 45, by then usually for small purses in tank towns. The day had come, Martin Kane wrote, "when only the courage remained." Arthur Daley called the elder Robinson "a distorted shadow of himself." And Gainford said, "Oh, my God, look at this man. He can do nothing anymore."

Sugar Ray Robinson, bloodied and weary, after losing a 15-round decision to Gene Fullmer in January 1957.

Robinson said, "I never had a day's pleasure out of fighting in my life . . . although I guess I owe everything to the ring. . . . I wanted to quit at the top, but you cannot choose your endings any more than your beginnings. . . . We been winners, we been losers. Other people lose, they go crazy. I always move ahead."

Rockne, Knute Kenneth
(1888–1931)

Knute (pronounced "Kuh-noot") Rockne was the most famous and most successful of all college football coaches. But, as Grantland Rice wrote, "He was more than a football coach."

Arthur Daley called him "genius in its purest form," and John Mooney wrote, "He did for football what Babe Ruth did for baseball." Pop Warner said, "No man has ever had a stronger or more magnetic personality." Allison Danzig called him "a man with intense convictions and the courage of those convictions." Paul Gallico wrote, "There were many other great football teachers in that era . . . but none of them had that extra star quality that he possessed and the ability to fuse 11 men into a unit representative of his own peculiar and often impish

spirit." Tim Cohane wrote, "He was an orator, an actor, a scientist, a teacher, a humorist, a psychologist, but most of all he was a salesman."

The product he sold was Notre Dame football, and he sold it so well that Notre Dame became the darling of millions who never went to college (a New York writer called them the subway alumni). In his 13 seasons (1918–30) as head coach, his teams won 105 games, lost 12 and tied five. Five of his 13 teams were undefeated and untied, and three were national champions. His teams were fast, precise, deceptive and clean. As John D. McCallum wrote, "Between the years of 1920 and 1930, football came into its own and Knute Rockne was its prophet."

He was eloquent and witty, a master psychologist celebrated for his pep talks at halftime. Once, when Notre Dame was losing, he stuck his head into the dressing room and said, "Fighting Irish? Bah!" Notre Dame went on to win. Once, under similar circumstances, he stuck his head into the dressing room and said, "Excuse me, girls." Of course, Notre Dame won. Once, before a game against Army, he told the story of George Gipp and asked his players to win one for the Gipper. Of course, Notre Dame won.

He was born in Norway and brought to America at the age of five. At 22, his hair almost gone, he started playing football for Notre Dame as a 5-foot-8-inch, 145-pound end and became a third-team All-American. In 1913 he caught so many passes from Gus Dorais that little Notre Dame upset Army, 35–13, and established the forward pass as a major part of every team's offense.

In 1914 he graduated *magna cum laude*. He played pro football and coached, and in 1951 he became a charter member of the College Football Hall of Fame. His success was legendary. So were many other things concerning him. Jack Newcombe wrote, "He was surrounded by a legend that has grown with the years until it has become hard to view the man as he really was."

Why was Rockne successful? "He was an innovator rather than an inventor," Francis Wallace

Knute Rockne (left) on the sidelines of a 1926 game.

wrote, "an adaptor who might pick up a new wrinkle from an opponent and use it to defeat that opponent the following year." Adam Walsh, who played for him, said, "He was tough as hell, a real taskmaster, but he was a perfectionist first, as tough on himself as on his men." H.G. Salsinger wrote, "He instilled a love for football in his players." Harry Mehre said, "He sold football to his players with a positive approach, not 'to die gamely' but to 'fight to live.'"

Allen Messick, the Notre Dame backfield coach when Rockne was a player, said, "He was basically a romantic with powerful emotions, which he usually kept under firm control. But where Notre Dame was involved, he sometimes found himself overcome."

"The breaks came my way," Rockne said, "when I had sense enough to take them, and while that's an unromantic way of explaining a career, it has the advantage of being the truth. . . . Football teaches a boy a sense of responsibility—responsibility as a representative of his college, responsibility to his teammates, responsibility in controlling his passions—fear, hatred, jealousy and rashness. Football brings out the best in everyone."

On March 31, 1931, the plane in which he was a passenger crashed in a Kansas cornfield, and Knute Rockne was dead at age 43. The King of Norway sent a personal representative to the funeral. Members of his last team carried him to his grave. An Atlanta newsboy refused to sell his papers because, he said, "I don't want my customers to read about Rock."

Gus Dorais, his old teammate, said, "Rock is not dead to me, any more than any great man really dies. The imprint of his charming, wonderful personality that he planted in the hearts of his boys will carry his gospel of clean living and fair play on and on after we are all gone."

Pat O'Brien playing Rockne in Knute Rockne—All American, *a popular 1940 film.*

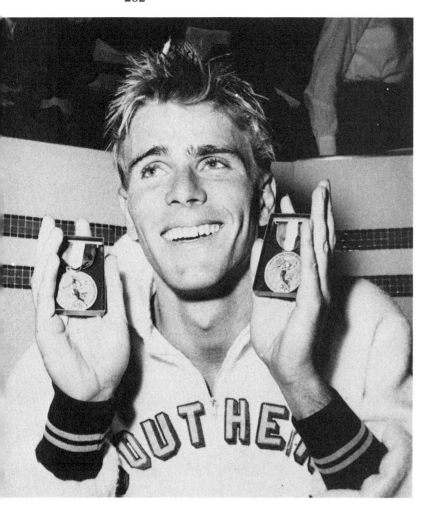

Rose, Iain Murray (1939–   )

Murray Rose was raised as a vegetarian. He ate only natural foods, mainly seaweed, brown rice, cereals and sunflower and sesame seeds. He ate no meat, poultry, fish or sugar. The diet may have helped him become a great swimmer, but his determination and unique tactical sense probably were more important.

He was born in England, but his family moved to Australia when he was one year old. In the 1956 Olympics he became the youngest swimmer in 32 years to win three gold medals. In the 1960 Olympics he won one gold medal, one silver and one bronze. In 1964 Australian officials demanded that he return for the Olympic trials if he wanted to make the team. He refused to leave his job in California and, despite an 18-month layoff, demonstrated his fitness by breaking two world records. The Australians refused to choose him, a decision that Arthur Daley called "the epitome of foolishness."

Murray Rose smiles with two of the three gold medals he won in the 1956 Olympics.

At three he could swim the length of a 50-yard pool. Using a classic, fluid stroke, he went on to set nine world free-style records between 1956 and 1964, and he held one world record or another for 12 years (1956–68). He was swimming captain at the University of Southern California, where he was named the outstanding scholar-athlete. He studied drama and television, and his charm and good looks helped him gain jobs in American movies and television.

Bob Kiphuth called him "the fastest man alive." Gus Stager called him "the greatest swimmer who ever lived, greater even than Johnny Weissmuller." "When he's right, no one can match him," said George Breen. Arlie Schlardt wrote, "He stands out among the newer swimmers like a Rolls-Royce in a traffic jam." Fred Isamu Wada of the Japanese Olympic Committee said, "Murray Rose one tremendous guy in Japan. Nobody like him since Babe Ruth. People break their back to see Murray Rose."

Rose said, "If you are racing a man, the object is to break him. . . . The big thing is to make him feel you are controlling the race. . . . If you can concentrate so that time is meaningless, a race will give you complete pleasure and you will feel no pain." He attributed his success to "hard work and long hours of training, nothing more."

Mauri Rose at Indianapolis in 1947.

Rose, Mauri (1906–   )

Mauri Rose was the third man to win the Indianapolis 500 three times, which certainly established his credentials as a race driver. But he considered himself more an automotive engineer than a driver.

Yet he drove for 24 years, starting on dirt tracks in his native Ohio. During most of those years he worked for auto manufacturers. He invented a device that allowed amputees to drive passenger cars, and when both of his children contracted polio in 1950 he invented an exercising device that helped them recover.

He was a slight man (5 feet 6 inches and 135 pounds) with a square black mustache. But as Robert Cutter and Bob Fendell wrote, "Under the big mustache, the ever-present pipe and the talk of engineering, there was the heart of a competitor."

He finished second at Indianapolis in 1934, and he won the national driving championship in 1936. In 1941, after switching cars in mid-race, he won at Indy. In 1947, semi-retired and racing for what he called "relaxation," he won again.

In that race he and Bill Holland drove cars owned by Lou Moore. With seven laps to go and the cars running 1-2, Moore had the pits flash "E-ZY" to both cars. Holland obeyed and eased up. Rose did not, and he passed Holland, who waved cheerfully (Holland thought he was one lap ahead). Rose won the race. Holland was second and furious. The next year Rose won again, beating Holland by a lap. In 1949, with Holland leading and Rose closing in with eight laps to go, a magneto strap broke and put Rose out of the race. In 1951 his car flipped. He escaped uninjured and quit racing.

Wilbur Shaw, another three-time winner at Indy, remembered Rose's strong ego. "According to him," said Shaw, "no one else knew half as much about racing as he did, and this was particularly irritating to me because I was equally certain I was the best in my business. Frankly, I have never known any top-ranking driver who didn't have such an opinion of himself, but he had not yet learned to voice his opinion with a proper amount of restraint."

Why did Rose, a brilliant engineer, race cars? "At first," he said, "I think of the money, but then, pretty soon, the dough is only part of it. You're like the dope addict who can't break away. After a while, you just can't quit."

Rosewall, Kenneth R.
(1934–)

For more than two decades, Ken Rosewall of Australia has been one of the best tennis players in the world. He is a little man (5 feet 7 inches, 142 pounds), and his friends kiddingly call him Muscles. He is quiet, proper and conservative, and he looks so unlike a sports hero that he has had to talk his way into many arenas past unbelieving guards.

He has flowing ground strokes, a classic backhand and patience. Rod Laver, a frequent opponent, said, "He beats you with consistency." Lance Tingay, an English tennis writer given to flowery words, wrote of "his immaculate purity of stroke, his superb mastery of the classic values of the game." Dave Anderson wrote, "Most of the time, he plays as if he were an automaton directed by an electronic brain."

The automaton had a brain of its own. René Lacoste, the former French player, said Rosewall was the best tennis player ever, "a complete athlete who combines intelligence with dexterity." Cliff Sproule, an Australian official, compared him to a chess player, saying, "He seems to be thinking a few shots ahead." Rosewall agreed. "This game is more than strokes," he said. "It's concentration. Medita-

tion, I guess you would call it. I try to blanket everything out of my mind except tennis."

His parents owned and operated three tennis courts in Sydney, and he started playing there at age seven. He and Lew Hoad, born nine miles apart, were prodigies together. At 17 he became the youngest winner of the French championship and at 18 the youngest winner of the Australian championship. At 21 he won his first United States championship. He never won at Wimbledon, but he was a finalist four times—once at age 19, once at age 39. In 1957 he became a touring pro, and in the early 1960s he was the number-one pro.

As Jerry Kirshenbaum wrote, "He has gone from child prodigy to geriatric phenomenon without losing either his schoolboy air or the quiet authority he has always exerted on the tennis court." Rosewall thought little had changed through the years except that he was "just a little heavier in the wallet." Of his longevity he said, "Probably the biggest reason I've lasted so long is that I learned the game the right way. . . . It's not often a man is lucky enough to do what he loves for so many years."

Wilma Rudolph sprints to victory in the 200-meter dash at the 1960 Olympics in Rome.

Rudolph, Wilma Glodean
(1940–   )

In 1960 Wilma Rudolph, known as Skeeter, won three sprinting gold medals in the Rome Olympics and became the darling of the world. On one trip to Germany, crowds had to be held back in Cologne by mounted police, in Wuppertal by police dogs. In Berlin souvenir hunters took her shoes—while she was wearing them.

She was tall and slender (5 feet 11 inches and 134 pounds), a charming, graceful beauty with a perpetual twinkle. Barbara Heilman wrote, ''She can command a look of mingled graciousness and hauteur that suggests a duchess, but, in a crowd that is one part Skeeter and 5,000 parts people, young men and babies will come to her in 30 seconds.''

When others succumbed to their nerves before a race, she was cool. Ed Temple, her coach at Tennessee State University, said, ''When the time comes to wake her, she sits down and yawns. She picks up a shoe and kind of looks at it. . . . She puts it on and yawns and looks at the other one.''

Miss Rudolph in 1969.

She was not always cast in the heroic mold. She was one of 19 children. She weighed 4½ pounds at birth. At four, suffering simultaneously from double pneumonia and scarlet fever, she lost the use of her left leg. At six, wearing special shoes, she hopped on one leg. She wore those shoes until she was 11.

At 13 she went out for basketball at Burt High School in Clarksville, Tennessee. To Coach Clinton Gray, she was more mosquito than basketball player. ''You're just like a skeeter,'' he said. ''You're little, you're fast and you always get in my way.'' She was twice all-state in basketball and unbeaten in three years of sprinting.

In college she broke world records for 100 and 200 meters. During the 1960 Olympics Italian newspapers called her *La Gazzella Nera* (The Black Gazelle). She won the Sullivan Award as America's outstanding amateur athlete, male or female. Later she hung her car keys from it.

Years later she set up athletic programs in Chicago for girls, including 14-year-old Yolanda Eldridge, the eldest of her four children. Speaking as coach and mother, she said, ''She looks just like me and she runs just like me.''

Miss Rudolph, "The Black Gazelle," winning the 400-meter relay for the U.S. at the 1960 games.

Rupp, Adolph Frederick
(1901–   )

He won more games than any other coach in college basketball history. He was the most popular man in Kentucky, and politicians tried to convince him to run for governor.

Adolph Rupp, the Baron, has always been colorful and outspoken, blunt and haughty, cantankerous and tough. He was a highly competitive coach who Zander Hollander called "a strange mixture of vanity and humility." His assistant, Joe Hall, cited "his extremely competitive desire and strong dread of losing." Joe Jares wrote, "He has a scowl that could freeze a basketball player in midair."

He is also a man of firm ideas, saying, "I don't plan to chaperone a bunch of boys around for an entire winter and not teach them to be successful in their undertakings. . . . Failure doesn't bother people today. In fact, we subsidize failure. The worse failure you are today, the better chance you have of getting on some of the subsidies we've got. . . . I know I have plenty of enemies, but I'd rather be the most hated winning coach in the country than the most popular losing one."

He had always been a winner. He played on Phog Allen's national champion teams at the University of Kansas. He coached for five years at high schools in Iowa and Illinois and in 1930 began a 42-year coaching career at the University of Kentucky. Using mostly home-grown talent, he won 874 games and lost 190. He produced 27 Southeastern Conference champions, a record 20 NCAA tournament teams, four national champions and 25 All-America players. Four times he was named coach of the year.

The university forced him to retire because of his age, prompting him to say, "If they don't let me coach, they might as well take me to the Lexington cemetery." Instead of the cemetery, he became an executive with Memphis and then Kentucky of the American Basketball Association. When a perforated ulcer slowed him, he said, "I didn't have time for ulcers when I was coaching."

He was stern with his players and would not get close to them. He did not take kindly to criticism. Instead, he believed that "To sit by and worry about criticism, which often comes from the misinformed or from those incapable of passing judgment on an individual or a problem, is a waste of time."

As his players watch, Rupp (left) receives the NCAA trophy in 1948 following Kentucky's victory in the tourney final.

Russell, William Felton
(1934–   )

Early in life Bill Russell became many things to many people. He was an extraordinary basketball player. He was the first black man to coach a major-league team in any sport. And he was a free thinker who spoke his mind and became a public personality.

Zander Hollander called him "the best defensive player in the game's history." Ronald L. Mendell wrote that his defense and shot-blocking revolutionized pro basketball. Red Auerbach, his pro coach, said, "He was the first man to actually block shots." "His forte was ball control and play-

making," Dick Joyce wrote. "In these categories, the game never produced an equal."

John Havlicek, a long-time teammate, said, "I've seen him in plays on a basketball court when he not only blocks the shot but controls the ball and feeds it to his forwards, and then he's up at the other end of the court trailing the fast break, and if there's a rebound, there he is, ready for it." Fred Katz said that his greatest accomplishment was to make defense a respectable part of the game. "He introduced a style of defensive play," Katz wrote. "Instead of playing a certain man, he played a certain zone, daring a man to come into it. . . . If he could prevent a player from driving on him, then he had won a battle without moving a muscle."

He was imposing at 6 feet 9⅝ inches, slim, sleek, goateed, always in command of himself. *The New York Times* said, "His main characteristics are pride, intelligence, an active and appreciative sense of humor, a preoccupation with dignity, moodiness, a capacity for consideration once his friendship or sympathy has been aroused, and an unwillingness to compromise whatever truths he has accepted."

As a 6-foot-2-inch, 128-pound high-school sophomore he could hardly play basketball. As a 6-5 junior he was third-string center. He improved enough to lead his college team, the University of San Francisco, to NCAA titles in 1955 and 1956 and 55 straight victories, and twice he made All-America.

Then he played 13 seasons (1956–69) at center for the Boston Celtics and led them to 11 National Basketball Association titles, eight in a row. Five times he was voted the league's most valuable player, and four times he led in rebounds. From 1966 until his retirement in 1969, he served as player-coach and won titles in two of the three seasons. He shrugged off his distinction of being the first black coach by saying, "I am just a man of the times."

After retirement he lectured at colleges for $1,500 to $2,500 a night, acted on television, tended to his rubber plantations in Liberia, did television commentary on NBA games and, in 1973, returned to the NBA as general manager and coach of Seattle. Of the television duties Larry Merchant wrote, "He is the best thing to happen to television sports since instant replay. . . . He has added a dimension of

Russell pulls down a rebound against the New York Knicks in 1957.

openness and fun to the job.'' Russell agreed about the fun part, saying, ''I believe in having a good time at the games.''

His long rivalry with Wilt Chamberlain, an even taller center, was legendary. He said with typical candor, ''Only the first year against Wilt was a challenge. Then it became clear that he was great—and I was better. . . . Players on his teams haven't loved playing with him.'' Jerry West, once Chamberlain's teammate, said, ''I think Wilt is the better all-round player, but for one game, I'd rather have Russell.''

''Before I came along,'' Russell said, ''there were virtually no blocked shots. . . . So, in effect, not only did I dominate my game . . . but I changed it altogether for all time. . . . I have lived up to all that society demands. I have achieved the absolute in my fields. I have been a good winner. I am affluent. I am concerned for my fellow man and have spoken out. I am articulate, make a good appearance and am relatively honest.'' But he added, ''I don't consider anything I have done as contributing to society. I consider playing professional basketball as marking time, the most shallow thing in the world.''

Coaching the Seattle SuperSonics in 1973.

Ruth, George Herman (1895–1948)

Babe Ruth was the most famous, the most exciting and perhaps the most gifted player in the history of baseball. Arthur Daley wrote that he was "greater even than the sport that spawned him." He was warm, generous, colorful and lovable. He loved kids and they loved him.

He established baseball's two most celebrated records—60 home runs in one season (1927) and 714 in a lifetime. Though Roger Maris hit 61 home runs in 1961 and Henry Aaron surpassed 714 career home runs in 1974, they captured Ruth's records but not his image. As Frank Graham wrote in 1954, "No matter what the record books of the future show, there certainly will never be another Babe Ruth. We were lucky there was one."

The home-run records were typical of a man who did everything in a big way. He inspired an adjective (Ruthian), a candy bar (Baby Ruth), a movie (*The Babe Ruth Story*) and countless books. His top salary was $80,000, by far the highest in baseball at the time and even higher than that of Herbert Hoover, President of the United States. "Why not?" Ruth supposedly said. "I had a better year." During World War II, when American GIs tried to infuriate Japanese soldiers to coax them out of their foxholes,

they yelled, "To hell with Hirohito." The Japanese stayed in their foxholes and yelled back, "To hell with Babe Ruth."

He played for the Boston Red Sox (1914–19), New York Yankees (1920–34) and Boston Braves (1935). He had a lifetime batting average of .342 in 2,503 games, and he is still the all-time leader in slugging (.690), home-run percentage (8.5 home runs in every 100 at bats) and runs batted in (2,217). He led the American League 13 times in slugging, 12 times in home runs, 11 times in bases on balls, eight times in runs and six times in runs batted in. He remains the single-season record-holder for slugging (.847 in 1920) and bases on balls (170 in 1923).

Had he not been such a home-run hitter, he might have become one of the great left-handed pitchers. He pitched, mostly for the Red Sox, well enough to compile a 94-46 record and 2.28 earned-run average. Once he won 23 games and once he won 24. His record of 29⅔ scoreless innings in World Series games lasted from 1918 until Whitey Ford broke it in 1961.

The Red Sox, near bankruptcy, sold him to the Yankees in 1919 for $125,000 plus a $350,000 mortgage loan. The Yankees made him a full-time outfielder and, wrote Fred Lieb, "He changed baseball from the stolen-base, play-for-one-run game to the home-run circuses of today." His home-run heroics brought the crowds into Yankee Stadium, the new ballpark the Yankees opened in 1923. People called it "The House That Ruth Built."

He was a splendid all-round player. He could hit, field, throw and run bases, and despite his big, round upper body and thin legs, he was all grace. He served the Yankees well, but when he wanted to manage them, they turned away. In 1935 he played 28 games for the Braves and then quit. "I wanted to stay in baseball more than I ever wanted anything in my life," he said. "But there was no job for me, and that embittered me. . . . I became a kind of ornament or antique of baseball history."

No one forgot his exploits, on the field or off. He did everything in excess—spend money, bet, eat, drink and carouse. He would breakfast on six eggs, two ham steaks, six slices of toast and four cups of coffee, then drive to the ballpark and tell the clubhouse boy to buy him a hot dog. Robert C. Ruark called him "a character straight out of Rabelais—a gross, profane, simple giant, whose

Babe Ruth, weakened by cancer, bids farewell to baseball in Yankee Stadium, "The House That Ruth Built," in 1948, two months before his death.

excesses violated every rule in the nice-nelly lexicon. . . . He was a gluttonous feeder, wencher and boozer.''

Claire Ruth, his widow, said, "He became a national baseball idol before he could vote, and he just wasn't prepared for it. . . . This was a robust man, and he wanted all the things robust men should want—unfortunately, in excess.'' But Jimmy Reese, a Yankee roommate, said, "I saw him half dead after some strenuous activities, but I never saw him drunk.''

With all the excesses, the public loved him. And the public loved his home runs, for they were unlike the home runs of others. "The dusty figures in the record books can never tell anyone what it was like to see Babe Ruth hit a homer," wrote Jack Sher. "They were the most complete and satisfying home runs ever hit. They were whacked so far and they sailed so high that nobody who ever saw Ruth belt one ever forgot it.''

No one ever forgot the man, either, even after his death in 1948 from throat cancer. His widow explained the Babe Ruth mystique by saying, "A nation loved him—not just because he hit 714 home runs and did all sorts of wonderful things on a baseball field, but also because the people knew that he was one of them. He had their faith and their weaknesses. They loved him because they sensed that he was, above all else, a great human being. And they were—and are—so right.''

Ryun strides to victory in world-record time in the 1,500-meter run at the U.S.A.–British Commonwealth dual meet in 1967.

Ryun, James Ronald (1947–   )

The record book shows that Jim Ryun is one of the most successful distance runners ever, a world record-holder, three-time Olympian, many-time national champion, a man who captured the imagination of America when he was a teen-aged prodigy and held it throughout a roller-coaster career. What the record book does not show is the complex personality that made him a success and then almost destroyed him, a personality that allowed the pressures to build up inside him and led, as one observer put it, to an "athletic death wish."

Jim Ryun is slim (6 feet 3 inches, 160 pounds) and boyish, shy and sensitive. He is an introvert and a straight arrow. In his most productive period he was unsophisticated and naïve, a grim, unsmiling, unhappy enigma. The pressure he faced took its toll. Dave Anderson wrote that he ran and lived within himself "as if a spring kept tightening inside him." Ryun said people had always put him on a pedestal. "They made me some sort of a super-something," he said. "And then they'd say, oh, how terrible, so young and so many pressures. Well, all the pressures were made by me. Inside pressures."

He grew up in a religious family in Wichita, Kansas. He attended church four times a week and was not allowed to drink, smoke or dance. In 1964, as a high-school junior, he ran a sub-four-minute mile, made the Olympic team and reached the Olympic semi-finals. He was 17 years old.

In 1965 he raced against Peter Snell, the world's best miler at the time, in the AAU national championships. When asked of Ryun's chances, Snell said, "I don't concern myself about schoolboys." He should have. Ryun beat him by two feet in 3 minutes 55.3 seconds.

In 1966, as a University of Kansas student, he went on a 13-month spree that brought him two world records in the mile, one at 880 yards and one at 1,500 meters. Kip Keino of Kenya, a frequent rival, explained Ryun's success by saying, "He run too fast." One of his few losses was to Keino in the 1968 Olympics, at Mexico City's 1½-mile altitude and after Ryun had been weakened by a severe bout with mononucleosis. His performance was remarkable. The public considered him a failure.

His real collapse came in 1969 at the AAU national championships. On the second lap of the mile he stopped running and stepped off the track. "I was pressuring myself too much," he said. "It was like going into the arena. If you don't win, the lions will eat you up." Bob Timmons, his high-school and college coach, said, "He created a situation where he was absolutely unbeatable. . . . A Ryun bandwagon developed, and he had to pull it."

Years later, Ryun said, "To have stopped running at that point may have been the best thing that ever happened to me. . . . I had to stop something that had been wrong for a long time. . . . My mental attitude was bad. I had to stop it. . . . I was putting pressure on what used to be Jim Ryun. I'm not so sure it was really the same person."

He retired for 19 months. When he returned in 1971 he ran fast one race and slow the next. In the 1972 Olympics he fell in his heat and could not catch up. In 1973 he joined the new professional track circuit, and suddenly he was relaxed and outgoing.

Paul Zimmerman wrote in the New York *Post*, "He smiles a lot these days, a fleeting smile that has as much sadness as humor."

He won often as a pro in 1973 but did not win a race in 1974. He said, "It was pretty disillusioning," and he looked forward to a projected $100,000 mile race in 1975. "It's not the money that's important," he said. "Actually, I think the money cheapens it. That's my Christian and amateur background showing, I guess."

What made Jim Ryun enigmatic? Dr. William Plummer, who headed the medical team at the United States training camp for the 1972 Olympics, thought Ryun demanded too much of himself and warned, "If he doesn't get help, he's apt to withdraw into a shell he'll never be able to break."

Ryun had his own thoughts. "People were never able to accept me when I started losing," he said. "I feel I have a God-given talent and I have a responsibility to develop it." With all his problems, he kept running. "All this about the pain and loneliness of the distance runner has been overemphasized," he said. "To me, running can be satisfying."

Jim Ryun plays in 1971 with his one-year-old daughter, Heather, while his wife, Anne, looks on.

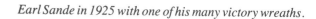

Sande, Earl (1889–1968)

His life was filled with highs and lows, the highs the product of his ability to ride a race horse, the lows often the result of his stubborness. At 5 feet 6 inches and big-boned, he was huge for a jockey, and he always had trouble keeping his weight down. But he had the hands and seat of a jockey, and Earl Sande, modest, shy, intense and a loner, was a jockey without peer.

Sande (pronounced "Sand-ee") rode from 1918 to 1932, and in 1953, at the age of 54, he made a brief comeback and won a race. In all, he won 967 of 3,663 races for an exceptional average of 26 percent. His horses finished in the money (first, second or third) 61 percent of the time, the highest average in history. He rode Man o' War, Zev, Gallant Fox, Grey Lag and Sarazen, and he won three Kentucky Derbies and five Belmont Stakes. Babe Ruth told him, "For a shrimp, you sure as hell get the fans stirred up."

In 1928, weak from constant dieting to make weight, he retired as a jockey and became a trainer. When the 1929 stock-market crash left him penniless, he became a night-club singer, trained more horses and rode again. He won the 1930 Kentucky Derby aboard Gallant Fox, inspiring Damon Runyon to poetry in the New York *American*: "Say, have they turned back the pages/ Back to the past once more?/ Back to the racing ages to a Derby out of yore/ Say, don't tell me I'm daffy./ Ain't that the same old grin?/ Why, it's that handy guy named Sande,/ bootin' a winner in."

In Sande's heyday Al Stump had written, "Being a hero meant everything to him." But Sande lived his later years in solitude, divorced, lonely and too proud to accept the many jobs offered by racing people who idolized him for the athlete and gentleman he was. "I know the fans liked me," he said. "They were great. But I never had many real close friends inside racing. . . . Don't call me a jockey. I'm a race rider, a member of a fine, honorable profession. I'm proud of it." But it was a profession that demanded sacrifices. "Making weight was so tough that I lived for just a couple of days out of the year. Those were the days I'd go on a food drunk—gorge myself with everything in sight."

Sande up on Crusade.

Sawchuk, Terrance Gordon
(1929–1970)

Terry Sawchuk's statistics were remarkable—21 seasons, 971 games and 103 shutouts, all National Hockey League lifetime records for goalies. They were even more remarkable considering his physical and psychological problems.

He was often injured. Facial wounds required more than 400 stitches. In three elbow operations, 66 bone chips were removed. His eyes were criss-crossed with scar tissue and stitch marks, and a flying puck almost cost him the sight of his right eye. His weight fluctuated between 166 and 228 pounds.

In the middle of the 1956–57 season, playing for the Boston Bruins, he contracted mononucleosis, a blood disease that often requires two months of rest. He returned to the ice in 12 days, still weak, suffered a nervous breakdown and missed the rest of the season. As Leo Monahan wrote, "One reason for his jangled nerves was the pressure of playing goal with a non-contending club where he was afforded little defensive protection." He was also highly volatile emotionally, easily inspired and easily upset. Gerald Eskenazi wrote, "One wonders how much greater his horizons would have been had he not succumbed so often to personal despair."

From 1949 to 1970, playing mostly for the Detroit Red Wings, he won four Vezina Trophies for goal-tending and seven all-star berths. Emile Francis, the New York Ranger coach, called him "the best goalie I ever saw." William Leggett wrote that he guarded his net "as if it were a precious tapestry that only he could protect."

Sawchuk had a style all his own. Andrew Crichton wrote of it this way: "He doesn't move so much as he explodes into a kind of desperate epileptic action: down the glove, out the arm, over the stick, up the glove, all in such rapid succession that it is difficult to watch him."

"Playing goal is like trying to catch a fastball pitcher without a mask," he once said. "You never know when you're going to get hit in the face. After a while, when you've seen a lot of rubber, you start to fret. . . . Then you start fighting the puck. Next thing you know, your whole game is shot. . . . The hardest thing to do is relax. . . . I'm not any more relaxed on the ice than I used to be, but I no longer consider it the end of the world when I lose."

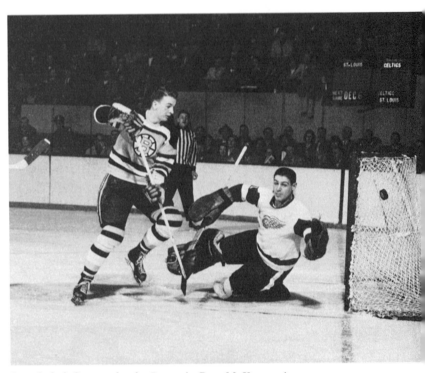

Sawchuk deflects a shot by Boston's Don McKenney in a 1957 contest.

Gale Sayers, University of Kansas, 1964.

Gale Sayers, Chicago Bears, 1970.

Sayers, Gale Eugene (1943–   )

"His days at the top of his game were numbered," Red Smith wrote, "but there was a magic about him that still sets him apart from the other great running backs in pro football. He wasn't a bruiser like Jimmy Brown, but he could slice through the middle like a warm knife through butter, and when he took a pitchout and peeled around the corner he was the most exciting thing in pro football."

Gale Sayers was twice an All-America halfback at the University of Kansas. At 6 feet and 199 pounds, he was solid and powerful. He was also a 26-foot long jumper, which meant he had speed. He was a warm man, celebrated in books and movies for his friendship with his ill-fated pro roommate, Brian Piccolo. He was once shy and withdrawn, and his wife, Linda, said, "We were married a year before I understood him."

He played seven years (1965–71) for the Chicago Bears and was earning $70,000 a year when he retired because of bad knees. As a rookie, he scored 22 touchdowns in a season (a National Football League record) and six in one game (tying the record). For his seven-year career he carried 1,001 times for 4,956 yards and scored 56 touchdowns.

His running style was spectacular. George Halas, the Bears' coach, said, "He detects daylight. The average back, when he sees a hole, will try to bull his way through. But Gale, if the hole is even partly clogged, instinctively takes off in the right direction. And he does it so swiftly and surely that the defense is usually left frozen."

George Donnelly, an opposing defensive back, said, "He doesn't look any different coming at you, but when he gets there, he's gone." John David Crow, once a leading runner and later a coach, said, "He has a sense of football, a feel for the game." Bob Oates, Jr., wrote, "His art, as all art, flows from being, not thinking."

Halas called the talent instinct, and Crow and Oates intimated as much. Sayers agreed. "I have no idea what I do," he said. "I hear people talk about dead leg, shake, change of pace and all that, but I do things without thinking about them."

Sayers was not overly impressed by his success and said he was not a great runner. Murray Olderman disagreed, writing, "No back in the history of pro football, not even Jimmy Brown, has so awed his contemporaries."

Gale Sayers slides into a hole and runs for a touchdown against the Minnesota Vikings in 1968.

Milt Schmidt of the Boston Bruins shoots against Terry Sawchuk of the Detroit Red Wings.

Schmidt, Milton Conrad

(1918–   )

He was a tenacious, powerful and courageous hockey player. *Sports Illustrated* cited "his fierce will to win," and Roger Barry wrote of his "fiery leadership on the ice." Referee Red Storey said, "I'd take five Milt Schmidts, put my grandmother in the nets and we'd beat any team."

Milt Schmidt played center for the Boston Bruins for 16 seasons between 1936 and 1955 and later coached them for 11 years. Starting in the 1937–38 season, he led the Bruins to four straight National Hockey League titles (and two Stanley Cups) and made the first or second all-star team four times. With Bobby Bauer and Woody Dumart, who grew up with him in Kitchener, Ontario, he formed the celebrated Kraut Line.

He was an inspirational player and coach. As Herbert Warren Wind wrote, "He had come to personify the Bruins in flesh and spirit as completely as Pee Wee Reese does the Dodgers or Sammy Baugh did the old Washington Redskins." When he was injured in 1949 a physician reported to the Bruins, "His knee is bad. His side is bad. But there's nothing wrong with his heart. He'll play."

And play he did. Jack McCarthy wrote, "He carries the puck faster than anyone in the game," and Art Ross called him the fastest playmaker of all time. "He is either a beauty or a beast," Al Hirshberg wrote. "If you're for him, he produces a response that borders on ecstatic effervescence. If you're against him, your baser nature is likely to show up in such an amiable avocation as aiming pop bottles at his head as he flies by on the ice."

Hockey always excited him. "You've got to have those butterflies in your stomach," he said. "You'll lose them the minute you hit the ice, but you've got to start with them or you'll never be able to get in the game." Of the Kraut Line he said, "We had grown up together, were lifetime friends and always felt that if each of us got exactly the same pay as the others, there would never be any jealousy or discontent among us. It worked, too. We eventually parted just as good friends as when we started out."

Schollander, Donald Arthur
(1946–   )

As a youth, as a maturing young man and as an athlete, he was almost unreal. He was handsome, fresh, vibrant, charming, intelligent, honest, poised beyond his years. And until his California teammate, Mark Spitz, he was the most successful swimmer in Olympic history.

Don Schollander was encouraged to swim by his mother, Martha, who did the swimming sequences for Maureen O'Hara in Johnny Weissmuller's Tarzan movies. By 1964 he had grown to 5 feet 11 inches and 175 pounds and developed a big swimmer's chest and a classic stroke, and he was breaking world records. That year, at 18, he won four gold medals in the Olympics at Tokyo, and for the next year he received 50 to 100 fan letters a day. He said later, "I always felt that I accomplished everything I wanted in the 1964 Olympics and that everything afterward has been anticlimactic. . . . The importance of swimming has diminished rapidly since then."

He entered Yale on a partial academic scholarship. He did not have to swim, but he did, even though he could devote only one and a half hours a day to workouts while rivals in other colleges were swimming up to four hours a day. He kept swimming until the 1968 Olympics, where he won one gold and one silver medal. Then he retired with 22 world records, 37 American records and a promise to try to make life easier for future swimmers.

He was an idealist who felt that amateurism was dead and the Olympic ideal dying. He had little tolerance for the establishment. Arthur Daley wrote, "His personal experiences have led him to feel let down by the inefficiencies of the Amateur Athletic Union, the lack of principle in the National Collegiate Athletic Association, the remoteness of the United States Olympic Committee."

He had lived under a peculiar type of pressure. "When a kid comes up," he said, "he is compared to me. When he's on the blocks, people wonder if he's going to beat me. So I have to swim not only to win but also not to lose."

Kim Chapin wrote, "He has turned into the rarest of swimming heroes—the champion who ages with grace and dignity and, despite the inevitable challenges, with considerable success."

Schollander dives into the water on the final leg of the men's 400-meter free-style relay trials at the 1968 Olympics as teammate Mike Wall completes the third leg below him.

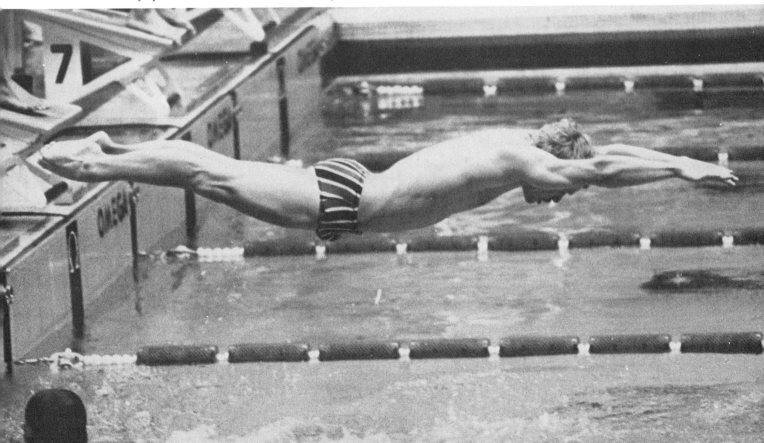

Seagren, Robert Lloyd (1946–   )

Bob Seagren has everything going for him. At 6 feet ½ inch and 178 pounds, he is handsome, fresh-looking and well scrubbed, with flirting blue eyes and a flashy, devilish smile. As a pole vaulter, he is graceful, durable, flamboyant and confident.

In 1966, at age 19, he broke the world records outdoors and indoors. From 1966 to 1972 he broke the world outdoor record five times, eventually raising it to 18 feet 5¾ inches. He won two Olympic medals—gold for first place in 1968, silver for second place in 1972. At the University of Southern California, he won two AAU and two NCAA titles. In 1973 he turned professional and became the top vaulter on the pro tour. Television has brought him into millions of homes in acting roles, commercials and the annual Superstars sport competition.

He started vaulting when he was in the fourth or fifth grade. "My brother Art and I went to the drugstore," he recalled, "and the druggist gave us the bamboo poles that his new rugs had been wrapped around. We piled boxes in our backyard, put up a small bamboo pole as a crossbar and we vaulted. We landed on the grass. I vaulted 6 feet 1 inch and Art didn't do much better." Eventually, Art did 15-9, the best among his peers but only second best in his family.

Brother Bob became a technically expert vaulter. "There are so many variables that can go wrong in vaulting," he said. "It's obviously the most highly technical event in track and field. You need more stamina, speed, strength, agility and coordination, and you have to be fearless with an inner recklessness." He became such an attraction that *Track and Field News* said, "What Jim Ryun did for the mile, Bob Seagren did for the pole vault."

He enjoyed vaulting. "I have to be in good humor to perform well," he said. "If I'm going to win, I might as well enjoy it. Some guys get nasty as hell and don't have any fun."

He was 21 when he said to Bill Toomey, the decathlon champion, "I'm in the heyday of my life. I'm having a great time." Toomey asked, "Don't all these meets seem more or less the same?" "Yes," said Seagren, "but I like to compete."

Seagren clears 17 feet ¼ inch at the 1967 NCAA indoor track and field championships.

Shaw, Warren Wilbur (1902–1954)

As a driver, he had the most impressive record ever achieved in the Indianapolis 500—three victories and three second places in eight years (1933–40). As an executive, he saved the Indianapolis Motor Speedway, the site of the 500, after World War II and helped make the race an American spectacle.

Wilbur Shaw was a dapper, photogenic man with a thin mustache, slight but muscular, charming, polished and well-spoken. Bloys Britt wrote, "He had implicit confidence in his ability as a race driver. His friends said he never hesitated to admit he was the best."

He recalled that when he first drove at Indianapolis in 1927 he was "scared to death." His first victory there came in 1937 in a Miller he co-owned, and he won in 1939 and 1940 in a Maserati. In 1941, driving the same Maserati, he tried to become the first driver to win three years in a row and four times overall. He almost succeeded. With 48 laps to go he was leading by a lap when wheel spokes loosened and his car crashed tail first into a retaining wall.

"My mind was in a turmoil," he said years later. "I couldn't move my legs. What if I could never race again? What if I was destined to be a wheelchair invalid? . . . I couldn't help thinking about all that cash which had been knocked out of my hands by the crash. I would have been in a position to collect between $150,000 and $200,000 simply by signing my name to some contracts."

Days after the accident, he tore off his cast and drove to California in a passenger car. But he never raced again. He became head of the aircraft division of the Firestone Tire and Rubber Company, but the sedentary life bored him. In 1946, when Eddie Rickenbacker was considering turning the Indianapolis track into an industrial park, Shaw convinced Anton (Tony) Hulman to buy it. For nine years Shaw was president and general manager, spreading the gospel of Indy. Al Bloemker wrote, "His perseverance and enthusiasm saved the Indianapolis Motor Speedway from a fate similar to that which engulfed Brooklands and other famous courses."

Shaw qualifying for the 1936 Indianapolis 500.

Shoemaker, Billy Lee
(1931–   )

Willie Shoemaker has won more races (almost 7,000), more stakes races (more than 600) and more $100,000 stakes races (more than 100) than any other jockey in history. He is quiet, efficient, unassuming and thoroughly professional, liked and respected by almost everyone in his business.

He weighed two and a half pounds at birth, and the doctor said he would not survive the night. Later, in a world of small men, he was one of the smallest—4 feet 11 inches, 95 to 100 pounds, size-1½ boot, 25-inch waist, boy's size-18 suit, boys' size-12 shirt. He plays golf (once shooting a 72) with women's clubs. Unlike most jockeys, he can eat all day and not gain weight.

He is gentle with horses. "Horses run for people who handle them intelligently and well," Joe Palmer wrote, "and not because of any personal affection. Horses run for him because he doesn't get in their way." Bennie Green said, "The horse does the running. He just rides." "He seems to understand what is going on with the horses," Leon Rasmussen wrote. R. H. McDaniel, a trainer, said, "He always takes care of your horse." Emmett Watson wrote, "He is the little man who talks to horses through the light, cool touch on the reins." Al Silverman wrote, "He has a wealth of common sense."

Shoemaker posts to victory aboard Royal Owl in 1972 for his 555th career stakes victory, breaking the record held by Eddie Arcaro.

"His hands . . . tell him everything about a horse," Eddie Arcaro said. Jimmy Cannon agreed, writing, "His touch is the secret." Shoemaker said, "I run when the horse wants to."

As a youth, his teeth were decaying and unsightly, and he talked little then or later. When he won the Santa Anita Maturity and a $15,000 share of the purse at age 19, a breathless announcer said to him, "The greatest day of your life, Willie. Tell us how you're going to celebrate tonight." Shoemaker replied, "Eat, I guess."

He is imperturbable. Once, at Santa Anita, his horse fell, and a flying hoof struck him. In the jockey room he discovered that his protective helmet had been split down the middle. He had escaped death by a fraction of an inch. Gordon Glisson recalled, "Shoe walked over to the billiards table and joined the game. He sank three balls on the first shot."

He has won three Kentucky Derbies, and he might have won in 1957 aboard Gallant Man had he not misjudged the finish line and momentarily stood in the saddle. "I just made a stupid mistake in judgment," he said. He has not made many of those.

Simmons, Aloysius Harry
(1902–1956)

Al Simmons, born Szymanski, picked his new name from a sign over a hardware store. The new name became famous because he was an outstanding slugger and a swaggering, confident man. As Arthur Daley wrote, "He was good and he knew it."

He played outfield for the Philadelphia Athletics (1924–32), Chicago White Sox (1933–35) and six other teams (1936–44). In 20 seasons he made 2,927 hits in 2,215 major-league games, with a lifetime batting average of .334. He batted over .300 15 times. In the seven seasons starting in 1925, mostly as cleanup hitter for Connie Mack's Athletics, he batted .384, .343, .392, .351, .365, .381 and .390, winning the American League batting title the last two of those years. During the 1940s he was a skilled third-base coach. In 1953 he was elected to the Baseball Hall of Fame.

He was best known for his odd batting stance. He batted right-handed. Starting with his feet close together, he took a long stride with his left foot, not toward the pitcher but toward third base. It was like stepping into a bucket. At first coaches on the Athletics tried to change the style, and his batting average dropped. Mack let him return to his way, saying, "It's hitting we want, not beauty, so let him alone."

He had many baseball virtues. Ralph (Cy) Perkins said, "I don't think he ever made a mistake." Leon (Goose) Goslin said he was at his best when a game was at stake. Joe Cronin said, "There never was a greater left fielder in going to the line and holding a double to a single." Joe McCarthy said, "He was the best left fielder I ever saw."

Art Morrow wrote, "He hated anyone—and everyone—who didn't wear the uniform he wore." Simmons agreed and cited a special target. "When I was hitting I hated pitchers," he said. "They were trying to take the bread and butter out of my mouth."

He was especially fond of Mack because, he said, "Mr. Mack seemed to look on me as his son." And he loved baseball, saying late in his career, "If I can't play and nobody will give me a coaching job, I'll shine shoes at the ball park."

Al Simmons crosses the plate after hitting a home run against the St. Louis Browns in the White Sox's 1933 season opener.

O.J. Simpson, carrying against the New York Jets in 1973, shatters Jim Brown's NFL single-season rushing record.

Simpson, Orenthal James (1947–)

At various times he has been known as O. J., Orange Juice (for his initials O. J.) or simply Juice. He has been acclaimed in polls as the greatest running back in college football history, and he has set all kinds of rushing records in the National Football League.

The man is just as impressive as the football player. He is handsome, warm, congenial, humble, articulate, sort of a black Frank Merriwell. Ralph Wilson, owner of the Buffalo Bills, said, ''He's a better person than he is a football player, if that's possible.'' Roone Arledge, president of ABC Sports, said, ''He always manages to say the right thing.'' He has the same sweet disposition as his mother's first cousin, Ernie Banks, once the Sunshine Kid of baseball.

He is imposing physically. At 6 feet 2 inches and 208 pounds, with especially strong legs, he has power and the ability to break tackles. In college he ran 100 yards in 9.4 seconds, and he combines that speed with quickness, balance and change of pace.

Most of all, he has running flair. Dick Cunningham, once a teammate, said, "He senses tacklers." Ron Fimrite wrote, "He is a swashbuckling runner who calls to mind the derring-do of Hugh McElhenny, Jon Arnett, Willie Galimore and Gale Sayers."

He drives defenses to distraction. Weeb Ewbank, a rival coach, said, "You have to think about him all the time, like you did with Jimmy Brown." Charlie Winner, another coach, said, "He'd be dangerous out there in a wheelchair." One reason is that he runs by instinct. "People are always asking me what I think about when I'm running," he said. "The answer is nothing."

He was a poor student in high school, and because his grades were not good enough to get into the University of Southern California, he spent two years at San Francisco City College. Then came two years at Southern California, where he carried 621 times for 3,124 yards, 33 touchdowns and the Heisman Trophy. He sometimes carried 30 or 35 times a game. Coach John McKay said, "He doesn't belong to a union. He can carry the ball as many times as we want him to."

In 1969 he was the first choice in the NFL draft. He wanted to play in Southern California, but he was picked by the Buffalo Bills. The Bills' coach, John Rauch, a stubborn man, made minimal use of him. As a result, wrote Pete Axthelm, "Simpson found himself on a floundering, leaderless team that lacked both confidence and ability."

When Lou Saban became coach in 1972, things changed. Simpson ran for 1,251 yards that year, and in 1973 he broke Jim Brown's record by rushing for 2,003 yards. After the record-breaking game, a news conference was arranged for him. With typical thoughtfulness and selflessness, he brought along his entire offensive unit.

He has been among the highest-paid players in football since joining the pros, and each year he has earned far more from outside interests than from football itself. He makes lucrative endorsements and appearances for Chevrolet and Royal Crown Cola. He provides commentary for sports on ABC television. He acts in movies and television shows. He is the first black athlete to cash in on so many commercial ventures.

"No athlete, black or white, ever has had so many deals at so young an age," *Sport* magazine said. "In the selling of O. J. Simpson," wrote Murray Olderman, "the commodity was more than a man with an extraordinary ability to carry a football." Yet with all that success, said Buffalo's quarterback, Joe Ferguson, "Nobody here is jealous of him. He hasn't got an enemy in the world."

Early in his pro career, when things were not going well, he said, "I've used football to make a lot of money and a good life for myself, and I know that football will use me. So whatever I get, I've got to get on my own." Then, when things improved, he said, "When I was a rookie, I really thought that five years in pro ball would be enough. But I have no limits like that in my mind now. I feel like I've just wasted the last few years. And now it's all in front of me."

What really motivates him? "Money never inspired me," he said. "Prestige did. I always wanted to be known. I wanted people to say, 'That's O. J. I like him. He's a great football player.' . . . Being the best is something I've lived with, and I like living with it."

In 1969, the Buffalo rookie sits on the bench awaiting his pro football debut.

Sisler, George Harold (1893–1973)

Branch Rickey, who had coached him in college, said years later of George Sisler, "There never was another first baseman who could match him in speed, reflexes, deftness and gracefulness. . . . He was the greatest player who ever lived."

If he was not the greatest, he was close to it. He played from 1915 to 1930, mostly for the St. Louis Browns. In 15 seasons he made 2,812 hits in 2,055 games, with a lifetime batting average of .340. In the six years starting in 1917, he batted .353, .341, .352, .407, .371 and .420. Then he missed the entire 1923 season because of a sinus infection that led to double vision. "I never was a real good hitter again," he said.

He started as a pitcher and once beat Walter Johnson, but like Babe Ruth, another left-handed pitcher of his era, he was too good a hitter to keep out of the lineup. He worked hard to become the great fielder he was. Bob Broeg called him "an athlete to whom good wasn't good enough." Frankie Frisch called him "true poetry in motion, the perfect player." "His game was consistency," Lee Greene wrote, "and no man ever used more skills more consistently over so long a period." Arthur Mann wrote, "His degree of baseball immortality is exceeded only by his reluctance to admit it."

In 1939, when he was among the first first baseman elected to the Baseball Hall of Fame, he said, "Maybe it will prove to be an inspiration to my sons." It did. Dick became a major-league first baseman-outfielder-coach, Dave a major-league pitcher, George Jr. a minor-league player and later president of the International League.

For 27 years their father was a scout and batting coach for the Brooklyn Dodgers and Pittsburgh Pirates, with such star pupils as Duke Snider and Roberto Clemente. His philosophy: "Hitters can't guess. They've got to think. They've got to look for the ball, not for a particular pitch."

He was W. C. Fields's favorite player. Once he visited Fields at a theater and was offered a drink. "I don't drink," he said. A disappointed Fields replied, "Oh, well, not even the perfect ballplayer can have everything."

Sloan, James Forman
(1874–1933)

Many racing people consider Tod Sloan the best of all jockeys. He may also have been the most innovative. It was Sloan who introduced the crouch (or monkey) seat, the method of crouching far forward on a horse that all jockeys use today.

He was a memorable character without these distinctions. He was a tiny man—less than 5 feet tall and 100 pounds—whose legs were short even for a jockey. He was a dandy who sported a monocle and changed clothes four or five times a day and a big spender who smoked made-to-order Havana cigars and gave a $25,000 party for Lillian Russell. A big gambler, he once lost $31,000 in an afternoon betting on horses and $30,000 that night at cards. At age 23 he lived year round in a $200-a-day hotel suite. He traveled to London to ride, accompanied by two valets, two financial advisers and a secretary.

He started riding in 1892. By 1901 he had lost interest in racing and in 1910 he stopped riding completely. In his day he earned $75,000 a year and made much more on stock tips from grateful horse owners. He was once worth more than a million dollars, but he eventually lost it all. John Warne (Bet-a-Million) Gates, the famous promoter and speculator, once bet half a million on him in one race. The Prince of Wales (later King Edward VII) offered him 6,000 guineas ($30,000) for first call on his riding services for one year. Max Hirsch, who rode against him and later became a celebrated trainer, said of Sloan, "He used to tell Mr. William Whitney and the others, 'You will come to me to ride that horse of yours,' and they often did, too."

Though he had a complex, unpredictable personality, he always went out of his way to be friendly with horses. Albert Abarbanel wrote that "He talked to horses in their own language," and Sloan tended to agree. "I use all my arts of persuasion on horses. I use the whip only rarely. It pains me to chastise a horse. . . . I always wanted to settle down and enjoy a gentleman's life, buy a stable of horses and train them. That's by far and away the best thing you can do."

Sloan's vision of a gentlemanly life never worked out. He wasted and drank away his fortune, and his two marriages went sour. He became a tout, a gambler and a drunk. He was found in a charity ward, at

Tod Sloan, a dandy and one of the best jockeys of all time.

age 59, suffering from cirrhosis of the liver aggravated by chronic alcoholism. Five weeks later the great Tod Sloan was dead.

Snead, Samuel Jackson (1912–)

When he was a high-school senior he broke his left hand playing football, and he started swinging a golf club to keep the hand from stiffening. When he was 21 he cleaned golf clubs and shoes and did odd jobs around the pro shop for $20 a month plus room and board. When he was 22 he took a $20 pay cut but was allowed to hustle hotel guests into lessons.

From those beginnings Sam Snead became a golf legend, even while he was playing on the tour. He has won 84 tour tournaments, more than any other golfer. From 1942 to 1954 he won the PGA championship three times, the Masters three times and the British Open once.

He has won every major tournament except the United States Open, and his miseries in the Open are part of golf lore. In 1939, needing a 5 on the last hole, he took an 8. In 1947 he missed a 30-inch putt

on the last hole. In 1949, needing pars on the last two holes to tie, he failed to get them.

In his 60s, he still plays occasionally on the tour. At 62 he led two tournaments going into the final round. "He's an absolute total freak," said Arnold Palmer. "I'm wearing glasses and not hearing so good at times, and there's Sam hitting the same old great shots. Who even wants to play that good when you're 60?"

Obviously, Snead wants to. "Sure, I want to win again, very badly," he said. "If I can get my putting to where it should be, I think I've got a chance. I know that from the green I can keep up with three-fourths of the golfers today. It's just the putting that marks the difference."

He had so much trouble putting that he turned to a side-saddle style in which he pushes the ball. Dan Jenkins watched him take that peculiar stance and wrote, "It made him look as if he were paddling his boat to a spot where the catfish were biting."

He is 5 feet 10 inches and 182 pounds, blocky and muscular, with long arms. He hits the ball with the sweetest swing in golf, and he hits with power. He describes himself as a hillbilly from the Back Creek Mountains of Virginia. Jimmy Demaret teases him by saying that Snead has buried all his tournament winnings in tomato cans in his backyard.

Snead is a positive thinker. "The bane of golf—and of life in general—is to remember your mistakes and not your right moves," he said. "If you know yourself to be a whiner, you'll never play up to your full ability. It takes guts to be an optimist in golf. He who thinks like a winner will win."

Speaker, Tristram E. (1888–1958)

Tris E. Speaker is generally regarded as the best center fielder of all time. Joe Williams wrote, "I saw Speaker and DiMaggio break in. Make mine Speaker." When Speaker was only a teen-ager in the minor leagues, Jimmy Ryan, a Chicago outfielder, said, "He is the greatest outfielder that ever lived." Marty McHale, a teammate, said, "It was an education and a thrill to watch him in the outfield." Sid Mercer said, "He was the daddy of them all."

When Speaker was ten years old he was thrown by a bronco and broke his right arm and collarbone, so he learned to pitch and bat left-handed. He learned well enough to play for the Boston Red Sox (1907–15), Cleveland Indians (1916–26), Washington Senators (1927) and Philadelphia Athletics (1928). In 22 years he played 2,789 games, made 3,515 hits and 793 doubles (still the major-league record) and batted .344. In his five best years he batted .389, .388, .386, .383 and .380.

People went to games just to watch him in the field. Bob Broeg wrote, "Never before nor since has an outfielder played so shallowly." Lee Greene wrote, "Crouched out there in shallow center field, so close to second base that he was virtually a fifth infielder, he looked like a poised bird of prey"

(perhaps that was the source of the nickname Gray Eagle). Speaker said, "I learned early that I could save more games by cutting off some of those singles than I would lose by having an occasional extra-base hit go over my head." A contemporary said Speaker's secret was "the greatest sense of baseball flight ever conferred on man."

During and after his baseball career, Speaker was creative, friendly and successful. As player-manager of the Indians (1919–26) he was a pioneer in platooning players. He was elected to the Baseball Hall of Fame in 1937, but he always championed the modern players ("I think the boys today may be a little better," he said). He became a broadcaster, batting coach and businessman. "The world has done all right by Tris Speaker," Gordon Cobbledick wrote. "He knew what he wanted, and he got it with a minimum of frustration and disappointment."

Spitz, Mark Andrew (1950–   )

He is the most successful swimmer, in and out of the pool, since Johnny Weissmuller. After he won a record seven gold medals in the 1972 Olympic Games at Munich, he began a career of commercial endorsements and public appearances expected to earn him at least $5 million. In the eight months after those Olympics, 300,000 life-sized posters of him wearing bikini swim trunks and his seven gold medals were sold for $2 and up (he earned 15 cents a poster). Yet for all his success, Mark Spitz has never been universally loved or respected.

He is broodingly handsome, like a younger Omar Sharif. He is graceful and exciting in the pool, often temperamental, immature, indiscreet and cold out of

Mark Spitz with five of the seven gold medals he won at the 1972 Olympics.

it. *Time* magazine described him as a "sullen, abrasively cocky kid." Susan Lydon wrote, "Apparently, to know him is not to love him." An Olympic teammate said of his success at Munich, "It could have happened to a nicer guy." In 1973 Joyce Haber called him "a 23-year-old Howard Hughes."

His sister, Nancy, also a swimmer, denied he was arrogant. Dave Edgar, a rival swimmer, said, "He talks a lot about himself, but how can you blame him? That's all people ever asked him." Gary Hall, a college and Olympic teammate, said, "He says what he means, and I respect that. Of course, sometimes he ought to watch who he says it to." Spitz himself said, "I just get all wound up sometimes."

His early life was dominated by his father, a scrap-metal dealer who moved family and household to put his son with the best coaches. "I've got my life tied up in this kid," said Arnold Spitz. "You think I created a monster? He's beautiful. There is nothing wrong with parents giving to their children. If people don't like it, the hell with them. . . . If I pushed Mark, it was part of his development. . . . Swimming isn't everything. Winning is. Who plays to lose? . . . Every outstanding person must have some egotism. Cassius Clay is obnoxious, but I love him."

In 1968 Mark Spitz went to the Olympics in Mexico City owning ten world and 28 American records and a conviction, which newspapers made public, that he would win six gold medals. Instead he won two gold (both in relays), one silver and one bronze. For someone else it would have been history. For Mark Spitz it was disaster. "I had the worst meet of my life," he said. "I tried not to believe all that I was reading about myself, but I wound up believing every word of it." Some Olympic teammates delighted in his failures. In training some had kicked him, elbowed him, spat at him and aimed anti-Semitic remarks at him. "I don't think it was hatred," he said, "just jealousy."

After the Olympics, a few days before Spitz entered Indiana University as a pre-dental student, Coach Doc Counsilman told his Indiana swimmers that there might be tense moments with Spitz and said they should not prejudge him. They cooperated, and Spitz seemed to mature. "He has accepted success graciously,'' said George Haines, once his coach. ''He was a little boy before,'' said Sherman Chavoor, his first and last coach. ''He has become a man.''

In 1972, at Munich, he swam in seven events, including relays, and won all seven in world-record time. People there wanted to see him so badly that they paid $50 for $12 tickets. But his performance, like so many before, was marred by his words. Asked before the Olympics how he, a Jew, felt in Germany, he said, ''Actually, I've always liked this country, even though this lampshade is probably made out of one of my aunts.''

As he had promised long before, he retired from swimming after the Olympics. Paul Zimmerman wrote from Munich, ''There are those who feel he is not enjoying his invasion of the history books, that he is having trouble coping with the mantle of destiny.'' Paul Hemphill wrote, ''When he flew home from Munich . . . America . . . was in need of milk-drinking heroes. He looked like the genuine article.''

The William Morris Agency, which handles show-business stars, became his manager. He endorsed electric razors and hair dryers (the contract guaranteed him $1 million), milk and clothes, swimming pools, swimming goggles and swimsuits. Susan Lydon called him ''a hero who was not born but made.'' ''I'm a commodity,'' Spitz said, but he said little else publicly because public-relations men, afraid he would say the wrong thing, seldom left his side.

Immediately after the Olympics he was asked, ''What about dental school?''

''I suppose I could always postpone it for a year,'' he said.

A year later, after he had married, acquired a $65,000 racing yacht, a new life style and new fame, he was again asked, ''What about dental school?''

''Are you kidding?'' he said.

Spitz swims to a world-record-breaking victory in the 200-meter butterfly at Munich.

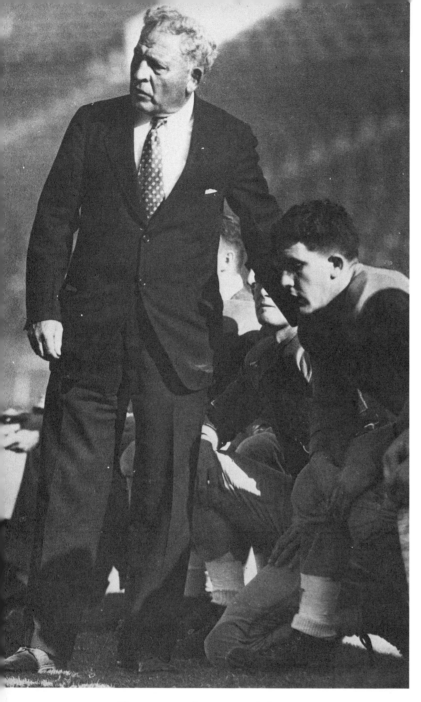

Stagg, Amos Alonzo (1862–1965)

Amos Alonzo Stagg coached college football longer than anyone else in history. With his integrity and creativity, he may have had a greater influence on college football than anyone else.

The New York Times called him "the most compelling single force for the tactical growth and ethical elevation of the game." The Chicago *American* said, "He exemplified so many things that are good and that seem to be going out of fashion—hard work, self-discipline, fairness, sportsmanship." *Sports Illustrated* said, "His lasting mark as a man is his unyielding idealism." And Frank Graham wrote,

Amos Alonzo Stagg, coach of College of the Pacific, sends in a substitute in a 1934 contest with Southern California.

"It is too bad that the ideals the old man has cherished all his life have taken such a beating elsewhere on the college scene."

Physically he was small (5 feet 6 inches, 160 pounds), but he played end for Yale for five years (1885–89) and was chosen in 1889 on Walter Camp's first All-America team. He pitched the Yale baseball team to five league championships and received six pro offers, but he rejected them because he did not like the character of the professional game and expected to become a minister. Then he decided against the ministry because he stammered, and he feared he could not speak easily before a group.

He became a football coach. For 57 years he was head coach at Springfield (1890–91), University of Chicago (1892–1932) and College of the Pacific (1933–46), never earning more than $8,500 a year. When Chicago retired him at 70 he refused a $3,000-a-year pension and moved to College of the Pacific. When he was retired there at 82 he became offensive coach at Susquehanna College in Pennsylvania for six years (his son Paul was head coach) and advisory coach at Stockton (California) Junior College for seven years. In 1960 he wrote a note to the Stockton coach, saying, "For the past 70 years I have been a coach. At 98 years of age it seems like a good time to stop."

Stagg reviews his troops during Pacific's game with the Alameda Coast Guard in 1943.

He was a true Spartan. His family was poor, and he lived on soda crackers at prep school and Yale until he was hospitalized with malnutrition. He gave up coffee in high school, and he did not drink or smoke. His strongest words were "jackass," "double jackass" and, in extreme cases, "triple jackass." He indulged only in sourballs and other hard candies. When he turned 98 friends gave him a power lawn mower. He returned it, saying, "I can still use the old one, and besides, I need the exercise."

Stella Stagg learned football to keep up with her husband. One Saturday, when she was in her 70s and the Staggs were at Susquehanna, she disappeared. Later that day she returned and said she had decided to scout Dickinson, the next opponent. "By the way, Alonzo," she said, "you can pass on their left halfback. He's slow." The following Saturday, Susquehanna defeated Dickinson with a fourth-quarter touchdown pass over the defensive left halfback, who was slow.

Amos Alonzo Stagg pioneered the forward pass and the T formation. He invented the tackling dummy, man in motion, shifts, onside kickoff, quick kick, field goal from placement (previously, they had been by drop kick only), fake field goal and the numbering of players. In baseball he invented the indoor batting cage and the head-first slide. He also invented troughs to catch swimming-pool overflow. He was the first football coach to have a field named for him and the first athletic director to achieve faculty status.

He was innovative and enduring (Milton Gross wrote, "He has made time stand still"). Most of all, he was strong of character. His son Amos Alonzo, Jr., like his father called Lonnie, said, "To disagree with my father was like breaking with God."

Amos Alonzo Stagg, the Grand Old Man of Football, said, "Winning isn't worthwhile unless one has something finer and nobler behind it. When I reach the soul of one of my boys with an idea or ideal or a vision, then I think I have done my job as a coach. . . . I would like to be remembered as an honest man."

Starr, Bryan Bartlett (1934–)

For 16 years (1956–71) he played quarterback for the Green Bay Packers, a bright, disciplined man who appeared to be the strong, silent type but was really much more.

"There is a softness in him, a sort of gentle manliness," said a teammate, Jerry Kramer. "But there is also an iron-hard spirit." Jack Zanger wrote, "The central fact about him is that he has infinite ability to adjust, to become what his quiet but driving ambition demands him to be."

Bart Starr needed that ambition because his career at the University of Alabama was spotty and the Packers did not draft him until the 17th round. Vince Lombardi, who became coach of the Packers and made them champions, said, "When I met him, he struck me as so polite and so self-effacing that I wondered if maybe he wasn't too nice a boy to be the authoritarian leader that your quarterback must be."

He proved to be a leader. He was smart, too, and he called half of his plays at the line of scrimmage. Bill Austin, a rival coach, said that his greatest asset was picking apart the defense. Dick Voris, another

coach, said, "You can't take any kind of gamble against him. A gamble produces a weakness and he always finds it."

He is 6 feet 1 inch and 197 pounds, with blue eyes, sandy hair and a boyish look. He does not smoke or drink, and he calls himself "a sensitive person basically." But, wrote Dave Wolf, "There is a grisly toughness behind his soft Alabama drawl."

He completed 1,808 of 3,149 passes for 24,718 yards and 152 touchdowns. He set one National Football League lifetime record by completing 57.4 percent of his passes, another by throwing 294 passes without an interception. More significantly, he led the Packers to five NFL titles in seven years and was voted most valuable player in the first two Super Bowl games (the Packers won both).

After retirement, he helped coach the Packers, ran an automobile dealership, made television commercials and, in 1975, became Green Bay's head coach. He loved the game, he loved the Packers and he could not say no. As he once said, "You have to have a sincere, burning desire to play the game. If you don't have a real love for it, you could never do the things you have to do in order to play it."

Bart Starr, the Packers' quarterback, confers with head coach Vince Lombardi during the 1967 Super Bowl.

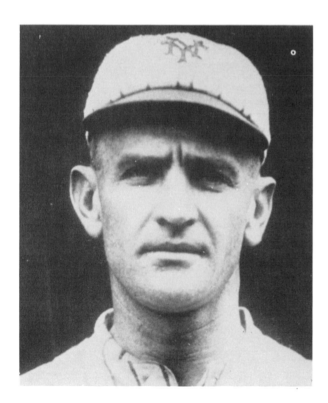

Stengel, Charles Dillon (1890–   )

He was the most successful of all baseball managers and the highest paid ($85,000 a year) of his day. In middle age he managed losers. In old age he managed the greatest winners of all. In older age he managed the greatest losers of all. And always he was that slightly ridiculous character with that delicious sense of humor, joy and vibrancy.

Sport magazine called him "a genius . . . he was unique." Ed Linn called him "an American monument." To Al Silverman, "He was a man for all seasons." Arnold Hano wrote, "The man is an original. . . . He had one of the great impish senses of humor of all time." Leonard Shecter wrote, "He can say anything better and funnier than anybody else, also longer." Maury Allen wrote, "Every time he appears tired, he gets a magic shot of youth."

Casey Stengel acquired his nickname from his home town of Kansas City (also known as K.C.). He has a wrinkled face, floppy ears, bright blue eyes, thick chest and bowed legs. When he hit an inside-the-park home run in the 1923 World Series, Damon Runyon wrote these words to describe him running the bases: "This is the way—His mouth wide open. His warped old legs bending beneath him at every stride. His arms flying back and forth like those of a man swimming with a crawl stroke. His flanks heaving, his breath whistling, his head far back."

He created a language of his own—Stengelese. It was a kind of doubletalk that violated most known rules of grammar, and it helped him avoid direct answers. He could speak perfect English, but he was happier entertaining the world with his gravelly voice passing along wisdom in Stengelese.

He spent his youth trying to become a left-handed dentist in a right-handed world. He studied three years at Western Dental College (Sally Rand said she dated him there) before turning to baseball. From 1912 to 1925 he played outfield for five National League clubs. He batted .284 in 1,277 games and was always good for a laugh. Once, he lifted his cap to the fans and a bird flew out.

He became a minor-league manager and major-league coach. Then he managed the Brooklyn Dodgers (1934–36) and Boston Braves (1938–43) and never got them into the first division. When he was struck by an automobile and missed the first half of the 1943 season, a Boston writer called the driver of the car "the man who has done the most for Boston baseball."

316

"The Old Professor" lecturing an umpire in 1963.

going up to take a nap,'' he once said. ''After the game, I might not be able to sleep.'' Another time he said, ''We got the World's Fair across the street. If you don't like the Mets' game in the second inning, you could finish there.''

When the Mets were bad, which was most of the time, his Stengelese was at its best. For example: ''The catching on this team before we got Gonder did not hit, but it receives better than last year and probably throws better. It commits less passed balls for a club that can't hit. . . . I'll tell you about youth. Look how big it is. They break a record every day. Don't tell me they don't get better. I am playing the youth of America if it can play. You can make the team here quick. Join the Mets.''

In 1966 he was voted into the Baseball Hall of Fame. At his induction he said, ''I want to thank my parents for letting me play baseball, and I'm thankful I had baseball knuckles and couldn't become a dentist. . . . I got $2,100 a year when I started in the big leagues, and they get more money now. . . . I chased the balls that Babe Ruth hit.''

He went back to managing in the minor leagues. Then, in 1949, at age 59, he was named manager of the New York Yankees. His team won the World Series his first five seasons, and in his 12 years they won ten American League pennants and seven World Series.

After the 1960 season he left the Yankees. They said he had retired; he said he had been fired because of his age. Years later, he said, ''Don't ask me about the Yankees. I made a living before the Yankees, and I made a living after the Yankees. I never think about the Yankees any more.''

In 1962, at age 72, he became the first manager of the New York Mets, and they finished last in the National League in each of his four years there. ''I'm

Stewart, John Young (1939–   )

In nine years (1965–73) of grand-prix racing, Jackie Stewart established himself as the most successful driver of his day. He won 27 of 99 grand-prix starts, a record. He won three world driving championships in five years—in 1969 in a Matra and in 1971 and 1973 in a Tyrrell. And then, at the height of his career, he retired.

Sports Illustrated said at that time, "He has brought to his sport a combination of qualities unique in its history—a marvelous physical talent, the intelligence and perspective to be an eminent spokesman for auto racing, and the discipline to retire at the peak of his career, a simple yet infinitely complicated personal act that few celebrated athletes have ever achieved."

He is a compact man (5 feet 8 inches, 145 pounds) who speaks with the burr of his native Scotland, mod, long-haired, bright and shrewd. He has a fine public-relations sense for himself and his sport. When he retired he was earning almost $1 million a year from racing, endorsements, promotion, consultations and television appearances. Since his retirement he has become more popular than ever.

When he barely failed to make Britain's 1960 Olympic trapshooting team, he turned to auto racing against his mother's wishes. In his first season as a professional he raced under the name of A. N. Other. But he was like no other.

Jim Clark, his close friend and rival, said, "Nobody ever had to teach him very much about driving a race car. It came naturally." Barrie Gill called him the most professional driver, on and off the course. Another writer said Stewart was an enthusiast "who enjoys himself so much that he just naturally succeeds. He controls his racing cars and his life exactly as he wants to."

According to Stewart, racing demanded such control. "The idea that there are men who risk their lives for the sake of winning is exciting," he said, "especially in modern society, which is so restricting. But basically, we're professionals. . . . You have to be quite mature mentally to be successful in this line of work. You have to be a thinker, with an almost computerized mind. If you aren't, you might never live long enough to become a top performer."

Racing to victory in the Canadian event with an average speed of 114 mph.

Jackie Stewart, winner in 1972 of his second straight Canadian Grand Prix.

Stokes, Maurice (1933–1970)

During his three years in pro basketball he was one of the game's great talents, a high scorer, aggressive rebounder and a three-time member of the all-pro second team. When an accident left him physically helpless, his 12-year struggle to recover inspired a nation.

Maurice Stokes was 6 feet 7 inches and 240 pounds, and at St. Francis College in Loretto, Pennsylvania, he was an All-American. Then he played professionally for the Royals in Rochester and Cincinnati. In the final regular-season game in 1958, he fell to the floor head first and was knocked out for three minutes. The next day, flying back to Cincinnati, he became violently ill and lapsed into a coma. He had suffered posttraumatic encephalopathy, brain damage to the motor-control center caused by a blow to the head.

For weeks he was close to death. He survived, but Mac Davis wrote, "He was little more than a vegetable." He spent the rest of his life in hospital beds or wheelchairs. He never walked again except for a few steps with heavy steel braces.

Jack Twyman, a teammate, became his legal guardian and raised hundreds of thousands of dollars to support him. The bills for hospital, doctors, nurses and rehabilitation reached almost $1,000 a week. Twyman marveled at Stokes's courage. "He doesn't feel sorry for himself," said Twyman. "He feels that what happened happened. He's going to beat this thing. I really believe that."

He beat it every way but physically. He learned to speak in slow, guttural sounds. He struggled five hours a day with therapy. He learned to make professional-quality ceramics. When Twyman bought him an electric typewriter, the first words he typed, painfully and laboriously, were: "Dear Jack, How can I ever thank you?"

His mind was keen. So was his sense of humor. Once, when Twyman was lifting him out of his wheelchair, he said to someone, "You better help Jack. He has bad hands." Once, when he saw Dolph Schayes, he touched his elbow and laughed. Schayes, who had two of the meanest elbows in basketball, laughed, too.

He was bitter only because some old friends had deserted him. "When I was in the headlines," he said, "they wanted to know me, but now that I can no longer shoot baskets they make themselves scarce. Maybe it's because they're afraid I'll ask them for money."

He asked nothing from anyone as he fought his battle for 12 years. Then his heart gave out, and at 36 he died. At his request, he was buried on the St. Francis campus.

Sullivan, John Lawrence
(1858–1918)

John L. Sullivan, the Boston Strong Boy, was the last of the bare-knuckled world heavyweight boxing champions and the first of the modern era. He was an imposing man who loved to talk and found a willing and appreciative public.

"He was a boozer and a bully and a braggart," Rex Lardner wrote, "and as such was loved by every red-blooded American." Jack Sher wrote, "He was incorrigible, childlike, loud and lovable, a hero made for the times." Nat Fleischer wrote, "He spoke as he fought—aggressively." Donald Barr Chidsey called him "a lowbrow, a tough, touchy and a very strong hick from a back street." Jack Sanders called him "a legend, the symbol of an era." To *Sport* magazine he was "a hero among heroes."

He became champion in 1882 by knocking out Paddy Ryan. In 1889, under a noonday sun in Mississippi (it was 104 degrees in the shade), he knocked out Jake Kilrain in 75 rounds that took 2 hours 16 minutes and 23 seconds. Then, for three years, he caroused and got fat.

In 1892 James J. Corbett, an opponent he failed to take seriously, knocked him out in 21 rounds and took the title. After the loss, the only one of his career, Sullivan called for silence and told the crowd, "I fought once too often. But I'm glad that it was an American who beat me and that the championship stays in this country. . . . I sincerely hope he won't lead the fast life I did." Corbett said, "I got him when he was slipping."

He never fought seriously after that. He was broke, he made a fortune as a stage actor and then he was broke again. He would stride into a saloon, buy a round for everyone and proclaim, "I can lick any man in the house." His appetite for food matched his capacity for drink, and he ballooned to 300 pounds. Later he quit drinking and lectured on temperance.

He gave this advice to youth: "If the young fellows of this world want to make good, tell 'em to let booze alone, let women alone, too, till you feel like getting married, and work hard on the job you're on, no matter what it is. Don't get the fool notion in your head that you ought to go to college. Keep out of politics and learn to box."

and lacrosse. He excelled in boxing, swimming and shooting, played golf in the 70s and bowled above 200. He was once described as "the fictional Frank Merriwell come to life."

He was five-eighths Sac and Fox Indian, a great-grandson of Chief Black Hawk, who had defeated the Osage and the Cherokee. In 1904 he was chosen to attend Carlisle (Pennsylvania) Indian School, which, though it had only the first 12 grades, soon would become a college football power.

In those days, when he was 15, he stood only 4 feet 10 inches and weighed 115 pounds. He worked in the Carlisle tailor shop and played for its football team. In 1907 and 1908 he was a varsity halfback. Then he left school for two years and played semi-pro baseball. He returned to Carlisle and became an All-America halfback in 1911 and 1912.

He helped Carlisle defeat such football powers as Harvard, Army, Pennsylvania, Penn State, Pittsburgh, Minnesota and Chicago. In the 1912 Army game, when he ran back the second-half kickoff 90 yards for a touchdown only to have a penalty wipe out the play, Army kicked off again and he ran it back 95 yards for a touchdown that counted. Army's sophomore halfback, Dwight D. Eisenhower, later

Thorpe, James Francis
(1888–1953)

In 1950, when the Associated Press asked sportswriters to choose the greatest athlete of the half-century, Jim Thorpe won in a runaway. He received one and a half times as many votes as Babe Ruth, three times as many as Jack Dempsey, six times as many as Ty Cobb, ten times as many as Bobby Jones.

Jim Thorpe was one of the most celebrated and most successful of all football players and track and field athletes. He was a major-league baseball player. In college he wrestled and played basketball

said, "He was the greatest football man I've ever seen."

In the 1912 Olympic Games at Stockholm he won the two most testing events in track and field—the decathlon (ten events) and the pentathlon (five). King Gustav V of Sweden told him, "You, sir, are the greatest athlete in the world." To which Jim Thorpe replied, "Thanks, King."

The next year it was discovered that he had played semi-pro baseball in 1910 for $15 a week, thus making him a professional and ineligible for the Olympics. He had to return his medals, and his records were expunged. "I was just a dumb Indian kid," he said later. "How was I to know playing baseball for money made me a professional in baseball and track?"

He was a National League outfielder from 1913 to 1919 and a football pro from 1915 to 1926 and in 1929. He was the first president of the league that in 1922 became the National Football League, and at $500 a game he was its highest-paid player.

"He didn't play for the money," Jack Cusack, a pro owner, said. "He played for the love of the game." When football was gone, the money was gone, too. He worked as a movie extra, bouncer, carpenter, factory guard and $4-a-day pick-and-shovel man. He drank heavily. As Murray Olderman wrote, "The legend obscures the man. . . . He was in reality a simple man who reveled in the playing of games, and when there were no games to play his useful days as a man were over."

He was happiest on the football field. There, said Joe Guyon, a teammate, "The modesty disappeared and aggressiveness came out." Alexander M. Weyand wrote, "The shock of combat filled him with joy. When the play was rough and the opposition strong, he was in his element." Percy Haughton called him "the theoretical super player in flesh and blood." Ralph Bernstein cited his one flaw when he wrote, "Sports to him were fun, and he refused to take games and events seriously."

Thorpe agreed, saying, "I played for fun." But he also said, "Thrills were mostly hard work for me. That's what I remember most about them. . . . I'd sure like to have those things I won. Haven't got much else any more. . . . I was in a lot of games in a lot of places."

Jim Thorpe, All-America halfback at Carlisle Indian School, in 1911.

Tilden, William Tatum 2d (1893–1953)

Allison Danzig hailed him as "the greatest tennis player the world has seen . . . the most complete player of all time." J. Gilbert Hall called him "the only genius the game has ever known." Big Bill Tilden was the tennis hero of the 1920s, the Golden Era of Sports. Between 1920 and 1930 he won seven United States and three Wimbledon titles and was ranked number one in the world for six straight years. In 1931 he became a touring professional.

He was lean (6 feet 2 inches and 165 pounds) and gaunt, a handsome, dynamic man. He was a clever player, a perfectionist who mastered every stroke. Maurice Brady wrote that his approach was more intellectual than instinctive, but almost every one of his matches involved histrionics, and the crowds loved it.

He came from wealth but lost most of his money financing and acting in plays ranging from Shakespeare to Dracula and writing tennis instruction books, drama and fiction. Vinnie Richards, who toured with him as a pro, remembered that "He was always broke, but there always seemed to be more where the last came from."

A great artist and a great actor, "He combed his dark hair with the air," John Kieran wrote. Will Grimsley wrote, "He was more than a mere striker of the ball. He was a tactician, an artist. The racquet was like a violin in his hands." Paul Metzler called him a flamboyant showman who "dramatized or burlesqued his way through many a match." George Lott, a leading player, wrote, "You either liked this man or you didn't."

At age 58 he played in a pro tournament. Two years later, in 1953, preparing to play in another tournament, he suffered a heart attack in his hotel room, and as Red Smith wrote, "Bill Tilden, who lived among the crowds, died alone."

Years earlier, in discussing tennis, Tilden revealed the strategy that helped make him great. "You cannot volley the serve. In any match between the perfect baseline player and the perfect net rusher, I would take the baseliner every time. . . . I am convinced that any player who wants to can master any stroke in the game. . . . At least 75 percent of the shots considered impossible are actually recoverable if the effort is made for them."

Bill Tilden, the retired tennis star, gives pointers to young enthusiasts at Forest Hills in 1946.

Toomey, William Anthony
(1939–)

Every four years the winner of the Olympic decathlon is widely hailed as the world's greatest athlete. By that standard Bill Toomey, the 1968 Olympic decathlon champion, was the world's greatest athlete. He is also gregarious, dedicated, sensitive, selfless, a Pied Piper who gathered decathletes from all over the world to train with him and benefit from his experience.

Success did not come easily. When he was five years old a piece of ceramic he was playing with shattered, severing nerves in his right hand. As an adult he contracted infectious hepatitis, spent five months in bed and almost died. When he recovered he caught mononucleosis. Later, he cracked both knees in an auto accident.

He competed at 6 feet 1½ inches and 195 pounds, with heavy muscles, heavy legs and horn-rimmed glasses. He won five straight Amateur Athletic Union national titles (1960–64) in the pentathlon (five track and field events in one day) and five straight (1965–69) in the decathlon (ten events in two days). In 1969 he raised the world decathlon record to 8,417 points.

"I didn't compete because I wanted to make a big name for myself," he said. "I did it because I loved

Bill Toomey flashes a victory sign after winning the 1,500-meter run in the 1968 Olympic decathlon.

Toomey, winner of the decathlon at the World University Games at Budapest in 1965.

the sport. People tell me, 'Stop running. If you lose now, you'll ruin your reputation.' Those people don't understand. I didn't do this for materialistic reasons. I ran for fun. I ran to achieve something on my own, something you can't put a price tag on. I wish I could keep on doing it."

He could not, at least in competition. After the Olympics he endorsed products, made television commercials, broadcast sports on television and became a marketing consultant, and the AAU declared him a professional. He said, "The AAU wants the amateur athlete to be so protected from what happens in real life that he becomes unprepared for anything that isn't measured in time or distance."

His friend, Frank Dolson, wrote, "Until he won the gold medal, he was one of the nation's best-kept secrets. . . . Success didn't change him, but it sure changed his life." He became wealthy. He drove a Rolls-Royce with the California license plate "BIL2ME." But he took a low-paying job as track coach at the University of California, Irvine, because, he said, "I started feeling like all I would become was a rich salesman."

Traynor, Harold Joseph
(1899–1972)

The verdict on Pie Traynor was near unanimous. "Unflinchingly, he was the greatest of all third basemen," Bob Broeg wrote. "He set the standard used today as the ultimate in third-base skill," wrote Lee Greene. "If I were to pick the greatest team player in baseball," said John McGraw, "it would have to be Pie Traynor."

At the age of six, Pie Traynor made his baseball debut, catching without a mask. The first pitch hit him in the mouth and he lost two teeth. A few years later he acquired his nickname because he loved pies. As an adult, he was handsome, slender, personable, articulate and always fit. He never drove a car because he feared he would stop walking and become lazy and soft.

He spent his entire major-league career (1920–37) with the Pittsburgh Pirates, playing only 62 games after 1934. In all he batted .320 in 1,961 games. "They always talk about my fielding," he said, "but I was a pretty good hitter."

He was an unbelievable fielder. Les Biederman wrote, "He covered more ground than any third sacker before or since." Charlie Grimm said he had the quickest hands and quickest arms of any third baseman. Telegraphers used to flash, "So and so doubled down the third-base line but was thrown out at first by Traynor." Traynor once said, "The best third baseman I've ever seen is Ken Boyer," but, as Bob Broeg wrote, "Pie, of course, didn't see Traynor."

He managed the Pirates from 1934 to 1939. Frankie Gustine recalled, "When I joined the team near the end of the season, there was no room in the clubhouse. He let me use his locker. Can you imagine a rookie using the manager's locker?"

His highest salaries were $14,000 a year as a player, $16,000 as a manager. After he was fired as manager, he spent most of his remaining 32 years as a Pirate broadcaster and scout. He was happy because, he said, "Baseball was never work for me."

In 1948, he was elected to the Baseball Hall of Fame, the only third baseman voted in by baseball writers rather than a special veterans' committee. Yet, Frank Graham wrote, "It is curious that his fame down through the years has not matched his skills."

Tunney, James Joseph (1898–   )

Gene Tunney was world heavyweight boxing champion, twice defeating Jack Dempsey in title fights. But he never won the hearts of boxing people of his day because they felt he considered himself too good for them. He did not socialize with them, he read classics and he wanted to be known as a boxer, not a prizefighter.

As *Sports Illustrated* said, "No athlete ever went to more pains to establish a public picture of himself but, incongruously, no athlete ever succeeded in obscuring his own great skills so completely."

He was a brilliant scientific boxer with agility, speed, quickness and power. Nat Fleischer called him "a ring scientist." Rex Lardner called him "a synthetic fighter" and wrote, "He studied, analyzed, rehearsed, pondered. He saw his opponent as a case history, a specimen, an anatomical subject."

In 1926, before his first fight with Dempsey, he said, "The heavyweight championship is the target at which I have aimed the shaft of my ambitions for the last five years." The fight, at Philadelphia, drew a crowd of 120,757. The return at Chicago in 1927 drew 104,943 and earned Tunney $990,445. He won both ten-round bouts on points, the second with the help of the famous long count (he was down at least 14 seconds) when Dempsey refused to go to the farthest corner.

A year later he retired, a rich man. He became a successful corporation executive and director. He and Dempsey became good friends and often attended functions together. "Jack and I have a very special kind of bond," he said. Paul Gallico recognized that bond, writing, "They were so necessary to one another to enable them to meet their destinies."

Tyus, Wyomia (1945–   )

Wyomia Tyus is a lithe, graceful runner with an economical style. She runs, said one observer, like a female Jesse Owens. *Sport* magazine said, "She helped lift American women's track and field from sports-page obscurity."

In 1964, in the quarter-finals of the Olympic 100-meter dash, she equaled the world record of 11.2 seconds. She won the final by two yards in 11.4, and Ed Temple, her Olympic and college coach, said, "By 1968 she will be unbeatable." By 1968 she was. She won the gold medal again, setting a world record of 11.0 and becoming the first sprinter, male or female, to win the same title in successive Olympics.

In 1965, two weeks after the 100-meter record had been lowered to 11.1, she tied it. In 1965 and again in 1968, she tied the 100-yard record of 10.3. She won four national titles outdoors and three indoors. In 1973, when pro track began, she immediately became the fastest woman pro.

She started in track as a high jumper and struggled to clear four feet. She tried sprinting and did better. In 1961 Temple saw her at the Georgia high-school championships. He recalled his impression of the

Miss Tyus with her four Olympic medals from the 1964 and 1968 games.

gangly 15-year-old: "At first, she looked like an average girl. Then I started to see things I liked. She was tall, she had lots of fight, and she wouldn't give up even when the race was lost. Determination—that's it. I thought she had a future." He made sure of that future when Tennessee State University, where Temple coached, gave her a full scholarship in 1963.

She stands 5 feet 7 inches and weighs 134 pounds, a quiet Georgia girl who has become tougher than she looks. She became a champion feared by opponents. As one rival, Margaret Johnson Bailes, said, "She bugs me. I get all psyched out when she is competing. Don't ask me why." Since the 1964 Olympics, said Miss Tyus, "Everything has been different. When I go into a meet, they're after me and not the other way around. But it makes me feel good. It makes me try harder, too."

No matter how hard she tried, she could not avoid comparisons with Wilma Rudolph of Tennessee State, who won three gold medals in the 1960 Olympics. She said simply, "Wilma was very good, very smooth. But I don't pay attention to comparisons. I'm not her and I can't be her. I'm just Wyomia."

Wyomia Tyus wipes her face in the rain at Mexico City after capturing a gold medal for her world-record-breaking time in the women's 100 meters.

Unitas, John Constantine
(1933–   )

Sport magazine chose him as the outstanding pro football player of the last quarter-century. The National Football League chose him as the greatest quarterback in professional history.

Sid Luckman called him "the greatest quarterback ever to play the game—better than me, better than Sammy Baugh, better than anyone." Baugh called him "the best there is today at beating a defense."

He was always in command. Murray Olderman wrote, "He has the elusive quality of being the boss when he's on the field." John Mackey, a long-time teammate, said that being in the huddle with him "is like being in the huddle with God."

Dave Anderson wrote, "He kept more than his cool. He kept his ice." Sid Gillman, a rival coach, said, "I don't know what he uses for blood, but I'll guarantee you it isn't warm. It's ice cold."

John Unitas was a self-made football player, and the player he created was one of a kind. In 18 seasons (17 with the Baltimore Colts), he completed 2,830 of 5,186 passes for 40,239 yards (almost 23 miles) and 290 touchdowns, all NFL records. He set another record by passing for touchdowns in 47 consecutive

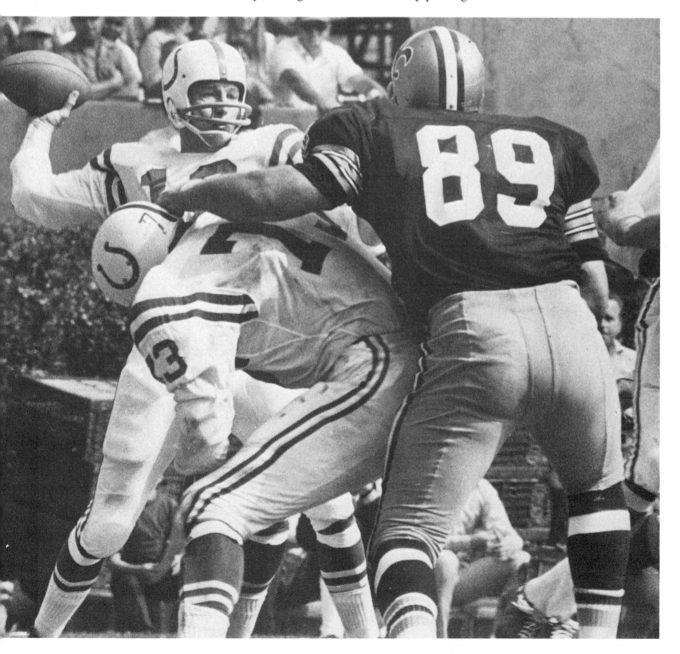

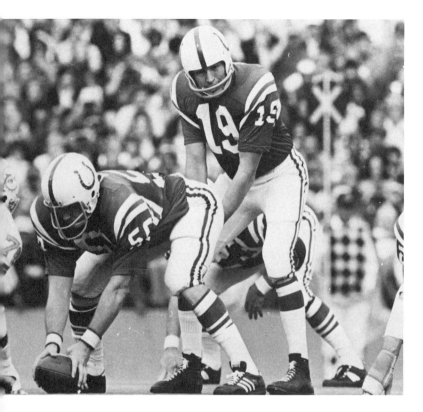

games (the previous record was 22). Three times he was chosen the NFL's most valuable player, and five times he was named all-pro.

The road to success was not smooth. He weighed only 145 pounds in high school, and he was turned down for an athletic scholarship as too light by Notre Dame, Indiana, Maryland and Lehigh. Pittsburgh accepted him, but he failed the entrance examination. He wound up at the University of Louisville, where he grew to 6 feet and 190 pounds.

In 1955 the Pittsburgh Steelers drafted him ninth, never played him and cut him in training camp. "Too dumb," said Coach Walt Kiesling. They gave him $10 for bus fare home. He saved the money by hitchhiking. He got a job as a piledriver and played Saturday nights in Pittsburgh for the semi-pro Bloomfield Rams for $6 a game.

In 1956 the Colts signed him as a free agent for $7,000 a year—if he made the team. He made it, and when George Shaw, the starting quarterback, broke his leg in the fourth game of the season, he got the job and kept it.

He had many things going for him. Vince Lombardi said, "He is uncanny in his abilities; under the most violent pressures, to pick out the soft spot in the defense." Frank Camp, his college coach, said, "He had the quickest reactions I've ever seen." Bill

McPeak, an enemy coach, said, "He is more willing to sacrifice himself for the sake of the contest than any quarterback I know."

His poise was celebrated. The 1958 NFL championship game between the Colts and New York Giants went into sudden-death overtime, and the Colts had the ball on the Giants' eight-yard line and needed only a field goal to win. Instead of playing it safe, he completed a pass to the one-yard line, and Alan Ameche crashed over on the next play for the winning touchdown. Why did he risk a pass interception? "When you know what you're doing," he said, "you don't get intercepted."

In 1973, when the Colts' new management started a youth movement, he asked to be traded. He and his high-topped black football shoes went to the San Diego Chargers, and he signed a two-year contract for $250,000 a year. He played five games that season, but in 1974, after five days at training camp, his legs were swollen and his knees popped, and he retired at age 41.

"You hate to quit playing football," he said. "I'd like to play another 30 years. Your mind is willing, but your body wears out."

In one sense he was relieved. "The game is a lot different than it was five or six years ago," he said. "It gets to where you don't know which end is up, what the hell their thinking is. The guys just don't have the dedication I would like them to have. You can't get them to do the things they should be doing. They don't seem to care whether they play football or not as long as they make the team and get their checks."

Van Buren, Stephen (1918–)

Earle (Greasy) Neale, his pro coach, said of Steve Van Buren, "He is the best halfback in modern times. Red Grange had the same ability to sidestep, but he never had Van Buren's power to go with it."

Steve Van Buren stood 6 feet 1 inch and weighed 208 pounds. He was a swarthy man with broad chest and shoulders, a bruising, crunching workhorse who ran with his head down, almost daring the opposition to stop him.

"Although he could finesse a tackler," Harold Rosenthal wrote, "more often than not he would drop him with a lowered shoulder or a forearm shiver." Lee Greene wrote, "He took an unholy pleasure in matching his flying bulk against any tackler." Allie Sherman, a pro teammate and later a coach, called him "the Jimmy Brown of his time. People didn't appreciate what he did." What he did, Murray Olderman wrote, "was usher in the era of the speedy big back who could take advantage of the quick-hitting T formation."

He was born in Honduras of American parents, and he lived there until he was orphaned at the age of ten. He had never heard of football, but he learned quickly and played in high school in New Orleans. At Louisiana State he was blocking back for two years (the star runner was Alvin Dark) and a running back for the last two.

He played for the Philadelphia Eagles from 1944 to 1951. He led the NFL in rushing in four of his eight years, and when he quit he held NFL rushing records for one game, career and playoffs. In 1965 he was elected to the Pro Football Hall of Fame.

He started with the Eagles at $4,000 a year and finished at $15,000. He never thought he was good enough to play pro football, and after his rookie season he had to be talked out of quitting. He was shy and modest. The Eagles once distributed a questionnaire to their players to get publicity ideas. To the question "What do you consider your outstanding football accomplishment?" Van Buren answered, "None."

He disdained the forward pass, saying, "The fellow who threw the first pass must have been all through as a football player, or just too tired that day to run with the ball. . . . I set a record every year I wasn't hurt." He made little money from pro football, saying, "Money meant nothing to me. I was stupid, that's why."

Andy Varipapa with one of the trick bowling shots for which he is famous.

entertain his audiences. Bill Fay, the writer, called him "The Talking Machine." But Lorraine Varipapa replied that "There's about as much ham in Pop as there is in a ten-cent drugstore sandwich." Varipapa himself said he acted because most fans expected it. "They think it's colorful. So I brag, put body english on the ball and jump in the air when I make a big strike. But believe me when I say I'd like to cut it out."

He stood 5 feet 6 inches and weighed 180 pounds, most of which seemed to be in his chest and shoulders. He came to America from Italy when he was ten and worked as a machinist, professional fighter and semi-pro baseball player before turning full time to bowling at age 33. He made movie shorts, taught bowling and gave trick-shot exhibitions, which left time for only three or four tournaments a year.

He became a champion at a time when bowling was becoming big time, and he helped make it so. As Stanley Frank wrote, "He deserves some credit for taking bowling out of the converted stables and rat-trap storefronts in which he found it and putting it into the elaborate recreation centers that have mushroomed all over the country."

After his all-star triumphs, he said, "They say I ought to retire undefeated. What does that mean? That you can't be beaten? No. It means that you quit before somebody beat you. Varipapa will keep on bowling."

Varipapa, Andrew (1894–   )

Andy Varipapa is a geriatric marvel. In 1947, at age 53, he won bowling's national all-star match-game championship. In 1948 he became the first to win the title in consecutive years.

That was enough to distinguish him. But championship bowling was only half, perhaps the lesser half, of his achievements. He was better known as the game's most celebrated trick-shot bowler, a distinction that annoyed the serious bowler in him but paid the bills. He was constantly giving exhibitions, rolling strikes blindfolded, with his back to the pins, right-handed, left-handed and two-handed. His ultimate feat involved three lanes and 14 pins, all of which fell victim to a single roll of one ball.

During his performances he kept up chatter to

Wagner, John Peter (1874–1955)

Physically, Honus Wagner was a sight. A Pittsburgh writer once wrote, "His legs were so bowed you could roll a barrel through them—but not a baseball. His hands hung like bunches of bananas at the ends of tremendously long arms." Another wrote that his legs "took off at the ankles in a curving sweep to meet in surprise at his waistline." Johnny Evers said his big hands were "like shovels."

Without dispute, he was the greatest shortstop ever, and according to John McGraw, Branch Rickey, Ed Barrow and Fred Clarke, he was the greatest player ever. Arthur Daley wrote, "He could play any position better than anyone else."

He was called Honus and Hans, contractions of the German "Johannes." He had a barrel chest, durability, great fielding range, surprising speed and surprising grace. He played in the National League for Louisville (1897–99) and the Pittsburgh Pirates (1900–17). In 2,787 games in 21 seasons, he batted .327 and led the league eight times in batting, seven in doubles, six in slugging and five in runs batted in, total bases and stolen bases. He batted .300 or higher in each of his first 17 seasons.

For all that, his highest salary was $10,000 a year. In 1936 he was one of the five men voted into the

In his 70s, Honus Wagner, Pittsburgh Pirate scout and coach, looks out of the dugout at Forbes Field.

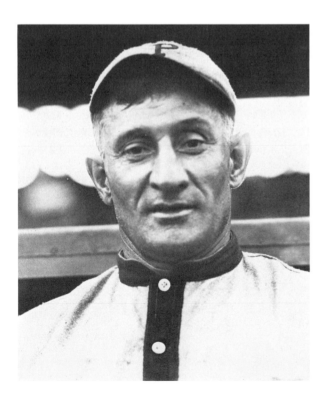

Baseball Hall of Fame in its first election. Months before his death he watched with tears as an 18-foot, 40-ton statue of him was unveiled in Pittsburgh.

When he left the Pirates he played semi-pro baseball for years, hitting a home run when he was 52. He was a Pirate coach from 1933 to 1951. Paul Waner recalled, "He was in his 60s, and goldarned if the old guy didn't get out there at shortstop every once in a while during fielding practice. A hush would come over the whole ball park, and every player on both teams would just stand there, like a bunch of little kids, and watch every move he made."

Jack Sher wrote of the elder Wagner, "In uniform, or near things related to baseball, he gives forth an aura of shining light, a special, ageless glory. He becomes the living symbol of the game, indestructible and forever young."

Walton, William Woodrow
(1950–   )

He was the most-talked-about player of his day in college basketball, and then he was the most-talked-about newcomer in professional basketball. Part of the reason for this fame is his extraordinary ability. Part of the reason is his personality and life style.

Bill Walton was a star from the beginning. In high school he was twice All-American. At UCLA, de-

spite knees plagued by tendonitis, he was three times an All-American and twice player of the year, and twice he led his team to NCAA titles.

He is a 6-foot-11-inch, 225-pound center with flaming red hair and, once he left college, a red beard. Like many of his generation, he was dissatisfied with the society created by his elders. He was an outspoken critic of the Vietnam war, and he was arrested during a student anti-war demonstration on the UCLA campus. When Richard M. Nixon was President, he circulated impeachment petitions, and he often answered his telephone by saying, "Impeach the President."

Later, he called the Federal Bureau of Investigation "the enemy" and urged "the world to join us in rejecting the Government of the United States." He said, "It is not the American people or the Constitution of the country that I think should be rejected. . . . This Government has done nothing to warrant the cooperation of the people it is supposed to represent. . . . My friends and I . . . think we have a responsibility to fight back. Not with guns, but with love, truth, compassion and education."

He refuses to eat meat, prompting Pete Axthelm to write, "While others savor the first-class travel and high-priced steaks that are part of the modern sports whirl, he moved at his own pace, tuning in to a very private drummer and nibbling at the dried fruits that he carries in a wrinkled brown paper bag."

He tries to keep his private life private, saying, "I think everyone . . . has a social responsibility in the way they live. . . . I'm trying to live a life that involves minimal consumption of material goods."

When he turned pro he signed for enough money to buy all the material goods anyone might want. The Portland Trail Blazers made him the first choice in the National Basketball Association's 1974 draft and signed him, even though the rival American Basketball Association was ready to move its San Diego franchise to Los Angeles if he would join it. Portland gave him between $2 and $2.5 million for five years, but his rookie season (1974–75) was filled with problems. A painful bone spur above the ankle kept him out of many games. He did not like Portland's rain and cold. As Charles Garry, his lawyer, said, "He's not happy unless he sees the sun. His energy comes from the sun."

Portland star Bill Walton shoots against the New York Knicks in 1974.

Waner, Paul Glee (1903–1965)

As Fred Lieb wrote, ''Paul Waner proved that a comparatively small man, by mastering timing and leverage, could outhit stronger and bigger athletes.'' He proved it so well that he was elected to the Baseball Hall of Fame in 1952.

He played for the Pittsburgh Pirates from 1926 to 1940 and for the wartime teams of the Boston Braves, Brooklyn Dodgers and New York Yankees. Waner was 42 and in his last season when Ted McGrew said, ''As long as he is able to drag himself and bat up to the plate, he'll be able to hit that ball.''

He was a line-drive hitter who made 3,152 hits in 2,549 major-league games, with a lifetime batting average of .333. He batted .309 or higher in each of his first 12 seasons, and in eight seasons he made 200 or more hits. He won three National League batting titles with averages of .380, .362 and .373.

For 14 seasons he played right field for the Pirates while his younger brother, Lloyd, played center field. He was Big Poison and Lloyd was Little Poison, but they were almost the same size—5 feet 9 inches and 150 pounds. He had been a pitcher until he threw his arm out in 1923. Then he became an outfielder, and Manager John McGraw of the New York Giants sent a scout to see him. The scout reported, ''That little punk don't know how to put on a uniform,'' but when McGraw looked for himself, he fired the scout and told him, ''I'm glad you did not scout Christy Mathewson.''

Waner liked late hours, good company and good liquor. Frank Graham wrote, ''He was a quiet little man on the field and a quiet little man off it, too, but he knew all the best places in all the towns, and if he didn't find joy in each, nobody ever did.'' Harold Parrott wrote, ''No other man in the history of the game has courted the highball and the pitched ball with such prolonged success.'' ''To him,'' wrote Nick Seitz, ''every night was Saturday night.'' Bob Broeg wrote that ''Drunk or sober, he could hit the finest pitcher of his day.''

Brother Lloyd said, ''He was absolutely the best hitter I ever looked at.'' Wilbert Robinson said, ''He's got eyes like a cat.'' Though Paul Waner seemed to enjoy it all, he said, ''There's a lot of happiness and a lot of sadness in playing baseball.''

Warmerdam, Cornelius Anthony
(1915–   )

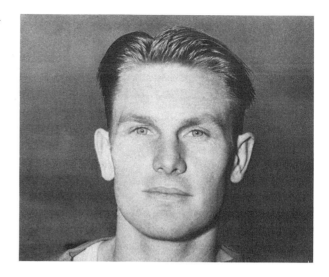

"In the entire history of track and field," wrote Cordner Nelson, "no athlete's superiority has been so unquestioned as Cornelius Warmerdam's." *Sport* magazine said, "He had atrocious form and lacked the compulsion to win. But he could jump." Arthur Mann called him "one of those super athletes who come along every so often and embarrass the complacent dictators of athletic techniques."

Cornelius (Dutch) Warmerdam, the son of Dutch-born parents, was the best pole vaulter ever. In 1940 he became the first to clear 15 feet, a height he achieved 43 times before his retirement in 1944. No one else made 15 feet until 1951, and no one did 16 feet until 1962, when springy fiberglass poles had replaced bamboo and aluminum.

He used an old bamboo pole patched up with tape. "It was a real wreck of a pole," Bob Mathias said. "I know, because I grew up right near his home town and saw him jumping when I was a kid." With that pole and a similar successor, he set world records of 15-0 and 15-1⅛ in 1940, 15-2⅝, 15-4¼ and 15-5¾ in 1941 and 15-6, 15-6⅞ and 15-7¾ in 1942. His world indoor record of 15-8½, set in 1943, lasted 16 years, his last outdoor record 15 years.

Bob Richards, the next generation's best vaulter, said, "He was part sprinter, part shock absorber, part acrobat and part strongman." Boo Morcom said, "I don't believe he was human." A quarter-century later, Brutus Hamilton said, "He would have been eight inches ahead of the field today, just as he was in his day."

He was modest, unassuming and thoughtful. His father was a farmer, and the youngster was discovered at the age of 18 vaulting 13 feet in his father's spinach patch. Despite his success, vaulting was a small part of his life, and he seldom practiced. Al Stump wrote, "He was a student of improved vaulting, rather than a disciple of victory."

He spent more than 25 years as assistant track coach and then head coach at Fresno State, his alma mater. He was not jealous of fiberglass vaulters because, he said, "It's always the man more than the equipment." The secret of vaulting in his day? "It's practically all speed," he said. Is there a limit to how high man can vault? "Probably," he said, "but I don't know what it is."

Warmerdam, the first man to pole vault 15 feet, shakes his fist at the 15-4 mark he failed to make at the 1943 Millrose Games. At the time he held the indoor record of 15-7¼.

Warner, Glenn Scobey (1871–1954)

For 44 years Pop Warner was a college football head coach and, in the words of Amos Alonzo Stagg, "one of the excellent creators." He invented the single wing and double wing, the reverse, naked reverse, crouching start, rolling block, clipping blocks, unbalanced line, screen pass, fiber padding, spiral punt, numbering of plays, mousetrap play, hidden-ball play and series plays.

He was a big man with a square jaw and a mane of hair. He was nicknamed Pop when he was a 21-year-old freshman at Cornell. He earned a law degree there in 1895. Then he was head coach at Georgia (1895–96), Cornell (1897–98), Carlisle Indians (1899–1903), Cornell (1904–06), Carlisle (1907–14), Pittsburgh (1915–23), Stanford (1924–32) and Temple (1933–38). His teams won 313 games, one fewer than Stagg's all-time record. He produced 47 All-America players, including Jim Thorpe and Ernie Nevers.

"He was not a dominant, forceful leader of men, as was Rockne, though he could win their affection and loyalty as could few others," Allison Danzig wrote. "His was the more contemplative and deliberate mind." Don Liebendorfer described him as "a strangely contradictory character whose gruff, sometimes almost surly and sullen, exterior concealed a big and very warm heart."

Red Smith called him "a gruff old gent, kind and forthright and obstinate and honest. He was one of the truly original minds in football coaching." Joe Williams wrote, "He was the best missionary college football ever had."

His philosophy guided a generation of coaches. He said, "I don't believe anyone can play two kinds of football—dirty and good—at the same time. I want my boys to play good football. . . . There is no system of play that substitutes for knocking an opponent down. When you hit, hit hard. . . . You play the way you practice. Practice the right way and you will react the right way in a game."

Glenn (Pop) Warner (left) and Jim Thorpe at the Los Angeles Memorial Coliseum in 1931.

Weber, Richard Anthony (1929–   )

Dick Weber has earned more prize money—close to a half-million dollars—than any other bowler in history. He has been an All-American ten times, and he has rolled 17 perfect games. Between 1961 and 1966 he won four All-Star titles and was three times named bowler of the year.

He hardly looked the part. In his prime he stood 5 feet 10 inches, weighed only 125 pounds and did not have great stamina. "He is forever fearful that his success may evaporate before he has fully savored it," Frank Graham, Jr., wrote. "Fatigue, a minor injury, a spell under unusual conditions, may rob him of his magic touch."

In high school he preferred baseball and basketball to bowling. In his sophomore year he was denied a baseball letter because he had accepted bowling prize money. As he explained, "I had been in a bowling league where you paid $1.55 to play three games. The games cost 30 cents each, and the league put 65 cents into the fund. At the end of the season I did get $20 in prize money. However, I had paid $40 into the kitty."

The incident was fortuitous. He concentrated on bowling and became probably the best bowler in Indiana, earning a living meanwhile as a $3,700-a-year postal clerk. At the invitation of Don Carter he quit the job to join the famous St. Louis Budweiser team in 1955. Pat Patterson, a teammate, recalled that he owned one suit, "with a wide pinstripe." He became a charter member of the Professional Bowlers Association and played in 1959 on the first tour, which consisted of three tournaments. He has won almost every year since.

Why has he been so successful? "He's got the best armswing in bowling," a fellow pro said. "It's like his arm wasn't really part of his shoulder at all, but something that was just bolted to it temporarily for the purpose of moving like a pendulum and delivering a bowling ball."

"Bowling is in the touch, the feel," Weber said. "The most important thing is concentration. After you have mastered the shots . . . you've got to learn to ignore everything but the lanes in front of you."

In the 1970s he was still one of the outstanding bowlers on the tour. "I still love to compete on the tour and I still love to win titles."

Dick Weber, one of the most successful pro bowlers in history, surrounded by his many awards.

"I was better than Mark Spitz is," he said. "I never lost a race. Never. Not even in the YMCA. The closest I ever came to losing was on the last lap of the Olympic 400 in 1924 when I got a snootful. But I knew enough not to cough. If you don't cough, you can swallow it."

Actually, he lost a few races early in his career, but losing does not fit with his image. "I'm supposed to be an idol to the kids," he said. "I'm supposed to be clean cut and set an example for them, if maybe their old man isn't so hot." Jerry Kirshenbaum wrote, "The truth is that he is probably too ingenuous to be a legend, or at least the kind of legend he talks about." He admits as much, calling himself "the original swinger."

"Sure, I've had my problems," he said. "Some bad investments. Four marriages that didn't last. Some battles with booze. But I'm a pretty tough guy to sink. I lived an exciting life and I've been an awfully lucky fellow. I just don't think I'd have been happy without the Hollywood part. I can't picture myself as a retired swimsuit company executive with a little place in the country and 18 grandchildren running around."

He remains an idol, especially since all the old Tarzan movies are shown on television. "All the kids know me," he said. "They grow up watching me every Saturday morning."

Weissmuller, Peter John
(1904–   )

He was the most celebrated swimmer of all time and, according to 250 sportswriters in an Associated Press poll, the greatest of the first half-century. He became more famous as Tarzan (making 19 movies in 17 years) and then as Jungle Jim (ten years on television).

Johnny Weissmuller is an imposing man—6 feet 3 inches, 195 pounds in his prime, with huge shoulders, long hair dyed brown and a high-pitched voice. He won three gold medals in the 1924 Olympics, two in 1928. In ten years of amateur swimming he won 52 national championships and broke 67 world records at free-style and occasionally at backstroke distances from 50 to 880 yards. His 100-yard free-style record of 51.0 seconds stood for 17 years, and he set it when there were no starting blocks, flip turns or lane ropes.

"Of all the sports stars of our time," wrote Frank Deford, "he is the most appealing. In his victories, which come often, he is reliable and accessible and humble. In his defeats, which are not many, he is never tragic, only vulnerable. . . . Personally, he is attractive, friendly, unassuming, gentle, loyal, popular and so forth and so on."

From 1957 to 1960 Jerry West led West Virginia University to three Southern Conference titles, made the All-America team twice and averaged 24.8 points per game. From 1960 to 1974, in 932 regular-season games for the Los Angeles Lakers, he scored 25,192 points and averaged 27.3 per game (the third highest total in history). He made the all-star team 12 consecutive times in 14 seasons and eventually earned $300,000 a year.

Late in his career he said, "I've been around so long. . . . It seems like basketball first, then family. . . . Everybody always says it's a kid's game, but, you see, it's a kid's whole life, too." He played it that way. His nose was broken nine times and his hands twice. He retired because of constant pain from weary knees and abdominal muscles. "There is no pressure now," he said. "There was a tremendous amount of pressure on me to play well all the time, and I don't miss that at all."

That pressure almost destroyed him. Fred Schaus, his college and pro coach, called him "a very complicated, wound-up spring, a bundle of nerves. He is so high strung that in all the time I have known him, I have never once seen him fully relaxed." Yet his ability in clutch situations was his greatest asset. "I know that I play well under pressure," he said. "I don't know why. Maybe the challenge stimulates me. . . . I want the ball. I know I can do something with it because I've done it before . . . and I'm proud of it."

West, Jerome Alan (1938–)

He was one of basketball's most skilled and exciting players, so smooth that he made everything look easy. He had a memorable jump shot, he could drive to the basket and he could play tight defense. He was a 6-foot-3-inch guard with 38-inch arms and an appreciative public.

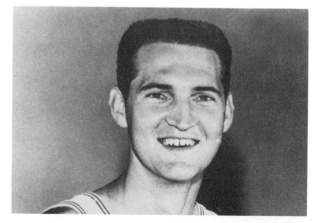

White, Byron Raymond
(1917–   )

As Whizzer White, he was a fabled football player in college and the pros. As Byron R. White, he is an Associate Justice of the United States Supreme Court. "Never before," wrote Alfred Wright, "has an American athlete of such fame risen to so distinguished a position in later life."

At tiny Wellington (Colorado) High School, all his grades were A or A+, and as valedictorian in his class of five, like all other valedictorians in the state, he received an academic scholarship to the University of Colorado. There he grew to 6 feet 2 inches and 190 pounds, with a square jaw and a scholarly, dignified look.

There, too, he was known for his character. Gene Moore, a football teammate, said, "Some guys—most of us—have a human instinct for taking that little edge if we can. He was always scrupulously honest. He played by the book and he never took the edge."

In college he received a B in Sociology, a B in Public Speaking and A's in everything else. He was student-body president, a member of Phi Beta Kappa and first in a class of 267. He won ten letters—four in basketball, three in football and three in baseball. In football he was an All-America triple-threat tail-

Byron R. White, in 1962, immediately before being sworn in as an Associate Justice of the U.S. Supreme Court.

Byron (Whizzer) White, All-American from the University of Colorado, in 1938.

back, leading the nation in rushing and scoring and averaging 31 yards returning punts.

He won a Rhodes Scholarship to study at Oxford University, but when he was allowed to delay his arrival there by four months he signed with the Pittsburgh Pirates (later known as the Steelers) for $15,000 a year, the largest salary in the National Football League since Red Grange's retirement. He led the league in rushing in 1938 as a rookie, sat out 1939 to study at Oxford and played in 1940 (when he again led in rushing) and 1941 with the Detroit Lions while attending Yale Law School.

Then came wartime service in Naval Intelligence, his last year at law school (he graduated *magna cum laude* and first in his class), a year as law clerk to Chief Justice Fred M. Vinson and finally private law practice. In 1960 he headed the National Citizens Committee for Kennedy, and when John F. Kennedy was elected President of the United States he named White Deputy Attorney General. In 1962 the President appointed him to the Supreme Court.

White believed in the values of football. "Few have suffered from it," he said. "Many have gained immeasurably." Of sports in general, he said, "The fundamental reason for playing competitive sports is to get some experience. The experienced people are better than the inexperienced. . . . When the whistle blows, you have only a limited amount of time to do what you have to do. You either do it then or you don't do it at all."

Kathy Whitworth recoils as she misses a putt during a 1969 pro-amateur tournament in Miami.

Whitworth, Kathrynne Ann
(1939–   )

Kathy Whitworth has won more pro tournaments (over 70) and more money (more than half a million dollars) than any other woman golfer in history. She led women golfers eight years in earnings and seven in scoring average, and six times she was named player of the year.

She is a willowy 5 feet 9 inches and 140 pounds, but she was not always so. In high school, where she played bass drum in the marching band, she was 5-7 and 215 pounds. She lost 40 pounds in five months, showing the determination and concentration that would mark her golf career.

She took up golf at the age of 15, won the New Mexico amateur championship at 18 and turned pro when she was 19. But professional stardom came slowly, and she was miserable. "I didn't think winning would be any problem," she recalled. "But it was terrible. I wanted to quit, but my mother and father always talked me out of it." After six months she finished 16th in a tournament and won her first prize money—$33.

When success came it came all at once. She won eight tournaments in 1963, nine in 1965, ten in 1966, eight in 1967, 11 in 1968 and eight in 1969. The only gap came in 1964, when she won only once. "I got a big head and thought they were going to hand me championships on a silver platter," she said.

She was the best and most consistent player in women's golf during the 1960s. One reason for her success was putting. Curry Kirkpatrick wrote that her putting was "the object of constant amazement among her fellow players." Sandra Haynie, one of those players, said, "When she has to have a putt, she gets it every time." Citing other attributes, Carol Mann, a rival, said, "She's not vulnerable emotionally. . . . She has great inner strength. She is probably a better competitor because she has to be. She is the best under pressure of anybody who ever played this tour."

Being so good created a pressure all its own. "When you're number one you're never allowed to have a bad round, and you're supposed to win all the time," she said. "I love to win. That's why I'm on the tour. But winning isn't something I can't live without. When I lose, it doesn't break my heart. . . . But I do want to play well all the time."

Wilkinson, Charles Burnham
(1916–   )

Bud Wilkinson's fame stems almost as much from his charm as from his unparalleled record as a football coach.

At 6 feet 2 inches and 190 pounds, he has a shy smile, a handsome, youthful face and a smooth and bright manner. He often speaks in platitudes and he never raises his voice. William Barry Furlong wrote of his "almost maddeningly flawless personality." Sam Lyle, an assistant, said, "He's the guy you wish you had for a father." Jim Weatherall, one of his best players, said, "What finer privilege could any kid want than to play under Bud Wilkinson?" Tim Cohane wrote that he was the kind of man who, "if he had set out to, might have become President."

At the University of Minnesota, where he was a non-scholarship student, he played guard (1934–35) and blocking back (1936) and was also golf captain and hockey goalie. Then he spent seven years as a college assistant coach and two years as a Naval officer at sea.

Bud Wilkinson, University of Oklahoma football coach, in 1959.

He was head coach and athletic director at the University of Oklahoma from 1947 to 1963. In 17 seasons his teams won 139 games, lost 27 and tied four, with separate winning streaks of 31 and 47 games. Three teams were national champions and four were unbeaten. His players included Darrell Royal, Eddie Crowder, Jim Owens, Wade Walker, Jack Mitchell and Dee Andros, all of whom became successful college coaches.

He quit coaching to enter politics and ran unsuccessfully for the U. S. Senate in 1964. He became a television broadcaster and chairman of the President's Council on Physical Fitness. Dave Condon called him "the most popular figure in Oklahoma since Will Rogers."

He believed that "Perfection is not attained at that point at which nothing else can be added, but at that point at which nothing else can be taken away. . . . When mental toughness has been rewarded by victory enough times, it adds up to the winning attitude or tradition, which is more important than personnel and coaching. . . . Football success is desire and speed and intelligence—and desire is 85 percent of it."

Charles Wilkinson, University of Minnesota guard, in 1935.

Willard, Jess (1881–1968)

Jess Willard was a giant of a man (6 feet 6 inches and 245 pounds) who became heavyweight champion of the world. Rex Lardner wrote, "He had plenty of courage in the ring and great durability." But, wrote Lester Bromberg, "He had no appetite for fighting." And as Nat Fleischer wrote, "Fight fans were quick to sense that the tiger instinct was altogether lacking in his make-up, and they resented a champion who was merely a good-natured boxer. . . . No man living ever possessed less of the knight-errant spirit."

He was a cowpuncher who turned to boxing at the age of 29. He had mild success, then took almost a year off and put on so much weight (he reached 320 pounds) that he waddled when he walked. He trimmed down to 263 for his 1915 fight in Havana with Jack Johnson, when he won the title on a 26th-round knockout tainted by rumors of a fix.

In 1919 he defended in Toledo against Jack Dempsey for a $100,000 guarantee. In the first round, Dempsey floored him seven times, broke his jaw and four of his teeth, closed one eye and bloodied his nose. The fight ended after three rounds. By then, wrote Damon Runyon, "The right side of Willard's face was a pulp."

Jack (Doc) Kearns was Dempsey's manager, and in his memoirs, published 45 years later, he said he had loaded Dempsey's gloves with plaster of paris from a can labeled "talcum powder." He said Dempsey never knew about it. Kearns stood to win $100,000 (he had put up $10,000) if Dempsey scored a first-round knockout and, he wrote, "I was a product of those days . . . when it was every man for himself." Dempsey called Kearns's story "ridiculous."

Willard once wrote to a friend, "God made me a giant. I never received an education, never had any money. I knew that I was a big fellow and powerfully strong. I just sat down and figured that a man as big as me ought to be able to cash in on his size, and that was what started me on the road to boxing. . . . I never liked it. In fact, I hated it as I never hated a thing previously, but there was money in it. . . . I never really knew how to fight."

Jess Willard takes the heavyweight title from Jack Johnson in the 26th round of their 1915 fight in Havana.

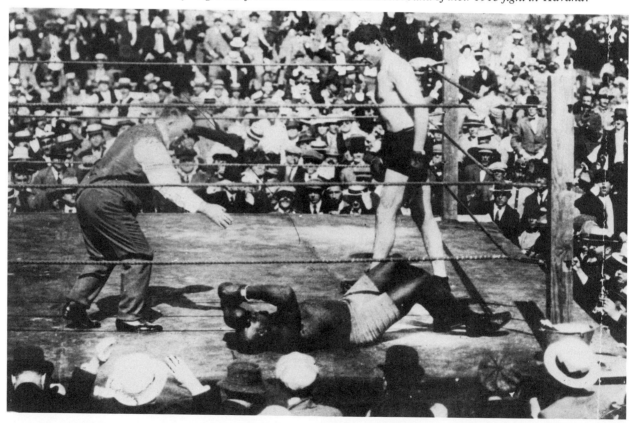

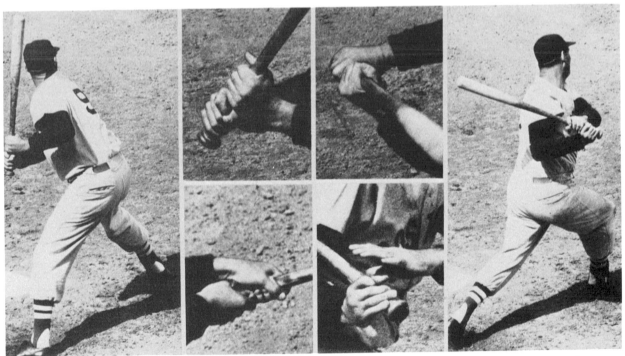

Ted Williams, baseball's last .400 hitter, with the grip that produced many American League batting titles. From upper left to lower right: his firm hold, level-off, follow-through, release.

Williams, Theodore Samuel (1918–   )

Ted Williams once said, "All I want out of life is to walk down the street and have people point at me and say, 'There goes the greatest hitter who ever lived.'" He was not disappointed.

Many pointed out other things about him. They considered him disagreeable, boorish, ungrateful. Jimmy Foxx once called him "a spoiled boy." Dave Sendler called him "a larger-than-life personality, a proud, abrasive man." Ed Linn wrote, "He was sometimes unbearable, but he was never dull."

There was another side of him. He helped raise millions of dollars for the Children's Cancer Hospital in Boston. He refused to endorse liquor and cigarettes because he wanted to be a good influence on youngsters. Arthur Daley wrote, "There's no more charming man in the world when he wants to be." Joe Reichler wrote, "He was a thoroughly honest soul who spoke his mind. . . . You always knew where you stood with him."

Ted Williams played outfield for the Boston Red Sox for all or part of 19 seasons between 1939 and 1960. He missed three years (1943–45) during World War II and most of the 1952 and 1953 seasons because of combat duty as a Marine Corps pilot. His first contract with the Red Sox called for $4,500 a year. His last called for $100,000.

In 2,292 games he posted a lifetime batting average of .344, the sixth highest ever and by far the best in the last generation. In only one season, at age 40, did he slip under .300. He ranks second to Babe Ruth in lifetime slugging (.634) and bases on balls (2,018). He hit 521 home runs. He led the American League nine times in slugging, eight in bases on balls, six in batting average and runs, four in home runs and runs batted in.

In 1941 he entered the final day of the season batting .39955. Rounded out, that would have been .400, a level last achieved by Bill Terry in 1930. Manager Joe Cronin said Williams could stay on the bench and preserve his .400 average. He declined, played the double-header against the Philadelphia Athletics, made six hits in eight at bats and finished with .406. No one has approached .400 since.

He was a left-handed pull hitter with a picture swing. "He used to swing so smoothly and surely," James S. Kunen wrote, "that it sometimes seemed as though he and the ball and the pitcher were all one part of a natural event, like the springing of a pine

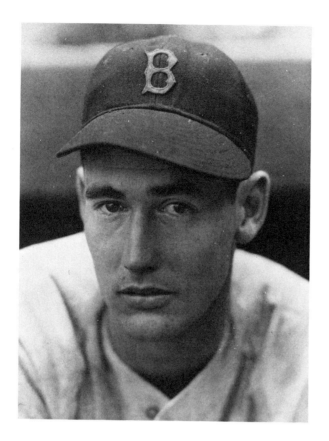

The Boston Red Sox slugger in 1941.

In 1960, before his final game, he was honored in ceremonies and almost tipped his hat. Later that day, in his last major-league at bat, he hit a home run and again refused to tip his hat. He said, "I vowed I'd never do it again when I realized that a lot of those guys cheering on a home run or a good catch were the same ones who led the boos at other times."

He was still a fine hitter when he retired at 42. Al Kaline said, "If they had the designated-hitter rule in his day, he could have kept hitting until he was 50." Carlton Fisk recalled when the 52-year-old Williams was a special batting coach. Fisk said, "He took batting practice and called hits. 'Here goes one off the 380-foot mark,' he'd say, and I swear he hit the 0 on one bounce."

In 1966 Williams was voted into the Baseball Hall of Fame the first year he was eligible. He managed the Washington Senators (who became the Texas Rangers) from 1969 to 1972.

In his autobiography, Ted Williams wrote, "I was and am too complex a personality, too much confusion of boyish enthusiasm and bitter experience to be completely understood by everybody." After he retired as a player, he said, "I don't think I'd do a single thing differently if I were starting out again."

bough when the sun has melted enough snow." Roger Kahn wrote, "Williams at bat is a human calculating machine. He measures each pitch, and if it is a quarter of an inch off the corner, he will not swing." He could measure the quarter-inch, too. Navy physicians said he had the eyes of one in 100,000.

When he batted, other teams often put three infielders on the right side of the infield, all but inviting Williams to hit to left field. He defied the so-called Williams shift and hit to right, though he once said, "Ty Cobb told me he would have batted about .900 if they ever had used that shift on him."

Crowds loved him and hated him. In 1957 he spit toward the fans and press box in Boston and was fined $5,000. He did the same in Kansas City and was fined again. Once, when a fan sitting behind third base heckled him during batting practice, he lined six straight fouls at the man. Sometimes he failed to run out grounders, and sometimes he took imaginary batting swings in the outfield, but he resented criticism.

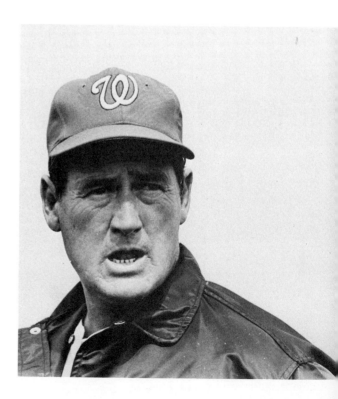

Manager of the Washington Senators in 1969.

Wills, Helen (1905–   )

In 1923, at age 17, Helen Wills won the first of her seven United States tennis titles. In 1938, at age 32, she won the last of her eight Wimbledon titles. In that 15-year span she became one of the world's most celebrated athletes and enigmas.

She was a trim woman, good-looking and well dressed. She was so impassive that one writer called her "the Calvin Coolidge of tennis." She was universally known as Little Miss Poker Face. Years later she said of that nickname, "I always thought it very clever, although I didn't think it applied and paid no attention to it."

She played a clean, smooth game with booming ground strokes. Elizabeth Ryan, a rival player, wrote, "She was all muscle, brute strength. She'd blow you off the court with her power." Helen Hull Jacobs, a frequent opponent, said of her style, "She fought on the court much as Gene Tunney fought in the ring—with implacable concentration and undeniable skill, but without the color or imagination of a Jack Dempsey or Suzanne Lenglen."

"There is a tense concentration in her every move, something that suggests the killer type of fighter," W. O. McGeehan wrote. "Somehow, she does not seem to be enjoying the game itself." But Paul Gallico wrote, "She loved to play tennis. . . . The cold, superior, emotionless sphinx evidently was her idea of how a famous lady athlete should comport herself." John M. Ross said, "Single-handedly, she led women's sports out of the forest of obscurity and contributed handsomely to the emancipation of American womanhood in general."

She was Phi Beta Kappa at the University of California. She found time away from tennis to write four mystery books and to paint in oil. She was divorced from Frederick Moody before her marriage to Aidan Roark, a polo player and writer. Ironically, her best-remembered matches were defeats by Miss Lenglen in 1926 and Miss Jacobs in 1933, when an injured back led her to default.

After the Lenglen match she said, "There will be other tennis matches. There are other years coming." After her loss to Miss Jacobs she said, "Animals and often humans prefer to suffer in a quiet, dark place." Of criticism she said, "Whatever is written is written." Of her career she said, "I'm awfully glad I played tennis."

346

Wooden, John Robert
(1910–   )

He is the only man in the Basketball Hall of Fame as both player and coach. The Helms Hall of Fame also named him to its all-time All-America. The teams he coached at the University of California, Los Angeles, became so successful that they made news not when they won national championships but when they failed to win them.

John Wooden is 5 feet 10 inches tall, a quiet, calm, scholarly man and church deacon who does not drink, smoke or swear. He looks like a high-school English teacher (which he once was) and a man with a heart ailment (which he has). "He is a man," said one observer, "cynics might call

square." But Dave Anderson wrote, "Under that peaceful appearance . . . is the cold heart of a competitor."

He was a three-time All-America guard at Purdue. Then he coached 11 years in Kentucky and Indiana high schools (his won-lost record was 218-42) and two years at Indiana State Teachers College (47-14).

From 1949 until he retired in 1975 he coached at UCLA and turned out such players as Lew Alcindor (later known as Kareem Abdul-Jabbar), Bill Walton, Gail Goodrich, Sidney Wicks, Curtis Rowe, Lucius Allen and Walt Hazzard (later Mahdi Abdul-Rahman). From 1964 to 1975 his teams won seven straight NCAA titles and ten in twelve years, and he was voted coach of the year six times. In 1974 UCLA ran its winning streak to 88 games, by far the longest in college history.

His 27-year record at UCLA was 620–147, and in 40 years as a head coach his record was 885–203. Yet, said Bob Boyd, a rival coach, "Even with the players UCLA has had, a lesser coach could have fouled it up." Jerry Tarkanian, a rival coach, said, "Maybe the basic part of his success is that he is very, very basic." Bill Becker explained his success by writing, "He believes that basketball is a game of taking chances, forcing the breaks and cashing in on them."

Wooden said, "We play as a unit. We always think of passing the ball before shooting it. . . . We don't try to make basketball a complicated affair because it isn't. We don't put that much emphasis on winning. We tell them to do their best and let winning take care of itself."

Sometimes, he made a different type of contribution. "He rides officials and players more than any other coach I have seen," said Coach Richard (Digger) Phelps of Notre Dame. "That's so bush league for a man of his stature, yet no referee has the nerve to reprimand him."

There were other dissenters, too. Abdul-Jabbar got along with him but said, "He had a terrible blind spot. He had this morality thing going. You had to be morally right to play. From that attitude came a serious inability on his part to get along with 'problem' players. If they didn't go to church every Sunday and study for three hours a night and arrive 15 minutes early to practice and nod agreement with every inspiring word the coach said, they were not morally fit to play, and they found themselves on the second team."

Wynn, Early (1920–   )

Early Wynn was a modern pitcher with the fiery temperament of a Ty Cobb. "He is a throwback to a time that is forgotten," wrote Jack Gordon. "He brings to pitching steel and granite, things that endure." Harry Jones described him "walking to the mound with the foreboding gait of an executioner." Roger Kahn wrote, "A cheerful, generous man within, he creates a surface impression akin to Vesuvius. . . . He has won a clubhouse reputation as the least happy loser in baseball."

He was called Gus, and he was a tough, burly man. He pitched for the Washington Senators (1939–48), Cleveland Indians (1949–57), Chicago White Sox (1958–62) and the Indians again in 1963. His 23 seasons tied the major-league longevity record for pitchers. He won exactly 300 games and lost 244, pitching many years with bad teams. He was a 20-game winner five times. He became a successful pitching coach for the Indians and Minnesota Twins, and in 1972 he was elected to the Baseball Hall of Fame.

He became obsessed with winning 300 games, a feat achieved only by Lefty Grove and Warren Spahn since 1930. "I may be the last ever to make it," he said. He almost didn't make it. In 1961, eight victories short, he popped an elbow tendon in June and pitched only five more games that season. In 1962, his pitching elbow so aching from gout that he combed his hair left-handed, he won seven games. In 1963, released by the White Sox just before the season started, he joined the Indians in June. He won only one game that year—his 300th. "I never slept the night before," he said. "The gout was killing me."

"There isn't a man in baseball which, if he is not stupid or lying, will not admit that he is afraid of him," Casey Stengel said. "He is not polite to hitters. He gives them that stare and he makes them duck, and I notice he isn't very friendly with even the hitters on his own team."

"They claim I knocked down my own mother," Wynn said, "and I tell them that Mom was a helluva curveball hitter. But that's not true. It wasn't my mother I knocked down. It was my son. The kid had just lined a good curve against the fence. . . . The first rule of pitching in the big leagues: The pitcher has to look out for himself."

Yost, Fielding Harris (1871–1946)

Fielding H. Yost was nicknamed "Hurry Up" because he was always in a hurry. So were the celebrated University of Michigan football teams he coached. His first five Michigan teams—from 1901 to 1905—won 55 games, lost one and tied one and scored 2,821 points to 42 for the opposition.

Tim Cohane wrote, "He had no sense of humor . . . unless he made the jokes." He was a self-centered man who talked slowly, seriously and incessantly. Grantland Rice once asked Ring Lardner, "Did you ever have a conversation with Yost?" "No," Lardner replied, "my parents taught me never to interrupt."

He grew up in a log cabin and was a teen-aged deputy marshal in rowdy mining towns in his native West Virginia. He played in the first football game he saw, and in an era of lax eligibility rules he played for Lafayette College, West Virginia University and Ohio Northern University at the same time.

He was head coach at Ohio Wesleyan in 1897, University of Nebraska in 1898, University of Kansas in 1899 and Stanford University in 1900 (he also coached the Stanford Freshmen, San Jose Teachers College, Lowell High School of San Francisco and the California Ukiah that year). Then he coached at Michigan from 1901 to 1926, except for a short retirement in 1924. In 29 years as a head coach, he produced superbly coached and inspired teams, with a record of 196-34-11.

Willie Heston, his greatest player, recalled, "He thought, talked and illustrated plays continually through every football season, with the exception of a few short hours each night when he was compelled to give way to sleep." Hugh Fullerton, Sr., wrote, "He had run the gamut of coaching methods from the 'tramp on the injured and hurdle the dead' days to today, when he ranks high as a preacher and practicer of the highest morality in sport. He has developed from a rough, fighting coach to an idealist." But another Big Ten writer wrote, "Yost was a schemer. . . . He was a sanctimonious man who preached a good line, then did what was necessary to win."

Yost said, "The athlete doesn't sacrifice anything by being out in the fresh air with a planned objective and work to do. That's the way to build a good, clean, sound body, mentally alert, with a will to fight for a place in the world."

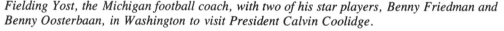

Fielding Yost, the Michigan football coach, with two of his star players, Benny Friedman and Benny Oosterbaan, in Washington to visit President Calvin Coolidge.

Young, Denton True (1867–1955)

Cy Young's major-league pitching record defies belief. He holds the all-time records for games won (511), games lost (315), games started (818), complete games (751), innings pitched (7,377) and hits allowed (7,078). He won 20 games or more for 16 seasons, 14 in a row. He won 32 or more games five times. He pitched more than 400 innings in five of his first six full seasons. He pitched three no-hitters, one a perfect game. He never had a sore arm and never had a rubdown. He was never sick until he had the flu at age 79. He never earned more than $5,000 a season.

"He stood astride the baseball world like a mighty oak tree," wrote Lee Allen and Tom Meany. "As long as baseball is played," wrote Frank Graham, "there will never be another pitcher like him. . . . In his time, there was no other even close to him." Al Simmons said, "He's not an immortal. He's a double immortal." Ty Cobb said, "He could pitch into a tin cup." Joe Williams called him "the invention of a bad baseball writer."

He pitched 22 seasons for Cleveland (1890–98) and St. Louis (1899–1900) of the National League, Boston (1901–08) and Cleveland (1909–11) of the American League and Boston (1911) of the National League. He was almost 44 when he pitched his last game, a 1-0 defeat by a rookie named Grover Cleve- land Alexander. In 1937 he was voted into the Baseball Hall of Fame.

When a youngster once asked him if he had been a pitcher, Young said, "Son, I won more big-league games than you are likely to see in your lifetime." He was a big, strong pitcher with speed and control. He recalled that when Lou Criger was his catcher, "We didn't have any signs. I told Criger we didn't need any. I said, 'I'll throw 'em and you catch 'em.' And he said, 'That suits me.' And that is how we operated." He pitched with two days of rest and never complained. But, he said, with the banning of trick pitches and defaced balls, "Pitching ain't what it was."

Zaharias, Mildred Didrikson (1913–1956)

She was the greatest woman athlete in history, slim (5 feet 6 inches, 135 pounds) yet muscular, long-legged and rawboned. She was uninhibited and unspoiled. She played sports, wrote Bert Rosenthal, with reckless abandon.

Westbrook Pegler, then a sportswriter, spoke of her "determination, courage, honesty and a candid but not immodest appreciation of her own superiority." Paul Gallico wrote, "She was apparently not made like other little girls of sugar and spice, but instead of whipcord, steel springs and Monel metal, enclosing the heart of a lioness. She had also the makings of an extraordinary woman."

Babe Didrikson Zaharias tried almost every sport and succeeded at everything she tried. She led the Dallas Cyclones to three AAU national championships in women's basketball and scored 106 points in one game. She pitched for the House of David touring baseball team and once struck out Joe DiMaggio. She made a cross-country billiards tour and several tours with a pro basketball team. Handball, swimming, diving, lacrosse, football, even boxing—she did it all. Her best were track and field and golf. "The best way to take athletics," she said, "is to like them all. Athletics are all I care for. I sleep them, eat them, talk them and try my level best to do them as they should be done."

She was the sixth of seven children of Norwegian immigrants. Her parents called her Baby, but when her mother decided she hit a baseball like Babe Ruth she changed the nickname from Baby to Babe.

Babe Didrikson became, wrote Grantland Rice, "truly the athletic phenomenon of our time, man or woman." Jack Newcombe called her "the first to prove that a girl can hold her own in strenuous competition and still remain very much a girl."

She was very much a girl in 1930 and 1931 when she won AAU national track and field titles in the long jump, hurdles, javelin throw and baseball throw. She entered the 1932 championships as a one-woman team representing the Dallas insurance company where she worked. She entered eight of the ten events and won five, finished second once and fourth once. She won the team title with 30 points. The second-place team had 22 athletes and 22 points.

In the 1932 Olympics, where she was limited to three events, she won the javelin throw with a world record and the hurdles with an Olympic record. She tied for first in the high jump, but her best jump was ruled illegal because she had dived over the bar (nothing in the rules forbid a dive). She got second place instead.

She played her first round of golf without a lesson and shot 95 for 18 holes. After three lessons she shot 83 and drove the ball 250 yards. In 1934, in her first tournament, she shot 77. She took the game so seriously that she spent 12 to 16 hours a day on weekends working on her shots. Often, she practiced until the blisters on her hands broke and bled.

She won 17 amateur tournaments in a row. In all, she won 55 tournaments, amateur and pro, in 15 years. She became a big attraction and helped steer the women's golf tour to its present importance. She won the women's United States Open three times, and five times she was chosen by the Associated Press as woman athlete of the year.

She was more than an athlete. She was good at

Babe Didrikson (right) en route to victory in the 80-meter hurdles at the 1932 Olympics.

Babe Zaharias in 1953, returning to the golf course after an operation for cancer. The next year she won the women's U.S. Open.

typing (86 words a minute), gin rummy, cooking, dancing, harmonica playing and crossword puzzles. "I never just wanted to be as good as somebody else," she said. "I always wanted to be better."

In January 1938 she was paired with George Zaharias, a 300-pound wrestler, in a golf match. Halfway through the round, he said, "You're my kind of girl." Eleven months later they were married, and for the first time she concerned herself with makeup and beauty parlors.

In 1953 she underwent surgery for rectal cancer. Within four months she was playing in golf tournaments. In 1954, still not at full strength, she won the women's United States Open by 12 strokes.

A year later the cancer returned. She promised she would beat it again, and her doctors said, "She is one of the world's indomitable spirits." But even her indomitable spirit was outmatched, and Babe Didrikson Zaharias, a great athlete and human being, died at the age of 43.

Zatopek, Emil (1922–   )

From his first race in 1941 to his retirement in 1958, he broke 18 world records for distance runs from 5,000 to 30,000 meters. He won the 10,000-meter run in the 1948 Olympics and three gold medals (for the 5,000 meters, 10,000 meters and marathon) in the 1952 Olympics.

Yet Emil Zatopek of Czechoslovakia made a greater impression with his looks than his accomplishments. He looked just awful. He was scrawny and awkward. When he ran he grimaced, his head wobbled, his shoulders hunched, his cheeks puffed and he looked pained. Cordner Nelson wrote, "He looked . . . as if he might be having a fit." To Kenny Moore, "He ran as if tortured by internal demons." William Johnson said, "He ran every step of a race as if there was a scorpion in each shoe." Allison Danzig wrote, "He runs like a man wasting no time getting out of a graveyard at the witches' hour with blood on the moon." Red Smith wrote that

Emil Zatopek strides to a pained victory in the 5,000 meters at an international meet in Karlsruhe, Germany, in 1955.

witnesses "still wake up screaming in the dark when Emil the Terrible goes writhing through their dreams, clawing at his abdomen in horrible extremities of pain."

In his early years in the military he trained at night, wearing army boots and carrying a flashlight. Once, en route to a meet, he stood all the way on a five-hour train ride, nourished only by beer and biscuits; he fell asleep on a streetcar taking him to the track and was awakened just in time to break the world record for 10,000 meters. In 1955, at age 32, he ran up to 90 400-meter sprints a day. He often spent hours riding a bicycle with 4.4-pound weights strapped to each foot.

He became a colonel in the Czechoslovak Army. In 1969, after he had supported the ill-fated, liberal Dubcek government, he was dismissed from the army, expelled from the Communist Party and given one menial job after another. The people still loved him, and when he worked as a garbage collector people recognized him and helped carry the garbage cans.

He believed that athletic success demanded hard work. "You must be fast enough," he said. "You must have endurance. So you run fast for speed and repeat it many times for endurance. . . . We forget our bodies to the benefit of mechanical leisure. . . . We have a magnificent motor at our disposal, but we no longer know how to use it. . . . Our children take a bus even if they need to go one kilometer."